Self, God,
and
Immortality

A Jamesian Investigation

EUGENE FONTINELL

Self, God, and Immortality

A Jamesian Investigation

The King's Library

TEMPLE UNIVERSITY PRESS · PHILADELPHIA

Temple University Press, Philadelphia 19122
Copyright © 1986 by Temple University. All rights reserved
Published 1986
Printed in the United States of America

The paper used in this publication meets the minimum
requirements of American National Standard for Information Sciences—
Permanence of Paper for Printed Library Materials,
ANSI Z39.48-1984.

Library of Congress Cataloging-in-Publication Data
Fontinell, Eugene.
Self, God, and immortality.
Includes index.
1. James, William, 1842–1910—Contributions in
immortality. 2. Immortality—History of doctrines—
20th century. I. Title.
B945.J24F66   1986   218   86-966
ISBN 0-87722-428-5 (alk. paper)

Two poetry epigraphs are used with the kind permission of the publishers:
To Chapter 7, from Alice Walker, "Goodnight Willie Lee, I'll See You in the Morn-
ing," Copyright © 1975 by Alice Walker, from the book *Goodnight Willie Lee, I'll See
You in the Morning* by Alice Walker. Reprinted by permission of Doubleday & Company,
Inc.
To Concluding Reflections, from Marie Ponsot, "The Great Dead, Why Not, May
Know," from *Admit Impediment* by Marie Ponsot, © by Marie Ponsot, 1981, published
by Alfred A. Knopf, New York.
The stanza from W. B. Yeats on page 21 is from "The Song of the Happy Shepherd,"
from the *Collected Poems of W. B. Yeats*, published in New York in 1956 by Macmillan,
and reprinted here with permission. The lines from Rilke's The Ninth Elegy on page
185 are reprinted from *Duino Elegies* by Rainer Maria Rilke, translated by J. B.
Leishman and Stephen Spender, with the permission of W. W. Norton & Company, Inc.
Copyright 1939 by W. W. Norton & Company, Inc. Copyright renewed 1967 by Stephen Spender and J. B. Leishman.

For
my parents
Helen and Ernest
and
my nieces
Justine and Flannery

Looking into Napoleon's eyes Prince
Andrew thought of the insignificance of
greatness, the unimportance of life which
no one could understand, and the still
greater unimportance of death, the meaning
of which no one alive could understand or
explain.

—Leo Tolstoy
War and Peace

The question of immortality is of its nature
not a scholarly question. It is a question
welling up from the interior which the
subject must put to itself as it becomes
conscious of itself.

—Soren Kierkegaard
Concluding Unscientific Postscript

CONTENTS

PREFACE

Can we who have been touched by the intellectual and experiential revolutions of the contemporary world still believe with any degree of coherence and consistency that we as individual persons are immortal? This is the central and controlling question of my essay, and I use the term "essay" primarily in its verbal connotation. A key assumption of the essay is that the gradual erosion of belief in personal immortality over the last several hundred years is bound up with the collapse of the dominant metaphysics of Western culture. This metaphysics combined a philosophy of the self as composed of a soul and body—the latter being material and subject to dissolution, and the former spiritual and essentially indissoluble—with a philosophy of an immutable, all-knowing, all-powerful God who, after a period of testing in the moral arena of "this world," sends the immortal soul to either eternal heaven or eternal hell. This view of the self and God, along with the metaphysics in which it is grounded—absolute and unchanging essences, values, principles, and laws—has been assaulted and undermined by a diversity of sciences and philosophies. In addition, it has become increasingly uncongenial to the experience of a variety of persons, including a number who view themselves as religiously concerned.

This situation has given rise to a variety of responses. At one end of the spectrum are those who consider the question of immortality closed. The most extreme expression of this denial of immortality, and some would say the most consistent, is that of nihilism—the total dismissal of all meaning, since "meaning" was intimately and inseparably bound up with faith in God and personal immortality. There are others, probably the majority, who, while denying that God and personal immortality are any longer live options, still strive to affirm meaning, though in completely immanentistic and humanistic terms—thus, in various modes of secular humanism. In recent years there has emerged a small but distinguished group of thinkers from within the major religious traditions who reject personal immortality but retain faith in God and the importance of religious activity, and endeavor to express meaning in those terms.

At the other end of the spectrum are those who still believe in personal immortality, and the meaning of whose lives is tied to this belief. Some of these simply accept personal immortality blindly and unquestioningly. Others, whether in sophisticated or unsophisticated form, retain the older metaphysics described above and find no existential or intellectual conflict. There are a few, however, who, aware of the problems accompanying traditional metaphysics, endeavor to be responsive to contemporary rejections of dualism, an absolutely immutable and transcendent God, and a mode of immortality belief that is thought to diminish the significance of the present life. These last, for the most part, are led merely to assert or juxtapose their belief in immortality with their acceptance of these contemporary views.

There is, I believe, a great need at present for a dialogue involving viewpoints that affirm and question personal immortality. These viewpoints may be located in different persons or, to some extent but not necessarily equally, within the same person, as they are in my case. Without such a dialogue, the important liabilities and possibilities of both the affirmation and the denial of personal immortality will not be faced adequately. This can only result in a continued thinning and flattening-out of the beliefs of those on both sides of the question. One important phase of such a dialogue will be reflective or speculative considerations of the implications of either belief in or denial of personal immortality. Since it is usually more fruitful, initially at least, to explore a question from one perspective, I have chosen—divided though I am—to approach the question from the side of one who affirms personal immortality.

The essay is subtitled "A Jamesian Investigation," and a word on my use of James is here in order. Early on I note that I am primarily concerned not to explicate James's metaphysics but rather to utilize his language, as well as that of others, "in the development of a 'self' open to the possibility of personal immortality." Nevertheless, I present an extensive explication of James's views because it is in James that I have found the richest resources for constructing a model of the self and God that renders belief in personal immortality plausible. It is necessary therefore, to describe carefully and in some detail several of James's central doctrines in order to show that they embody a subtlety, complexity, and plausibility that a more superficial presentation of James misses. Since in these instances I am making James's doctrine my own, the establishment of the fundamental reasonableness of his doctrine reinforces mine.

If James is to be a resource rather than a weapon, I must consider those aspects of his thought that threaten as well as support my hypothesis. For example, it is necessary to deal with the contention that James's philosophy of the self is properly interpreted as a materialistic or "no-self" doctrine. Unless I can make a reasonable case for an alternative reading, my claim for the congeniality of a Jamesian field-self open to personal immortality is seriously undermined. Similarly, by showing that the view of the self that emerges in James's later works is consistent with the view in his earlier *Principles of Psychology,* though more developed and refined, I am simultaneously showing that there is a doctrine of the self that is sensitive and responsive to "scientific," "metaphysical," and "religious" concerns. Such a view of the self must allow for the reality of a unique and continuing individual while avoiding both dualism and atomistic individualism. Hence, the bedeviling, controverted, and elusive question of "personal identity" must be touched upon. Finally, since no plausible belief in immortality is possible unless the individual self is related to and partially constituted by a "wider self," the reality, character, and role of "God" must be considered.

In those chapters in which James's thought receives detailed description and analysis, what is of primary importance is not whether I present a fundamentally correct interpretation of James—though I think I do—but whether there emerges from my reading of James, supplemented by a number of other thinkers, an intrinsically reasonable doctrine of a self that is open to personal immortality. This is the justification for such detailed consideration of the James texts. In following James as he attempts to affirm a nondualistic self without falling into materialism, to affirm personal identity while avoiding any Soul Substance view, and to affirm a God who does not diminish the significance of individual human actions, we are engaged in questions that are still very much alive. No claim, of course, is made that these issues are definitively resolved by either James or me. The more modest but still rather ambitious claim is that by showing that there is in James a coherent and consistent philosophy of world, self, and God, I am simultaneously showing that there is available a necessary and indispensable framework within which belief in immortality can be explored and affirmed.

The essay is divided into two parts, both concerned with personal immortality: the first part, "Possibility and Credibility," indirectly; the second, "Desirability and Efficacy," directly. I contend that these two distinct but not separate aspects of immortality belief belong together and that the two parts of the essay, when read whole, reinforce each other. It is crucial first to establish as "reasonable" the doctrines of a processive-relational or "field" metaphysics that allows for a *continuity* of narrower and wider dimensions of *one* world, of a holistic self that avoids both an unacceptable dualism and a reductionistic materialism, and of a God intimately and existentially intertwined with human lives. Unless this is done, the claims that immortality belief is not escapist, that it directs human energies toward rather than diverting them from the crucial tasks confronting us here and now, that such belief is not an expression of an out-moded soul-doctrine, and that we are cooperatively acting with God in the creative process—all such claims are reduced to mere pious assertions. An important consequence, then, of my considering immortality belief within the processive-relational view of the self and God is that such belief plays a significantly different role within this view than it does within the traditional view of self and God. In sum, the doctrines developed in the first part of the essay give depth and support to the extrapolations advanced in the second part; and the extrapolations presented in the second part give specificity and concreteness to the doctrines developed in the first part.

One final point: though I have argued for the viability of belief in personal immortality, I have made no effort to mask or sugarcoat those features of human experience that threaten or tend to undermine such belief. Indeed, I have endeavored to present as strongly as I could what I consider the more serious objections to this belief. These objections are not merely abstract or "intellectual" but concrete and existential. They pervade the thought and experience of any reflective contemporary believer, and there are no absolutely compelling arguments I know of that can completely overcome them. Thus, particularly in the second part of the essay, a number of the speculations are quite tentative and characterized by a degree of incompleteness. This is consistent, however, with the central claim of the essay, which is that belief in personal immortality for those conscious of and sensitive to the distinguishing features of the contemporary world inevitably and inescapably involves unresolved and perhaps unresolvable tensions.

ACKNOWLEDGMENTS

If one of the central claims of this essay is valid, then I must acknowledge a debt to everyone with whom I have been related in any way, since who we are as individual persons is inseparable from a multiplicity and diversity of relations, past and present. Of course, not all the relations that enter into the constitution of our selves are equally important. Hence I owe a special debt to a number of friends who, over the years, directly and indirectly, consciously and unconsciously, have in varying degrees contributed to the formation of whatever reflective life I may possess.

My oldest professional debt is to the late Robert Pollock, who introduced me to William James and American philosophy many years ago at Fordham University. Whether teaching medieval, modern, or American philosophy, Pollock possessed a genius for orienting his students to the living features of thinkers within these periods. My own efforts to teach James have benefited from the questioning and criticisms of my students at Queens College, City University of New York. Over many years and in different ways, my colleagues in the Philosophy Department have been responsible, often unknowingly, for my thinking and rethinking many of the issues with which this work is concerned.

Three friends of long standing have been continually and crucially supportive. Joseph Cunneen who, with his wife Sally Cunneen, has edited the journal *Cross Currents* for more than thirty-five years, encouraged me at the earliest stage of the project. Versions of Chapters 7 and 8 appeared as articles in *Cross Currents* (Summer 1981; Spring 1982). Those articles and the sections of this book that incorporate them were edited creatively by William Birmingham. He also read an early, very rough draft of the manuscript and made suggestions for its organization and development that were of inestimable value.

My debt to John J. McDermott is threefold. First, I am in debt to him, as are all students of William James, for his comprehensive edition of James's writings (*The Writings of William James,* New York: Random House, 1967), which appeared almost a decade before the first volumes of the superb Harvard University Press edition of James's works. Second, both through his essays and personal communications over the years, I have been led to even new appreciation of the range and subtlety of James's thought. Finally, McDermott's criticisms of my views, even when they were in conflict with his own, were always constructive and aimed at helping me give these views their strongest articulation—with never an attempt to turn them toward his own concerns.

Everyone at Temple University Press with whom I have had any dealings has been exceptionally gracious and helpful. I must, however, single out several persons. Jane Cullen, senior aquisitions editor, reviewed the manuscript in a rough, unfinished form at a time when I had set it aside because of other concerns. Her recognition of its possibilities and enthusiastic support and encouragement gave me the impetus to bring the project to closure. Mary Denman Capouya, production editor, continually kept me informed of the myriad details connected with turning a manuscript into a book and gently but firmly pressed me to maintain the production schedule. Patricia Sterling's copyediting was sensitive and insightful; her changes and suggestions invariably served to clarify and further my intentions.

My brother, F. J. Fontinell, was of great help in the onerous tasks of rechecking the numerous textual citations and the reading of the proofs against the manuscript. Further, his chastening wit kept me laughingly aware of the gap between the scope and complexity of the issues under consideration and my treatment of them.

Finally, I wish to express a word of appreciation to Joseph Armenti, editor of *The Papin Gedenkschrift: Dimensions in the Human Religious Quest* (Ann Arbor: University Microfilms International, 1986), which includes a memorial essay incorporating segments of several chapters, principally from Chapter 5.

LIST OF ABBREVIATIONS

Where available, *The Works of William James* has been used. This critical edition of James's writings is being published by Harvard University Press with Frederick Burkhardt, General Editor, and Fredson Bowers, Textual Editor. Each volume of the *Works* includes the definitive critical edition of the text, extensive editorial notes, and an introduction by a distinguished scholar. Where a second date appears, it is the year of the work's original publication.

CER   *Collected Essays and Reviews,* New York: Longmans, Green, 1920
EP   *Essays in Philosophy,* 1978
ERE   *Essays in Radical Empiricism,* 1976; 1912
HI   *Human Immortality: Two Supposed Objections to the Doctrine,* 2d ed., with preface, Boston: Houghton Mifflin, 1899
LWJ   *Letters of William James,* 2 vols., ed. Henry James, Boston: Atlantic Monthly Press, 1920
MS   *Memories and Studies,* New York: Longmans, Green, 1911
MT   *The Meaning of Truth,* 1975; 1909
P   *Pragmatism,* 1975; 1907
PBC   *Pscyhology: Briefer Course,* 1984; 1892
PP   *Principles of Psychology,* 2 vols., 1981; 1890
PU   *A Pluralistic Universe,* 1977; 1909
SPP   *Some Problems of Philosophy,* 1979; 1911
VRE   *The Varieties of Religious Experience,* 1985; 1902
WB   *The Will to Believe,* 1979; 1897

Introduction

Oh, why is not man immortal? . . . Why these brain centers and their convolutions, why vision, speech, feeling, genius, if all this is destined to go into the ground, ultimately to grow cold together with the earth's crust, and then for millions of years to whirl with it around the sun without aim or reason? Surely it is not necessary, merely for the sake of this cooling and whirling, to draw man, with his superior, almost godlike intelligence, out of oblivion and then, as if in jest, to turn him into clay.

—Anton Chekhov
Ward Six

Thus our personality shoots, grows and ripens without ceasing. Each of its moments is something new added to what was before. We may go further: it is not only something new, but something unforeseeable.

—Henri Bergson
Creative Evolution

There would seem to be rhythms of emphasis in the history of Western thought that manifest pendulumlike swings. These can be broad and cultural or narrow and technical. Usually they are both. Among the most persistent swings is the rationalistic-romantic, which takes many forms. One of the earliest was the Hellenic-Hellenistic; even earlier was the mythological-rational. The primacy of the mythological or religious should be noted; then, with the Greek creation of philosophy, there begins a dialectic that is never pure and never identical in its repeated manifestations but continues to the present. From the first moment that an alternate mode to the mythological account of the world emerges, the dialectic begins. The mythological is never completely eradicated even from Greek philosophy at its apex, but there is surely a shift in dominance. If it can be said that even Plato and Aristotle retain certain mythological dimensions, they are surely diminished from those found in the pre-Socratics. In broad cultural terms, it would seem that Nietzsche is right—something is killed, never to return in precisely the same form, by "Socratic rationalism." However fulfilling and satisfying the exercise of "reason" may have been for an elite group of philosopher/scientists, it failed to satisfy the generality of human beings. The emergence and persistence of the Orphic and Eleusinian mystery religions alongside and concurrent with Greek philosophy is an early indication that some aspect of human experience, some need, is not met by "reason." Whether or not the Hellenistic period was a "failure of nerve," it represents a period of varied and competing claims for human allegiance, only one of which is the "rational." Nevertheless, the rational henceforth will be at least *one* of the claims and will fulfill at least *one* human need. Once this mode of consciousness has emerged, there is no possibility of ever again completely suppressing it. It may and indeed will be transformed and modified, but it remains one of the continuing characteristics of the human situation. More, it has shown itself, particularly in the West, to be one of the two

3

serious claims—the esthetic being the other—able to serve as alternatives to religion.

The emergence of Christianity out of the Hellenistic context moves the dialectic to a new stage. Very early the tension and outright conflict between reason and faith appears. This faith/reason dialectic has continued down to the present. Within the culture at large, we have two simple and clear positions: faith alone is sufficient; reason alone is sufficient. For most of Western history, however, the dominant views have made attempts to account for both. The Tertullian antirationalistic position expressed what has been a continuing claim, but the view of Clement of Alexandria that faith *and* reason are both good and necessary has been the one that has held most Christians as well as most Jewish and Islamic thinkers. Of course, the abstract assertion that faith and reason cannot be in *real* conflict is one thing. Concrete demonstration that existential and intellectual conflicts are only *apparent* is quite another matter. I would suggest that no formal expression of the relation between faith and reason can ever be permanent or definitive. At best these expressions can serve as guidelines, as regulative ideals. Only in the individual person can the two be lived with a degree of relative harmony and reconciliation; and even there the tendency has been for juxtaposition rather than existential synthesis or fruitful dialectic.

During the Middle Ages and while the Church was the dominant formative factor, culturally and individually, the disputes concerning the proper relation between faith and reason were for the most part confined to university circles. All this began to change with the rise of the scientific revolution. Whatever the merits of the technical questions that emerged concerning claims for the new science, this revolution was to have an effect far beyond the intellectual milieu from which it originated. Ironically, the anti-Galileo ecclesiastics saw or sensed this more perceptively than many defenders of science, incluing Galileo himself. What was coming to an end was a world, a world in which theistic faith (if not myth) was the central and controlling factor not only in matters explicitly religious but in all aspects of human life—political, economic, familial, and artistic. While during the Middle Ages philosophy/science had to show that it could be reconciled with religion, from the eighteenth century on it was increasingly the other way around: religion had to show that it could be reconciled with science or reason. In place of an earlier view that faith *alone* was sufficient, the Enlightenment brought forth a counterclaim that reason *alone* was sufficient. Just as earlier fideists had viewed reason as a threat to the integrity of faith, so the new rationalists viewed religious faith as a threat to the integrity of reason.

The success of the new science and the new claims for reason can hardly be exaggerated; there is no aspect of Western culture—and soon one will be able to say of the world—that has remained untouched, for better or worse or both, by science and its consequences, proximate and remote. Again, however, as in the Greek period, religion did not fold its tent and silently slip away. The responses among those who still affirmed religion, as in the earlier period, were varied and diverse, ranging from complete rejection of scientific or rational claims, insofar as they touched upon any fundamental religious or moral values, to a complete rationalization of religion as the highest flowering of reason. Between these extremes were numerous efforts to modify the claims of both science and religion in such a way as to show that both were justifiable.

The present situation presents a bewildering array of positions reflecting most of the previous responses plus a number peculiar to the age. The comparison of this age to the Hellenistic is well taken: it is a period characterized by supreme and near miraculous achievements in science and technology combined with a profound sense of alienation, frustration, and despair (perhaps unexceeded in human history), giving rise to a variety of cults, religious and other, all promising personal salvation. It has been pointed out by a number of thinkers that as our knowledge of the cosmos has increased, our knowledge of ourselves has not. Earlier in the century, Max Scheler noted that for the first time in history, man had become profoundly problematical to himself. Paradoxically, knowledge or knowledge claims pertaining to the human have become so massive and conflicting as to undermine almost completely our earlier confidence in the human species as well as in individuals.

To the earlier question "What am I?" and the somewhat more recent "Who am I?" has been added, whether from Eastern sources or Western deconstructionist sources, the question "Am I?" There is perhaps no more astounding shift in such a short period than the twentieth-century shift of the radicalizing segment of the Western intellectual community from humanistic existentialism to an antihumanistic structuralism or poststructuralism. In the first half of the twentieth century, some of our most creative thinkers were insisting on the reality of the human subject and defending it against various modes of objectification, whether from science, mass culture, technology, or intellectualism. For about the last twenty-five years, however, *some* of the most brilliant and creative thinkers have heralded the disappearance of the subject, the self, the ego, the individual, and the like. The human sciences, it is claimed, must surrender the human "subject" if the human is to be an "object" of science. Thus we are confronted with a situation in which "no-self" doctrines are advanced by subtle and sophisticated thinkers. A feature of some Eastern religions that is said to show their superiority to Western religions is that they are not egocentric, that they recognize the illusory character of the individual self.

To suggest, at this time, not only that the individual self is real but that it may possess a reality such that its existence will not be restricted to its present spatio-temporal conditions, is probably more foolish than daring. And yet, and yet . . . it must be done if for no other reason than the fact that the question of *my* person seems to me unavoidable. If, of course, this is an isolated and idiosyncratic feeling, then my efforts will have only a personal therapeutic effect at most. But I do not believe that it is only *my* question, and the only way to find out is to ask, however haltingly and inadequately, and listen for a response. Of course, if the only task were to ask a pollster-like question about the afterlife, it would be quite simple and, for some, reassuring: it would seem that a surprisingly high number of human beings still *say* they believe in an afterlife. But while such data are not completely irrelevant, they do not take us far in relation to the crucial question: namely, can we who have been touched by the intellectual and experiential revolutions of the contemporary world still believe with any degree of coherence and consistency that we as individual persons are immortal? To respond to this question—it is not a question that has an "answer"—is to participate, in however modest a way, in that long and continuing effort to show that one's faith is not only not in essential conflict with the best insights and achievements of contemporary thought and experience but that indeed this faith is deepened and enriched by such insights. It is not false modesty to say that the most I can hope to do is to hint at, or point to, or suggest how such a harmonization might be realized. Whatever the merit of any particular effort to realize consistency between "faith" and "reason," I share with John Herman Randall, Jr., the view that it is an eminently worthwhile effort. This attempt to bring "religious beliefs into accord with philosophic truth" is designated by Randall "rational" or "philosophical theology." As he states: "Its worth lies not in the formulations of the moment—they will soon give way to others. It lies rather in the conviction that it is supremely important to make the never ending effort to understand."[1]

No response to the question, "Is the individual person immortal?" is possible without a prior response to the question, "What is the nature of the individual person?" Or, in keeping with the kind of objections already referred to, "Are there such realities as individual persons?" In raising this question, one opens a Pandora's box, for there emerges a bewildering variety of allied questions—some with long histories, and others that involve very technical matters. Among these questions are the following: Are human beings completely accounted for in terms of matter (bracketing the question as to what matter is)? Are human beings composed of both matter and spirit, body and soul? If so, what is the role and relation of each? Are these really distinct principles or only distinct functions? What is the nature of consciousness? Is it substantive or only epiphenomenal? Are mind and brain identical? If not, how can they be differentiated? What is the nature of the human body? Is there personal identity? If so, how can it be accounted for? Is there a distinction between the individual and the person? If so, what is it? Is the human being identical with and reducible to her or his behavior? Is the human being reducible to the various social structures that constitute it?

The literature on these questions is vast, varied, and in many instances highly technical, both philosophically and scientifically. Yet one can say with reasonable assurance that there is no one position concerning the nature of the human person, philosophical or scientific, that has anything approaching a definitive consensus. Perhaps there will someday emerge an understanding of the human so overwhelmingly persuasive that only cranks will dissent. For the foreseeable future, however, anyone reflecting on this question will have to make some crucial choices, assumptions, or acts of faith. At what might be called the relatively unreflective level, "you picks your horse and bets your money" and let it go at that. Some will accept without question that we are merely what can be seen and touched, weighed and measured; others who insist that we are more than our bodies will simply *assert* that this "more" is spirit or soul. The first group does not even consider immortality. Its view is expressed succinctly in such time-honored phrases as "seize the day," or "you only live once," or "eat, drink, and be merry for tomorrow we die," or "when you're dead you're dead." The second group has its own time-honored phrases: "What shall it profit a man if he shall gain the whole world and lose his own soul?"; "this life is but a preparation for the next"; "the visible world is temporal while the invisible world is eternal"; "I'm but a stranger here—heaven is my home."

Both views have a variety of more or less reflective and sophisticated expressions, but they can be broadly reduced to two classical modes: namely, materialism and dualism. Materialism has no difficulty with the question of immortality, since it is ruled out from the start. Whatever versions of materialism are advanced, they all share the view that the individual human self has no reality apart from or beyond the particular material complex called the "body." The situation with dualism is a bit more complex, because while all materialisms exclude immortality, not all dualisms affirm immortality. Aristotelian dualism, for example, apparently does not, or at least does not clearly, allow for immortality. Thomistic or Cartesian dualism, on the other hand, affirms at least the ontological possibility if not the necessity of personal immortality.

Perhaps any affirmation of immortality must involve some mode of dualism. If so, the defender of immortality must face the formidable antidualistic views that have proliferated in the twentieth century. The various critiques of any form of Cartesian "ghost in the machine" have come close to an antidualistic consensus. Such issues, however, are not settled by a head count, even if those heads are impressive philosophical or scientific ones; hence, it would be simply incorrect to say that dualism has been philosophically or scientifically refuted. Arthur Lovejoy's *The Refutation of Dualism,* written over fifty years ago, in which the claims of a variety of impressive philosophers to have overcome dualism are seriously and subtly challenged, still stands as a caution against those who would lightly dismiss dualism. In addition, the work of such respectable contemporary dualists as H. D.

Lewis, Peter Geach, and Roderick Chisholm serves as evidence that dualism remains a respectable philosophical option.

Even though dualism does not necessarily entail personal immortality, there can be no question that it is eminently congenial to it, and that any doctrine of immortality may be at least implicitly dualistic. This would be so if dualism were defined so broadly as to include any view claiming that the reality of the individual self is not confined to its visible spatio-temporal coordinates. Such a definition of dualism, however, seems unwarrantedly broad since many philosophies that claim to be antidualistic—such as various forms of phenomenology—deny along with Martin Heidegger that the self is enclosed within the envelope of the skin. As I see it, there are numerous and often conflicting efforts to devise a doctrine of the self that escapes both classical materialism and classical dualism. These efforts, in my opinion, offer the richest possibilities for an adequate doctrine of the self. My particular concern is whether they inevitably exclude the possibility of personal immortality. That most of them claim to do so is unquestionable; whether a non-dualistic doctrine that does not exclude immortality is plausible is the question with which I am concerned.

What I would like to suggest and broadly sketch is a doctrine of the self that is reasonably consistent with at least one mode of contemporary antidualism—namely, pragmatism (princiaplly as expressed in the work of William James and to a lesser extent in John Dewey)—and yet is open to the possibility of belief in personal immortality. If such belief can be reasonably justified, therefore, it would not find itself in conflict with or merely juxtaposed to a doctrine of the self essentially uncongenial to such belief. I think doctrines of the self and immortality are needed that mutually reinforce one another. Hence, while I do not believe it possible to construct a view of the self that logically entails immortality, I do not think it enough to have a self that *merely* does not positively and absolutely exclude immortality. What is needed is a self that would be essentially enhanced by its extension to life beyond the visible present. By the same token, an immortality belief merely juxtaposed or tacked on to the existential self will not do. Such belief must be shown to be *here and now* significant and effective; it must not merely refer to some future realization—though it will involve the future—but be a contributing factor to the ongoing existential constituting of the self.

My essay, therefore, has two broad divisions, distinct but not separate: the possibility of immortality, and the desirability of immortality. The first will focus on the nature of the self and endeavor to construct a doctrine or model that is internally coherent, reasonably consistent, and also congenial to immortality. A crucial corollary of this doctrine of the self is an organically related doctrine of God, since it will be argued that only a self that has as one of its constituent relations the relation to God has the *possibility* for immortality. The second part of the essay will attempt to show that immortality is desirable, both in pointing toward an attractive mode of life and in energizing human beings here and now.

PRAGMATISM'S METAPHYSICAL ASSUMPTIONS

Before presenting doctrines of the self and God, it will be necessary to indicate something of how I view the character of the "world" or "reality." Why, it may be asked, if one is concerned with the question of immortality, is it necessary to take on such all-encompassing and overwhelming questions as "What is the world?" or "What is reality?" To do so is to leap into that intellectual thicket in which many formidable thinkers have become hopelessly lost or to step into an intellectual quicksand that has relentlessly consumed precious human energies. To put it crudely, why open up the metaphysical "can of worms"? The simplest response is to note that a world from which personal immortality is excluded and a world in which it is possible are radically different—and that difference gives rise to experiential consequences of great significance.

Does this mean that unless we can present a fully developed and systematic metaphysics, we are prohibited from reflecting on the question of immortality? I sincerely hope not, for such an accomplishment is much beyond the intellectual capability not only of most reflective humans but of most professional philosophers. There is, however, a less formal sense of metaphysics that touches, in various degrees, practically all of us. I refer to metaphysics as an "angle of vision" or perspective from which we view the world and by means of which we interact with and perhaps constitute the world. This perspective involves a number of fundamental assumptions which, though for the most part unquestioned, influence our lives in their various spheres and activities—assumptions, for example, that there is a world; that this world is independent of us; that we can know this world; that there is truth and error, right and wrong; that we as individuals exist. I use the term "assumptions" deliberately because most people simply take for granted, without question, the principles or values by which they live.

Of course, that human activity which has been designated "philosophy" has always had as part of its task the questioning of those assumptions, and the various positions taken in regard to them have given rise to a rich variety of philosophies. While in one sense this is quite obvious, in another sense it is less so. Nietzsche perhaps overstated the case, but not by much, when he accused philosophers of failing to question their assumptions. Philosophers have never been hesitant to question other philosophers' assumptions, but they have often claimed that their own were "given" or "self-evident" or "proved" (by them). Most philosophers today are more modest than that about their philosophical claims, but while few would maintain that absolute certitude is realizable, most reject skepticism, radical subjectivism, and destructive relativism.

We might designate two broad tasks as involved in any philosophical endeavor. The first is to clarify, articulate, and describe the metaphysical assumptions that govern one's inquiry. While these principles are not, strictly speaking, provable and are in a sense acts of faith, they must nevertheless be reasonably coherent and consistent with data from all kinds of experience—ordinary, scientific, esthetic, religious, and moral. The second task, therefore, is to present evidence and/or arguments in support of these assumptions or principles and to draw out their implications—theoretical and practical. The diverse ways in which these tasks are executed result in the variety and diversity of philosophies manifest in every age but particularly in the twentieth century.

One twentieth-century way has been designated "pragmatism"—which does not tell us very much, since there are probably as many distinct, though not totally different, pragmatisms as there are pragmatists. But since I claim that my approach to the question of personal immortality is "pragmatic," I must indicate what I am presupposing when I use the term. The mode of pragmatism—though it is but one version—to which I incline and which I am presupposing for the purposes of this essay can be described as processive, relational, personalistic, and pluralistic.

Additionally, I will understand pragmatism as both a metaphysics and a method of evaluation. I use the phrase "method of evaluation" rather than "theory of truth" in order to bypass the long, tortuous, and often contentious criticism of pragmatism as a theory of truth. I would, however, insist on one point: regardless of whether one speaks of "pragmatic truth" or "pragmatic evaluation," neither can be dealt with adequately without acknowledging the distinctive metaphysics that accompanies and is inseparable from them.

Now to speak of "pragmatic metaphysics" may seem oxymoronic, since it is well known that pragmatism is antimetaphysical if metaphysics is understood in its classical sense as knowledge of the ultimate and unchanging character of being- or reality-in-itself. In this sense of the term, pragmatism at most can be described as a mode of metaphysical agnosticism, since it denies that we can know what is, or whether there is, "ultimate reality"—that is, reality constituted in itself unrelated to human experience;[2] further, though pragmatism describes reality in terms of processes, it remains agnostic concerning any ultimate origin or end of the world process or processes. Nevertheless, pragmatism does not hesitate to venture some metaphysical guesses or construct some metaphysical myths by way of extrapolation from concrete experience as to what characterizes reality or the world. While, on the basis of what is available to human experience, there can be no absolute origin or absolute end, still we can discern and/or speculate about possible directions and opt to work for some directions and against others. Such efforts, of course, must be energized by beliefs and hopes which, though not "provable," are nevertheless "reasonable."

This last point brings us back to "pragmatic evaluation," which I will consider a bit later. First, let me return to the four features of pragmatism as I define it. Instead of viewing them as features of pragmatism, however, I will treat them as characteristics of reality or the world; thus, the world presupposed throughout this essay is processive, relational, personalistic, and pluralistic. The first two characteristics are developed throughout the body of the text; in summary, a world of processes and relations contrasts sharply and importantly with a world of permanent or unchanging substances, laws, essences, and values. Pragmatism's world excludes both metaphysical dualism wherein reality is divided into changing and unchanging or temporal and eternal realities, and any atomistic individualism wherein beings (atoms or gods) exist as essentially unrelational, isolated, self-enclosed, or self-sufficient. In the language of James, this is an "unfinished universe" or a "world in the making" and is thereby open to radical novelty. All modes of human activity take on a potentially creative role in such a world. What the world will be depends, at least in part, on our thoughts, beliefs, loves, hopes, hates, and actions. The nature and role of immortality belief within such a world is, of course, a central concern of this essay.

WORLD OR REALITY AS "PERSONALISTIC"
There is a stronger and a weaker sense in which the world or reality can be designated "personalistic." In the weaker sense we would have a world that includes or gives rise to some beings categorized as "persons." A personalistic world in the stronger sense would be one in which all real beings are characterized by "personhood." For most people, the first claim is obviously true and the second obviously false. Which of these senses would express pragmatism's meaning of "personalistic world"? As stated, neither; properly modified, however, pragmatism's meaning would be closer to the strong sense. Pragmatism's version of such a world claims to find in personal experience traits common to all realities. There are hints, though no developed presentation, of such a view in James, Dewey, and Alfred North Whitehead, who—on this point at least—can be brought under the umbrella of pragmatism. Before reviewing texts in which these three thinkers maintain that any metaphysical generalizations must be grounded in immediate experience, it is important to understand what is meant by "experience" throughout this essay, particularly because much of what will be said about self, God, and immortality will be extrapolated from personal experience.

The nature and role of "experience" within pragmatism is a story in itself, a long and not always clear one. For present purposes, a few key points will suffice. "Experience," for the pragmatists, is not identical with the "experience" of classical empiricism stemming from David Hume and John Stuart Mill. The differences are described clearly and sharply by Dewey in a 1917 essay entitled, "The Need for a Recovery in Philosophy."[3] He contrasts what I shall call the traditional and the pragmatic views on five points. First, whereas experience in the traditional view is primarily a "knowledge-affair," for the pragmatist it is "an affair of the intercourse of a living being with its physical and social environment." Second, experience from the traditional perspective is primarily psychical and permeated by "subjectivity"; to the pragmatist, experience suggests an objective world modifying and modified by human actions and sufferings. Third, experience is traditionally seen as tied to the past or as "given"; in its pragmatic mode it is experimental, oriented to changing the given and thereby having connection with a future as its salient trait. The fourth point of contrast is between an "empirical tradition committed to particularism" and one for which experience is "pregnant with connections." Finally, experience and thought are antithetical terms from the traditional perspective, whereas pragmatism's experience is "full of inference" and thereby renders reflection "native and constant."

Stated most succinctly and in Deweyan language, experience for the pragmatist is an organism–environment transaction.[4] Since there are a variety and diversity of such transactions, there is a variety of experiences differing in scope and quality, such as cognitive experience, esthetic experience, affective experience, and religious experience. While we can distinguish these various experiences, they never operate in complete isolation, nor do they relate to separate modes of reality. How these different modes of experience relate, overlap, and interpenetrate is a most complex question and can never be described with definitive clarity. Any distinctions between them are never made "for their own sake" or in an attempt to mirror the way these experiences allegedly are "in themselves." Rather, the distinctions can only be justified pragmatically insofar as they deepen, enrich, and illuminate the quality of human life.

Bearing in mind this view of experience as transactional, let us look at a few texts that point toward pragmatism as a "metaphysics of experience." In his essay "The Philosophy of Whitehead," Dewey notes that whatever their other philosophical differences, "the background and point of departure seems to be the same for both of us." The crucial point held in common is that "the traits of experience provide clews for forming 'generalized descriptions' of nature." Dewey goes on to emphasize the importance of this shared claim:

> The idea that the immediate traits of distinctively human experience are highly specialized cases of what actually goes on in every actualized event of nature does infinitely more than merely deny the existence of an impassable gulf between physical and psychological subject matter. It authorizes us, as philosophers engaged in forming highly generalized descriptions of nature, to use the traits of immediate experience as clews for interpreting our observations of non-human and non-animate nature.[5]

There is little doubt that Dewey has correctly represented Whitehead's perspective, for early in *Process and Reality* we are told that "the elucidation of immediate experience is the sole justification for any thought; and the starting point for thought is the analytic observation of components of this experience."[6] Elsewhere, Whitehead states: "The world within experience is identical with the world beyond experience."[7]

Earlier than either Dewey or Whitehead, James insisted that personal experience is the crucial pathway to whatever reality is available to us. In his last work, unpublished at the time of his death, James asks "whether we are not here witnessing in our own personal experience what is the essential process of creation?" (*SPP*, 108).[8] And in the last work he published, he maintained that "the only material we have at our disposal for making a picture of the whole world is supplied by the various portions of that world of which we have already had experience" (*PU*, 9). A similar point had been expressed elsewhere: "No philosophy can ever do more than interpret the whole, which is unknown, after the analogy of some particular part which we know" (*CER*, 469).

I will later discuss the well-known—some might say notorious—Jamesian notion that life or experience "exceeds our logic" and its corollary that experience or feeling brings us to a deeper and richer reality, to "more" reality, than we are ever able to verbalize or conceptualize. Here I would like merely to touch upon this theme insofar as it indicates a dimension of what is implied in the claim that we live in a personalistic universe.

Ralph Barton Perry does not hesitate to say that the priority of original experience over representations or descriptions is "the most general principle in James's philosophy."[9] James himself emphasized "the gaping contrast between the richness of life and the poverty of all possible formulas" (*TC*, II:127), and maintained that "something forever exceeds, escapes from statement, withdraws from definition, must be glimpsed and felt, not told" (*TC*, II:329). It is in religion that the personal and feeling characteristics are most in evidence, for "the religious individual tells you that the divine meets him on the basis of his personal concerns" (*VRE*, 387). Further, "feeling is the deeper source of religion," and that is why James calls theological formulas secondary. He doubts that any philosophic theology would ever even have been framed "in a world in which no religious feeling had ever existed" (*VRE*, 341).[10]

The point I particularly wish to stress here is that while the personal and experiential are preeminently found in religion, they are not exclusively found there. James maintains that scientific and religious truths are consistent and homogeneous because, insofar as their final appeal is to experience, they are both "truths of experience" (*TC*, I:451). A more important, and surely more controversial claim is that our deepest and fullest grasp of reality is by means of the personal rather than the impersonal: "So long as we deal with the cosmic and the general, we deal only with the symbols of reality, but *as soon as we deal with the private and personal phenomena as such, we deal with realities in the completest sense of the term*" (*VRE*, 393). Thus, from James's perspective, the "impersonality of the scientific attitude" is shallow.

But James does not consider the impersonal world described by modern science as the last word, even for science.

> The spirit and principles of science are mere affairs of method; there is nothing in them that need hinder science from dealing successfully with a world in which personal forces are the starting-point of new effects. The only form of things that we directly encounter, the only experience that we concretely have, is our own personal life. . . . And this systematic denial on science's part of personality as a condition of events, this rigorous belief that in its own essential and innermost nature our world is a strictly impersonal world, may, conceivably, as the whirligig of time goes round, prove to be the very defect that our descendants will be most surprised at in our own boasted science, the omission that to their eyes will most tend to make *it* look perspectiveless and short. (*WB*, 241)

In sum, then, pragmatism's universe can be said to be "personalistic" or "experiential" because transactional activity, which is most immediately and richly evidenced in personal experience, is generalized or posited as "metaphysical": that is, as constitutive of all realities. "Human" experience, therefore, is not in some magical fashion superadded to nature; rather it is but one of a multiplicity of modes of transactional activity. Hence, James insists that the "word 'activity' has no imaginable content whatever save these experiences of process, obstruction, striving, strain, or release, ultimate *qualia* as they are of the life given us to be known." We cannot, therefore, suppose activities to go on outside our experience unless we suppose them in forms like these (*ERE*, 84). The metaphysics presupposed by pragmatism, then, might properly be designated "transactional realism."

PLURALISTIC UNIVERSE
The processive-pluralistic character of reality will be in evidence throughout the body of the text. We shall come to see in more detail that in the world presupposed by pragmatism there is a multiplicity of centers of activity, no one of which is completely isolated or unrelated and no one of which includes all the others. If we designate this "ontological pluralism," then we can call its correlative pluralism "epistemological." Inasmuch as this is a "pluralistic, restless universe," the entire universe cannot be encompassed within any single point of view (*WB*, 136). According to James, "We have so many different businesses with nature that no one of them yields us an all-embracing clasp" (*PU*, 19).[11] Experience shows us that the universe is "a more many-sided affair than any sect, even the scientific sect, allows for" (*VRE*, 104). Since "to no one type of mind is it given to discern the totality of truth" (*WB*, 224), James is led to suggest that "common sense is *better* for one sphere of life, science for another, philosophic criticism for a third" (*P*, 93). Such epistemological pluralism is, of course, a mode of perspectivism, but it is not—or at least not obviously—a mode of destructive relativism and superficial subjectivism. Pragmatism acknowledges that every thought

claim is perspectival and partial, but it does not thereby concede that we are prohibited from making reasonable choices among such claims or perspectives. Which brings us to the nature and role of "pragmatic evaluation."

PRAGMATIC INQUIRY AND EVALUATION

Any pragmatic inquiry is indefinitely open-ended, particularly when dealing with such issues as self, God, and immortality. The initial stage might be designated "probative" or "exploratory." In this stage, a hypothesis must be constructed that is not glaringly contradictory or inconsistent. The evidence in favor of the hypothesis must be broadly described and its possible fruits indicated. This stage will, for the most part, bracket or move gingerly over many technical details and difficulties to which the hypothesis gives rise. (It is within this stage that, for the most part, the present essay will be located.) Subsequent stages of a pragmatic inquiry will have to deal with these difficulties and either overcome them or modify the hypothesis accordingly. Concurrently, the projected "fruits" will have to be evaluated. This meeting of difficulties and evaluation of fruits will be continuous and ongoing, and the hypothesis will remain viable only as long as, "on the whole," the difficulties are not insuperable and the fruits are sufficiently abundant.

In regard to the investigation and evaluation of personal immortality, the pragmatist insists upon two things. First, it cannot be either proved or disproved. Second, and more important, believers have the obligation to evaluate their belief and to search out its "justifying reasons."[12] Such evaluation must eventually relate to concrete experience. More specifically, it must respond to the extent possible to the overwhelming mass of cumulative experience, whether quotidian, historical, artistic, scientific, moral, or religious. Any conclusions reached in this evaluative process will always be tentative and subject to modification under the press of future experience, but we are not thereby excused from making the most "reasonable" case possible at any moment.[13]

Without pretending to present a fully developed description of pragmatic inquiry and evaluation, I would like to call attention to a few crucial points both for the purpose of clarification and to avoid a gross misunderstanding of the claims of pragmatism. To begin with, whatever the difficulties associated with pragmatism's "method"—and they are numerous and well documented—there is no possibility of understanding it unless one remains aware of its metaphysical assumptions, already alluded to. Pragmatism posits a processive-relational world, an "unfinished universe," a "world in the making." Within such a world, pragmatism opposes—in the language of Dewey—any "partitioning of territories" whereby "facts" are assigned to science and "values" to philosophy and religion. It denies that science is grounded on reason while morality and religion are grounded on faith.[14] Pragmatism very early surrendered the great Western dream, brought to a crescendo by René Descartes and reprised by Edmund Husserl, of grounding philosophy/science on an absolutely certain foundation.[15] This rejection does not lead the pragmatist to embrace either irrationalism or subjectivistic relativism. Reason has a crucial and indispensable role to play in human life; it is, however, but one mode of experience, one mode of transaction between poles of reality, and it neither exists nor operates in isolation from other modes.

For pragmatism, the world is neither simply "rational" nor "irrational," though it involves dimensions of both. There is evidence for believing that the world is *becoming* more rational and that humans have a crucial role to play in that rationalizing process. "The world," James tells us, "has shown itself, to a great extent, plastic to this demand of ours for rationality." He goes on to say that the only means of finding out how much more it can become rational is to try out our conceptions of moral as well as mechanical or logical necessity (*WB*, 115).[16] In surrendering the quest for absolutes—whether foundations, truths, values, or ends—pragmatism is not surrendering its quest for "reasonableness."[17] Further, the denial of final closure on any question does not exclude the possibility of—indeed, the necessity for—intellectual and existential judgments and decisions. All nontrivial judgments and decisions will have the characteristics of incompleteness and tentativeness and will lack the feature of absolute certitude.[18] Of course, if probability and provisionality were merely characteristics of pragmatic inquiry and evaluation, it would hardly be of moment. Pragmatism insists, however, that the limitations of inquiry are due not to the incompetence of pragmatists but to the nature of the world within which inquiry and evaluation are exercised. James concedes that pragmatism can be legitimately reproached with "vagueness and subjectivity and 'on-the-whole'-ness," but he quickly adds that the "entire life of man" is liable to the same reproach. "If *we* claim only reasonable probability, it will be as much as men who love the truth can ever at any given moment hope to have within their grasp" (*VRE*, 266, 267).[19]

All pragmatic evaluations, whether of ideas, beliefs, values, or institutions, are always open to modification and correction. As stated by Dewey: "Any one of our beliefs is subject to criticism, revision, and even ultimate elimination through the development of its own implications by intelligently directed action."[20] If pragmatism's method can be said to be modeled on that of modern science, it is insofar as it shares with science the feature of self-correction. This is a community process with "later views correcting earlier ones" (*PP*, I:191), resulting in a continually cumulating experience.[21] This cumulative experience enables us to build on earlier successes, however partial, in an effort to engender new successes, however partial. While "there are no successes to be guaranteed" (*VRE*, 299) and no certain, uncorrectable conclusions to be reached, we are not thereby "playing into the hands of skepticism." James insists that it is one thing "to admit one's liability to correction" and quite another "to embark upon a sea of wanton doubt" (*VRE*, 267).

Granted that pragmatism excludes any definitive "once and for all" mode of evaluation, how might it be described more positively? Stated simply, much too simply, we can say that within the processive-relational world presupposed by pragmatism, ideas, beliefs, symbols, and institutions—all of which originate in experience—can be judged only on the basis of the experiential consequences or quality of life they bring forth. This is expressed most succinctly in Dewey's pragmatic test for any philosophy: "Does it end in conclusions which, when they are referred back to ordinary life-experiences and their predicaments, render them more significant, more luminous to us, and make our dealings with them more fruitful?"[22] The consequentialism that distinguishes pragmatism is by no means crystal clear and consistent, nor does it have an identical meaning in Charles Sanders Peirce, James, and Dewey. Without making any attempt to delineate what the methods of these three pragmatists share and where they diverge, let me simply draw on a few texts of James, since his approach is most congenial to my purposes.

To begin with, there is a well-recognized ambiguity in James's pragmatic method that allows for both a positivistic and a personalistic reading. Thus Elizabeth Flower and Murray G. Murphey note a certain relaxation of the pragmatic criterion whereby it is broadened "from verifying consequences in particular sensible experiences to consequences for the quality of human living."[23] It is the personalistic or humanistic emphasis to which I am attracted and which I consider more faithful to the full range of James's notion of experience. Something of this is expressed by H. S. Thayer: "The particularly extraordinary feature of *Pragmatism* . . . is its reflection of James's ardent concern to bring philosophic thought into immediate contact with the real perplexities, the uncertainties and resurgent hopes that permeate ordinary human experience" (*P*, xxxvii). Perry, in noting that for James "the basic dogmas of religion are not wholly without evidence," adds that James compiles this evidence by "appealing to experience in the broad sense, and rejecting that narrower or positivistic version of experience which already presupposes a naturalistic world-order."[24] This broadened meaning of experience is expressed in what was perhaps James's last formulation of the "pragmatic rule": "The pragmatic rule is that the meaning of a concept may always be found, if not in some sensible particular which it directly designates, then in some particular difference in the course of human experience which its being true will make" (*SPP*, 37).

In stressing the practical consequences, for "anyone," of an idea or a belief, James left himself open to the charge of fostering a narrow and destructive subjectivism. There can be no doubt that his failure to make some crucial distinctions lent some support to this charge,[25] though I am persuaded that the weight and totality of his thought is against it. James surely intended to make satisfaction of the individual a crucial factor in any pragmatic evaluation, but what is not usually adequately stressed is that James rejected the atomistic individualism that is a necessary component of the kind of subjectivism with which he was often charged. It is the burden of a large segment of this essay to spell out a relational view of the individual self which was, as a minimum, *implicit* in James's thought. Judging what is "satisfactory" or "satisfying" for such a self is immensely more complex than describing what *appears* to satisfy some imaginary or psychically isolated ego. In a letter to Perry, written a few years before his death, James expressed his dismay at being misunderstood.

> The pragmatism that lives inside of me is so different from that of which I succeed in wakening the idea inside of other people, that theirs makes me feel like cursing God and dying. When *I say* that, *other things being equal,* the view of things that seems more satisfactory morally will legitimately be treated by men as truer than the view that seems less so, *they quote me as saying* that anything morally satisfactory can be treated as true, no matter how unsatisfactory it may be from the point of view of its consistency with what we already know or believe to be true about physical or natural facts. Which is rot!! (*TC,* II:468)

Because James's relationalism was so often overlooked, his pragmatism is reduced to such crude formulations as "anything is true or good if it makes someone feel good." Inasmuch as emotionally "feeling good" is but one of a number of relevant factors in the situation of any individual, it can never serve as the sole criterion of what is judged "good." James quite explicitly rejected such a view when he said that "what immediately feels most 'good' is not always most 'true,' *when measured by the verdict of the rest of experience. . . .* If merely 'feeling good' could decide, drunkenness would be the supremely valid human experience" (*VRE,* 22; italics added). The same failure to acknowledge the relational context that James takes for granted results in reducing pragmatism itself to crude formulas: "whatever works for the individual is good," for example. In support of such an interpretation one might cite James's claim that pragmatism's "only test of truth is what works best in the way of leading us." What would be left out in such an interpretation, however, is the rest of the sentence in which James adds some qualifications: "what fits every part of life best and combines with the collectivity of experience's demands, *nothing being omitted*" (*P,* 44; italics added). He expresses the same acknowledgment of the complexity of evaluation as follows: "*If theological ideas prove to have a value for concrete life, they will be true, for pragmatism, in the sense of being good for so much. For how much more they are true, will depend entirely on their relations to the other truths that also have to be acknowledged*" (*P,* 40–41).[26]

I am not for a moment suggesting that James achieved such complex evaluation of any of our religious or moral beliefs, and I am most certainly not suggesting that I will realize such achievement in what follows. I am suggesting, however, that whatever shortcomings pragmatism may have, it cannot properly be charged with taking the easy road to evaluation. Indeed, it points toward a method that for even partial realization would be immensely demanding and rigorous. In *The Varieties of Religious Experience,*

James designated three tests that are applicable to religious truth: immediate luminousness, philosophical reasonableness, and moral helpfulness (*VRE* 23). Perry noted that "these are new names for criteria of knowledge which appear repeatedly in James's philosophy" (*TC*, II:334). In *A Pluralistic Universal*, James said that "rationality has at least four dimensions, intellectual, aesthetical, moral and practical." He added that "to find a world rational to the maximal degree *in all these respects simultaneously* is no easy matter." The task would be to get "a conception which will yield the largest *balance* of rationality rather than one which will yield perfect rationality of every description" (*PU*, 55). Since I am suggesting that "pragmatic evaluation" claims to be a mode of "rational" evaluation, these last texts serve to reinforce my claim that pragmatism, while affirming personal experience as its ultimate touchstone, involves a diversity of subtle criteria in its effort to reach any concrete evaluation of the lived consequences of an idea, belief, or institution.

It is against such background presuppositions that I will maintain throughout this essay that the worth of any belief in immortality (or its counterbelief) must be evaluated in relation to human experience. Louis Dupré has suggested that "the belief in life after death appears to have grown out of actual experiences more than out of reasoning processes."[27] Whether or not Dupré is correct concerning the origin of this belief, I would maintain that in the past it has been a significant belief only to the extent that it has borne directly or indirectly upon personal experience. By the same token, it has tended to become insignificant in proportion to its distance from the ongoing lives of human beings. A pragmatic inquiry into the nature and worth of belief in personal immortality must, therefore, bring forth the positive and negative, actual and implicit, consequences of such belief. This kind of approach, it is important to note, is not restricted to description, even assuming that such description could be more nearly complete than it ever is. Pragmatic inquiry also includes a speculative or critical component that suggests possibilities for a future course of action. Put simply, on the basis of the way things are and have been, the pragmatist ventures a guess as to how they might be—"guessing" that takes the mode of extrapolation.

PRAGMATIC EXTRAPOLATION
Any effort to talk about a future mode of the individual self or the cosmic process, or even about this process considered as a totality or as a whole, takes us beyond both direct experience and inferential reasoning, strictly considered.[28] Such a movement might be designated speculation, imagination, or the term employed here, extrapolation. Any pragmatic extrapolation of the future, as I have pointed out elsewhere,[29] must fulfill at least four conditions. First, it must proceed from data given in experience. Second, this projected future must be plausible—that is, it must not be in fundamen-

tal conflict with the data from which it is an extrapolation. Third, the future state must be sufficiently different from the present state so that the future is not merely the present indefinitely extended. Fourth and most important, the extrapolation must render our present life—in both its individual and communal aspects—more meaningful, more significant, and more rich.[30]

Since the goal of extrapolation in the present endeavor is to produce a *model* of the self and the cosmic process which is open to immortality, a word should be said about how "model" is to be understood. Ian Barbour has given us an excellent description of the nature and role of models in both science and religion. Although I cannot claim Barbour for the pragmatic tradition—he calls himself a "critical realist"—I will appropriate some of his language concerning models which I find eminently congenial to pragmatism.

> Broadly speaking, a model is a symbolic representation of selected aspects of the behaviour of a complex system for particular purposes. It is an imaginative tool for ordinary experience, rather than a description of the world. . . .
>
> Models are taken seriously but not literally. They are neither literal pictures of reality nor "useful fictions," but partial and provisional ways of imagining what is not observable; they are symbolic representation of aspects of the world which are not directly accessible to us.
>
> Models in religion are also analogical. They are organizing images used to order and interpret patterns of experience in human life. Like scientific models, they are neither literal pictures of reality nor useful fictions. . . . Ultimate models—whether of a personal God or an impersonal cosmic process—direct attention to particular patterns in events and restructure the way one sees the world. (*MMP*, 6–7)[31]

The kind of pragmatic model called for would not pretend to give us either a pictorial or a conceptual representation of reality. Its chief function will be to enable us to participate more creatively in and with reality. Such a model must result from an extrapolative process that begins in and relates back to concrete experience.[32] Like any pragmatic evaluation, it will be subject to criticism in terms of consistency, coherence, and continuity of experience, but its ultimate worth will be determined by the quality of life that it suggests, encourages, and makes possible.[33]

PERSONAL IMMORTALITY

One final introductory point: the concern of this essay is *personal* immortality—by which is meant simply and crudely the survival of the "I" or the "me."[34] At least five other modes of immortality have been suggested: absolute spirit immortality (we are immortal insofar as we are absorbed with the Eternal Spirit, or the Everlasting God, or the One); cosmic immortality (we are immortal insofar as we emerge from and return to the cosmos or nature); ideal immortality (we are immortal insofar as we participate in timeless values or eternal ideals); achievement immortality (we are immortal through our creative acts or deeds); posterity immortality (we are immortal through our children, or the community, or the race).[35]

Now whatever their differences and however valuable their respective insights, these five modes all have one thing in common—the individual person will cease to be, he or she will be without remainder, at the moment of death.[36] My contention, in contrast though not totally in opposition, is that the loss involved in such modes of *personless* immortality is directly proportional to the worth of the individual person; further, failing personal immortality, that there are no adequate surrogates which can serve to alleviate the pain of loss. Assuming that human persons are precious realizations of nature or the cosmic process, the failure to maintain these persons in that mode of individuality upon which their preciousness depends may be a harsh truth to be endured but surely not to be celebrated. Finally, while beliefs in immortality through ideals, achievements, nature, humankind, or God have been known to and can continue to inspire and energize a portion of humanity, the exclusion of the individual person from these modes cannot but have a radically diminished pragmatic efficacy for the overwhelming number of human beings.[37]

Further, the contemporary awareness of the probable obliteration, naturally or humanly induced, of the earth and its inhabitants has deprived at least three modes of immortality (cosmic, achievement, posterity) of much of their attraction even for these select groups. From among the numerous expressions of pessimism concerning the earth's future, it will suffice to cite two, one from a philosopher (Bertrand Russell) and one from a poet (W. B. Yeats).

> That all the labor of the ages, all the devotion, all the inspiration, all the noonday brightness of human genius, are destined to extinction in the vast death of the solar system, and that the whole temple of Man's achievement must inevitably be buried beneath the débris of a universe in ruins—all these things, if not quite beyond dispute, are yet so nearly certain, that no philosophy which rejects them can hope to stand.[38]

> The wandering earth herself may be
> Only a sudden flaming word,
> In clanging space a moment heard,
> Troubling the endless reverie.[39]

There is perhaps no more plaintive cry against any kind of immortality that excludes the individual person than the one found in *The Brothers Karamazov*: "Surely I haven't suffered, simply that I, my crimes and my sufferings, may manure the soil of the future harmony for somebody else. I want to see with my own eyes the hind lie down with the lion and the victim rise up and embrace his murderer. I want to be there when everyone suddenly understands what it has all been for."[40]

There is a certain irony here, of course, in that Dostoevsky puts these

words in the mouth of Ivan—the "unbeliever." Whatever Fyodor Dostoevsky's overt belief, or overbelief, in personal immortality, his artistic expression is more ambiguous and more characteristic of the modern sensibility. "There is only one supreme idea on earth," he tells us in *Diary of a
Writer,* "the idea of the immortality of the human soul, since all other 'highest' ideas man lives by derive from it." Further, "without the belief in the
existence of the soul and its immortality human existence is 'unnatural' and
unbearable."[41] Unequivocal as this statement is, it cannot be taken in complete isolation from Dostoevsky's literary expressions. As Ralph Harper
notes, "In spite of the superficial orthodoxy of Dostoevsky, he, not Nietzsche, was the first to outline the consequences of the absence of God and
immortality."[42] One need not accept Harper's evaluation of Dostoevsky's
orthodoxy to acknowledge that no one could describe this absence so vividly and sensitively unless he had in some fashion experienced it. This an-
guished ambiguity is, in my view, the inevitable condition of those attempting to be responsive to contemporary thought and experience while
themselves believing in God and personal immortality.

PART I

*Personal
Immortality:
Possibility and
Credibility*

CHAPTER 1

World or Reality as "Fields"

Now I will do nothing but listen,
To accrue what I hear into this song, to let sounds
    contribute toward it.
I hear bravuras of birds, bustle of growing wheat,
    gossip of flames, clack of sticks cooking my meals,
I hear the sound I love, the sound of the human voice,
I hear all sound running together, combined, fused or following,
. . . .
I am cut by bitter and angry hail, I lose my breath,
Steep'd amid honey'd morphine, my windpipe throttled
    in fakes of death,
At length let up again to feel the puzzle of puzzles,
    and that we call Being.
                            —Walt Whitman
                            "Song of Myself"

We know existence by participating in
existence. . . . Existence then is the primary
datum. But this existence is not my own
existence as an isolated self. If it were, then the
existence of any Other would have to be proved,
and it could not be proved. What is given is the
existence of a world in which we participate.
                            —John Macmurray
                            Persons in Relation

Some years ago John J. McDermott suggested that it was "unfortunate that James did not stay with the language he utilized in preparing for his Psychological Seminary of 1895–1896. At that time, he resorted to the metaphor of 'fields' in order to account descriptively for the primal activity of the process of experience."[1] While I share McDermott's view, my concern here is not primarily to explicate James's metaphysics in terms of fields but to utilize his language as well as that of others to construct a "field" model, for which my primary purpose is to employ it in the development of a "self" open to the possibility of personal immortality. Since a key feature of both the self and the mode of immortality I wish to suggest is their continuity with the experienced world or reality, it will be necessary first to present the distinguishing characteristics of this world, beginning with "fields" as the primary

25

metaphor, in an effort to understand all reality. It must be stressed that there is no pretense of giving a mirror image of some outer "reality in itself" when reality or the world is described as a plurality of fields. A pragmatic approach consciously employs its primary terms metaphorically, having as its chief aim the development of a metaphysical language that will serve to expand, deepen, and enrich human life through varied and diverse modes of participation in reality, rather than claiming that such language gives us a conceptual "picture" of a reality essentially independent of human experience.

Let me begin with a consideration of James's notes for the Psychological Seminary, in which "fields" is employed as the central category.[2] James considers three suppositions necessary "if . . . one wants to describe the process of experience in its simplest terms with the fewest assumptions." Before looking at these suppositions, we should focus on the sentence just cited. As so often happens with James, his graceful style and felicitous expression mask the profound and complex question with which he is struggling. In this instance, of course, it is nothing less than the perennially simple and recurring question: "What is reality?" For James, this question, like all questions, must be answered in terms of experience, but that attempt immediately gives rise to the allied question, "What is experience?"

Now one might concede that such ponderous questions are the stock-in-trade of those usually genial but often peculiar beings called philosophers, but for those who live by "common sense," they are of little concern. As I have already indicated, though few of us—even those involved in the philosophical game—are metaphysicians in the full sense of that term, we are all metaphysicians in the sense of thinking and acting within a set of ideas, principles, and assumptions. When James and other pragmatists suggest a language shift, then, they are not trying to refute "common sense" so much as they are trying to make us aware of ways of looking at reality that are obstacles to richer ways of living. While the concern of this essay is not with the technical specifics and the historical polemics in which the pragmatists were engaged, it is still important to note that they were attempting to bring forth ways of thinking that were in sharp conflict with many deeply ingrained perspectives and intellectual customs.

This is best illustrated, perhaps, by presenting James's three "field" suppositions and indicating some of the notions to which they are opposed.

(1) "Fields" that "develop," under the categories of continuity with each other—[categories such as]: sameness and otherness [of] things [or of] thought streams, fulfillment of one field's meaning in another field's content, "postulation" of one field by another, cognition of one field by another, etc.

From the first part of this supposition we learn that reality is pluralistic ("fields"), processive ("develop"), and continuous ("continuity"). If we add "relationality," which is implied in the categories described, we have four distinctive features of the world within which I will develop my views on the self and immortality. For the moment it is sufficient to note that what is implicitly rejected by this field, or processive-relational, view is any reality that is unchanging or unrelated.

(2) But nothing postulated whose whatness is not of some *nature* given in fields—that is, not of field-stuff, datum-stuff, experience-stuff, content. No pure ego, for example, and no material substance.

In this supposition we have James's radical rejection of all modes of essentialism, whether materialistic, idealistic, or dualistic. The fuller implications of this supposition will emerge as the character and role of fields is described, but it is already evident that to view reality as "fields" excludes any underlying substance having universal and unchanging essential characteristics.

(3) All the fields commonly supposed are incomplete, and point to a complement beyond their own content. The final content . . . is that of a plurality of fields, more or less ejective to each other, but still continuous in various ways.[3]

The importance of this supposition for my purposes cannot be exaggerated. It provides the ground for the recognition of individuals while avoiding any atomistic individualism or isolating egotism. While all fields are "incomplete" and continuous with others, they are not so continuous that reality is reduced to an undifferentiated monistic flux. "Plurality" is just as real as "continuity," and when we add to these three suppositions James's later notes that there is "around every field a wider field that supercedes it . . . (the truth of every moment thus lying beyond itself)," we are presented with a world that can be most succinctly described as "fields within fields within fields. . . ."[4]

"What have we gained," James asks, by substituting fields "for stable things and changing 'thoughts'?"

We certainly have gained no *stability*. The result is an almost maddening restlessness. . . . But we have gained concreteness. That is, when asked what we *mean* by knowing, ego, physical thing, memory, etc., we can point to a definite portion of content with a nature definitely realized, and nothing is postulated whose nature is not fully given in experience-terms.

The goal of "concreteness"—fidelity to concrete experience—would appear to be simple and easy of realization, but it is deceptively so, as a diverse group of late modern and contemporary philosophers have attested. John Herman Randall, Jr., maintains that metaphysics can best be described as "the criticism of abstractions." He further claims that this is

the metaphysical method of Bradley, Dewey, Whitehead; of the Hegel upon whom they all draw; of the continental post Hegelians, criticizing the "intellectualism" of the Hegelian tradition in the light of "life" (the *Lebensphilosophie* of Nietzsche and Dilthey) or *Existenz* (Kierkegaard); of the phenomenologists, criticizing the formalism of the Neo-Kantians (Husserl), and of the existentialists (Heidegger, Jaspers, Tillich); of Bergson, opposing experienced *durée* to "The 't' of physics," and of William James opposing "immediate experience" to the empiricism of Mill; and of many other late nineteenth– and early twentieth-century philosophies of experience.[5]

Randall is not suggesting that the specific features of the views of such a variety of thinkers are identical or even always compatible. Whatever the differences, however, the importance of their converging emphasis upon the primacy of concrete experience and the rigorous reflection demanded for its apprehension should not be minimized. Throughout this essay, therefore, I will repeatedly stress the necessity of relating any speculations, extrapolations, or models to the experienced world within which we live, think, and act. What attracts me to James is his passionately relentless effort to be as faithful as possible to the range and varieties of experience. Something of this effort is expressed by Ralph Barton Perry:

> Thus by the inclusion of experiences of tendency, meaning, and relatedness, by a recognition of the more elusive fringes, margins, and transitions that escape a coarser sensibility, or a naive practicality, or an unconsciously artificial analysis—by such inclusion, the field of immediately apprehended particularity becomes a continuum which is qualified to stand as the metaphysical reality. (*TC,* I:460)

Another important aspect of James's emphasis upon and quest for concreteness is its strongly personalistic character. Many years ago, Robert Pollock stressed this relation between James's concern for concrete reality and his celebration of personal activity:

> Evidently, for James, pragmatism is an "attitude of orientation" by which man can achieve a vital contact with concrete reality and along innumerable paths, by aiming not simply at the abstract relation of the mere onlooker but at a relation that is personal, direct and immediate, and involving participation with one's whole heart and being. . . . James was endeavoring to take seriously the fact that reality does not address itself to abstract minds but to living persons inhabiting a real world, to whom it makes known something of its essential quality only as they go out to meet it through action. It is this concrete relation of man and his world, realized in action, which accounts for the fact that our power of affirmation outruns our knowledge, as when we feel or sense the truth before we know it. To James, therefore, pragmatism was a doctrine designed to enlighten the whole of human action and to give meaning to man's irrepressible need to act.[6]

One final point concerning the centrality of concrete experience in the thought of James has to do with differentiating his view from narrow and excluding modes of empiricism. A text from Perry will suffice to underline the openness of James's world: "This fluid, interpenetrating field of given existence, as James depicts it, embracing the insight of religious mysticism and of Bergsonian intuition, is far removed from the sensationalistic atomism of the discredited empiricists" (*TC,* I:461).

CHARACTERISTICS OF "FIELDS"

There is an inevitable circularity involved in discussing or analyzing any alleged "ultimate" category of reality. For example, if reality is best described in terms of "fields," as is being suggested here, then it would seem that we must describe fields themselves in terms of "fields." Since pragmatism does not aim at or believe possible any definitive conceptual description of reality, however, this circularity is neither vicious nor particularly unsettling. The aim of pragmatism is participation in, rather than abstract representation of, reality. Any circularity involved in the analysis of fields, therefore, must be judged on its ability to expand and enrich experience in both its explanatory and lived dimensions.

Bearing in mind that "field" is a metaphor and that images or concepts are employed in its analysis for the purposes of insight and utilization rather than definitive description, let me touch briefly upon the chief characteristics of a "field." A field can be described as a processive-relational complex, but this term would be grossly misleading if we imagined that "things" called processes and "things" called relations have combined to make a field. Nor is it adequate to posit a plurality of processes that subsequently enter into relations such that fields result. Given the limitation of language and its inevitable tendency to reify and detemporalize reality, perhaps the best we can do is to express the constitution of fields dialectically. Hence, we must insist that processes are relational and relations are processive. There are no unrelated processes and no nonprocessive relations. The concrete reality (actually realities) is always a unity involving an ever changing multiplicity. Depending on the specific field, these multiple "elements" will be variously named: for example, electrons, neutrons, and protons in the atomic field; molecules, cells, and genes in the organic field; planets in the solar field.

Now negatively speaking, this field view rejects any "ultimate" elements or atoms or particles understood as indivisible, impenetrable, unchangeable units. This does not, however, exclude all modes of metaphysical atomism. Whitehead, for example, maintains that "the ultimate metaphysical truth is atomism. . . . But atomism does not exclude complexity and universal relativity. Each atom is a system of all things."[7] Whitehead's label for these ultimate atoms is "actual entities," which he describes as "drops of experience, complex and interdependent" (*PR, 28*).

The field metaphor that I am constructing must acknowledge a character of interdependence both "within" and among fields (I use quotation marks to call attention to the relative character of "withinness"). An adequate field theory, from my perspective, must allow for a multiplicity of distinct individuals while avoiding any enclosure or isolation of these individuals. As the James text with which we began indicates, fields are continuous with other fields; hence there are no absolute, definitive beginnings and endings of any individual field. Whitehead expresses something of this continuity: "When we consider the question with microscopic accuracy, there is no definite boundary to determine where the body begins and external nature ends. . . . The body requires the environment in order to exist."[8] Of course, it must be quickly added that discreteness is just as real and fundamental as continuity. We cannot sharply mark off the borders of an individual field—there are no such borders to be marked off, given that fields insensibly shade into other fields; nevertheless, fields really are distinct (not separate) from each other, and pluralism—not monism—is the metaphysical view suggested here. Given this perspective, there must be a real and significant sense in which we can speak of discrete individuals having irreducible centers. This point will be extremely important to the view of the individual self that I will present, but for the moment I wish to maintain that whatever discrete realities exist, they are all characterized by being "centers of activity." As James expressed it in his unpublished notes: "Be the universe as much of a unit as you like, plurality has once for all broken out within it. *Effectively* there are centers of reference and action. . . . and these centres disperse each other's rays" (*TC,* II:764). In a similar vein, Dewey states: "In a genuine although not psychic sense, natural beings exhibit preference and centeredness."[9]

Note that Dewey does not equate centered activity with psychic activity. To the end, James flirted with panpsychism, and there is a difference among the commentators as to whether or not he succumbed. I think that Dewey's approach is the more fruitful and thus would suggest that panactivism is a more accurate description of reality than panpsychism. Panactivism excludes any completely passive entities or Whiteheadian "vacuous actualities" and, while affirming centered activity as the mark of all real beings, restricts "psychic" to a specific mode of such activity. In a world of "fields within fields," of course, a field that has its own center of activity will simultaneously be a constituent of another field with its own center of activity. This is most simply illustrated in the case of an organism where the individual cells are centers of activity while also constituting organ or tissue fields, which in turn are constituents of the organism as a "whole," which also has its distinctive center.

DEWEY'S "SITUATION"
While not using field language as his dominant terminology, Dewey does present a mode of field metaphysics. A brief consideration of Dewey's meaning and use of "situation" will illustrate this and amplify certain field characteristics already introduced. Dewey suggests that his use of the term "situations" antedated "the introduction of the field idea in physical theory."[10] What is important, however, is not priority of use but the utility of Dewey's situational view for the construction of an adequate field metaphysics.

"Situation," Dewey maintains, "stands for something inclusive of a large number of diverse elements existing across wide areas of space and long periods of time, but which, nevertheless, have their own unity."[11] Elsewhere, Dewey emphasizes the nonisolational character of situations, objects, and events. Objects and events are never experienced or known in isolation "but only in connection with a contextual whole . . . called a 'situation.'" Dewey does not deny the reality of objects and events but insists that they are special parts, phases, or aspects "of an environing experienced world—a situation." Hence, there is "always a *field* in which observation of *this* or *that* object or event occurs."[12]

I mentioned earlier that a field view must acknowledge interdependence both within fields and between or among fields. This "interdependence" is most forcefully expressed in Dewey's notion of "transaction." In 1949, he coauthored a work with Arthur F. Bentley in which "transaction" was introduced as a more apt term than "interaction" for purposes of describing reality and knowing.[13] "Interaction" was judged inadequate because it conveyed the impression that change involves action between substantially complete and unchanging entities. From a situational, contextual, or transactional perspective there are no such independent entities; therefore, "in a transaction, the components themselves are subject to change. Their character affects and is affected by the transaction."[14] As another commentator expressed it: "Within the various transactional situations, the related aspects are indeed mutual and completely interdependent, as they are in any 'field.'"[15] Hence, when terms are "*understood transactionally,* . . . they do not name items or characteristics of organisms alone, nor do they name items or characteristics of environments alone; in every case, they name the *activity* that occurs *of both together*" (*KK,* 71).

Reverting to field language, we can say that it is the "nature" of every field to flow into or shade off to other fields in such fashion that the fields so related are mutually constitutive of each other. This will be of crucial importance later, when I will extrapolate a relation between the human and divine fields that renders belief in personal immortality plausible. To prepare the ground for this extrapolation, let me here draw upon Dewey's insightful descriptions of the relationship between an organism and its environment. Because this is, of course, a transactional relationship, what he says about it can serve to reinforce points already made. "We live and act," Dewey tells us, "in connection with the existing environment, not in connection with isolated objects" (*L,* 68). When experience is viewed as an organism-environment transaction, this must not be understood as the coming together of two essentially complete and separate realities—"organism" *and* "environment." Indeed, we can now more aptly describe this relationship as between wider and narrower fields that are *distinct* though not *separate.* Thus Dewey is led to say that "an organism does not live *in* an environment, it lives by means of an environment" (*L,* 25). When Dewey elsewhere speaks of seeing "the organism *in* nature, the nervous system in the organism, the brain in the nervous system, the cortex in the brain," he quickly adds that "when thus seen they will be seen *in,* not as marbles are in a box but as events are in history, in a moving, growing never finished process" (*EN,* 295).[16]

It should be noted that "environment" is an open-ended term as Dewey uses it. "Environment,"we are told, "is whatever conditions interact with personal needs, desires, purposes and capacities to create the experience which is had" (*EE,* 42). Another aspect of Dewey's transactional experience that I will utilize in my later extrapolation (though in a way that would probably not please Dewey) is his description of organic life as a process of activity involving an environment as "a transaction extending beyond the spatial limits of the organism" (*L,* 25).

Throughout this section I have stressed the characteristic of transactional mutuality among all related fields, and the following texts indicate how far Dewey was willing to push this mutuality.

> Adaptation, in fine, is as much adaptation *of* the environment to our own activities as our activities to the environment.[17]

> Habits are like functions in many respects, and especially in requiring the cooperation of organism and environment. Breathing is an affair of the air as truly as of the lungs; digesting an affair of food as truly as of tissues of stomach. Seeing involves light just as certainly as it does the eye and optic nerve. Walking implicates the ground as well as the legs; speech demands physical air and human companionship and audience as well as vocal organs.

> Honesty, chastity, malice, peevishness, courage, triviality, industry, irresponsibility are not private possessions of a person. They are working adaptations of personal capacities with environing forces.[18]

Such phenomena as are described in these and other field-supportive texts constitute in part the experiential ground from which I will extrapolate the transactional character of the relations between the divine and human fields.

JAMES'S "PURE EXPERIENCE" AS PRIMORDIAL FIELD
It is one thing to call attention to the difficulties of an ontological dualism and quite another to show how such a dualism is to be overcome. Nowhere is this more evident than in James's radical empiricism or theory of pure experience. This theory is notorious for its lack of clarity, its inconsistencies, and its incompleteness; to render it clear, consistent, and complete would be a formidable achievement.[19] No pretense of doing this or even showing that it is possible is here made. In keeping with my general approach, I will consider James's theory of pure experience insofar as it can contribute to the construction of a field model of the self. More specifically, I will indicate those aspects of the pure experience doctrine that seem in conflict with an adequate field metaphysics and those that are congenial with and supportive of such a perspective.

We have already suggested that James's primary philosophical concern was to devise a method that would enable us to have greater access to and more intimate participation in "the concrete"—which, as I have noted and will continue to stress, is the feature of a "fields" model that most commends it to the purposes of this essay. A quest for the concrete was the dominating motive in James's construction of his theory of pure experience. There is an irony of sorts here in that this is perhaps the most technical and vague of James's doctrines, and often characterized by that very "abstractness" which he frequently criticized in others.

Of course, James is not the only twentieth-century thinker who in an effort to realize concrete experience has *appeared* to bring forth the airiest of abstractions. Henri Bergson, Edmund Husserl, and Martin Heidegger immediately come to mind. One might justifiably say of these thinkers, *mutatis mutandis,* what McDermott said of James: "He does not utilize the notion of 'pure experience' to close off the analysis of the real but to give it new impetus and send it away from traditional but narrow categories. Perhaps he meant it as a heuristic device, as a sort of waiting game" (*WWJ,* xlv). These words are equally applicable to the incipient field theory which is the focus of our concern. I would add, and hope to show, that had James employed more widely and consistently his "field" language rather than his "pure experience" language, he would have better realized his goals while avoiding some unfortunate interpretations of his doctrine. As already noted, however, my concern throughout my exposition of James's doctrines is not with these doctrines in themselves but insofar as they, as I interpret them, are a rich resource for doctrines of self and God that are congenial to and consistent with belief in personal immortality.

James was of the opinion that the traditional doctrines and assumptions of dualism, idealism, and materialism had run their course. Without denying that each had its insight and relative utility, he maintained that each gave rise to problems that were unsolved and would remain insoluble unless certain fundamental presuppositions were surrendered. The key presupposition was that mind and/or matter are ultimate substances or essential modes of being. The dualist held that both are "real"; the idealist, that mind alone is "real"; the materialist, that matter alone is "real." Of course, James was not denying that mind and matter are *in some sense* "real," but the metaphysical question was, "In what sense are they real?" While it is not quite accurate and indeed, as we shall see, is misleading, let us give an initial Jamesian response to this question within the framework of the classical quest for the "*urstoff*" or ultimate character of reality. Thus we would say that reality is ultimately neither mind nor matter, neither subjective nor objective, but is instead "pure experience" or "pure experiences." We would then account for mind and matter, subjective and objective, in terms of pure experience, showing how they are derived from this reality as a result of diverse functions and relations.[20]

James presented his doctrine of pure experience in a series of essays published individually between 1905 and 1907 and later collected under the title *Essays in Radical Empiricism*. Though much in these essays is technical, elusive, inconsistent, and misleading, a few texts from them, combined with some unpublished notes, will be sufficient for my purposes.

In an unpublished note written around 1904, James indicates the intention of his theory of pure experience.

> By the adjective "pure" prefixed to the word, "experience," I mean to denote a form of being which is as yet neutral or ambiguous, and prior to the object and the subject distinction. I mean to show that the attribution either of mental or physical being to an experience is due to nothing in the immediate stuff of which the experience is composed—for the same stuff will serve for either attribution—but rather to two contrasted groups of associates with either of which . . . our reflection . . . tends to connect it. . . . Functioning in the whole context of other experiences in one way, an experience figures as a mental fact. Functioning in another way, it figures as a physical object. In itself it is actually neither, but virtually both. (*TC*, II:385)

In his well-known if not well-understood essay "Does Consciousness Exist?" James contends that in answering this question negatively, he means "only to deny that the word stands for an entity, but to insist most emphatically that it does stand for a function. There is, I mean, no aboriginal stuff or quality of being, contrasted with that of which material objects are made, out of which our thoughts of them are made" (*ERE*, 4).

Consistent with his perspective, James could also have written an essay entitled "Does Matter Exist?" Had he done so, he would have denied *and* affirmed the reality of matter in the same sense in which he denied and affirmed consciousness. James did not write such an essay, because he believed that his point concerning matter as an ultimate substance had already been made by George Berkeley: "*Consciousness as it is ordinarily understood does not exist, any more than does Matter to which Berkeley gave the coup de grâce*" (*ERE*, 271).

Well, if ultimate reality is neither mind nor matter, what is it? James's answer appears to be quite simple: "There is only one primal stuff or material in the world, a stuff of which everything is composed, and . . . we call that stuff 'pure experience'" (*ERE*, 4). And elsewhere, after denying the heterogeneity of thoughts and things, he adds: "*They are made of one and the same stuff, which as such cannot be defined but only experienced; and which, if one wishes, one can call the stuff of experience in general*" (*ERE*, 271). The simplicity of this answer, of course, is most deceptive, for in the same essay in which he speaks of "private stuff,"he states that "there is no *general* stuff of which experience at large is made. There are as many stuffs as there are 'natures' in the things experienced" (*ERE*, 14).

Whether employed in the singular or the plural, the notion of "pure experience" gives rise to a host of difficulties and inconsistencies at worst, and at best is grossly misleading when it is understood as the ultimate substance(s) out of which all things are made. James must unquestionably be held at least partially responsible for this result, but it must be borne in mind that he made no pretense of having given a finished doctrine. Further, he was persuaded of the need to break out of the classical cul-de-sac, and there is a decided exploratory and experimental cast to all his writings concerned with pure experience. Some of the confusion, I would suggest, arises from his tendency to conflate the epistemological and ontological perspectives. I am not contending that they can be completely separated, but methodologically, at least, they must be distinguished.

Let us briefly consider an epistemological explanation and show how, when this is taken without further qualification as an ontological explanation, we land in a doctrine that would seem to be unreconcilable with James's overall philosophy. After asserting "that there is only one primal stuff" and designating "that stuff 'pure experience,' " James goes on to say that "knowing can easily be explained as a particular sort of relation towards one another into which portions of pure experience may enter. The relation itself is a part of pure experience; one of its 'terms' becomes the subject or bearer of knowledge, the knower, the other becomes the object known" (*ERE*, 4–5). It would seem that, for James, "pure experiences" become either physical or psychical depending on the context or relations into which they enter. Thus, he maintains, "experiences are originally of a rather single nature." When, however, these experiences "enter into relations of physical influence . . . we make of them a field apart which we call the physical world." When they enter into a different set of relations, when "they are transitory, physically inert, with a succession which does not follow a determined order but seems rather to obey emotive fancies, we make of them another field which we call the psychical world" (*ERE*, 270).[21] James expresses this same view concerning the "neutrality" of experiences considered in themselves in "How Two Minds Can Know One Thing":

> This "pen," for example, is, in the first instance, a bald *that*, a datum, fact, phenomenon, content, or whatever other neutral or ambiguous name you may prefer to apply. I call it . . . a "pure experience." To get classed either as a physical pen or as some one's percept of a pen, it must assume a *function*, and that can only happen in a more complicated world. (*ERE*, 61)[22]

Whatever the uses this doctrine might have as an epistemological or phenomenological expression, it is most inadequate if translated without qualification into an ontological doctrine. As such it suggests that reality in itself is a multiplicity of "thats" or "pure experiences," which are transformed into mind or matter as a result of their relations and functions. A. J. Ayer, among others (beginning with Bertrand Russell), labels this theory "neutral monism."[23] Richard Stevens comments that "Ayer seems to imply that James envisaged the units of pure experience as a series of ontologically neutral building blocks . . . as elementary atomic particles" (*JH*, 17–18).

While I think Stevens suggests a more fruitful interpretation of the doctrine of pure experience, there can be little doubt that James gives good grounds for interpreting his radical empiricism as a mode of "neutral monism," though this is quite evidently in conflict with other aspects of his philosophy. James stated that "the pure experiences of our philosophy are, in themselves considered, so many little absolutes" (*ERE*, 66).[24] John Wild, commenting on this passage, notes that as "little absolutes" these "pure experiences" would be "without relations to anything outside." Such a view, Wild correctly points out, would lead to "that abstract atomism" that James so often attacked. "How can this be reconciled," Wild asks, "with the field theory, according to which every focused experience is surrounded by a halo of fringes from which it cannot be separated except by a reductive abstraction?"[25]

It is James's desire to describe mind empirically, to avoid locating it "outside" or "beyond" experience, that undoubtedly contributes to the unacceptable interpretation of his doctrine of pure experience labeled "neutral monism." As a minimum, therefore, we can say (with Elizabeth Flower and Murray G. Murphey) that "the point he is making is that experience is what is given before any categorization at all—before the divisions of internal-external, subjective-objective, apparent-real, and therefore certainly before phenomenal-physical and the rest."[26] While it would not have "solved" the related problems, James might have at least avoided some of the confusion to which his doctrine of pure experience has given rise if he had used the more neutral term "field" or "fields" to call attention to that inclusive feature of reality *within which* categorizations such as those just listed are constructed. I will return to this when discussing pure experience as "primordial field," but first a word should be said about the ambiguity of experience and of the term "experience."

Stevens notes "an unresolved ambiguity" in James's use of the term "experience." In the *Principles of Psychology*, James makes personal ownership the first characteristic of consciousness: "It seems as if the elementary fact were not *thought* or *this thought* or *that thought*, but *my thought*, every thought being *owned*" (*PP*, I:221). Stevens points out, however, that "elsewhere, James seems to mean by 'experience' a kind of neutral and unowned givenness which is prior to the emergence of any act of personal appropriation. This linguistic ambiguity may account for the obscurity which seems to permeate his insufficiently articulated theory of pure experience" (*JH*, 92).[27]

James might well reply that the terminological ambiguity is grounded in experiential ambiguity. Several texts from his essay "The Place of Affectional Facts" will indicate the direction such a response might take.

> There is no original spirituality or materiality of being, intuitively discerned, then; but only a translocation of experiences from one world to another; a grouping of them with one set or another of associates for definitely practical or intellectual ends (*ERE*, 74).

If "physical" and "mental" meant two different kinds of intrinsic nature, immediately, intuitively, and infallibly discernible, and each fixed forever in whatever bit of experience it qualified, one does not see how there could have arisen any room for doubt or ambiguity. But if, on the contrary, these words are words of sorting, ambiguity is natural. . . .

The obstinate constroversies that have arisen . . . prove how hard it is to decide by bare introspection what it is in experiences that shall make them either spiritual or material. It surely can be nothing intrinsic in the individual experiences. It is their way of behaving towards each other. Their system of relations, their function; and all these things vary with the context in which we find it opportune to consider them. (*ERE*, 77)[28]

Had James utilized his field language in the considerations expressed in these passages, I think he would have retained his focus upon the concrete, would have taken account of the ambiguity and fluidity accompanying such terms as "physical" and "mental," "spiritual" and "material," while safeguarding his doctrine against any metaphysical atomism or metaphysical dualism. This would have necessitated, however, affirming relation, function, context, and the like as fundamental features of all realities rather than additions to some ultimate realities designated "pure experiences."

But if we do not understand "pure experiences" as irreducible metaphysical atoms, how are we to understand this doctrine? Charlene Seigfried makes a most helpful suggestion by noting that James has submitted "pure experience" as a supposition or hypothesis. Further, she points out that to use "the words 'stuff' and 'material' in connection with pure experience is misleading. It is not a clay-like *materia prima* out of which other things are fashioned" (*CC*, 39). Seigfried goes on to say that "James is not asserting a metaphysical sub-stratum" (*CC*, 40). but is presenting pure experience as a hypothesis that "gives a better explanation of knowing, of subject and object, thought and thing, perception and conception, than does the alternate hypothesis of primordial dualism" (*CC*, 50).

If pure experience is taken as a hypothesis, we are faced with the rather peculiar consequence that it is neither "pure" nor "experience": that is, as "pure" it is not experienced, and as experienced it is not pure. Let me try to indicate the difficulty by considering texts where James does appear to claim instances in which experience can be had in its purity.

The instant field of the present is always experienced in its "pure" state, plain unqualified actuality, a simple *that*, as yet undifferentiated into thing and thought, and only virtually classifiable as objective fact or as someone's opinion about fact. (*ERE*, 36–37)

The instant field of the present is at all times what I call the "pure" experience. It is only virtually or potentially either object or subject as yet. For the time being, it is plain, unqualified actuality or existence, a simple *that*. (*ERE*, 13)

The inclusion of tensed language in these passages—"as yet," "for the time being"—suggests an interpretation fraught with great difficulty: namely, the positing of an existential "that" which is not a "what." The difficulty would seem to be compounded if we posit a multiplicity of heterogeneous "thats," for this would seem to imply that, for example, the pure experiences of "pen" and "table" are differentiated in the absence of any essential (what) differentiating characteristics. Despite his language, therefore, James would not seem to be saying that literally there is a time in which we grasp a "that" which is chronologically prior to our grasping it as a "what."

The closest he comes to saying something like this is in the following text: "Only new-born babes, or men in semi-coma from sleep, drugs, illnesses, or blows, may be assumed to have an experience pure in the literal sense of a *that* which is not yet any definite *what*, tho' ready to be all sorts of whats" (*ERE*, 46). The operative phrase here is "may be assumed," for while (as I will shortly indicate) there are some experiential grounds for this assumption, its hypothetical or suppositional character must be constantly kept in mind. Seigfried is again helpful here, for after asking in what sense pure experience can be spoken of meaningfully if it is never "pure as experienced," she replies, "I think that it can be as a limit concept which enables James to dethrone dualism as the primordial beginning of all experience" (*CC*, 49). Seigfried goes on to refine the nonexperiential character of pure experience:

> James does not say that pure experience is never experienced, but that it is never immediately experienced and communicated as such because as soon as anyone is conscious in a human sense, he already structures that consciousness according to conceptual and verbal categories. Pure experience is indeed the immediate flux of life which furnishes the raw material to later reflections, which is inextricably intertwined with conceptual categories. (*CC*, 51)

In pointing out that the "immediate flux of life" can be experienced but not communicated, she is indicating what I believe to be one of the more fruitful features of James's radical empiricism. Attention was earlier directed to James's claim that experience exceeds logic, that verbalization and conceptualization—however necessary and useful—are never adequate to nor exhaustive of the concrete flow of experience.[29] When the doctrine of pure experience is grasped as an effort to keep us open and present to reality in its overwhelming richness, depth, and experience, the difficulties previously noted are not removed but become peripheral and secondary. Even, then, if "pure experience" can never be experienced "as such," postulating it serves the purpose of keeping us aware of the fact that categorizations, conceptualizations, theories, and the like are not mental representations of concrete reality. The further recognition that categories, concepts, and theories are derived from a wider, everflowing field gives a measure of "experiential" justification for postulating pure experiences that are neither physical nor mental, subjective nor objective, spiritual nor material. In this way dualism, idealism, and materialism are, if not disproved, at least shown to be themselves derivative modes of human thought and experience.

It is, however, when pure experience is treated as a primordial flowing field(s) that it offers the richest possibilities for a field metaphysics. The phenomenological grasp and description of this field as the immediately given or immediately present or immediate appearance is congenial to a speculative effort toward the construction of a metaphysics of fields. While it is not their principal concern, both Stevens and Seigfried in their analyses of pure experience can be useful in the development of such a metaphysics. Though it is merely a matter of emphasis, I wish to rely on Stevens in describing the "givenness" of this primordial field and Seigfried in stressing its flux or processive character. In both instances, of course, relations are inseparably present.

Stevens maintains that James's "resolute return to the data of experience" is a "rediscovery of an absolute sphere of givenness, which antedates every entitative distinction" (*JH,* 15).[30] If the "original field of givenness, i.e., the data of pure experience," is rigorously analyzed, we do not discover the dualistic "distinction between a subject-entity and independent-object entities." We find "only interrelated patterns of givenness" (*JH,* 68).[31] As an "absolute sphere of givenness, which embraces both mind and body, conscious states and their contents," pure experience cannot be reduced to or identified with "a subjective stream" (*JH,* 12). Hence, as we saw earlier, "pure experience is intrinsically neither objective nor subjective, but a larger area within which the *functional* differences between consciousness and the physical world can be defined." As Stevens notes, this "larger area" or pure experience is viewed by James as "a neutralized sphere or field" (*JH,* 10).

One further point concerning this primordial field is noted by both Stevens and Wilshire: namely, the phenomenological, though not necessarily ontological, self-sufficiency and self-containedness of this field. Stevens contends that "the whole purpose of James's theory of Radical Empiricism was to promote the discovery of an absolute field of experience, a zone of pure givenness which would depend upon nothing beyond itself for justification" (*JH,* 115). In a similar vein, Wilshire writes:

> I think that James' notion of the "originals of experience," which he develops in the *Principles,* is the root-notion of his later metaphysics of pure experience. The key idea of that metaphysics is that experience is pure in the sense that "it leans on nothing"—it is the self-contained foundation. A pure experience is a "specific nature"—a "fact" in the sense that it has an irreducible meaning, *not* in the sense that it is necessarily a truth about the actual physical world. (*WJP,* 167)

Let me suggest now how this primordial given might be expressed in more speculative and metaphysical field language. Suppose we postulate

pure experience as a primordial inclusive field(s) capable of being differentiated into distinct fields such as the mental and the physical. Since both the
mental and the physical are *within* the field of pure experience, there is no
ultimate ontological dualism. This in itself, of course, does not tell us what
it is that determines fields to be physical or mental, but it keeps us focused
upon concrete experience in our effort to make such determination. By having to make any distinction such as mind and body, subjective and objective, spiritual and material in terms of distinct functions and relational processes, we are enabled to continually expand our awareness of the concrete
while not confusing it with any theoretical entities such as sense data, physicochemical atoms, ideas, and the like. Any distinctions made will be recognized as derivative rather than ultimate and will have to be justified in terms
of their experiential fruitfulness rather than as allegedly mirroring or corresponding to different ontological entities or orders of being. By grasping
reality or experience relationally rather than atomistically, we are led to recognize both its continuities and its discontinuities. By grasping it processively, we avoid locking reality into one form or another but instead
recognize its characteristics of shifting, overlapping, fusing, and separating.

As I indicated in the general discussion of "fields," a larger field is always
constituted by narrower fields that are both continuous with and distinct
from the wider field. This wider field is homogeneous, being neither reducible to nor simply identical with its narrower fields. Since the wider
field, like all fields, is dynamic, it is continually giving rise to new fields.[32]
Hence, for example, one "portion" of this field acting upon another gives
rise to a distinction that can be designated as knower and known, or meaning and content, or subject and object. The important point in terms of
James's radical empiricism is that there is no need to go outside or beyond
experience (ever widening field) to account for "real" distinction and difference of function of one portion of this field (experience) upon another.
They are really distinct because they are two different functions involving
two distinct sets of relations, but they are not ontologically different because
they are and remain two different functions of the *same* experience (field).[33]

Just as important as the "givenness" character of the primordial field(s) of
pure experience is its "flux" character. James's recognition of and emphasis
upon the processive, changing, or developmental features of reality are present in his earliest writings, but only in his final years does he draw out the
full metaphysical implications of the experience of reality as changing. For a
period of about two and a half years between 1905 and 1908, James recorded
his reflective efforts to meet certain criticisms of his doctrine of "pure experience."[34] In a 1906 note, James raises against himself a crucial question:
"May not my whole trouble be due to the fact that I am still treating what is
really a living and dynamic situation by logical and statical categories?" He
goes on to say that "if life be anywhere active, and if its activity be an
ultimate characteristic, inexplicable by aught lower or simpler, I ought not

to be afraid to postulate activity" (*TC,* II:760). In his Hibbert Lectures—delivered in 1908–09 and later published under the title *A Pluralistic Universe*—James, encouraged by his encounter with Bergson, bites the metaphysical bullet and makes "flux" the heart of his metaphysics. In doing so, he does not deny the utility and necessity of concepts and conceptualization, but he explicitly rejects their ability to give us reality in its "thickness." He readily grants that direct acquaintance and conceptual knowledge are complementary,

> but if, as metaphysicians, we are more curious about the inner nature of reality or about what really *makes it go,* we must turn our backs upon our winged concepts altogether, and bury ourselves in the thickness of those passing moments over the surface of which they fly, and on particular points of which they occasionally rest and perch. . . . Dive back into the flux itself, then, Bergson tells us, if you wish to *know* reality, that flux which Platonism, in its strange belief that only the immutable is excellent, has always spurned; turn your face toward sensation, that flesh-bound thing which rationalism has always loaded with abuse. (*PU,* 112–13)

James goes on to say that "the essence of life is its continuously changing character," and it is this distinctive feature of reality as given "in the perceptual flux which the conceptual translation so fatally leaves out." Since "our concepts are all discontinuous and fixed," we can make them coincide with life only by supposing that life intrinsically contains "positions of arrest." This effort to make our concepts congruent with life or reality is doomed to fail, since "you can no more dip up the substance of reality with them than you can dip up water with a net, however finely meshed" (*PU,* 113).

This "flux" emphasis is already present in James's doctrine of "pure experience": in "The Thing and Its Relations," published early in 1905, he states, "'Pure experience' is the name which I gave to the immediate flux of life which furnishes the material to our later reflection with its conceptual categories" (*ERE,* 46). I earlier called attention to Seigfried's suggestion that "pure experience is a limit concept, an explanatory hypothesis which can be postulated but not experienced as such." Given the definition of pure experience "as the instant field of the present, the immediate flux of life before categorization," she further points out that "the stream of consciousness provides an experiential correlate which comes closest to pure experience and therefore is a useful model for explicating the more obscure hypothesis." A fruitful consequence of "proposing a continuous, unbroken flux as the basic paradigm of experience" is that we will thereby "be induced in our ordinary, interpreted experience to take continuity and flux seriously and will, consequently, experience the transitions and not be fixated on the objectified world" (*CC,* 51–53).[35]

James's evident concern—indeed passion—for the concrete in no way diminishes the importance of concepts, abstractions, theories, symbols, beliefs, and the like; rather it increases their importance so long as we continue to recognize that these are not ends or entities in themselves but processes or activities by which we are enabled to participate ever more fully in that ongoing reality whose depth can be touched and appreciated but never exhausted through either perception or conception.

Later, with specific reference to personal immortality, the important implications and consequences of this continuing dialectic between the human field(s) in its individual and collective modes and the wider field(s) of reality will be explored. For now, let me call attention to the character of "activity" as belonging to all fields. "Bare activity," Seigfried points out, "is predicable of the world of pure experience." Such distinctions as actor and acted upon, cause and effect, do not apply to experience in its immediacy, though they can quite properly be introduced "when the field of experience is enlarged." Seigfried contends—quite correctly, I believe—that "the meaning of activity, in its immediacy, is just these experiences of process, obstruction, strain and release" (*CC*, 96). This phenomenological description seems to me supportive of a metaphysical extrapolation that would postulate activity as characteristic of *all* realities. As mentioned above, panactivism rather than panpsychism would seem to be a more fruitful way of characterizing James's metaphysics, despite his own language. Bruce Kuklick interprets *A Pluralistic Universe* as an affirmation of panpsychism and a rejection of neutral monism.[36] I find Kuklick closer to James's tendency on this matter than Perry, who laments James's compromising the "theory that mind is a peculiar type of relationship among terms which in themselves are neither physical nor mental . . . through identifying the continuum of experience with consciousness great and small" (*TC*, II:592). It is just this identification that Kuklick reads as expressive of James's view as expressed in his last philosophy. Having gotten beyond conceptualization, James found that "neutral experience was now not neutral, but throbbing, alive, constantly coalescing and recoalescing. This conscious experience was not unitary but contained ever-widening spans of consciousness within some of which human consciousness might lie" (*RAP*, 333).

This notion of "ever-widening spans of consciousness" is most important for the purposes of this essay. It is not necessary, however, to posit spans of consciousness as coextensive with reality. Here again, field language can keep us open to this feature of reality without universalizing it and giving rise to the problems attached to panpsychism. To employ Kuklick's language, we might say that all fields—from electronic to divine—are "throbbing, alive, constantly coalescing and recoalescing." There is no need, however, to conclude that all fields are "conscious" as long as we do not, a priori, identify "consciousness" and "activity." Further, there is an ambiguity in the way Kuklick employs the term "neutral." While "pure experience" can be neutral as regards the physical or psychical, it cannot be neutral as regards process and relation. By this I mean that pure experience is open to manifestation as either physical or psychical, but it is not open to being non-processive or nonrelational. Since *all* fields, as we have seen, are processive and relational, hence "constantly coalescing and recoalescing," reality has a continuity and commonness that exclude ontological dualism. Since, however, the processes and relations constituting any field are multiple and variegated, we avoid any monism, affirming instead metaphysical pluralism. Our distinguishing conscious fields from nonconscious fields, therefore, must be based upon distinct functions rather than ultimately different kinds of being.

CHAPTER 2

Toward a Field Model of the Self

> What an abyss of uncertainty, whenever the mind
> feels overtaken by itself; when it, the seeker, is at
> the same time the dark region through which it
> must go seeking and where all equipment will
> avail it nothing.
> —Marcel Proust
> *Remembrance of Things Past*

> When I find myself, I always find that self
> coexisting with something facing that self,
> something in front of it and opposing it; the
> world or the circumstance, the surroundings. It
> is certain that this something does not exist by
> itself, apart from me. . . . But neither do I ever
> exist alone and within myself; my existing is
> coexisting with that which is not I. Reality, then,
> is this interdependence and coexistence.
> —José Ortega y Gasset
> *Some Lessons in Metaphysics*

It is, perhaps, a suggestive irony that we live in an age characterized by both an obsessive concern for the ego or individual self and a denial that there is any such reality. The first characteristic is manifest in the charges that contemporary experience is best described as narcissistic, or that the present generation is the "me" generation, or that ours is a hedonistic culture in which self-satisfaction is the dominant if not exclusive value. The denials of the ego or the individual self come from the more intellectually sophisticated segments of the community, taking such various forms as Buddhist "no-self" doctrines and structuralist and deconstructionist movements. Both perspectives have validity not only as descriptions but, more important, as expressions of significant human concerns, neither of which can be ignored in any effort to construct a viable view of the human self. Yet the sharp contrast and conflict between these apparently opposed perspectives, combined with the multiplicity of technical problems involved, should temper any hopes for the emergence in the near future of anything approaching a definitive doctrine of the self. "Everything one says about the self," as Ralph Harper perceptively notes, "should be regarded as tentative, born in swirling mists of conflict and self-conflict."[1] Such a cautionary warning is even more necessary in an effort whose deliberate purpose is the construction of a model of the self that is open to the possibility of immortality or, as a bare minimum, does not conclusively exclude a belief in immortality or resurrection.

CONCERNING A "FIELD MODEL" FOR THE "SELF"

My modest but still relatively ambitious aim here is not to present a "theory" of the self, or even a "model" in the more technical and developed sense of these terms, but rather to describe the broad outlines of what a "field-self" ought to involve. The development and detailed filling-out of this sketch would necessitate relating and applying it to a variety of disciplines and areas of human experience. For example, it would be necessary to relate the constructed model to data and theories in physics, chemistry, biology, psychology, and sociology. Further, one would have to show that this model is suggestive and illuminating as regards moral, political, and religious questions. Most important would be to indicate how it might allow for fruitful transactions between and among those various disciplines and distinct spheres of experience. As with any theory or model, therefore, a field model of the self would have to be tested and then developed, modified, or rejected in terms of its experiential fruits. This testing, of course, is really a collective, long-run testing and is not to be realized by any individual or restricted group of individuals. Indeed, within the pragmatic frame, the most that could be hoped for would be a relatively complete confirmation in the form of an ever expanding and enriching dialectic between cumulating diverse data and the relatively stable but ever developing fields that constitute the self. The open-ended character of such an endeavor is in keeping with the kind of world already described.

The most that can be claimed for what follows is that it suggests a direction and something of what might be achieved by the utilization of the "fields" metaphor in relation to the human self. As such, it might be designated an ontological or metaphysical speculation which though distinct from must also be consistent with both empirical and phenomenological inquiries. Needless to say, such a speculation neither supplants nor substitutes for either of these activities. Finally, a particular concern of this speculation will be to open up ethical and religious possibilities and indicate how these activities might be justified.

Even in this rather vague, initiating stage of speculative inquiry, however, one must do more than advance airy generalizations or gratuitous hypotheses. Hence, the model constructed must be "reasonably" coherent and consistent; that is, it must not involve gross illogicalities, and it must not be in conflict with well-attested and firmly grounded data from the various intellectual disciplines. Further, it must flow from, be consistent with, and help develop the processive-relational world that is being presupposed. In sum, in keeping with the assumed pragmatic perspective, this model of the self must do—or at least allow for the possibility of doing—the following:

1. preserve individuality without falling into atomistic individualism or egocentric isolationism;
2. account for change, growth, and development;
3. account for a range and diversity of relations;
4. account for continuity, identity, sameness, and difference;
5. account for a variety of structures or dynamic systems such as the psychological, personal, historical, cultural, social, and religious;
6. indicate how individuals *both* make and are made by language, history, art, science, religion, and other institutions;
7. allow for creative participation in wider processes or fields;
8. allow for radical transformation without obliteration or absorption into another reality or process.

Now what, it might be asked, does such a self have to do with immortality or resurrection? The claim made is that such a self is not necessarily prohibited from continuing its reality and activities beyond the parameters of what is customarily described as "this world." At the same time, any concern for immortality must be shown to deepen and intensify rather than diminish participation in the "here and now." Hence, given the kind of world or reality already described, continuance in a new life is not in itself in conflict with such participation. The kind of world, therefore, in which personal immortality is a possibility would be a richer and more variegated world than one from which it is definitively excluded.

SELF AS "FIELDS WITHIN FIELDS . . ."
Let me try to describe this self explicitly as "fields within fields. . . ." I want to suggest that a self is composed of submicroscopic, microscopic, macroscopic, and ultramacroscopic fields. Without any pretense to an exhaustive enumeration, we can list the following fields as continuous and overlapping but nevertheless distinct. Among the submicroscopic fields would be found atoms, electrons, neutrons, protons, and whatever may be the latest particles designated by the physicists. Cells and molecules are, of course, microscopic fields, themselves constructed of the submicroscopic fields just mentioned. We enter the realm of macroscopic fields when we focus on organs such as the brain, heart, and liver as well as muscles and bones. Again, these macroscopic fields are constituted by distinctive cell fields and in turn constitute the individual organism, itself a macroscopic field. At this point it might be useful, to distinguish between "inner" and "outer" macroscopic fields that enter into the reality of the individual organism. Those just listed would, of course, be "inner"; among the "outer" would be atmospheric and environmental fields such as oxygen, hydrogen, water, foodstuffs, and other organisms. We move into the realm of ultramacroscopic fields when we locate the multiplicity of macroscopic fields

within the earth field. This field in turn is located within the solar field, which is within the galactic field, which is within the universe field, which is within . . . .

To this point the description of the self is most uncontroversial, but it is also most incomplete: uncontroversial because I have included only those fields whose "observability" and "reality" evoke a high level of consensus; incomplete because I have not included those fields that most distinguish human selves from other organic fields. When we focus on any human organism, we are compelled to acknowledge additional fields: the unconscious, the dispositional, the conceptual, the social, the personal, the cultural, the religious, the historical, and the like. I have deliberately avoided labeling these fields as physical and psychological or mental, in order to avoid any ontological dualism. It may be useful later to reintroduce such distinctions as functional categories; for the moment, however, I wish simply to stress that *all* these fields are real and interdependent, and are involved in the structure of the self. Any reductionism that would give an ontological priority to any field or group of fields is unacceptable. This is not to say that all these fields must have the same degree of intimacy in relation to the self. Whether they are all *inseparable* from the reality of the self is a speculative question that must be addressed later.

For the moment, it will suffice to describe the various aspects characterizing the self from the field perspective. When James speaks of the self as "all shades and no boundaries," he is rejecting any encapsulated self—any self enclosed within the envelope of the skin or in some inner ego or mind.[2] As John Herman Randall, Jr., has noted: "It is indeed amazing that students of man should ever have convinced themselves that the mechanisms of human behavior are located exclusively within the skin of the organism, or within a private and subjective 'mind,' in view of the obvious fact that everything that distinguishes man from the other animals is a common and social possession."[3]

It is this image of the self as radiating "outward" and overlapping and being overlapped by numerous other fields that must constantly be kept in mind as we focus our attention on particular aspects. Initially and tentatively, therefore, let us understand "the self"[4] as the widest and most inclusive field in relation to the plurality of subfields mentioned earlier. Of course, it is wide and inclusive only in relation to these subfields, because in relation to suprafields it is itself a subfield. Whether this "field-self" is a postulate and what grounds there are, if any, for such a postulate are questions that can be addressed only after we have attempted to describe the distinguishing characteristics of this self.

THE FIELD-SELF AS NONDUALISTIC

As the history of philosophy repeatedly attests, any shift in perspective or any new idea emerges and can be understood only in reference to the perspective or idea it is endeavoring to replace. The Introduction notes that a process view of reality rejects any metaphysical or ontological dualism whereby reality is bifurcated into the changing and the unchanging, the temporal and the eternal. Similarly, a field view of the self resists such dualisms as mind-body, psychical-physical, spiritual-material, subjective-objective, insofar as these terms refer to essentially different orders of reality.[5] This is not to suggest that these distinctions have no meaning or utility, or that there is no difference between, for example, thinking and walking, or willing and running. The question is how to account for such differences, and a nondualistic view denies that they must be accounted for by dichotomizing the self and the world in such a manner as to locate one set of activities in a realm designated spiritual and the other set in a realm designated material. More positively, the field view suggested here will attempt to account for these real differences and distinctions in terms of functions and processes, so that while rejecting various modes of ontological dualism, it will not hesitate to affirm a variety of *functional* dualisms.

Of more immediate concern is whether, given the stated aim of this essay, it will be possible to avoid attributing features to the self that render this model vulnerable to some of the objections raised against dualism.[6] Since I intend to describe or construct a model that does not exclude the possibility of the self's continuing and participating in a life beyond the parameters of what we customarily call "this world," some will see such effort as a "bad faith" attempt to escape contemporary arguments against dualism. Hence, let me say immediately that if any view of the self that allows it a reality and life not confined to the explicitly localizable and identifiable parameters of "this world" is called "dualism," then of course my view must be so designated. While I believe such a definition unjustifiably restrictive, what is important in the final analysis is not the particular label but whether persuasive evidence and arguments, as well as plausible speculations, can be marshaled in support of a field-self.

PRAGMATIC OBJECTIONS TO DUALISM

Whatever the differences between Greek, medieval, and modern expressions of dualism, they all affirm the reality of an immaterial substance or substantial principle. Whether designated mind, intellect, or soul, this principle or entity is made of a kind of being and belongs to an order of reality essentially different from the body to which it is joined—mysteriously or naturally. The nonexistence of such a principle cannot, of course, be proved, and pragmatism makes no such claim. "Our reasonings," James conceded, "have not established the nonexistence of the Soul; they have only proved its superfluity for scientific purposes" (*PP,* I:332). We miss the thrust and bite of James's criticism if we understand "scientific" in a narrow positivistic sense, which would leave open the possibility of accounting for the soul by a "philosophical" method. It is the uselessness of the "soul" for the purposes of the broadest intellectual inquiry that leads the pragmatist to exclude it from any explanatory effort. James expresses this view: "My final conclusion, then, about the substantial Soul is that it explains nothing and guarantees nothing" (*PP*, I:331). Many years later, with his customary philosophic generosity, James conceded that "some day, indeed, souls may get their innings again in philosophy," but this will happen "only when someone has found in the term a pragmatic significance that has hitherto eluded observation" (*PU*, 95–96). James is, perhaps, being unduly gracious here, since "souls" with "pragmatic significance" would not be the same "souls" as those being rejected.

Now a defender of a soul theory would undoubtedly reply that the soul is posited precisely *because* of its explanatory power and pragmatic significance. The soul serves as a rational explanation of why an organic being has unity, identity, continuity, and individuality. The pragmatist, as we shall see, must indeed account for these characteristics of the self and give some indication of how this might be done *without* positing a substantial soul. Even apart from these features, however, it might be argued that great pragmatic significance attaches to an immaterial substance or soul insofar as its simplicity and incorruptibility guarantees its natural immortality. James does not deny that such a soul would be immortal; his claim is that the immortality would be such that most people would not desire it.

> The Soul, however, when closely scrutinized, guarantees no immortality of a sort *we care for*. The enjoyment of the atom-like simplicity of their substance *in saecula saeculorum* would not to most people seem a consummation devoutly to be wished. The substance must give rise to a stream of consciousness continuous with the present stream, in order to arouse our hope, but of this the mere persistence of the substance *per se* offers no guarantee. (*PP*, I:330)

I will explore this text more fully in presenting a substantive self as a more fruitful model than a substantial soul. For the moment, let it serve to indicate why, from a pragmatic perspective, the substantial soul is considered devoid of significant experiential fruits.

The oldest, most persistent, and strongest argument for the existence of an immaterial substance stems from that intellectual activity which distinguishes human beings from other conscious beings. The argument takes a variety of forms, but as Randall describes it, the contention is basically that since humans are able to grasp universals which are simple and immaterial, they "must 'have' or 'possess' a 'single unextended immaterial spiritual principle' [called 'Mind'] *with which* to do it!" (*NHE*, 218). Randall presents three major reasons why this argument does "not seem to present-day metaphysicians very fruitful."

The first reason is that to posit a distinct principle for every distinct activity would destroy the possibility of explanation and intelligibility: "Every distinguishable process of Nature would then have to be accomplished by a principle unique and proper to itself." Such an indefinite multiplication of principles would lead to intellectual chaos, rendering it impossible to "explain" any phenomenon. Randall asks us to imagine what physics would look like "had Nature been really so constituted that each of her distinguishable productions required a specifically different mechanism as its necessary condition!" (*NHE*, 218–19).

Randall's second reason for rejecting the characterization of "Mind" as an immaterial substance is that to do so is "to convert the operation of a 'power' into its own mechanism and conditions." The argument here is that merely to posit "mind" as the "power" to act "is to remain with a mere statement of the observed facts, without attempting any further analysis of the complex mechanisms involved." In other words, to attempt to explain thinking by saying we have the "power" to think is to say and explain nothing. Randall considers such a view analogous to the famous satirical example of Molière "of trying to 'explain' the observed action of opium upon the human organism as due to its 'dormitive powers' " (*NHE*, 219).

Randall's final objection is that construing "Mind" as a unique kind of substance makes the factors involved in thinking "wholly private and inaccessible" and thereby "obscures all the cultural and environmental factors which are in reality necessary conditions of any 'functioning mentally' " (*NHE*, 219–20). In sum, then, the objections raised by Randall, which accurately reflect the views of both James and Dewey, not only call attention to the emptiness of the substantial soul principle but, more important, emphasize that the positing of such a principle tends to divert energy from more concrete and fruitful avenues of investigation.

Dewey was particularly sensitive to what might be called the existential consequences of any ontological dualism. He notes how such a perspective leads to the extremes of both objectivism and subjectivism, which, though opposed, give impetus and justification one to the other. The location of the "objective" and the "subjective" in essentially different and discontinuous orders of reality results in reciprocal excesses. "An objectivism which ignores initiating and re-organizing desire and imagination will in the end only strengthen that other phase of subjectivism which consists in escape to the enjoyment of inward landscape." This ontological split inevitably leads to a split in philosophy whereby we have a "realistic" philosophy "for mathematics, physical science and the established social order; another, and opposed philosophy for the affairs of personal life" (*EN*, 241). Dewey goes on to say:

> The objection to dualism is not just that it is a dualism, but that it forces upon us antithetical, non-convertible principles of formulation and interpretation. If there is a complete split in nature and experience then of course no ingenuity can explain it away; it must be accepted. But in case no such sharp division actually exists, the evils of supposing there is one are not confined to philosophical theory. Consequences within philosophy are of no great import. But philosophical dualism is but a formulated recognition of an impasse in life; an

impotence in interaction, inability to make effective transition, limitation of power to regulate and thereby to understand. (*EN*, 241–42)

The years since Dewey wrote these words have hardly served to diminish the potentially disastrous consequences of dividing reality and human experience into two worlds having such basically different constitutions and touching and communicating with each other only indirectly, accidentally, and incidentally. As the allegedly "impersonal" and "objective" orders of science, technology, and society have grown to overwhelming proportions, there has emerged in response the passionate call for the recognition and practice of activities that flow from and depend almost totally upon allegedly "inner experience" or "personal faith" or "humanistic insight" or "religious revelation." At no time in history, perhaps, has there been a greater need to overcome the isolating opposition of these distinct "aspects" of reality and experience, and to create fruitful means and channels of transaction and communication. This, needless to say, is a formidable task that demands the fullest participation of a diversity of human beings bringing their distinctive experiences to bear upon this question. There will be no shortcuts and many deadends, as there are in any kind of experimental activity. As a minimum, however, an effort must be made to rid ourselves of that deeply ingrained prejudice that has converted distinct functions and processes, which flow into and overlap one another, into discontinuous realms of reality and experience.

FIELD-SELF AND MATERIALISM

There have been three metaphysical accounts, though with many variations, of reality and human beings. In addition to the dualism just discussed, there have been two forms of monism. Idealistic monism maintains that all reality is ultimately reducible to mind or is a mode or manifestation of mind or idea. Materialism, as the polar opposite of idealism, has insisted that all reality is reducible to matter—including mind, which is nothing but a mode or manifestation of matter.[7] Where are we to locate field metaphysics? My suggestion is that while partaking of aspects of all three of these traditional views, field metaphysics is not reducible to or completely identifiable with any of them. Abstractly considered, a field model is indifferent to these three views and hence could quite easily be employed by any or all of them. Only after I have spelled out in more concrete detail a field model that I judge adequate will we be able to see what is shared and not shared with these other views. Yet inasmuch as both James and Dewey can be and have been read, at least in part, as materialists, a few preliminary words are in order.[8]

The various expressions of contemporary materialisms are a long way from the relatively clear-cut materialism of Democritus, in which atoms of varying sizes and shapes alone were considered real and the apparent differences we experience due solely to the arrangement of these atoms. When the anthropology of Claude Lévi-Strauss and the history of Fernand Braudel are described as materialisms, it is evident that something much more subtle is at work.[9] Fortunately, it is not the task of this essay to delineate the distinguishing features of these intellectual expressions. I need only indicate a few broad and relatively unrefined meanings of materialism to differentiate it from the field metaphysics that is here proposed.

Reductive materialism is the oldest and most unequivocal expression of materialism. Simply stated, it claims that everything real is reducible to whatever happens to be understood as "matter." Thus, however different things may appear, ultimate analysis reveals them to be *nothing but* the basic constituents of matter variously organized. This reductionist perspective is succinctly and explicitly expressed by a character in one of Stanislaw Lem's science fiction short stories.

> Are not we as well, if you examine us physically, mechanistically, statistically, and meticulously, nothing but the miniscule capering of electron clouds? Positive and negative charges arranged in space? And is our existence not the result of subatomic collisions and the interplay of particles, though we ourselves perceive those molecular cartwheels as fear, longing, or meditation? And when you daydream, what transpires within your brain but the binary algebra of connecting and disconnecting circuits, the continual meandering of electrons?[10]

Such a reductive materialism is subject to rather widespread criticism,[11] and among its critics we can safely place pragmatism with its field metaphysics. We have already asserted that all fields or relational processes are real and that the task of inquiry is to discover the distinctive features of these fields and their relations and transactions without assigning metaphysical priority or exclusivity to any of them. Materialism, as Randall indicates,

> illustrates where one gets when one does not take activities and processes as primary and irreducible subject-matter. A sound metaphysics would say, activities, operations, and processes "exist," and are effected by means of mechanisms distinguished as factors involved in those processes. "Materialism" locates the means and mechanisms involved; then by reductive analysis, holds that *only* these mechanisms can be said to "exist"—what they *do* does not "exist," but is merely something else. (*NHE*, 206)[12]

James raises what might be called an existential or moral objection to materialism:

> A philosophy whose principle is so incommensurate with our most intimate powers as to deny them all relevancy in universal affairs, as to annihilate their motives at one blow, will be even more unpopular than pessimism. Better face the enemy than the eternal Void! This is why materialism will always fail of universal adoption, however well it may fuse things into an atomistic unity, however clearly it may prophesy the future eternity. For materialism denies

reality to the objects of almost all the impulses which we most cherish. The real *meaning* of the impulses, it says, is something which has no emotional interest for us whatever. (*WB*, 70–71)

Now while it is clear that pragmatism's field metaphysics escapes the net of reductive materialism, it is not so evident that it escapes what might be called "effective materialism." By this I mean any view which, while denying that the self and its activities are identical with or reducible to the physicochemical fields to which they are intimately related, also denies that the self and its activities can have any existential reality apart from these *specific* physicochemical fields.

Such a view, of course, undermines the chief concern of this essay.[13] It is incumbent upon me to construct a field model of the self that does *not exclude* the possibility of the self's continuing to exist independently of *some* of the fields with which it is presently involved. Note that there will be no claim of *proving* that such an existence is possible. The task is to show that this is an open possibility, thereby allowing for a reasonable "faith," which will have to be supported by grounds other than those that emerge from the analysis and construction of a field-self. I will continue to draw principally upon James and Dewey in the construction of a model of the field-self. Remember, the intention is not to show that either of these thinkers has a fully developed view of the self but rather to utilize often inconsistent aspects of their thought. This means that I may apply their insights and ideas in ways that are not explicit in their texts and that may even in some instances be in opposition to some of their conclusions.

Overall, this will be so in the case of Dewey more than of James. The question of effective materialism is a good example. James, though often inconsistent in details, is surely open to the kind of field-self here suggested, particularly when his thought is considered in all its aspects, including the ethical and the religious. Dewey, on the other hand, will have to be classified as an effective materialist, since he holds "that all the subject-matter of experience is dependent upon physical conditions."[14] Nevertheless, the issue is not as clear-cut and unequivocal as it first appears, and I wish to show that much in Dewey is congenial to a field view of the self in spite of his unsympathetic attitude toward any speculation about immortality.

DEWEY'S RELATIONAL VIEW OF "MIND" AND "MATTER"

Dewey gives two closely connected reasons as to why he did "not come out frankly and use the word *materialism*." Together, they are a succinct expression of his more developed relational view of "mind" and "matter." His first reason for rejecting the label of materialism is that philosophies so designated posit a metaphysical view of *substance* in which matter is a substance and "the only substance." Since Dewey rejects *all* modes of metaphysical substantialism, he also rejects materialism as a mode of substantialism.

Dewey's second reason is but an empirical specification of the first. Materialism is an antithetical position opposing matter to the psychical and mental posited as *spiritual*. Having abandoned this antithetical perspective, Dewey fails "to see what meaning 'matter' and 'materialism' have for philosophy." He goes on to note that "*matter* has a definite assignable meaning in physical science. It designates something capable of being expressed in mathematical symbols which are distinguished from those defining *energy*." The generalizing of this definite meaning of "matter" into the philosophical view of materialism is no more legitimate than "generalizing what is designated as energy in physics into spiritualistic metaphysics." If one employs the term "matter" as philosophically, therefore, "this meaning . . . should be to name a *functional* relation rather than a substance." It would then be appropriate to use the term "matter" as "a name for existential conditions in their function *as* conditions of all special forms of socio-biotic activities and values" (*EKV,* 605).

Whatever difficulties this doctrine might pose for the field view of the self, the following text clearly expresses Dewey's rejection of reductionistic materialism.

> But recognition that all these activities and values are existentially conditioned—and do not arise out of the blue or out of a separate substance called spirit—is far from constituting materialism in its metaphysical sense. For it is only by setting out from the activities and values in experience just as they *are* experienced that inquiry can find the clues for discovery of their conditions. Denial that the former are just what they are thus destroys the possibility of ascertaining their conditions so that "materialism" commits suicide. It is quite possible to recognize that everything experienced, no matter how "ideal" and lofty, has its own determinate conditions without getting into that generalization beyond limits which constitute metaphysical materialism. (*EKV,* 605)[15]

Over a decade earlier, Dewey had presented his ideas on the mind–matter question in his great metaphysical work, *Experience and Nature.*[16] This rich, subtle, and complex text does not admit of easy summarization or articulation; my concern is to highlight a few passages that point in the direction of a field metaphysics and a field view of the self. In doing so, of course, I must touch upon and quickly pass over a number of questions and aspects of Dewey's philosophy that merit much fuller treatment. Among these would be the nature and role of "events" in his metaphysics; the question of "meaning"; the importance of "quality"; the distinction between "having" and "knowing" and the allied doctrine that there is no immediate knowledge; and the nature and role of "mind," "matter," "consciousness," "spirit," and the like.

Dewey maintains that the tendency of modern science to substitute "qualitative events" for "the older notion of fixed substances" points "to the idea of matter and mind as significant characters of events presented in different contexts, rather than underlying and ultimate substances" (*EN,* xi).

At first glance, it might seem that Dewey is positing "events" as the ultimate constituents of reality, neither mental nor material but becoming so according to the context into which they enter. Such an interpretation would be similar to the "neutral monism" interpretation of James's doctrine of "pure experience" and would be subject to the same criticisms. Again, therefore, I would suggest understanding "events" as fields—as processive-relational realities. For Dewey, such events can be "had" or immediately grasped, but they cannot be "known."[17]

Nevertheless, by seeing nature as a complex of events, we are kept aware of its processive-relational character and can avoid identifying it with or reducing it to any specific quality. Thus, Dewey tells us, "when nature is viewed as consisting of events rather than substances, it is characterized by *histories*, that is, by continuity of change proceeding from beginnings to endings" (*EN*, xi–xiii). Further, "events, being events and not rigid and lumpy substances, are ongoing and hence as such unfinished, incomplete, indeterminate" (*EN*, 159).[18]

When Dewey comes to describe mind and matter, he assigns both to "the complex of events that constitute nature" (*EN*, 75). He finds "the notion that the universe is split into two separate and disconnected realms of existence, one psychical and the other physical . . . the acme of incredibility" (*EN*, 267–68). If one begins with the assumption that mind and matter are "two separate things," then one has the task of restoring the connection between them. Both "mechanistic metaphysics" and "spiritualistic metaphysics" begin with this assumption, though they account for the restoration in diametrically opposite ways. For the former, the "cause" that accounts for the other's existence is "matter"; for the latter, it is "mind." In both instances there is "a breach in the continuity of historic process," which can be avoided by simply observing such processes as "growth from infancy to maturity, or the development of a melodic theme" (*EN*, 273–74). It is the notion of growth, according to Dewey, that enables one "to detect the fallacy in both views."

> The reality *is* the growth-process itself; childhood and adulthood are phases of a continuity, in which just because it is a history, the latter cannot exist until the earlier exists ("mechanistic materialism" in germ); and in which the later makes use of the registered and cumulative outcome of the earlier—or, more strictly, *is* its utilization ("spiritualistic teleology" in germ). The real existence is the history in its entirety, the history as just what it is. (*EN*, 275)

In stressing the processive character of reality, Dewey is not affirming a doctrine of chaotic, undifferentiated flux. We can distinguish and differentiate realities and aspects of realities on the bases of "rates of change" and breadth of connections or relations. Not all processes change or proceed at the same rate. "The rate of change of some things is so slow, or is so rhythmic, that these changes have all the advantages of stability in dealing with more transitory and irregular happenings" (*EN*, 71).[19] Dewey finds it a mark of "sound practical sense" when the slower and regular events are designated "structure" and the more rapid and irregular ones "process." But this is a "relational and functional distinction" that both spiritualistic ide-alism and materialism treat "as something fixed and absolute. One doctrine finds structure in a framework of ideal forms, the other finds it in matter" (*EN*, 71–72).

Just as "structure"and "process" are differentiated on the basis of a "rela-tional and functional distinction," so are "mind" and "matter." Dewey, along with a number of other contemporary thinkers, has called attention to the misleading feature of language whereby we are led to posit substantive things or entities wherever we encounter nouns: "It is a plausible prediction that if there were an interdict placed for a generation upon the use of mind, matter, consciousness as nouns, and we were obliged to employ adjectives and adverbs, conscious and consciously, mental and mentally, material and physically, we should find many of our problems much simplified" (*EN*, 75).

Note that Dewey does not claim that our problems would be "solved" by a mere shift in terminology but that they would be "much simplified." We might at least avoid a number of dead-end "solutions" which, while giving us a kind of abstract coherence or rationality, divert our attention and ener-gies from the more concrete experiential aspects of reality. I have suggested that such refocusing is a definite fruit of describing reality in terms of fields, of processive-relational complexes, rather than in terms of essentially differ-ent "things" or orders of being, and this is the direction of Dewey's reflec-tions on mind and matter.

Dewey urges us to think "of both mind and matter as different characters of natural events, in which matter expresses their sequential order, and mind the order of their meanings in their logical connections and dependencies" (*EN*, 74).[20] Again, we must avoid thinking of "natural events" as the ulti-mate, irreducible constituents of reality that combine in different ways called "mind" and "matter." Recall the point made earlier concerning "fields": namely, that you do not have "processes" and "relations" that com-bine to make a field, but rather that all processes are relational and all rela-tions are processive. This processive-relational or field view is evident, I believe, in the following analogy:

> The "matter" of materialists and the "spirit" of idealists is a creature similar to the constitution of the United States in the minds of unimaginative persons. Obviously the real constitution is certain basic *relationships* among the ac-tivities of the citizens of the country; it is a property or phase of these *processes*, so connected with them as to influence their rate and direction of change [italics added]. But by literalists it is often conceived of as something external to them; in itself fixed, a rigid framework to which *all* changes must accom-modate themselves. (*EN*, 73)

Dewey rejects the view "that matter, life and mind represent separate kinds of Being," maintaining instead that they are manifestations of "levels of increasing complexity and intimacy of interaction among natural events" (*EN*, 261). Here again, I think Dewey's doctrine is congenial to and supportive of a metaphysics that describes reality as "fields within fields within fields. . . ." Thus Dewey contends:

> While there is no isolated occurrence in nature, yet interaction and connection are not wholesale and homogeneous. Interacting-events have tighter and looser ties, which qualify them with certain beginnings and endings, and which mark them off from other fields of interaction. Such relatively closed fields come into conjunction at times so as to interact with each other, and a critical alteration is effected. A new larger field is formed, in which new energies are released, and to which new qualities appertain. (*EN*, 271–72)

Dewey goes on to distinguish "three plateaus of such fields," the physical, the living, and the mental. The physical field is constituted by "narrower and more external interactions," which are articulated in "the mathematical-mechanical system discovered by physics." The second level is that of life, which manifests "qualitative differences, like those of plant and animal, lower and higher animal forms." The distinguishing characters of the third plateau are "association, communication, participation." This mental level "is still further internally diversified, consisting of individualities. It is marked throughout its diversities, however, by common properties, which define mind as intellect; possession of and response to meanings" (*EN*, 272).[21]

While each of these levels "having its own characteristic empirical traits has its own categories," Dewey insists that "they are not 'explanatory' categories, as explanation is sometimes understood; they do not designate, that is, the operation of forces as 'causes.' They stick to empirical facts noting and denoting characteristic qualities and consequences peculiar to various levels of interaction" (*EN*, 272–73).[22]

The field character of Dewey's metaphysics is also implicit in his notion "that a higher organism acts with reference to a spread-out environment as a single situation." The crucial point being emphasized is that an organism acts with reference to a temporal spread as well as a spatial spread. "Thus an environment both extensive and enduring is immediately implicated in present behavior. Operatively speaking, the remote and the past are 'in' behavior making it what it is. The action called 'organic' is not just that of internal structures; it is an integration of organic-environmental connections" (*EN*, 279).[23] To express this in field language, we might say that an organism is constituted by and through participation in a diversity of fields varying in complexity and spatial and temporal scope, overlapping and shading into each other. The continuing intellectual task is the delineation of these fields in terms of their distinctive characteristics, activities, and relations without losing sight of the concrete and unique situation that they constitute. This, of course, is an open-ended task that becomes increasingly tentative as we focus on wider and more complex fields, such as human selves.

We might cite Dewey's distinction between "mind" and "consciousness" as an example of delineating fields of different spread and scope.

> Mind denotes the whole system of meanings as they are embodied in the workings of organic life; consciousness in a being with language denotes awareness or perception of meanings; it is the perception of meanings; it is the perception of actual events, whether past, contemporary or future, *in* their meanings, the having of actual ideas. The greater part of mind is only implicit in any conscious act or state; the field of mind—of operative meanings—is enormously wider than that of consciousness. Mind is contextual and persistent; consciousness is focal and transitive. Mind is, so to speak, structural, substantial; a constant background and foreground; perceptive consciousness is process, a series of heres and nows. (*EN,* 303)[24]

Of course, Dewey does not mean by this last sentence that mind is a static structure related to a processive consciousness. Bearing in mind the "functional and relational distinction" previously made between "structure" and "process," we might say that mind is a field characterized by a slower process and a wider and more numerous set of relations in comparison with the processes and relations that characterize the field of consciousness.

To illustrate the relation between mind and consciousness, Dewey asks us to reflect upon what happens when we read a book. In our reading we are immediately conscious of meanings that come to be and pass away; these existential meanings Dewey calls *ideas.* We are able to have such ideas, however, only "because of an organized system of meanings of which we are not at any time completely aware." Our ideas or particular apprehensions, then, are possessed and determined by systems of meaning, examples of which would be "mathematical mind" or "political mind." There is, Dewey concludes, a continuum or spectrum between these containing systems "and the meanings which, being focal and urgent, are the ideas of the moment." Dewey faults the "orthodox psychological tradition" for "its exclusive preoccupation with sharp focalization to the neglect of the vague shading off from the foci into a field of increasing dimness" (*EN,* 305). He later gives the following description of the concrete situation:

> If we consider the entire field from bright focus through the fore-conscious, the "fringe," to what is dim, sub-conscious "feeling," the focus corresponds to the point of imminent need, of urgency; the "fringe" corresponds to things that have just been reacted to or that will soon require to be looked after, while the remote outlying field corresponds to what does not have to be modified, and which may be dependably counted upon in dealing with imminent need. (*EN,* 311)[25]

One final text, from *Human Nature and Conduct,* will serve to illustrate how radical and pervasive was Dewey's processive-relational doctrine of mind. He points out that we cannot but be perplexed "by the problem of how a common mind, common ways of feeling and believing and purposing, comes into existence," assuming that "we start with the traditional notion of mind as something complete in itself." This would mean that we have a multiplicity of essentially independent minds, and we must then account for the fact that they realize the character of "commonness" or shared perspective and feeling.

> The case is quite otherwise if we recognize that in any case we must start with a grouped action, that is, with some fairly settled system of interaction among individuals. The problem of origin and development of the various groupings, or definite customs, in existence at any particular time in any particular place is not solved by reference to psychic causes, elements, forces. It is to be solved by reference to facts of action, demand for food, for houses, for a mate, for someone to talk to and listen to one talk, for control of others.[26]

Processes and relations, therefore, are not realities added on to separate individual minds, thereby bringing them together in a loosely federated common mind. Rather, processes and relations are the constitutive factors present from the beginning of the emergence of any mind. Thus minds are formed transactionally and always involve concrete environmental factors in their formation. Shared perspectives, customs, feelings, and values are to be expected, then, since the minds that share them come to be and develop through the transactional emergence of these perspectives, customs, feelings, and values. A mind isolated from or completely independent of such features is an empty abstraction. I will later address the question of whether a field view that excludes the possibility of any *isolated* mind or self also excludes the possibility of any *individual* mind or self.

CHAPTER 3

James: Toward a Field-Self

An ulterior unity, but not a factitious one. . . .
Not facititious, perhaps indeed all the more real
for being ulterior, for being born of a moment of
enthusiasm when it is discovered to exist among
fragments which need only to be joined
together; a unity that was unaware of itself,
hence vital and not logical, that did not prohibit
variety, dampen invention.
—Marcel Proust
Remembrance of Things Past

The self in which I believe with a primordial
certainty is not a thinking thing enclosed within
itself. It is open to a field of independent persons
and things with which I am intimately and really
connected by my cares and concerns.
—John Wild
"William James and the
Phenomenology of Belief"

On the surface, James's doctrine of the self would seem to have developed through three stages. Beginning with a methodological dualism in his *Principles of Psychology,* James apparently moved to a "no-self" doctrine in the *Essays on Radical Empiricism,* and finally to the affirmation of a substantive self in *A Pluralistic Universe.*[1] This three-stage view is basically sound and helpful as long as it is not understood as suggesting any clear, linear, and unequivocal development. In fact, there are tensions, shifts, inconsistencies, and even contradictions, not only between but also within these broad stages. Throughout, James is much less clear and confident about his positive affirmations and solutions than he is in describing the problems and what he wishes to avoid.[2]

The most serious threat to the interpretation suggested in this essay, as we shall later see, is found in those texts in which James appears to opt for a materialistic or behavioristic account of the self, or in which he seems drawn toward a denial of the reality of the "self" or the "ego." While in other texts he affirms opposition to such views,[3] it will only be by keeping in mind his overall philosophy, including his ethical and religious doctrines, that we can confidently deny materialistic or "no-self" interpretations of James's philosophy of self.[4] It is also important to remember that fidelity to experience in all its variations and ambiguities was his primary concern, rather than any systematic conceptual consistency. Ralph Barton Perry has well noted that James feared "thinness" much more than "inconsistency."[5]

Rather than attempting to follow the twists and turns, the argumentative subtleties and obscurities that accompany the historical development of James's doctrine of self, let us simply assume that he is from the first moving toward a field view of the self. Hence, I will select and concentrate on those texts and aspects of this thought which contribute to such a field view and ignore or minimize whatever may point in another direction.

James at times speaks primarily in terms of experience that is neither mental nor physical, and at other times in terms of consciousness. Both terms can easily and properly be encompassed under the rubric of "field," which, as we have already seen, is one way of understanding "pure experience" and which, as we shall see, is also one way to understand "consciousness." In what follows, we must keep in mind what has previously been said about fields as processive-relational complexes. Most important is the point that if the self is a complex of fields—"fields within fields within fields . . ."— then there is no "self in itself." This does not, of course, solve traditional questions such as "who" or "what" is doing the acting or thinking—questions that gave rise to doctrines of the substantial soul or transcendental ego or to the denial that there is any "who" or "what." A field perspective or assumption does, however, shift the focus of our attention and present us with the task, at least initially, of *describing* the characteristics of those activities constituting the self.

If we were restricted to citing one text from James that describes most concretely the field character of the self, the following would do as well as any:

> My present field of consciousness is a centre surrounded by a fringe that shades insensibly into a subconscious more. I use three separate terms here to describe this fact; but I might as well use three-hundred, for the fact is all shades and no boundaries. Which part of it properly is in my consciousness, which out? If I name what is out, it already has come in. The centre works in one way while the margins work in another, and presently overpower the centre and are central themselves. What we conceptually identify ourselves with and say we are thinking of at any time is the centre; but our *full* self is the whole field, with all those indefinitely radiating subconscious possibilities of increase that we can only feel without conceiving, and can hardly begin to analyze. The collective and disruptive ways of being coexist here, for each part functions distinctly, makes connexion with its own peculiar region in the still wider rest of experience and tends to draw us into that line, and yet the whole is somehow felt as one pulse of our life,—not conceived so, but felt so. (*PU*, 130)

This passage includes explicitly or implicitly most of the characteristic features of the self that I will be emphasizing. First, however, I wish to focus briefly on the implication of the last phrase of the text—"not conceived so, but felt so." That implication is the primacy and pervasiveness of "feeling" throughout the life and work of James. This point was touched upon earlier when we discussed James's acceptance, in his last work, of Bergson's invitation to "dive back into the flux." We noted then that, for James, the "thickness" of reality could not be grasped by means of concepts or conceptualization. Stating this point now in more positive language, we might say that the "thickness" of reality can be "felt" but cannot be known conceptually, since there is a "gaping contrast between the richness of life and the poverty of all possible formulas" (*TC*, II:127).

I earlier called attention to pragmatism's concern for the concrete; in James's stress upon the primordiality of "feelings" in contrast—though not in opposition—to concepts, we have further evidence of this concern. In any effort to describe our experience, of course, we are compelled to use words and concepts, and this gives rise to the danger that James designated "vicious intellectualism." The perennial temptation of the rationalistic temper is to confuse "reality" with the concepts that we necessarily employ in our efforts to render more satisfactory our transactions with and within reality. James's concern for the concrete and his suspicion of abstract concepts were present almost from the start of his intellectual journey, but it was only in his later years and with the aid of Bergson that James felt that he had broken the "edge" of intellectualism. In *A Pluralistic Universe*, the last full-length work published during his lifetime, he unequivocally affirms that "feeling" exceeds both conceptualization and verbalization. After all the talking, James tells us, "I must *point*, point to the mere *that* of life, and you by an inner sympathy must fill out the *what* for yourselves" (*PU*, 131). If we break reality into concepts, we can "never reconstruct it in its wholeness." There is "no amount of discreteness" out of which it is possible to "manufacture the concrete." On the other hand, "place yourself at a bound, or *d'emblée*, as Bergson says, inside of the living, moving, active thickness of the real, and all the abstractions and distinctions are given into your hand" (*PU*, 116).

James's concern for the concrete and his recognition that "life exceeds logic" should not be interpreted as a mode of irrationalism or antiintellectualism except insofar as rationalism and intellectualism are understood as confusing concepts or ideas with the full richness of experience and reality. Similarly, his insistence on the centrality of "feelings" should not be understood as a mode of "emotionalism" or "pseudo-mysticism." This is not to say, of course, that James denies the reality and importance of our emotive or affective life, as well as authentic mystical experiences. What is important, however, is that his insistence on taking mysticism seriously stems from his profound desire to explore concrete experience in all its richness, depth, variety, and vagueness. In *Some Problems of Philosophy*, published posthumously, James maintains that "the deeper features of reality are found only in perceptual experience. Here alone do we acquaint ourselves with continuity, or the immersion of one thing in another, here alone with self, with substance, with qualities, with activity in its various modes, with time, with cause, with change, with novelty; with tendency, with freedom" (*SPP*, 54).

For our purposes "feeling" and "perceptual experience" can be considered the same,[6] and this text and its implications will be repeatedly reflected when we come to discuss more specifically the various aspects of James's "self." The point here is that "feelings" is the term James employs to keep us focused on and open to original experience. Perry has emphasized this and at the same time cautioned against a narrow reading or misreading of James's use of "feelings."

> It may, I think, be said that James' works contain the most thoroughgoing attempt which has ever been made to carry all the terms of discourse back to the original data of sense, or to other immediately discriminated *qualia*. Like Whitehead, he suggested that "feelings" was the best term to employ for these originals. "Sensation" is too narrowly associated with apprehension through recognized end-organs. "Thought," "ideas," and "representations," all of which have been used for this or a similar purpose, are too closely associated with the processes of the intellect. If the term "feelings" is used, this term must also be freed from its own characteristic limitations, its exclusive association, namely, with affective or emotional states. The term must be used in a sense that makes it natural to speak of a "feeling of relation," or a "feeling of identity," or a "feeling of drink-after-thirst," or a "feeling of pastness and futurity."[7]

Are "feelings," then, physical or psychical? As with "experiences," we must say, at least initially and descriptively, that they are neither and both, the purpose of this paradoxical response being to prod us to look "beyond" the traditional categories of "physical" and "psychical." Thus, by employing the term "feelings," James alerts us to the irreducibility of our concrete experiences. "It is hard to imagine," he tells us, "that 'really' our own subjective experiences are only molecular arrangements, even though the molecules be conceived as beings of a psychic kind." How much more difficult it would be to imagine, James implies, if molecules were conceived as beings of a material kind. He continues by noting:

> A material fact may indeed be different from what we feel it to be, but what sense is there in saying that a feeling, which has no other nature than to be felt, is not *as* it is felt? Psychologically considered, our experiences resist conceptual reduction, and our fields of consciousness, taken simply *as such,* remain just what they appear, even tho facts of a molecular order should prove to be the signals of appearance. (*SPP*, 78)[8]

The distinctiveness and irreducibility of "feelings" are further manifested in the fact that we can feel more than we can name. Thus James contends that "namelessness is compatible with existence."

> There are innumerable consciousnesses of emptiness, no one of which taken in itself has a name, but all different from each other. The ordinary way is to assume that they are all emptinesses of consciousness, and so that same state. But the feeling of an absence is *toto coelo* other than the absence of a feeling; it is an intense feeling. (*PP*, I:243–44)[9]

This last sentence succinctly and vividly illustrates that some phenomena are available only through immediate experience. No kind of "argument" or "external" evidence could possibly compel one to affirm what is here described. I will later suggest that there is a "depth" or character to the self which a field view illuminates even if it does not "explain" it. Something of this "depth" is indicated, though in dualistic language, in James's claim that "tendencies" are grasped from "within" as well as from "without":

> Now what I contend for, and accumulate examples to show, is that "tendencies" are not only descriptions from without, but that they are among the *objects* of the stream, which is thus aware of them from within, and must be described as in very large measure constituted of *feelings of* tendency, often so vague that we are unable to name them at all. (*PP*, I:246)[10]

> It is . . . the reinstatement of the vague and inarticulate to its proper place in our mental life which I am so anxious to press on the attention. (*PBC*, 150)

James's desire to reinstate the "vague and inarticulate" is therefore not a defense of obfuscation or romantic cloudiness. Paradoxically, it is an effort to describe our experience as rigorously as possible and to avoid any procrustean cutting of experience so as to fit it neatly into what can be named or conceptualized. Thus, in our attempt to construct a field model of the self we will draw generously from James's descriptions and his approach, which takes seriously our own experience. Robert Ehman has noted that James "is suspending consideration of those dimensions of the self that are accessible through inference or through the observation of a third-person witness. He appeals to our own first-person experience and describes the self as it appears prior to theoretical elaboration."[11] This in no way denies the legitimacy and even necessity of extrapolating from or speculating upon our personal experiences. It does, however, caution against explaining away that which is present in our immediate experience. We must begin from this experience; indeed, we must return to it—though if our speculative and imaginative forays are successful, the experience to which we return will be immeasurably richer and more complex than that from which we began.[12]

THE "SELF" OF THE *PRINCIPLES*
The chapter entitled "The Consciousness of the Self," one of the longest chapters in *The Principles of Psychology* (*PP*), is filled with a richness of detailed description and observation which to this day remains worthy of reflective consideration, quite apart from its technical and theoretical aspects. James presents us with a view of the self that has been read by some as

anticipating behaviorism and by others as proto-phenomenology. Without doing violence to the text and in keeping with the fundamental thrust of James's thought, I believe it can also be read as moving toward a doctrine of the self as a complex of fields. The processive-relational characteristics of all fields is much in evidence in every important feature of James's "self." Whatever obscurities, inconsistencies, and gaps attach to this doctrine, it is quite clear that it excludes any view of the self as a finished, permanent, essentially enclosed entity or thing. At the outset, James notes "that we are dealing with a fluctuating material" (*PP,* I:279).[13] This is not surprising, given all we have previously said about James's process metaphysics. It is not accidental that the chapter on the self immediately follows the most famous chapter in the *Principles,* the one in which "stream" is introduced as the primary metaphor for "thought" or "consciousness."[14]

As already noted, throughout the *Principles* James assumes a methodological dualism, which he will deny in his later metaphysics, but there is widespread agreement among the commentators that the more imaginative and insightful aspects of the book resist being incorporated within any ontological dualism. Let us assume, therefore, that any dualistic language we encounter is to be read only as expressing a diversity of functions—a functional dualism. Hence, the implicit dualism in the phrase "steam of consciousness" is easily circumvented, and is more in keeping with James's fundamental intentions, by designating it "stream of experience."[15] Similarly, when we find James speaking of the "me" as objective and the "I" as subjective, we will remember that in his more developed metaphysics he views "objective" and "subjective" as functionally rather than ontologically distinct. Thus, in discussion of the "me" or the "I," the "object" or the "subject," it will be understood that we are not referring to different orders of being but rather focusing on different aspects or functions of the self. As James himself noted: "the words *I* and *me* signify nothing mysterious and unexampled—they are at bottom only names of *emphasis*" (*PP,* I:324n.).

The field or processive-relational character of James's doctrine of the self is present at the outset of the "Self" chapter: "*In its widest possible sense . . . a man's Self is the sum total of all that he CAN call his,* not only his body and his psychic powers, but his clothes and his house, his wife and children, his ancestors and friends, his reputation and works, his lands and horses, and yacht and bank-account" (*PP,* I:279). Recall that in Chapter 1, I made the point that "relations" are not extrinsic to the "essence" of a being, something accidentally added on to its substance. Rather, they are constitutive of it; they enter into the very fabric of a being, making it what it is. Let us look at the text just cited within this perspective. There is no "self" to which are extrinsically added a body, clothes, wife, or lands; these are relations that continue to form and fashion, build and diminish, expand and narrow, enrich and impoverish that reality referred to as "the self."[16]

The legitimacy of such a field reading is borne out by the ways in which

James describes "the Constituents of the Self." These are first divided into "the empirical self" (me) and the "pure Ego" (I), with the former further divided into the material, social, and spiritual selves. I will first consider the empirical self and its constituents; after an excursus on "the body" I will return in the next chapter to the "pure Ego" in relation to James's important but controversial doctrine that the thinker is the "passing Thought."

To begin with, we must be on guard against understanding the terms "material," "social," and "spiritual" in a traditional, commonsense, or dualistic manner. Not surprisingly, James tells us that "the body is the innermost part of *the material Self.*" What is a bit surprising—and may be an effect of James's Victorian milieu—is that "clothes come next," after which he adds family, home, and property (*PP,* I:280). Now it is not for a moment being suggested here, or in the consideration of the other selves, that all constituting relations are on the same plane and enter into the self with the same degree of intimacy. The role played by different relations and their relative weight in the determination of the self cannot be determined a priori; nor are these set once and for all. The self is a constantly changing self, and a relation that may be an intimate constituent today may be peripheral tomorrow and nonexistent the day after. Whether there are any relations without which an individual self would cease to be is a question that must be considered later when we focus more explicitly on the possibility that the self is immortal. The point to be stressed here is that the relations being described are "real" constituents of the self—in a sense each *is* the self or at least a part of the self. "Our immediate family," James states, "is a part of ourselves. . . . When they die, a part of our very selves is gone. If they do anything wrong, it is our shame." This is no pious or sentimental or romantic expression on James's part, for he also insists that our clothes, home, and property are "with different degrees of intimacy, parts of our empirical selves" (*PP,* I:280–81).

Turning to the "social self," we see that the ways in which we are regarded by our fellow humans determine us to be the selves we are. Just as we should properly have spoken of our material *selves* (rather than *self*), we should speak of our social *selves,* since "*a man has as many social selves as there are individuals who recognize him* and carry an image of him in their mind" (*PP,* I:281–82).

Whatever one may think of the suggested interpretation of the material and social selves, the phenomena described by James are relatively unproblemed, and most thinkers would agree that they have some bearing upon the self, though the precise nature of this bearing might be disputed. The case of the "spiritual self" is quite different, beginning with the very designation "spiritual," for it is James's description of this self that lends the support to a materialistic or behavioristic reading.

He begins innocently enough: "By the Spiritual Self, so far as it belongs to the Empirical Me, I mean a man's inner or subjective being, his psychic faculties or dispositions, taken concretely" (*PP*, I:283). Nor is it particularly upsetting, despite a degree of vagueness, when James goes on to speak of the feeling that we have of "a sort of innermost centre within the circle, of a sanctuary within the citadel, constituted by the subjective life as a whole" (*PP*, I:285). When he asks, "*What is this self of all the other selves?*" his initial description seems appropriate to a self that is designated "spiritual." He notes that "probably all men would describe it" as

> the active element in all consciousness. . . . It is what welcomes or rejects. It presides over the perception of sensations, and by giving or withholding its assent it influences the movements they tend to arouse. It is the home of interest. . . . It is the source of effort and attention, and the place from which appear to emanate the fiats of the will. (*PP*, I:285)

The basic consensus begins to dissipate, however, when an effort is made to define more accurately the precise nature of this central self. "Some would say that it is a simple active substance, the soul, of which they are conscious; others, that it is nothing but a fiction, the imaginary being denoted by the pronoun I; and between these extremes of opinion all sorts of intermediaries would be found" (*PP*, I:286). James puts to the side for the moment the question of what this "central active self" *is*, preferring to begin by attempting to describe as precisely as possible how it is felt, for "this central nucleus of the Self, . . . this central part of the Self is *felt*." His general description of how "this palpitating inward life" feels is still relatively free of problems. "I am aware," James tells us, "of a constant play of furtherances and hindrances in my thinking, of checks and release, tendencies which run with desire, and tendencies which run the other way" (*PP*, I:286–87). The bombshell is dropped (at least for those who resist a materialistic or behavioristic interpretation of James) when he tells us that forsaking general descriptions and

> coming to the closest possible quarters with the facts, *it is difficult for me to detect in the activity any purely spiritual element at all. Whenever my introspective glance succeeds in turning round quickly enough to catch one of these manifestations of spontaneity in the act, all it can ever feel distinctly is some bodily process, for the most part taking place within the head.* (*PP*, I:287)

Now what is significant here is that James explicitly includes acts of attending, assenting, negating, making an effort, remembering, and reasoning. These acts usually designated mental or immaterial or spiritual are felt by James "as movements of something in the head" or nearby. Thus the rather startling conclusion is reached that the central nucleus of the "Spiritual Self," the "'*Self of selves,' when carefully examined, is found to consist mainly of the collection of these peculiar motions in the head or between the head and throat.*" James quickly adds that he does "not for a moment say that this is *all* it consists of," and a few pages later he concedes "that over and above these there is an obscurer feeling of something more." I will later attempt to exploit this "something more," which is a recurring phenomenon in James's thought, in favor of a nonreductionistic field-self. It must be acknowledged, however, that in this section of *The Principles of Psychology,* James is perilously close to a denial of the subject or self and an affirmation of a reductionistic behaviorism.[17] This becomes manifest when he speculates on the consequences of what he concedes is a hypothesis: namely, "*that our entire feeling of spiritual activity, or what commonly passes by that name, is really a feeling of bodily activities whose exact nature is by most men overlooked*" (*PP,* I:288). The key consequence of this hypothesis would be that "*all* that is experienced is, strictly considered, *objective*"; hence, it would be more appropriate to describe the stream of thought as "a stream of *Sciousness*" rather than "*consciousness*," which would be a "thinking its own existence along with whatever else it thinks." It would follow, according to James, that "the existence of this thinker would be given to us rather as a logical postulate than as that direct inner perception of spiritual activity which we naturally believe ourselves to have." He goes on to say that such a speculation violates common sense and that he will henceforth avoid it (*PP,* I:291). When we come to consider his notion of the thinker as the "passing Thought," however, we will again have to ask whether James's doctrine can be utilized in the construction of the kind of substantive self that would allow for a belief in immortality.

Ehman makes a corrective criticism of James's view of the self that would have to be incorporated in the model of the self suggested in this essay. Briefly stated, the criticism is that in his description of self-feeling and self-love James overlooks the reflexive character of these experiences and hence loses, or appears to lose, the "self." A central feature of James's doctrine is that the material, social, and spiritual selves are all manufactured out of "objects" that are interesting and arouse the desire to appropriate them "for their own sakes." In bodily self-love, social self-love, and spiritual self-love, what is loved is always some object—a comfortable seat, the image of me in another's mind, my loves and hates. In none of these instances do I love a pure principle of self or a Pure Ego (*PP,* I:303–7). Ehman does not deny the accuracy of James's description, but he does question whether it is exhaustive. What James fails to recognize is "the felt reflexivity, the felt reference back to self, that is present in all self-feeling and self-love on the adult human level" (*NEP,* 260). Ehman makes a similar point concerning James's claim that the "present pulse of our conscious life" can become an object of knowledge only when it has passed. Conceding this, Ehman nevertheless insists that our present pulse can "feel prereflectively its own existence in its very act."

> The present pulse must feel itself as the central self; it cannot have the central self as a mere object before it. For in this case it could not in a radical sense feel bodily motions, sensations, attitudes, and locations as its own; and in appropriating peripheral objects to its bodily center, it would not appropriate them to *itself.* In order for the present pulse to feel the warmth and intimacy of the

body and bodily life, it must feel that this is close to itself. There is a moment of self-relation in the very experience of intimacy: intimacy is intimacy *to;* and for an anonymous, nonreflective consciousness everything would simply appear as present, as objective; nothing would appear warm and intimate. The body would always in this case appear as an external object, never as its own body, as the location of its own life. (*NEP,* 263–64)[18]

I believe that Ehman is here more faithful to the overall thrust of James's thought than is James himself when he suggests that the self may be nothing more than a collectivity of "objects" within an impersonal stream of consciousness. Recall the earlier stress placed upon James's notion of "feelings" and his insistence that we can feel more than we are able to conceptualize. He is consistent in denying that the self can be known directly, since through reflective consciousness we are always presented with "objects." To say, therefore, that we can directly know the self or the subject of our activities would be to say that the subject can be known as an object. This is why James (as well as Hume) can never discover the self through an introspective or reflective act. But given the weight that James (unlike Hume) attaches to "feeling," it is not inconsistent to acknowledge a prereflective felt awareness that accompanies all our conscious acts.[19]

This crucial notion of the self's felt awareness will be considered again when the "passing Thought" and its relation to unity, continuity, and identity are analyzed. Before doing so however, I must briefly discuss a most complex and bedeviling topic: the "body" and how it might be understood within a field view of the self.

EXCURSUS: "THE BODY"
We have already seen that James has described the activities of the "spiritual self" in terms of bodily feelings. I wish to consider those and other texts in which James apparently presents the "self" and the "body" as interchangeable. My purpose is to underline the ambiguity involved in James's use of the term "body" and try to show how a field interpretation of "body" is more consistent with his thought than is a materialistic or behavioristic interpretation.

First, however, I would like to call attention to the fact that any ambiguity attached to the term is by no means unique to James. In the West this explicit ambiguity goes back at least as far as Paul, who, in response to the question, "How are dead people raised and what sort of body do they have when they come back?" answered by distinguishing "earthly bodies" from "heavenly bodies."[20] Christian thinkers have been debating and speculating on Paul's meaning from the earliest times, and they continue to do so. Not surprisingly, there is a great range and variety of interpretations; in spite of this diversity, however, it is safe to say that on one point there is a consensus— the "resurrection body" cannot be simply and unequivocally identical with the body as it is commonly known and experienced.[21]

The absence of univocal meaning in "body" language is not, of course, found only in the West. In Eastern thought there are lengthy treatises on the "astral," "subtle," and "etheric" bodies, all of which are differentiated from the "physical" body. In addition, there is a long tradition within Buddhism of the "Triple Body of the Buddha."

Since Plato, the Western philosophical tradition has endeavored to restrict the meaning of the term "body" so as to highlight the nonbodily aspect of human nature usually designated "soul," "spirit," "reason," or "mind." In a sense, this effort culminated in Descartes's "clear and distinct" division of human beings into two essentially different substances—mind and body— to which subsequent modern philosophy has responded in one of three ways: acceptance of two ultimate substances (dualism); reduction of matter to mind (idealism); reduction of mind to matter (materialism). It is only in the twentieth century that there have emerged various philosophical efforts to articulate an understanding of "the body" that does not easily fall into any of the three traditional classifications. I believe that pragmatism is one such effort.

The movement that has brought forth the most explicit, developed, and technical expression of the ambiguity belonging to "the body," however, is phenomenology. Any in-depth consideration of this issue is beyond both the limits of this essay and the competency of its author. Still, since I will later utilize several phenomenological commentators on James in suggesting a field interpretation of his use of the term "body," it might be helpful to show from the works of prominent phenomenonlogists that James is not alone in referring to the body in ambiguous, vague, and even confusing ways.

The indispensable insight in all "soul" views is that the human person or self is "more" than what is commonly understood as "the body": that is, an object that can be weighed, measured, located in mathematically exact spatial and temporal coordinates, and reduced to precise kinds and quantities of chemicals. The task confronting all nonmaterialistic philosophies is to account for this "more" in a way that does not create such problems as the classical Cartesian one of having to explain how two essentially different substances can interact in such a way as to form one being. Without claiming to be able to prove that James and the phenomenologists succeed in this task, I believe it is important to keep in mind what they are attempting if we are to make any sense of their often elusive language. Negatively, they wish to overcome the difficulties and lack of adequate explanatory power in dualism, materialism, and idealism. More positively, they wish to describe human beings in a manner distinct from but not in opposition to science, and faithful to human experience in its most concrete and subtle expressions.

The explicit distinction between "thing-body" and "lived body" probably originated with Max Scheler,[22] but the phenomenon he describes is a concern of all phenomenologists. A few excerpts from the thought of Jean-

Paul Sartre, Maurice Merleau-Ponty, and Gabriel Marcel will suffice to indicate a similarity of intent and direction among these thinkers and between them and James, the differences of overall philosophy and technical language notwithstanding. For my purposes, a key similarity is that all these thinkers speak in terms of processes and relations—fields—rather than in terms of underlying substance and unchanging principles or essences.

Sartre distinguishes between the body as a "being-for-itself" and a "being-for-others," and he insists that "they cannot be reduced to one another."

> Being-for-itself must be wholly body and it must be wholly consciousness; it cannot be *united* with a body. Similarly being-for-others is wholly body; there are no "psychic phenomena" there to be united with the body. There is nothing *behind* the body. But the body is wholly "psychic."[23]

Whatever else may be said about this far from self-evident text, it is clear that Sartre is calling attention to a phenomenon—the body as being-for-itself—that eludes both scientific and commonsense observations. One other passage can be cited to exemplify the relational character of the body as being-for-itself: "We know that there is not a for-itself on the one hand and a world on the other as two closed entities for which we must subsequently seek some explanation as to how they communicate. The for-itself is a relation to the world" (*BN*, 306).

The irreducible distinctiveness of the lived body as well as its processive-relational character is also affirmed by Merleau-Ponty:

> The outline of my body is a frontier which ordinary spatial relations do not cross. This is because its parts are interrelated in a peculiar way: they are not spread out side by side, but enveloped in each other. . . . Psychologists often say that the body image is *dynamic*. Brought down to a precise sense, this term means that my body appears to me as an attitude directed towards a certain existing or possible task. And indeed its spatiality is not, like that of external objects or like that of "spatial sensations," a *spatiality of position*, but a *spatiality of situation*.[24]

Whether Gabriel Marcel can properly be called a phenomenologist is perhaps open to dispute, but there can be no doubt that his reflections on the body, halting and unsystematized as they may be, are strikingly relevant to the concerns of this essay. One aspect of Marcel's view of the body is of particular importance: his strong personalistic emphasis. Thus he reminds us that "it is not *a* body, but *my* body, that we are asking ourselves questions about." He goes on to say that "speaking of my body is, in a certain sense, a way of speaking of myself"; hence, it is proper to say, "I *am* my body." As soon as we do so, however, we encounter that ambiguity to which we have previously referred, and Marcel is explicit in denying that the identification with "my body" can be properly understood as a mode of materialism.[25] "I *am* my body only in so far as for me the body is an essentially mysterious type of reality, irreducible to those determinate formulae (no matter how interestingly complex they might be) to which it would be reducible if it could be considered merely as an object" (*MB*, I:103). Marcel concedes that there is a strong temptation to treat the body in a detached fashion as a "kind of instrument . . . which permits me to act upon, and even intrude myself into, the world" (*MB*, I:99). On the contrary,

> I *am* my body in so far as I succeed in recognizing that this body of mine *cannot*, in the last analysis, be brought down to the level of being this object, *an* object, a something or other. It is at this point that we have to bring in the idea of the body not as an object but as a subject. (*MB*, I:101)

These views of Marcel, expressed in his Gifford Lectures of 1949, were anticipated many years earlier in his *Metaphysical Journal*.[26] In a note written in 1923 he acknowledged the nonconceptualizable and nonobjectifiable character of "my body."

> Since the fact for my body of being my body is not something of which I can genuinely have an idea, it is not something that I can conceptualize. In the fact of *my body* there is something which transcends what can be called materiality, something which cannot be reduced to any of its objective qualities. . . . The non-objectivity of *my body* becomes clear to our mind as soon as we remember that it is of the essence of the object as such that it does not take me into account. In the measure in which it does not take me into account my body seems to me not to be my body. (*MJ*, 315–16)

Two other aspects of "my body" as understood by Marcel should be noted: namely, "my body" as "felt," and as extending beyond the envelope of the skin. Marcel maintains "that *my* body is *mine* inasmuch as, however confusedly, it is felt. . . . If I am my body this is in so far as I am a being that feels" (*MJ*, 243). A key idea in Marcel is "feeling as a mode of participation." While he only hints at it, he does suggest that we participate in reality only insofar as we are bodies; more, we "feel" reality only insofar as we feel our bodies.

> From this point of view it seems, therefore, that my body is endowed with an absolute priority in relation to everything that I can feel that is other than my body itself; but then, strictly speaking, can I really feel anything other than my body itself? Would not the case of my feeling something else be merely the case of my feeling *myself* as feeling something else, so that I would never be able to pass beyond various modifications of my own self-feeling? (*MB*, I:101)

The "felt" character of "my body" is closely bound up with its relational character; that is, the fact that it cannot be localized within narrow spatial and temporal coordinates. "I am inclined to think," Marcel tells us, "that there can only be a body where there is an act of feeling, and for there to be this feeling the distinction between the *here* and *there* needs to cease to be rigid" (*MJ*, 270). I will later argue that the self's relations to a more encompassing reality are the grounds for a plausible belief in its immortality. The experiential ground for such an extrapolation, however, is the evidence that we are here and now constituted by relations that extend the reality of the self "beyond" the confines of the "skin." This "transcending" relational feature has already been noted in reference to James's doctrine of "selves." The following text from Marcel can be cited as reinforcement for such a view:

> I *am* my body; but I *am* also my habitual surrounding. This is demonstrated by the laceration, the division with myself that accompanies exile from home (this is an order of experience that Proust has expressed incomparably). Am I my body in a more essential way than I am my habitual surrounding? If this question is answered in the negative, then death can only be a supreme exile, not an annihilation. This way of stating the problem may at first sight seem childish. But that, I think, is mistaken. We must take in their strictest interpretation words such as *belong to* (a town, a house, etc.): and the word *laceration*. It is as though *adhesions* are broken. (*MJ*, 259)

Marcel and James, I suggest, use a similar phenomenon in their "belief," "faith," "extrapolation" concerning the divine. What is significant, however, is that the phenomenon itself is recognized by many who would not also share the "faith" of a James or a Marcel. Sartre bears this out: "My body is everywhere: the bomb which destroys *my* house also damages my body in so far as the house was already an indication of my body" (*BN*, 325).

JAMES'S "BODY-TEXTS"
Let us return now to the previously cited body-texts of James to see how they may be interpreted so as to avoid a materialistic or physicalistic interpretation. Recall that James referred to the "Spiritual Self" as the "central active self," the "central nucleus of the Self," and "this self of all the other selves." The startling and confusing feature of James's doctrine emerges when, in attempting to describe this self as concretely as possible, all he "can ever feel distinctly is some bodily process." Even such acts as attaining, negating, and making an effort are—so James claims—"felt as movements of something in the head." It is not surprising, then, that those sympathetic to materialism as well as many unsympathetic to it should interpret James's doctrine of the self materialistically or behavioristically. "There is perhaps nothing in James," Ehman contends, "that has been more radically misinterpreted than his account at this point, and he has often been taken as a mere materialist." Ehman insists that there is no materialism here, "no denial of thought or emotion, but simply the observation that we are unable to grasp these as purely psychical, as nonbodily" (*NEP*, 262).

While I obviously share Ehman's rejection of a materialistic reading of these texts, the issue is, I believe, a bit more complicated. The complication is evident as soon as we ask not what James is denying but what he is affirming. It is always easier to see what a creative thinker is denying than what he is affirming, and James is no exception. James shared the difficulty of our own contemporary thinkers who desire to overcome dualism but are hampered in their efforts by the dualistic language that is so deeply embedded in the culture and in our psyche-body. Still, the direction is evident, whatever difficulties James and we have in articulating that direction. Ehman helpfully proposes that "when James asserts that the 'acts of attending, assenting, negating are felt as movements in the head,' the term *as* ought to be taken literally" (*NEP*, 262).[27] This at least suggests that James cannot be understood to assert any simple unequivocal identity between the "self" and the "body." Indeed, James seems to acknowledge a distinction when—a few lines before describing the feelings of the spiritual self as bodily movements—he states that "when it [the spiritual self] is found, it is *felt;* just as the body is felt" (*PP,* I:286).

In spite of the fact that materialism cannot be reconciled with James's overall philosophy and that, as we have seen, he explicitly rejects it as inadequate to fundamental human needs, textual support for a materialistic interpretation of his doctrine of the self is not confined to a few passages in his early work, *The Principles of Psychology.* In an equally notorious text from his essay "Does Consciousness Exist?"—some fourteen years after publication of his *Principles*—James added more fuel to the flames of the controversy. In the penultimate paragraph, and after conceding that "to many it will sound materialistic," he states:

> I am as confident as I am of anything that, in myself, the stream of thinking (which I recognize emphatically as a phenomenon) is only a careless name for what, when scrutinized, reveals itself to consist chiefly of the stream of my breathing. The "I think" which Kant said must be able to accompany all my objects, is the "I breathe" which actually does accompany them. . . . Breath, which was ever the original of "spirit," breath moving outwards, between the glottis and the nostrils, is, I am persuaded, the essence out of which philosophers have constructed the entity known to them as consciousness. (*ERE,* 19)

Harsh words, indeed ("and some would walk with him no more"), but as with an earlier sayer of "harsh words," it is not perfectly clear what is being said. The more tender-minded will take comfort in James's acknowledgment that these words will *sound* materialistic, to which the more tough-minded will make the "if it looks like a duck . . ." response. The phenomenologically oriented commentators (who can be classed as either tender tough-minded thinkers or tough tender-minded ones) are, I believe, responsive to the texts under consideration while remaining consistent with James's broader philosophical concerns and congenial to a field view of the self. To begin with, there is no dispute concerning James's effort to find an alternative to the traditional "soul." Richard Stevens suggests:

> Such crudely materialistic language seems to have been chosen by James as part of a strategy designed to eliminate the last vestiges of soul-theory which

he felt led infallibly to a misunderstanding of the body. If spiritual activity is attributed to an incorporeal separate entity, then the body is inevitably looked upon as a mere instrument.[28]

The next point of agreement is that James "refuses to view the body, in the fashion of traditional dualism, as an extended mass in space" (*JH*, 73).[29] Closely allied to this is that the "body" James is positively affirming is, in less technical language, the "lived body" of the phenomenologists. "It is not," John Wild maintains, "the body of traditional dualistic thought, the mere mass of matter extended in space. It is the moving, living, conscious body which expresses our emotions, and is the non-objective centre of my world." Thus, according to Wild, James came to see "that the self is neither a physical body, nor a separated consciousness, nor any combination of the two. . . . It is a living, sentient body dependent on the things among which it has been thrown, and inseparable from the world in which it exists."[30]

Finally, there can be little doubt, as Ehman has pointed out, that

> James opens the door to misunderstanding by failing to distinguish clearly between the body as a mere physical object as studied by physiology and the body as we feel and live through its movements in our actual conscious experience. The body as a physiological entity containing the central nervous system and brain is an object for the detached attitude of science; it is not our localized, felt subjective self. (*NEP*, 262)

An important aspect of all of this is that the ambiguity of James's body references is not *merely* a terminological ambiguity. Earlier, in discussing his doctrine of pure experience, I made the point that the terminological ambiguity "is grounded in experiential ambiguity"; in support, I cited several passages from his essay "The Place of Affectional Facts," in which James maintains that "our body is the palmary instance of the ambiguous. Sometimes I treat my body purely as part of outer nature. Sometimes, again, I think of it as 'mine.' I sort it with the 'me,' and then certain local changes and determinations in it pass for spiritual happenings" (*ERE*, 76).[31] I suggested that James's doctrine would have benefited from the use of field language, and I would like now to expand this point a bit with reference to his doctrine of the "body."

Bruce Wilshire points out that James "treats the body as a topic known always as the same within an Object that has field-like as well as stream-like characteristics" (*WJP*, 128).[32] A brief consideration of the manner in which James understands "topic" and "Object" will clarify Wilshire's statement and indicate some grounds for the field view being suggested. The terms "topic," "kernel," and "fractional object" all mean the same for James. They point to or express a "part" of the *Object* which is really the thought's "entire content or deliverance, neither more nor less." James illustrates this point with the thought, "Columbus discovered America in 1492." Most people, if asked what in such a case is the object of one's thought, would reply "Columbus" or "America" or "the discovery of America." According to James, however, "it is nothing short of the entire sentence, 'Columbus-discovered-America-in-1492.'" Further, if we wish to feel the idiosyncrasy of this thought, we must reproduce it just "as it was uttered, with every word fringed and the whole sentence bathed in that original halo of obscure relations, which, like an horizon, then spread about its meaning" (*PP*, I:265–66). Now if, as Wilshire suggests, "the Object in its prereflective totality" is the "field of consciousness" (*WJP*, 128), and the body is a "topic" within an "Object," it seems apt to describe it as a "field within a field." Such a description receives support, I believe, from James's claim that our bodies "are percepts in our objective field—they are simply the most interesting percepts there. What happens to them excites in us emotions and tendencies to action more energetic and habitual than any which are excited by other portions of the 'field'" (*PP*, I:304).

Remember, I am not claiming that James is here, or in the other texts cited, consciously and deliberately constructing a field doctrine of the self. I am and will continue suggesting, however, that these experiential descriptions lend themselves to incorporation within such a field metaphysics, and the utility of these texts for fashioning such a metaphysics—rather than the explicit intention of James—is my primary concern. Consider, for example, the way in which he speaks of the multiplicity of selves that constitute the empirical self or "me" (we have still to consider that other constituent of the self—the pure Ego). Surely James does not mean that each of these is an entity somehow stacked up within a container self. No physicalistic imagery will convey the fact that each of these selves is the self through and through. But a field metaphor would seem eminently appropriate here, since fields are overlapping and inclusive, able to come and go with both continuity and discontinuity. As I have repeatedly acknowledged, the utilization of the field metaphor does not "explain" how such overlapping simultaneity of multiple yet unified realities is possible (though it does turn us away from a number of dead-end pathways while keeping us focused upon the concrete experiential flow)—no more, for example, than does speaking of the "lived" or "live body" explain how, according to Merleau-Ponty, "its parts are inter–related in a peculiar way: they are not spread out side by side, but enveloped in each other."[33] Whatever they are trying to say, it is clear that when James and Merleau-Ponty refer to "parts," whether of the self or of the body, they do not mean "parts" in the same sense as when speaking of parts of an automobile or even parts of our object-body.

There remains one other crucial body-text to consider—a text at once a suggestion of and an obstacle to the field view of the self. What I would like to do is to read this text in terms of the field assumptions previously posited, conceding the somewhat procrustean character of such an effort. The text in question is part of a lengthy footnote to "The Experience of Activity," originally delivered in 1904 as the Presidential Address to the American Psychological Association.[34] In this note James is responding to a critic who had taken him to task "for identifying spiritual activity with certain muscular feelings," basing the charge on the text we have already discussed. James's first point is that his intention was to show that "there is no direct evidence that we feel the activity of an inner spiritual agent as such." He goes on to distinguish three "activities." First is the activity in "the mere *that* of experience, in the fact that something is going on." For my purposes, I will refer to this as the stream of experience—the general flowing field of reality. Within that field James further distinguishes "two whats, an activity felt as 'ours,' and an activity ascribed to objects." He insists that in the disputed text his concern was to determine which activity within the "total experience-process" could properly be designated "ours." In language whose surface sense is surely materialistic or behavioristic, he states: "So far as we are 'persons,' and contrasted and opposed to an 'environment,' movements in our body figure as our activities, and I am unable to find any other activities that are ours in this strictly personal sense."

James concedes that there is "a wider sense in which the whole 'choir of heaven and furniture of the earth,' and their activities, are ours, for they are our 'objects.'" In this sense, however, "'we' are . . . only another name for the total process of experience, another name for all that is." This last has an almost monistic ring to it insofar as it suggests that there is one process constituting all that is. When James's later doctrine concerning the self-compounding of consciousness is considered, we will encounter this notion again and with a pantheistic flavor. It will be seen that James is eager to stress the "intimate" character of the divine but in a way that does not deny the reality of individuals. Hence, there will be an overlapping of consciousness ("fields within fields") that allows for both individuality and the encompassing character of the divine. I am contending that the note under consideration anticipates this later doctrine and that in both instances James's insight is better expressed in field language. To illustrate further, let us return to the text in which James says that it is not "we" as the "total process of experience" but the individualized self that was the focus of his concern in the previously cited texts concerning the spiritual self and movements in the head. He then reinforces his early expression:

> The individualized self, which I believe to be the only thing properly called self, is a part of the world experienced. The world experienced (otherwise called the "field of consciousness") comes at all times with our body as its centre, centre of vision, centre of action, centre of interest. Where the body is is "here"; when the body acts is "now"; what the body touches is "this"; all other things are "there" and "then" and "that." These words of emphasized position imply a systematization of things with reference to a focus of action

and interest which lies in the body. . . . The body is the storm centre, the origin of co-ordinates, the constant place of stress in all that experience-train. Everything circles round it, and is felt from its point of view.

Recalling the previously made distinction between the "thing-body" and the "lived body," our initial response to this text is, "To which of these bodies is James referring?" The question is seriously misleading, of course, if it implies that there are two bodies; it would then land us back in that ontological dualism James was continually striving to overcome. On the other hand, if we take "body" in the scientific or commonsense meaning, we cannot avoid materialism. If there is implicit in James, as the commentators have maintained, a distinction between the body as a physiological entity and as "lived," then it can only be a distinction of focus and function. The thing- or object-body can only be the lived body viewed more narrowly, viewed as a limited field within a more inclusive field. James is pointing, I believe, to that more inclusive body field which, while not separate from the "thing-body," is also neither reducible to nor simply identical with it.

In Stevens's commentary on the text under consideration, there is, in my opinion, support for the kind of field reading being presented: "These terms designate a network of positions, a system of coordinates, whose focal point is always the body. No experience is possible for us, unless it fit into this oriented system of references" (*JH*, 74). While he does not say so explicitly in this passage, Stevens is clearly referring to the lived body, as is evident in a later passage in which he states that Husserl and James "both agree on the ambiguous situation of the animate body which reveals itself simultaneously as a Thing in the world and as the center of coordinates to which the rest of the world is related" (*JH*, 88).[35] Stevens describes the body as "the functional center of my consciousness," and as "the zero-point, the locus of every field of consciousness" (*JH*, 143, 86).[36]

One other segment of James's lengthy footnote merits consideration. It immediately follows the last passage cited:

> The word "I," then, is primarily a noun of position, just like "this" and "here." Activities attached to "this" position have prerogative emphasis, and, if activities have feelings, must be felt in a peculiar way. The word "my" designates the kind of emphasis. (*ERE*, 86n.)

Apart from the relational character of the "I," this passage can be read as implying, or at least not foreclosing, the reality of a personal self that is "more" than an object in what Ehman called "an anonymous stream of consciousness" (*NEP*, 263). Recall that Ehman criticized James for the failure to acknowledge "the felt reflexivity, the felt reference back to self," in many of our experiences. In his desire to stress that when we reflect, we always encounter the self as an object within the stream of experience, James flirts with a "no-self" doctrine. The corrective for this tendency, as Ehman insists, is to acknowledge the self's prereflective awareness of its own existence. Does the passage just cited recognize this awareness? It depends, I believe, on how we understand the "peculiar way" in which the activities attached to the "I" are felt. Is the "prerogative emphasis" an act of prereflective self-reference without which the self would be reduced to just another object in "an anonymous stream of consciousness?" If so understood, it would certainly soften the "materialistic" implications of those passages previously cited.

Important as they are, I do not believe that James's doctrine of the self can be constructed from these "body-texts" alone. Nevertheless, I have dwelt upon them at some length in order to show that they need not be read in a materialistic or behavioristic sense and that they can properly be read as pointing toward a field view of the self. Since I have chosen to speak in terms of "self" rather than "body"—even "lived body"—it is important to reemphasize why James was attracted to "body" language. The point has repeatedly been made that James wished to account for the data of experience without recourse to any nonexperiential spiritual or transcendental principle or any immaterial soul. But he also had a more positive reason for describing experience in bodily terms: namely, that such language keeps us aware of the concreteness, immediacy, otherness, uniqueness, and centeredness that characterize the stream of experience while protecting us against a deenergizing absorption in empty abstractions.[37]

These are also the features James wishes to emphasize when he makes sensation, as Perry says, "the prototype of experience." But Perry notes the same kind of ambiguity attached to "sensation" that was earlier noted in reference to "body." Sensory experience is not, for James, what it is for those empiricists who "reduce the concreteness of experience to sensational atoms" or "limit the *qualia* of experience to the 'six senses' " (*SWJ*, 47–48). Nevertheless, according to Perry, "sensory experience is still typical of existence in respect of that character of fullness, direct presence, and shock of externality which distinguishes it from thought, memory and imagination" (*SWJ*, 70).[38] Since concreteness and its allied characteristics are the claimed advantages of the field metaphor, and inasmuch as it has been suggested that the body can be understood in field terms, why use, as I do, "self language" instead?

To some extent the difference in speaking of "self field" or "body field" is only terminological. Nevertheless, I would maintain that in view of the aims of this essay (and I would say the overall aims of James's philosophy), "self" is a less misleading term than "body" for referring to the *full* reality of the human being. Notice that I say "less misleading," for the danger in speaking of the "self" is that while it is a more palatable term for contemporary thinkers than "soul" or "spirit," it may simply mask an unacceptable dualism. Still, I believe the likelihood that "body" terminology will eventuate in materialistic reductionism is greater than that "self" terminology will dissipate into vacuous spirituality. The reason for this, I would suggest, is that we apparently have more "exact" language for the body both in science and in common sense.[39] The very vagueness of the term "self" is an advantage in that it keeps us open to dimensions of human reality never adequately grasped when speaking of the "body." This is reflected, I believe, in ordinary language that expresses a long-standing belief, insight, intuition, or perhaps prejudice that we are "more" and "other" than our bodies.[40]

But the distinction between the self and the body is not restricted to common sense or to the various forms of dualism. George Herbert Mead, who is within the pragmatic tradition, shares many assumptions and principles with James and Dewey, and has given us a very rich philosophy of the self as social. Nevertheless, he explicitly asserts that "we can distinguish very definitely between the self and the body," since "the self has a character which is different from that of the physiological organism proper."[41]

Finally, it is more consistent with and faithful to James's more developed view of the self, which will be presented later, to speak in terms of the self rather than the body. Hans Linschoten has pointed out that "to James, the Self was a property of a body, although it can, and sometimes even must, be described as something different from the body."[42] Even in that section of *The Principles of Psychology* in which James describes the spiritual self as "movements in the head" or "bodily feelings," he still seems to distinguish, as previously noted, the spiritual self from the body: when insisting that the spiritual self "is *felt*," he immediately adds, "just as the body is felt" (*PP,* I:286). If this were an isolated text, it would prove nothing, but it is consistent with the kind of distinct meaning that belongs to what James will later call the "*full* self" (*PU,* 130).[43]

CHAPTER 4

James: Personal Identity

Who is it that can tell me who I am?
—William Shakespeare
King Lear

For every man alone thinks he hath got
To be a Phoenix, and that then can bee
None of that kinde, of which he is, but hee.
—John Donne
"An Anatomy of the World"

To find wherein personal identity consists, we
must consider what person stands for; which, I
think, is a thinking intelligent being, that has
reason and reflection, and can consider itself as
itself, the same thinking thing, in different times
and places.
—John Locke
*Essay Concerning Human
Understanding*

Having had his say concerning the empirical self (me) and its constituent
selves (material, social, spiritual), James next declares that the decks are
"cleared for the struggle with that pure principle of personal identity," the
pure Ego (I) which has been repeatedly alluded to but whose description
was postponed. After noting that "ever since Hume's time, it has been justly
regarded as the most puzzling puzzle with which psychology has to deal,"
James concedes that whatever solution he adopts "will fail to satisfy the
majority of those to whom it is addressed" (*PP*, I:314).[1]

There is hardly a more crucial issue for the purposes of this essay than that
of personal identity. Unless a "reasonable" case can be made for a continually changing self that nevertheless embodies a significant mode of
"sameness" or "identity," any belief in immortality or resurrection would
be characterized by emptiness and blindness. Before explicitly considering
"personal identity," however, and the solution that James adopts in *The Principles of Psychology*, I would like to recall and reemphasize some crucial principles and presuppositions of his more general philosophy.

Again and again throughout the *Principles*, James insists that he is concerned only with the psychological, not the metaphysical, dimensions of the

various problems under consideration. Again and again, however, he merges the two, and he later realized that they cannot be kept completely apart regardless of one's methodological intentions.[2] Without completely conflating the psychological (descriptive) and the metaphysical (speculative), I have suggested that the deeper thrust and significance of James's position on such specific questions as truth, self, and God can be grasped only by surfacing the metaphysical presuppositions that permeate his more particularized responses.

Recall the earlier contention that the pragmatists in general and James in particular are best understood within the framework of a metaphysics of process and relations, a metaphysic of "fields." Again, I make no suggestion that this is a fully developed and systematized metaphysics, or that individual pragmatists—especially James—have been perfectly consistent in pursuing the implications of a radically changing and relational world. Still, the hypothesis governing this essay is that when pragmatism is understood as presupposing such a world, it offers rich resources for the treatment of a range of questions, including those that fall under the heading of "philosophy of religion"—and among these is the question of personal immortality. I will attempt, therefore, to illustrate this point more concretely in the consideration of James's doctrine of personal identity.

James's insistence that he is presupposing dualism in his psychology gives rise to the oft-noted conflicts and inconsistencies that populate *The Principles of Psychology*. I have suggested that for the purposes of this essay, James will be read in the light of his later rejection of ontological dualism; therefore, his dualistic language, which cannot be completely avoided, will be understood functionally rather than ontologically. There is one self with a variety of functions; hence, I maintain that the distinction between James's "objective *me*" and "subjective *I*" is a distinction of focus and function. An extremely important implication of this perspective, as we shall see, is that inasmuch as functions are "real" and are neither epiphenomenal nor in need of some underlying substantial principle, then if there are real I-functions, there is a real I.

Another central presupposition, already touched upon, is that the deepest features of reality—its "thickness"—are grasped in "feelings," sometimes referred to as immediate or perceptual experience. The self, insofar as it is an identity-in-diversity, a sameness-amidst-differences, a unity-within-plurality, must be "felt." "*Whatever* the content of the ego may be," James states, "it is habitually felt *with* everything else by us humans, and must form a *liaison* between all the things of which we become successively aware" (*PP*, I:235).[3] Just how "feeling" is to be understood and whether it is adequate to account for personal identity are and are likely to remain matters of intense dispute, but—following James—I believe it highly unlikely that any claim to establish the reality of personal identity will be able to dispense completely with feeling or something akin to it.[4] An important aspect of James's understanding of "feeling," of course, is that it must be seen within his metaphysics of experience and not as some esoteric activity that is imported from a realm beyond experience when reason fails us.[5]

To say that personal identity is felt is not to make any exclusive claims for the experience of self. "In James," Perry states, "the personal subject loses all of its special privileges. It must submit to the common test. If it is there at all it must give evidence of its existence, and this evidence furnishes, so far as it goes, the only clue to its nature and character."[6] The "ground" evidence, for James, is what is felt or what is presented in perceptual experience. While this feeling or perceptual experience never admits of exhaustive exposition, it is not a representation of some kind of noumenon lying behind or beyond the phenomenon. As he wrote to Hugo Münsterberg in 1900, "My fundamental objection to your philosophy is that I still believe the immediate living moment of experience to be as 'describable' as any 'scientific' substitute therefor can be" (*TC*, II:150). It is this crediting of experience that led James to affirm the importance of John Locke insofar as he had "made of 'personal' identity (the only practically important sort) a directly verifiable empirical phenomenon. Where not actually experienced, it *is* not."[7] My point here is not to maintain that this assertion is unproblemed but simply to stress the centrality of perceptual experience or feeling in James's doctrine of personal identity.

One further point in this regard is that identity or sameness as "felt" must be distinguished from the identity or sameness that characterizes concepts. It was only in James's last philosophy that he thought he had finally broken loose from the "logic of identity" that so hampered his efforts to describe the flux of experience: "What, then, are the peculiar features in the perceptual flux which the conceptual translation so fatally leaves out?" James responds that the essence of life is its continuously changing character, while concepts are discontinuous and fixed. "When we conceptualize, we cut and fix, and exclude everything but what we have fixed . . . whereas in the real concrete sensible flux of life, experiences compenetrate each other so that it is not easy to know just what is excluded and what is not" (*PU*, 113).[8] James brings out the importance of the distinction in his description of the continuity and sameness that belong to personal experience.

> What I do feel simply when a later moment of my experience succeeds an earlier one is that tho there are two moments, the transition from one to the other is *continuous*. Continuity here is a definite sort of experience; just as definite as is the *discontinuity-experience* which I find it impossible to avoid when I seek to make the transition from an experience of my own to one of yours. . . . Practically to experience one's personal continuum in this living way is to know the originals of the ideas of continuity and sameness, to know what the words stand for concretely, to own all that they can ever mean. (*ERE*, 25–26)

But it is this experiential sameness and continuity that are, according to the rationalists, excluded by logic. "'Sameness,'" they have said, "must be a stark numerical identity; it can't run on from next to next. Continuity can't mean mere absence of gap; for if you say two things are in immediate contact, *at* the contact how can they be two?" These thinkers end up "by substituting a lot of static objects of conception for the direct perceptual experiences" (*ERE,* 26).[9] They consider it absurd to maintain that the "self-same" functions differently with and without something else, "but this is sensibly seems to do." James does not deny that *"qua* this an experience is not the same as it is *qua* that . . . but the *quas* are conceptual shots of ours at its postmortem remains." In its sensational immediacy, however, "everything is all at once whatever different things it is at once at all." It is only when concepts are substituted for sensational life that intellectualism apparently triumphs through its claims to prove "the imminent-self-contradictoriness of all this smooth-running finite experience" (*PU,* 120–21).

A central and disputed feature of James's doctrine of the self is that the "passing Thought is the thinker." I will later analyze this and suggest an interpretation congenial both to a field metaphysics and a belief in personal immortality. A crucial feature of that analysis will be James's notion of the "specious present"—the claim that in immediate experience we grasp both the receding past and the emerging future. Again I wish to stress that this is not a conceptual grasp but a felt grasp: "The tiniest feeling we can possibly have comes with an earlier and a later part and with a sense of their continuous procession." James insists that the "passing" moment is the minimal fact and that "if we do not feel both past and present in one field of feeling, we feel them not at all" (*PU,* 128). This "temporal" character of experience and reality, explicitly articulated in James's later philosophy, is implicit in and a key to understanding his earlier views on the self. At the heart of this temporality is "continuous transition" or "change," which, as I have been stressing, can be immediately experienced or felt but cannot be grasped through concepts. This is an extremely important point as regards any attempt to understand the nature of the self; as James notes, "personal histories are processes of change in time, and *the change itself is one of the things immediately experienced"* (*ERE,* 25).

The general point I am attempting to make in these introductory remarks to a description of James's doctrine of the self as presented in *The Principles of Psychology,* is that this doctrine is much enriched when read within the incipient field metaphysics of James's later philosophy. In the *Principles,* James maintains that he is restricting himself to a description of experience, to the structure of the mind; he is bracketing the question of "external" reality. When he jettisons this ontological dualism in the *Essays in Radical Empiricism,* he is able to ask, somewhat rhetorically, "Should we not say here that to be experienced as continuous is to be really continuous, in a world where experience and reality come to the same thing?" (*ERE,* 30). In recalling here that for the pragmatists experience is the only pathway to any speculation or extrapolation concerning the general character of reality, I am stressing how different is the claim that change or continuous transition is felt when that claim is understood not merely as a psychological description but as an expression of our deepest and most intimate penetration into reality. Consider, for example, how significantly different are the implications of the following text, depending on which of these perspectives is assumed: "In the same act by which I feel that this passing minute is a new pulse of my life, I feel that the old life continues into it, and the feeling of continuance in no wise jars upon the simultaneous feeling of novelty. They, too, compenetrate harmoniously" (*ERE*, 46–47).

The fuller implication of the self's feeling its own continuity, whereby its dimension of pastness is intimately bound up with its dimension of newness, can be appreciated only after we have described James's effort to account for the unity, continuity, and identity of the self in terms of the "passing Thought." I will at that time suggest that when these metaphysical presuppositions are related to the "passing Thought," we are able to avoid accounting for personal identity through the substantialist's underlying principle or the transcendentalist's propertyless transcendental ego. Also avoided, however, will be that "thinness" and radical ephermerality that accompanies a narrow phenomenalist interpretation of the "passing Thought."

THE SENSE OF PERSONAL IDENTITY

In the eighteenth century, Thomas Reid asserted that "the conviction which every man has of his identity, as far back as his memory reaches, needs no aid of philosophy to strengthen it, and no philosophy can weaken it, without first producing some degree of insanity."[10] Whether philosophy can strengthen or weaken this conviction may be disputed, but there can be no doubting that personal identity has been a matter of continuing philosophical controversy. "Evidently," Whitehead states, "there is a fact to be accounted for"; hence, every philosophy "must provide some doctrine of personal identity."[11] This holds even if one concludes that personal identity is an illusion, for one would still have to explain why human beings are so universally and persistently saddled with such an illusion—the task of such thinkers as the Humeans and the Buddhists, who deny the reality of the self.[12] James himself has been interpreted as presenting, if only implicitly, a view of the self that denies the reality of the subject, or ego. I will contend that in spite of a number of misleading texts, such an interpretation is in conflict with the deeper strains of his philosophy when considered in its overall thrust.[13] Unless I can establish this claim, my effort to employ James's doctrine of the self as a ground for belief in personal immortality will be radically undermined. Hence the necessity for the close and detailed consideration of some subtle and elusive features of James's doctrine.

Recall that the central feature of James's description of the empirical self (me) was that in all its manifestations it is experienced as an object. The question that inevitably follows, of course, is *who* or *what* is doing the experiencing,[14] which finally brings James to a consideration of "the I, or pure Ego," which he had bracketed while describing the empirical self. In his *Psychology: Briefer Course,* James admits that "the I, or 'pure ego,' is a very much more difficult subject of inquiry than the Me. It is that which at any given moment *is* conscious, whereas the Me is only one of the things which it is conscious *of.*" He goes on to say that the reference here is to the *Thinker,* which immediately gives rise to the question, "*What* is the Thinker?" James will eventually answer, the "passing Thought" or the "passing state of consciousness." At the outset, however, he acknowledges that the passing state is the embodiment of change, "yet each of us spontaneously considers that by 'I,' he means something always the same" (*PBC,* 175). It is this sense of sameness or personal identity that must now be explored in order to determine whether there is an alternative to the three traditional accounts of this phenomenon—substantialism, transcendentalism, and associationism.

There can be no doubt that I *feel* I am the same person today that I was yesterday, but it may be asked whether this feeling expresses fact or illusion, whether in reality "*I am the same self that I was yesterday*" (*PP,* I:316). Or, as James expressed it later, "*Is the sameness predicated really there?*" (*PBC,* 180). It must be determined just what is meant when consciousness "calls the present self the *same* with one of the past selves which it has in mind." The key here is the feeling of "warmth and intimacy" that characterizes our present thought or self. We receive "an unceasing sense of personal existence" from the "warmth" that characterizes "the feeling which we have of the thought itself, as thinking," and/or "the feeling of the body's actual existence at the moment." We identify with those *distant* selves who are remembered with warmth and intimacy, and those alone are so remembered who were initially experienced with warmth and intimacy. James illustrates this point by comparing our thoughts to a herd of cattle. Just as at roundup time the owner picks out from a larger herd those cattle bearing his brand, so we gather together out of a larger collection of thoughts those bearing our brand—"warmth and intimacy." When we add the feeling of *continuity* that we remember when referring to more distant selves and perceive as our present self continually fades into the past, we have the two characteristics of personal identity—resemblance and continuity (*PP,* I:316–18).

Now it should be noted that James maintains at this point the same criteria for the sameness perceived in the self and the sameness perceived in other phenomena. Further, James cautions us against claiming more unity or sameness than is warranted by experience, such as "metaphysical or absolute Unity in which all the differences are overwhelmed. The past and present selves compared are the same just so far forth as they *are* the same, and no farther." There is then *both* generic unity and generic difference coexisting so that "from the one point of view they are one self, from others they are as truly not one but many selves." Finally, this sense of personal identity vanishes when "the resemblance and the continuity are no longer felt" (*PP,* I:318).

In so describing personal identity, James notes that he has only given a version of "the ordinary doctrine professed by the empirical school."[15] At this point, however, he diverges from the traditional empircists, charging that "these writers have neglected certain more subtle aspects of the Unity of Consciousness" (*PP*, I:319). What is missing from the empirical doctrine is the character of ownership belonging to our thoughts. Reverting to his herd metaphor, James states: "No beast would be so branded unless he belonged to the owner of the herd. They are not his because they are branded; they are branded because they are his." It is this recognition that thoughts are owned which leads common sense to posit "a pure spiritual entity of some kind" as the "real Owner" (*PP*, I:319–20). Stated in other terms, what is absent in traditional empiricism is an acknowledgment that a multiplicity of individual thoughts can be integrated only by means of a medium. In contradistinction to this empirical doctrine, James maintains that in his account "the medium is fully assigned . . . in the shape of something not among the things collected, but superior to them all, namely, the real, present onlooking, remembering, 'judging thought' or identifying 'section' of the stream" (*PP*, I:320–21).[16]

Though yielding much, according to James, this assumption still does not satisfy the demands of common sense, since the unity achieved by the Thought (the present mental state) "does not exist until the Thought is there." This is equivalent to a new settler lassoing wild cattle and owning them for the first time. But the claim of common sense is that past thoughts were *always* owned, and this suggests that the Thought has a "*substantial* identity with a former owner,—not a mere continuity or resemblance . . . but a *real unity*." While James concedes that the "Soul" and the "Transcendental Ego" are attempts to satisfy this urgent demand of common sense, he advances an alternative hypothesis to account for "that appearance of never-lapsing ownership" (*PP*, I:321). How would it be, he asks, "if the Thought, the present judging Thought, instead of being in any way substantially or transcendentally identical with the former owner of the past self, merely inherited his 'title,' and thus stood as his legal representative now?" (*PP*, I:321).

James goes on to suggest that just as a long succession of herdsmen might come into possession by the rapid transmission of the original title of ownership, so might "the 'title' of a collective self be passed from one Thought to another." Something very much like this patently occurs when "each pulse of cognitive consciousness, each Thought, dies away and is replaced by another." In this stream of succession each later Thought, recognizing the earlier Thoughts as "warm," appropriates them and greets them saying: "Thou art *mine,* and part of the same self with me." Hence, "each Thought is thus born an owner, and dies owned, transmitting whatever it realized as its Self to its own later proprietor." James is suggesting, then, a process of "adoption" or "appropriation" whereby the present "passing Thought" adopts or appropriates the previous Thought and all it includes, which Thought had in turn adopted the previous Thought all the way back to the initial moment of Thought. James concludes: "Who owns the last self owns the self before the last, for what possesses the possessor possesses the possessed" (*PP*, I:321–22).[17]

While claiming that this sketch includes all the *verifiable* features in personal identity, James does admit that the *act of appropriation* is somewhat obscure, inasmuch as "a thing cannot appropriate itself; it *is* itself." Still less, James continues, can it disown itself, since "there must be an agent of the appropriating and disowning." This agent has already been named: "it is the Thought to whom the various 'constituents' are known" (*PP*, I:322–23). Nevertheless, this Thought cannot be an object to itself, nor can it ever appropriate or disown itself: "It appropriates *to* itself, it is the actual focus of accretion, the hook from which the chain of past selves dangles, planted firmly in the Present, which alone passes for real, and thus keeping the chain from being a purely ideal thing" (*PP*, I:323).

The present moment of consciousness, however, is "the darkest in the whole series," for "nothing can be known *about* it till it be dead and gone." James concedes that "it may feel its own immediate existence"; nevertheless, "its appropriations are . . . less to *itself* than to the most intimately felt *part of its present Object, the body, and the central adjustments,* which accompany the act of thinking, in the head. *These are the real nucleus of our personal identity*" (*PP*, I:323). With this text that ambiguity of the body, previously discussed, surfaces again. Further, despite the qualification "less to itself" concerning the Thought's appropriations, and the fact that a few lines before he maintained that the Thought "appropriates *to* itself," it is easy to see why James's doctrine of the "passing Thought as the Thinker" might be interpreted as a "no-self" doctrine.

If all doctrines that deny the presence in the stream of experience of any essentially unchanging principle remaining absolutely identical at all moments of its existence are designated "no-self" doctrines, then James's view falls into this classification. This notion of identity, however, which by definition restricts it to unchanging realities, is what James is challenging. His challenge here is part of his broad metaphysical challenge to the view that reality in its essential structure is permanent or immutable. If existential beings are essentially changing beings, then the only identity they can possess must be that peculiar to such beings. The numerical or substantial identity characteristic of static beings must be distinguished from the relative or functional identity characteristic of changing beings. Hence, James maintains that the identity discovered by the "I" can be only "a relative identity, that of a slow shifting in which there is always some common ingredient retained."

He goes on to say that the identity which the "I" finds in its "me" is only "a loosely construed thing, an identity 'on the whole'" (*PP*, I:352).[18] In his *Psychology: Briefer Course*, James denies any *substantial* identity between yesterday's and today's states of consciousness, "for when one is here the other is irrevocably dead and gone." They do possess *functional* identity, however, since both know the same objects—including the bygone me—to which they react in an identical way, calling it their own in opposition to all the other things they know. James concludes: "This functional identity seems really the only sort of identity in the thinker which the facts require us to suppose. Successive thinkers, numerically distinct, but all aware of the same past in the same way, form an adequate vehicle for all the experience of personal unity and sameness which we actually have" (*PBC*, 181).[19] Thus, James's "passing Thought" doctrine excludes any view of the self as *substance*, but I will later suggest that when combined with the views on the self that emerge in his last philosophy, the "passing Thought" can be reconciled with a *substantive* view of the self.

First, however, it will be helpful to consider briefly James's arguments against the three traditional accounts of personal identity. I am concerned here not so much with the historical accuracy or fairness of his interpretation but rather with what his criticisms tell us about his own doctrine and their implications for the field model of the self that I am endeavoring to construct.

James begins with an analysis of substantialism, which posits the soul as the nonphenomenal, underlying, unchanging principle allegedly responsible for the unity, continuity, and identity belonging to the self. In my earlier treatment of pragmatism's rejection of dualism, I noted that James does not claim to prove the nonexistence of the soul; rather, he rejects it because he judges it useless as an explanatory principle. For example, the soul would fulfill the need for that medium of union that James found absent in associationism, but in merely asserting that distinct ideas and experiences are unified "by a unifying act of the soul, you say little more than that now they *are* united, unless you give some hint as to *how* the soul unites them" (*EP*, 85). It is this "how," James maintains, that his "passing Thought" hypothesis accounts for, and does so without positing any principle behind or beyond the "phenomenal and temporal facts" (*PP*, I:326–27). Consider the claims of simplicity and substantiality made for the soul. James has described his "Thought" by the metaphor "Stream" to convey its absence of "*separable parts.*" Hence, it can be said to be "simple." As for substantiality, "the present Thought also has being,—at least all believers in the Soul believe so— and if there be no Being in which it 'inheres,' it ought itself to be a 'substance.'" Despite these similarities, if similarities they indeed be, the differences between the two doctrines is even more striking.

> The Thought is a perishing and not an immortal or incorruptible thing. Its successors may continuously succeed to it, resemble it, and appropriate it, but they *are* not it, whereas the Soul-Substance is supposed to be a fixed unchanging thing. By the Soul is always meant something *behind* the present Thought, another kind of substance, existing on a non-phenomenal plane. (*PP*, I:327)

What James is affirming may not be completely clear, but what he is rejecting most certainly is. Whatever the self may positively be, it is not "a fixed unchanging thing" or shadow reality located in a world ontologically different from the world we experience.

James begins his consideration of the associationist theory by commending Locke for having grasped that "the *important* unity of the Self was its verifiable and felt unity," accompanied by a *consciousness* of diversity. It was Hume, however, who "showed how great the consciousness of diversity actually was." Nevertheless, Hume ends up as the mirror image of the substantialists: they say "the Self is nothing but Unity," while he says "it is nothing but Diversity." Hume denies the phenomenal "thread" of resemblance "or core of sameness" that James contends is acknowledged in his "passing Thought" hypothesis. The crucial deficiency in Hume and all the other associationists is their failure to recognize the connectedness that is given in experience. According to Hume, *"All our distinct perceptions are distinct existences, and . . . the mind never perceives any real connection among distinct existences."*[20] James, however, insists that within the stream of experience the connections are just as "real" as the separations. This is the crucial point at which the difference in the meaning of "experience" significantly separates James and the other pragmatists from the classical empiricists. This difference is explicit in the statement of fact and generalized conclusion that characterizes James's radical empiricism.

> The statement of fact is that the relations between things, conjunctive as well as disjunctive, are just as much matters of direct particular experience, neither more so nor less so, than the things themselves.
> The generalized conclusion is that therefore the parts of experience hold together from next to next by relations that are themselves parts of experience. The directly apprehended universe needs, in short, no extraneous trans-empirical connective support, but possesses in its own right a concatenated or continuous structure. (*MT*, 7)

This is a key example of a claim presented as "psychological" in *The Principles of Psychology* having become "metaphysical" in *The Varieties of Religious Experience*. Prescinding from the psychological/metaphysical question, the important point here is that James makes relations of connection just as much matters of direct experience as relations of separation. Both the associationists and the transcendentalists presuppose an experience comprised of a succession of separate or discrete ideas or sensations. The associationists, maintaining that these "distinct existences" are unconnected, must limit any connection or unity to some psychological act in accordance with vague "laws of association." The transcendentalists, on the other hand, accepting the same assumption of experience as a succession of discrete psychic atoms, posit a "transcendental Ego" as the necessary condition for uniting this multiplicity. James discusses John Stuart Mill and Immanuel Kant as representatives of these two approaches.

Though an associationist, Mill, according to James, comes perilously close to positing something like the Soul when he speaks of "the *inexplicable tie* . . . which connects the present consciousness with the past one." Since Mill goes on to refer to this "tie" as "something in common" and "permanent" (*PP*, I:338), James sees here "metaphysical Substance come again to life."[21] But Mill makes the same blunder as Hume: "The sensations *per se,* he thinks, have no 'tie.' The tie of resemblance and continuity which the remembering Thought finds among them is not a 'real tie' but 'a mere product of the laws of thought'; and the fact that the present Thought 'appropriates' them is also no real tie" (*PP*, I:340).

James takes Kant as representative of the transcendentalist theory. Kant posits the transcendental Ego as necessary to bring unity to the original manifold of sensation. Note again the assumption that the basic building blocks of knowledge—the data of sensation—are in themselves unconnected and hence in need of some transcendental principle of unity, which for Kant is the pure Ego.[22] This is not the Soul, however, since we can know nothing positive about it, inasmuch as it "has no properties, and from it nothing can be deduced." Granting that "knowing must have a vehicle" by which the "many" is known, the complete emptiness of the transcendental Ego excuses James from accepting it rather than his own "present passing Thought." In unusually harsh language for James, he dismisses the Ego as "only a 'cheap and nasty' edition of the soul . . . as ineffectual and windy an abortion as Philosophy can show" (*PP*, I:341–45).

In sum, then, James's view of the structure of experience and/or reality is concatenated and continuous as well as disconnected and discontinuous. All experiences and realities are connected and continuous with other experiences and realities, but every experience and reality is not immediately or directly connected and continuous with every other experience and reality. Given such a world, there is no need to posit either a substantial or transcendental "glue" to hold together ontologically separate realities. The soul and/or transcendental Ego have been presented as the "glue" that holds the discrete elements of the Self together, and God or the Absolute has been claimed necessary to account for the unity of the world.

If substantialism and transcendentalism felt compelled to go beyond experience to account for the "medium of union" or the "vehicle of knowing," associationism failed to recognize the need for such a medium or vehicle. James can claim to both agree and disagree with elements in all three theories, since he maintains the need for a "medium" but locates it within the stream of experience—that "section" of the stream that he has designated the "passing Thought." This is by no means a problem-free claim; as previously mentioned, the notion of the "passing Thought" has been viewed as inclining James in the direction of a "no-self" doctrine. I would like now to explore the "passing Thought" in relation to the self with a view to seeing it as, if not fully consistent with the more substantive self of James's later philosophy, at least not in irreparable opposition to it.

FIELD-SELF: EARLY SIGNS

Milic Capek maintains that "the distance between the 'perishing thought' of *The Principles of Psychology* and 'the full self' of *A Pluralistic Universe* is considerable."

> In the first period, we find consciousness floating over a limited region of the brain, following passively the shifting maximum of the physiological excitations along the neural paths; it is a "perishing pulse of thought" about which we are not even certain whether it has its own autonomous and causally efficient reality or is a simple epiphenomenon of the brain. In the last period, we face a genuinely creative activity whose conscious moment is only a limited manifestation of the whole personal life, embedded in the larger cosmic self without being absorbed in it.[23]

I will later focus on James's "full self" doctrine, which Capek, in opposition to Dewey and other behavioristic interpreters, has most persuasively emphasized. His essay remains a splendid description of the various stages of the development of James's doctrine of the self, as well as of the conflicts and inconsistencies both within and among the various stages. Nevertheless, as other passages in Capek's essay would show, the description of the "first period" in the text just cited is quite misleading if taken as the full story of the self in James's early philosophy. My concern, as frequently noted, is not to present James's doctrine with all its shades and variations but rather to select from his writings those features I believe most serviceable for the construction of a field view of the self. While it is not possible to completely ignore certain shifts and difficulties, I will continue to touch upon these only insofar as they contribute to my central purpose. Showing that even in those places where James's doctrine seems most congenial to a behavioristic or "no-self" interpretation there are resources for a field-self strengthens the case for the latter view. Similarly, indicating at least the lack of any essential opposition between the more "empirical" self of the early James and the more "mystical" self of the late James protects the former from positivistic closure and the latter from floating off into a realm of merely wishful abstractions.

Recall now a few of the earlier stated assumptions in terms of which I am describing James's self. The three fundamental field suppositions suggested by James himself were "(1) 'Fields' that 'develop,' under the categories of continuity with each other. . . . (2) But nothing postulated whose whatness is not of some *nature* given in fields. . . . (3) All the fields commonly supposed are incomplete and point to a complement beyond their own content" (*TC*, II:365). I earlier suggested that the self be understood as the widest encompassing field in relation to the plurality of the constituting subfields within its compass but not in relation to the wider fields within whose compass the self exists.

Bearing these presuppositions in mind, let us see how we might understand the self described in *The Principles of Psychology*. James gives two summary statements of his view. In the first he says that "personality implies the incessant presence of two elements, an objective person, known by a passing subjective Thought and recognized as continuing in time. *Hereafter let us use the words* ME *and* I *for the empirical person and the judging Thought*" (*PP,* I:350). Later in the same chapter he states: "The consciousness of Self involves a stream of thought, each part of which as 'I' can (1) remember those which went before, and know the things they knew; and (2) emphasize and care paramountly for certain ones among them as '*me,*' and *appropriate to these* the rest. The nucleus of the 'me' is always the bodily existence felt to be present at the time" (*PP,* I:378).

Now how are we to understand these far from clear and distinct texts? First, they might be understood dualistically, in which case the "I" and the "me" would be two essentially different principles, the "I" being the underlying principle that unifies the phenomena into a "me." Second, they might be understood epiphenomenally, in which case the objective body would alone be real, while the "I" would be merely an epiphenomenon emerging as the result of the activity of the body, in particular the brain. While there are grounds in James for both these interpretations, I believe there are far better grounds for another: namely, a transactional or field interpretation.

In a transactional or field view, the primary reality is the concrete flowing field or stream *within* which specific fields or functions are distinguished. Let us understand "the self" as this concrete flowing field or stream with the caution that "within" is not to be understood as "within a container." The self is not a container but a field or relational process constituted by a multiplicity of such processes. Further, since all processes, in accordance with one of our key metaphysical assumptions, are transactional, there are no processes or fields existing "in themselves." All fields or realities are relational, and while the poles of the relation can be distinguished, they cannot be separated. Thus any unity possessed by a field is inseparably bound up with a multiplicity of functions or subfields. When the texts cited above are viewed from this field or transactional perspective, the "I" and the "me" are seen to have their reality only correlatively or in transactional activity. Neither the "I" nor the "me" has any reality apart from the other, since *that* they are and *what* they are is determined by processes of co-constitution. The distinction, however, is proper and defensible because the "I" and the "me" refer to different functions and perspectives of one and the same self. The self is thus subjective-objective, these being derivative relational functions of the concrete flowing field or stream. The important point here is that the "subjective *I*" and the "objective *me*" are equally real since, as correlatives, it is not possible to have one without the other. Hence the empirical, objective self considered apart from the subjective "I" is just as much an abstraction as the subjective "I" considered apart from the empirical objective self. While for a particular purpose it might be legitimate to focus on either of these poles without specific reference to the other, when we are faithful to the experience of the self in its concreteness, both must be held together.

It is misleading, therefore, to take James's view on the "passing Thought as the thinker," isolate it from the full self, and interpret it as a doctrine of egolessness or of "the vanishing subject." There is a sense in which James dissolves and denies the ego, and it is the same sense in which he dissolves and denies consciousness: he denies both insofar as they are understood as entities, but he affirms both insofar as they are understood as processive-relational functions.[24] Thus we might say that there is a function or activity of the self whereby the self grows, cumulates, appropriates, and inherits, and this activity is designated the "passing Thought" or the "I." The "I," then, is as real as these functions and subject to the same metaphysical conditions; that is, it has no reality in itself or in isolation from its "objects," key among which is the "me."[25] To question the reality of the "I" because it cannot be directly known as it is in itself apart from its activities is to restrict the meaning of "I" to either a substantial principle or a transcendental Ego. It is just such a restriction that is denied by the effort to describe the "I" as a transactional process located within the concrete stream of experience.

I believe that James was at least moving toward such a transactional Ego even in *The Principles of Psychology*: "The unity, the identity, the individuality, and the immateriality that appear in psychic life are thus accounted for as phenomenal and temporal facts exclusively, and with no need of reference to any more simple or substantial agent than the present Thought or 'section' of the stream" (*PP*, I:326–27). Two points to note here are, first, that while James denies the need for a "substantial agent" as a transempirical reality, he does affirm the reality of an agent; second, that this agent is the "present Thought," which is a "section" of the stream of experience. These same two features were encountered earlier when James, in opposition to the associationists, insisted on the need for a "medium" of unity and identity. He described this medium as "the real, present onlooking, remembering, 'judging thought' or identifying 'section' of the stream" (*PP*, I:321). If we are to make any sense of this view we must constantly resist the tendency to think in terms solely of static concepts and continually bear in mind James's admonition that the flux of experience can be participated in and pointed at but can never be adequately described in concepts or words which by their very nature tend to be static.

Take, for example, James's use of the term "section" in referring to the passing Thought or identifying activity. It is not accidental that this term is placed in quotation marks, since to take it literally would be nonsensical. The "I" as a "section" of the stream cannot be unqualifiedly the same as "Queens" as a section of New York City. Yet the use of the term "section" has some legitimacy, since James is trying to point to that activity within the stream of experience whereby the stream appropriates and unifies. This expression has the advantage of avoiding any transempirical "I" while taking account of a distinctive activity or process of the self or stream of experience.[26] Hence, the distinction between the "I" and the "me" is one of focus and function. This avoids any dualistic reification as well as any dissolution of the "I" into an illusory epiphenomenon or grammatical fiction accidentally attached to a totally objective "real" self.

All of this has been by way of suggesting that even in James's early doctrine, the "self" was wider and more inclusive than the "passing Thought." The self, therefore, is inclusive of the "I" and the "me" in such fashion as to be wholly both, that is, the self is "I" through and through and "me" through and through. If this makes any sense at all, and I am not sure it does, it makes sense only in light of the previously described transactional relation between "I" and "me." The self as "I" does not possess an *additional* part called "me," or vice versa. It is one and the same self, whether grasped as "I" or "me." When it experiences itself as object or as the receptor of other activities, it says "me." When it feels itself as subject or as the initiator of activities, it says "I." While acts do not happen to "I" and "me" does not act, it is one and the same self that acts and is acted upon. If the "I" remains elusive in such a view of the self, it is because the self as continuously changing is always in a sense ahead of itself. This is why, when James introspectively turns, he can not locate any reality other than the objective reality of the empirical self or "me."[27] The "acting part" of the self, the "I" has already moved on, as it were, and becomes "known" only in its residual mode of past selves. Throughout this process, however, there is a feeling of the process, an experience of activity, a feeling of tendencies, a feeling of effort, none of which reduces to objectively known realities. It is the self as a temporal or continuously changing process—which, though real, defies objectification—that is a central feature of the field-self suggested in this essay.

SELF AS CENTERED-ACTIVITY FIELD
Assuming, now, that the "passing Thought" is a function of a wider, fuller, and more inclusive self, I will henceforth refer to the "self" without attempting to restrict the characteristic under consideration to any specific aspect or function of this self. I am, of course, proceeding within the previously described framework of a metaphysics of fields in which the self is understood as a complex of fields or relational processes. Further, as we have already seen, this self has a unity and identity proper to such a complex: that is, a unity amidst plurality and an identity amidst change. In what follows, I will increasingly though not exclusively draw upon the later James. When I do utilize texts from *The Principles of Psychology*, I will not use them in their earlier, more restricted sense. My justification for this is that whatever can properly be predicated of a particular function of the self can also be predicated of the whole or fuller self. Thus, for example, if it is correct to say that the "passing Thought" cumulates or appropriates past selves, then it is also correct to say that the self is characterized by a cumulating or appropriating activity whereby it is continually changing while retaining in some fashion its earlier modes of being.[28]

The first characteristic of selves that might be noted is that they are centers of activity. This, of course, does not distinguish them, for as we earlier saw, all discrete realities are centers of activity. Concerning that plurality which is a feature of the universe, James pointed out that "*effectively* there are centres of reference and action" (*TC*, II:764). Also noted was Dewey's contention that "in a genuine although not psychic sense, natural beings exhibit preference and centeredness."[29] I suggested that panactivism is a more accurate description of reality than panpsychism. Thus, while centered activity is affirmed as the mark of all real beings, thereby excluding any completely passive entities,[30] the term "psychic," or "conscious," will be restricted to describing a specific mode or modes of centered activity. Selves as centers of activity, therefore, are not unique or distinctive, since reality is a plurality of such centers. Inasmuch as we have rejected any ontological dualism, the distinctive character of selves cannot be located in a realm or mode of being "outside" or "beyond" the stream of experience. Any distinction, therefore, must be due to the scope and complexity of the self field that determines its powers of communication and initiation. Hence, consciousness will not be some totally new or completely different kind of being unrelated to and radically discontinuous with nonconscious entities or fields; rather, consciousness will be an activity of those fields that have a wider range and greater complexity than the fields that are encompassed by consciousness and with which it is continuous.

In describing the self as a centered-activity field, of course, there is no positing of any static, unchanging center. Again, the controlling field metaphor must be kept in mind. The "center" of a field has no reality apart from the relations that constitute the full field as well as the center itself. Hence, inasmuch as the field is continually changing and shifting in relation to other fields, so the center of every field is also continually changing and shifting. This is not to suggest that all relations are changing at the same rate or that all centers change and shift at the same rates; there is a vast range of differences both among fields and within a particular field. These differences are manifested in the variations in stability among individuals. In *The Varieties of Religious Experience*, James calls attention to both the reality of and the shifts in our centers of energy. He notes that even among the Buddhists and Humeans, for whom "the soul is only a succession of fields of consciousness: yet there is found in each field a part, or sub-field, which figures as focal and contains the excitement, and from which, as from a centre, the aim seems to be taken."

James goes on to speak of "the hot place in a man's consciousness, the group of ideas to which he devotes himself, and from which he works," and he calls this "*the habitual centre of his personal energy*. . . . It makes a great difference to a man whether one set of his ideas, or another, be the centre of his energy; and it makes a great difference, as regards any set of ideas which he may possess, whether they become central or remain peripheral in him"

(*VRE*, 161–62). The particular use to which James was putting this notion of a "centre of energy"—in this case, religious conversion—is not here of concern. Independently of this use, what is described is a self whose life is always centered, however much the center may change or shift.

In stressing the fact that the self's center is constituted by sets of ideas, James is presupposing a crucial distinction between what might be designated "activity" and "action."[31] "Sustaining, persevering, striving, paying with effort as we go, hanging on, and finally achieving our intention—this *is* action" (*ERE*, 92). Though James does not explicitly and formally make the activity-action distinction that has been articulated by contemporary "action theory" philosophers, he recognizes this distinction in rough form. He designates as "bare activity . . . the bare fact of event or change." If there is such activity, it would be devoid of direction, actor, and aim.

> But in this actual world of ours, as it is given, a part at least of the activity comes with definite direction; it comes with desire and sense of goal; it comes complicated with resistances which it overcomes or succumbs to, and with the efforts which the feeling of resistance so often provokes; and it is in complex experiences like these that the notions of distinct agents, and of passivity as opposed to activity arise. (*ERE*, 82–83)[32]

At stake here, of course, is whether the self can properly be considered an actor, an agent, a center of initiation and origination whose conscious, deliberate action makes a difference both to itself and to the world. This issue, variously described as "causal efficacy" or the "feeling of effort," was a major concern for James from the beginning to the end of his philosophical life. As Perry points out, "James' scientific studies disposed him to accept the view that man is a 'conscious automaton.' . . . Consciousness is present, but has no vote; it supervenes but does not intervene" (*TC*, II:25). But James began very early to distrust this view; in an 1879 article, "Are We Automata?"[33] he presents empirical evidence for the efficacy of consciousness. In *The Principles of Psychology*, he finds it "quite inconceivable that consciousness should have *nothing to do* with a business which it so faithfully attends" (*PP*, I:140). To itself, at least, every actually existing consciousness seems "to be a *fighter for ends*, of which many, but for its presence, would not be ends at all" (*PP*, I:144). James is willing to concede that "the feeling of effort certainly *may* be an inert accompaniment and not the active element which it seems"; no measurements are ever likely to be made showing that effort "contributes energy to the result." But while granting to the mechanist that our feeling of having an effect on reality may be an illusion, he insists that the mechanist grant that it may *not* (*PP*, I:428–29). Even in the *Principles*, then, James was convinced that "however inadequate our ideas of causal efficacy may be, we are less wide of the mark when we say that our ideas and feelings have it, than the Automatists are when they say they haven't it" (*PP*, I:140).

Some years later, after James had articulated his radical empiricism more explicitly, he again affirmed the reality of causal efficacy, not with certainty but surely with more confidence. The increased confidence clearly flowed from his more assured attitude concerning "feelings" or perceptual experience. James was not unaware that many able thinkers insisted that merely to feel active is not to be active and that "agents that appear in the experience are not real agents, the resistances do not really resist, the effects that appear are not really effects at all." Nevertheless, James expressed his own view with passionate firmness:

> No matter what activities there may really be in this extra ordinary universe of ours, it is impossible for us to conceive of any one of them being either lived through or authentically known otherwise than in this dramatic shape of something sustaining a felt purpose against felt obstacles, and overcoming or being overcome. What "sustaining" means here is clear to any one who has lived through the experience, but to no one else; just as "loud," "red," "sweet," mean something only to beings with ears, eyes, and tongues. The *percipi* in these originals of experience is the *esse;* the curtain is the picture. (*ERE,* 85)

Later in the same essay, James states "that real effectual causation as an ultimate nature, as a 'category,' if you like, of reality, is *just what we feel it to be*" (*ERE,* 93).[34] In the posthumously published *Some Problems of Philosophy,* James maintains that it is from "our own personal activity-situations" that the notion of causation is derived.

> In all these what we feel is that a previous field of "consciousness" containing (in the midst of its complexity) the idea of a *result,* develops gradually into another field in which that result appears as accomplished, or else is prevented by obstacles against which we feel ourselves to press. . . . It seems to one that in such a continuously developing experiential series our concrete perception of causality is found in operation. If the word has any meaning at all it must mean what there we live through. (*SPP,* 106)[35]

Another way of expressing all of this is to say that as selves we are initiators of actions and lives of action that really make a difference in the character and course of the world. Stated more simply, we are to some extent, at least, free beings who have the possibility of playing a role in the development of ourselves and of reality. Thus, as Edie notes, freedom, for James, "came to mean the *deliberate achievement* of the ability *to act:* on himself, on others, on the world."[36] And James himself tells us that "the whole feeling of reality, the whole sting and excitement of our voluntary life, depends on our sense that in it things are *really being decided* from one moment to another, and that it is not the dull rattling off of a chain that was forged innumerable ages ago" (*PP,* I:429). In affirming "freedom," James insists that he is not positing some "transphenomenal principle of energy." Rather, he is describing that novelty which emerges from fresh "activity-situations."

If an activity-process is the form of a whole "field of consciousness," and if each field of consciousness is not only in its totality unique (as is now commonly admitted) but has its elements unique (since in that situation they are all dyed in the total), then novelty is perpetually entering the world and what happens there is not pure *repetition*, as the dogma of literal uniformity of nature requires. Activity-situations come in short each with an original touch. (*ERE*, 93n.)

It should be noted that a pluralistic-processive world, an "open" and "unfinished" universe characterized by chance and novelty, is one that does not reduce freedom to a subjectivistic or psychological aberration. The particular kind of world acknowledged by James and the other pragmatists is one in which there are "original commencements of series of phenomena, whose realization excludes other series which were previously possible" (*CER*, 31). In another place, James states: "Free will pragmatically means *novelties in the world*, the right to expect that in its deepest elements as well as in its surface phenomena, the future may not identically repeat and imitate the past" (*P*, 60). This insistence on the relation between freedom and novelty appears again in *Some Problems of Philosophy*, where James maintains that the difference between monism and pluralism rests on the reality or unreality of novelty. He goes on to say that the "doctrine of free will" is "that we ourselves may be authors of genuine novelty" (*SPP*, 74–75).

Needless to say, I am not presuming to handle the issue of freedom and determinism by citing these few texts. My point is simply to indicate that the kind of self proposed here is an agent capable through its *efforts* of bringing some degree of novelty into this ever changing world. James goes so far as to suggest that "effort seems . . . as if it were the substantive thing which we *are*," that it is perhaps "the one strictly underived and original contribution which we make to the world!" Thus it is that "not only our morality but our religion, so far as the latter is deliberate, depend on the effort which we can make. '*Will you or won't you have it so?*' is the most probing question we are ever asked. . . . We answer by *consents or non-consents* and not by words" (*PP*, II:1181–82).

One final point concerning human causal activity has to do with what might be called its "metaphysical implications." Earlier, I stressed that for pragmatists such as James and Dewey, whatever can be predicated of reality or the world in general must in some fashion be given in experience. This is reflected when James asks, in reference to the novelties that result from human activity, "whether we are not here witnessing in our own personal experience what is really the essential process of creation. Isn't the world really growing in these activities of ours?" (*SPP*, 108). I have already suggested that a world or reality that is continually growing can be viewed as giving meaning to the belief in personal immortality, particularly when human persons are viewed as here and now participating in that growth. There is, of course, no *necessary* connection between present participation in the growth of reality and everlasting life. Still, given the obvious scope and magnitude of the reality process, the possibility of continuing participation beyond the short time allotted in "this life" would seem to enhance rather than diminish the meaning of our present participation. This crucial and controversial claim that belief in personal immortality is life-enhancing is discussed at length in later chapters.

CHAPTER 5

James: Full Self and Wider Fields

> Pulses of mind lay beating and absorbing beside
> my own little pulse, and together we were a
> whole, connecting within this wholeness with
> the myriad differing wholes that each of these
> people had formed in their lives, were
> continuously forming in every breath they took,
> and through this web, these webs, ran a finer
> beat, as water ran everywhere in the stone city
> through channels cut or built in rock by men
> who were able to grade the lift or the fall of the
> earth.
> —Doris Lessing
> *Briefing for a Descent into Hell*

> But it is not man alone who can be properly said
> to "connect," nor is it human powers alone that
> are the necessary condition of the functioning of
> Connectives. It is existence cooperating with
> man that "connects."
> —John Herman Randall, Jr.
> *Nature and Historical Experience*

It is my contention that a plausible belief in personal immortality is intimately bound up with a belief in God. More specifically, I will argue that
the relation between the person and God must be such that a belief in personal immortality has experiential grounds—not grounds in the sense of
offering a compelling necessity to infer immortality, but in the softer sense
of being basically consistent with and open to such belief. In keeping, then,
with this experiential methodology, there must be some "justifying" evidence for the extrapolated belief in a divine-human relationship. The principal grounds for such extrapolated belief are found in the view of the self
that emerges in James's later writings.

What I wish to do now is try to construct the essential features of what
James himself calls the "full self." In making this attempt, I will draw principally upon material from *The Varieties of Religious Experience, Essays in
Radical Empiricism,* and *A Pluralistic Universe,* without dealing with important differences of concern and context among these works. Nor will I deal
with inconsistencies, real or alleged, or with a number of technical ques-

tions (particularly in *Radical Empiricism*), which a close textual and systematic study would demand.[1] I wish simply to indicate that there is a common thrust to these works, as well as to *Some Problems of Philosophy* and several essays on psychical research and mysticism. This thrust, as we shall see, is toward articulating both the self and reality in terms of overlapping fields of consciousness. An alternative way of describing this is as the temporalization of reality. The stream or process character of consciousness or experience described in *The Principles of Psychology* is extended to all reality. Thus, as Ralph Barton Perry notes, "Radical empiricism consists essentially in converting to the uses of metaphysics that 'stream of consciousness' which was designated originally for psychology" (*TC*, II:586).[2] One way of viewing the relation between James's *Principles* and his later "metaphysical" works is that in the former, immediate personal experience or feeling is viewed psychologically within a dualistic metaphysics; in the latter, this experience becomes the paradigm for all reality as well as the pathway to reality in its depth and "thickness." In *A Pluralistic Universe*, James insists that "Bergson is absolutely right in contending that the whole life of activity and change is inwardly impenetrable to conceptual treatment, and that it opens itself only to sympathetic apprehension at the hands of immediate feeling" (*PU*, 123n.).[3]

EXPERIENCE OF "SOMETHING MORE"

I have already tried to show that even in those sections of *The Principles of Psychology* where James's view of the self is most capable of a behavioristic or materialistic interpretation, there is evidence of a self much fuller and richer. I suggested that reading these early texts from a field perspective keeps James's doctrine open to the more inclusive self. When we turn to the later James, the case is much more compelling for a field view of the self that more clearly and successfully escapes the egoless, epiphenomenal tendencies earlier evidenced. I noted that even in those bedeviling texts in which James seems to identify the self with the body—where the self is "*found to consist mainly of the collections of these peculiar motions in the head or between the head and throat*"—even here James quickly adds that not for a moment is he suggesting "that this is *all* it consists of." A bit later he explicitly concedes "that over and above these there is an obscurer feeling of something more" (*PP*, I:288, 292).[4]

In exploring this "more," I hope to show that the processive-relational or field character of James's "self" becomes increasingly more explicit and central. This is due in great part, I believe, to the fact that James becomes more conscious of and confident about those metaphysical presuppositions that he derived from personal experience. Having flirted with the notion of an egoless self and an epiphenomenal consciousness, in *A Pluralistic Universe* he speaks in field language, which is much more congenial to a "substantive" view of the self and consciousness that is open to the possibility of personal immortality.

I have already noted that when selves are viewed as transactional centers of activity—as fields—consciousness is not merely an epiphenomenon, nor is it imported from some transempirical realm of being. Consciousness is itself a field continuous with both conscious and nonconscious fields, the distinction between the conscious and nonconscious fields being determined on the basis of range, complexity, and modes of selectivity and initiation. The task remains of phenomenologically describing the specific characteristics of those fields designated "conscious," but the distinct advantage of such a field approach is that there is no need to go "outside" experience in describing consciousness in order to avoid a materialistic or behavioristic reductionism. Thus, in the final analysis, the scope and complexity of human consciousness can be determined only experientially. Here, however, a crucial distinction must be made: one repeatedly referred to as the distinction between the descriptive or phenomenological and the extrapolative or speculative. It is the same distinction that is at work, as we shall see, when James distinguishes what is religiously *experienced* from overbeliefs concerning this experience.

I wish to utilize this descriptive-extrapolative distinction in considering the self as it emerges in James's later writings. The first task will be to describe as faithfully as possible what can be immediately experienced and then to suggest plausible extrapolations from this experience. It must be stressed at the outset, however, that this is a functional distinction, the borders of which are shifting and can vary from time to time as well as from person to person. For example, following James, I will contend that the reality of God is an extrapolation or overbelief, but a mystic would make a stronger experiential claim.[5] The key point here is that if James's position is legitimate, the need for extrapolation or overbelief may be due only to an accidental, nonpermanent limitation in the development of human consciousness. The possibility that the mystics' experiential claim is a delusion cannot, of course, be definitely excluded. Given James's experiential criteria, then, nothing short of immediate experience of the divine would be adequate or completely satisfying. In the present stage of the human condition, however, the most that can be claimed philosophically is that such an experience is a possibility that not only does not conflict with reality as immediately experienced and metaphysically articulated but also is consistent with such experience—indeed, is possibly an enrichment, a deepening and continuation of our narrower quotidian experiences.

While everyone might agree that what is immediately experienced is beyond dispute, it is quite evident that just what it is that is immediately experienced is a matter of great dispute. This is made obvious by the variety of competing, inconsistent, and even contradictory claims of immediate experience. James and a host of twentieth-century phenomenologists have significantly deepened our awareness of how difficult it is to describe with complete fidelity the characteristics of experience. There would be no such difficulty if immediate experience were clear, distinct, and unambiguous instead of being characterized by obscurities, shades, margins, fringes, penumbras, and what James has called "the vague and inarticulate"—which returns us to the question of the "more" that accompanies all experiences. "All that is," James tells us, "is experiences, possible or actual. Immediate experience carries a *sense of more*. . . . The 'more' develops, harmoniously or inharmoniously; and terminates in fulfillment or check." He goes on to say that "the problem is to describe the universe in these terms" (*TC* II:381).

In his own effort to describe the universe in such terms, James moves nonsystematically from the immediately evident "more" that is present as "margin" or "fringe" to such perceptual fields as the visual and auditory; to the "more" that is involved in epistemological-ontological questions such as objective reference, knowing two things together, knowing other minds; to the "more" involved in metaphysical-religious questions such as the "wider self" and overlapping consciousnesses, including divine and human. James's doctrine of the "full self" must include all of these "mores." It is obvious that there is not an equal consensus regarding these diverse "mores"; that is why James, or anyone attempting to construct a doctrine of the self along Jamesian lines, must first establish the general character of this experiential "more" from experiences where the evidence is most widely compelling before considering experiences of "more" that are less universal and more controversial. James's central claim, and the one crucial for the purposes of this essay, is that the structure of our visual fields, for example, is in some respects the same as the structure of mystical experience.

"Our fields of experience," according to James, "have no more definite boundaries than have our fields of view. Both are fringed forever by a *more* that continuously developes, and that continuously supersedes them as life proceeds" (*ERE*, 35). Let us follow James as he describes this marginal "more" that accompanies our field of experience. This will serve as the paradigm to be employed later in his consideration of mystical experience.

> My talk is merely a description of my present field of experience. That field is an experience of physical things immediately present, of "more" physical things "always there beyond" the margin, of my personal self "there," and of thoughts and feelings belonging to the self, together with "other" thoughts and feelings connected with what I call "your" personal selves. Of these various items some, as fully realized, are "sufficients"; others, the physical things "beyond" and "your" thoughts, come as insufficients—they connect themselves with the marginal "more." But . . . that marginal "more" is part of the experience under description. No one can use it mystically and say that self-transcendency or epistemological dualism is already involved in the description—that the "more" is a reference beyond the *experience*. The "more" is more than the vividly presented or felt; the "beyond" is beyond the centre of the field. (*TC*, II:371)

James's use of the term "mystically" in this text might be misleading if taken as his own understanding of mystical experience. He is here using it, as it is often used, to convey the introduction of a nonexperiential realm of being. He is opposed to this notion of "mystical" just as he is opposed to introducing a transcendental Ego or substantial Soul to avoid accounting for the experiences just described in behavioristic or epiphenomenalist terms. The "sense of more" that belongs to all the self's experiences is an indication of relations with a wider reality than is currently in focus. It is the task of metaphysics and religious philosophy, of course, to suggest just what the scope and character of this wider reality is, and we shall later follow James as he describes it in terms of wider fields of consciousness. The only point to be made at this time is that James's affirmation of a wider reality or wider consciousness or wider self does not involve inferring or postulating a reality or realm of being that is essentially, completely, and permanently discontinuous with the experiential.

The reality of "something more" in our immediate experience is evidence of that continuity that characterizes the self. We have already noted James's contention that the felt experience of one's own continuity is the most intimate grasp of that continuity that is characteristic of reality or the world. Again, this is a variation on James's processive or temporalistic metaphysics. Perry calls continuity "one of the master keys to the understanding of James' thought. It is the dominant feature of his last metaphysics" (*TC*, I:524). This is another instance of a feature that James first delineates psychologically and phenomenologically and later comes to utilize metaphysically. A metaphysical expression of continuity is found in the first and third "field" suppositions, which were presented earlier: "(1) 'Fields' that 'develop' under the categories of continuity with each other," and "(3) All the fields commonly supposed are incomplete and point to a complement beyond their own content. The final content . . . is that of a plurality of fields, more or less ejective to each other, but still continuous in various ways" (*TC*, II:365).

A processive or "growing" world, like a processive or growing self, must involve continuity. This continuity, however, is neither the abstract continuum of mathematics nor the permanent, unchanging substantial principle of an earlier metaphysics. Dynamic continuity involves an overlapping of fields and an appropriation or inheritance of past fields by present ones.[6] This is not to suggest that everything is continuous with or immediately related to everything else. There are discontinuities as well as continuities, and there are diverse modes of both. The way in which a self is continuous with its own experiences is not identical with the way in which it is continuous with another's experiences.[7] The distinctive continuity whereby the self appropriates to itself its previous fields of experience is what in part, at least, constitutes the self's individuality. But since there is no self-continuity that does not simultaneously involve continuity with other fields (air breathed, objects known, persons encountered), we have a world of radically plural individuals without atomistic or isolating individuation. The crucial aspect of this question for my purposes is whether there is a sense in which the divine and human consciousnesses can be continuous.

CONSCIOUSNESS AS SELF-COMPOUNDING

In order to arrive at some understanding of how James, in his later writings, saw the relation between the divine and human fields of consciousness, we must follow him—however briefly and superficially—as he considers a question with which he had wrestled for many years: the question of whether "states of consciousness, so called, can separate and combine themselves freely, and keep their own identity unchanged while forming parts of simultaneous fields of experience of wider scope" (*PU*, 83). In *The Principles of Psychology,* he had apparently answered in the negative when he rejected the "mind-stuff" or "mind-dust" theory: that is, the theory that our higher mental states are composed of smaller states. James insisted there that each psychic state was a unit—novel, unique, and individual—and not a collection of primordial atoms of sensation that remained unchanged in themselves while entering into various combinations. For example, according to the "mind-stuff" theory, the taste of lemonade would be simply the atomistic sensations of water, lemon, and sugar conjoined. According to James, however, the taste of lemonade is new and unique, and does not contain the atomistic sensations of water, lemon, and sugar. In spite of James's statement in his Presidential Address to the American Psychological Association in 1894 that in the interest of harmony he was giving up his principle that mental states cannot compound (*EP*, 88), it would be more accurate to say that he came slowly to modify it.[8]

In *The Principles of Psychology,* as previously noted, James was allegedly adhering to a methodological dualism. Hence, though each thought or mental state was unique, two minds could know a common object. In *Essays in Radical Empiricism,* James claims to surrender the dualism between thoughts *and* things, contending that reality is composed of pure experiences which in themselves are neither mental nor physical but can become either, depending on the context or relational functions. For example, the pure experience "pen" is in itself neither mental nor physical, belongs to neither your mind nor my mind. But since it is the "same" pen that is known and is written with, and the "same" pen that you and I know, it would appear that "an identical part can help to *constitute* two fields." This doctrine, of course, is in conflict with the position of *The Principles of Psychology,* which denies that mental states can have "parts." It was B. H. Bode and Dickinson Miller who, according to James, picked up the contradiction, and their objections led James to keep notes—totaling several hundred pages over two and a half years, in which he continually struggled with the problems involved. In a 1905 note, he asks, "How can two fields unite if they contain this common part?" And he immediately adds, "We must overhaul the whole business of connection, confluence and the like, and do it radically" (*TC*, II:750). James ends these notes during his writing of the Hibbert Lectures, which were delivered several months later and subsequently published as *A Pluralistic Universe.* It is in this work that James advances his radical overhaul of the character of confluent consciousness and allied questions.

This "radical overhaul" was actually a somewhat more consistent and explicit articulation of insights and concerns that had been present in some form in James's earliest reflections. "He was simply reaffirming," Bruce Kuklick quite correctly notes, "the primacy of the concrete and immediate over the abstract and the derived"[9]—and, we might add, the pervasiveness of processes and relations that an acute attention to the concrete brings to awareness. Recall that one of the advantages of employing a field model of reality is that it enables us to be more faithful to the "concrete." It is interesting to note that in his reflections on the "Miller-Bode Objections," James wonders whether he might not be guilty of that "sin of abstraction" (*TC*, II:759) with which he had so often charged others. In *A Pluralistic Universe*, he comes to realize that "the difficulty of seeing how states of consciousness can compound themselves . . . is the general conceptualist difficulty of any one thing being the same with many things, either at once or in succession, for the abstract concepts of oneness and manyness must needs exclude each other" (*PU*, 127). This "conceptualist difficulty" is bound up with the traditional "logic of identity," which James finally feels compelled to give up "fairly, squarely, and irrevocably" (*PU*, 96).[10] The central charge against this logic is that it denies the continuous universe, which was a concern of James throughout his reflective life: "That secret of a continuous life which the universe knows by heart and acts on every instant cannot be a contradiction incarnate. If logic says it is one, so much the worse for logic" (*PU*, 94).

EXPERIENCE OVERFLOWS CONCEPTS

A running theme in James's thought, which reaches its crescendo in *A Pluralistic Universe*, is that various modes of rationalism or intellectualism have repeatedly endeavored to substitute clear, distinct, and changeless concepts for the rather murky, messy, and ever changing experiences of ongoing life. James, noting that "framing abstract concepts is one of the sublimest of our human prerogatives," goes on to find it understandable that earlier thinkers have forgotten that "concepts are only man-made extracts from the temporal flux"; as a result, however, they ended up treating concepts "as a superior type of being, bright, changeless, true, divine, and utterly opposed in nature to the turbid, restless lower world" (*PU*, 98–99). When we conceptualize, we cut out a section of the flux of experience and fix it in a static form, thereby excluding everything else in experience but that which we have fixed. In contrast, experiences in the real sensible flux of life "compenetrate each other so that it is not easy to know just what is excluded and what is not" (*PU*, 113). James maintains that intellectualism, after "destroying the immediately given coherence of the phenomenal world," finds itself unable to realize coherence through its conceptual substitutes and hence must "resort to the absolute for a coherence of a higher type." May there not, however, be present in the flux of sensible experience an overlooked rationality? Instead, then, of disintegrating concrete experience through intellectualist criticism and substituting "the pseudo-rationality of the supposed absolute point of view," the real remedy is to focus more attentively and intelligently upon the immediate flow of experience (*PU*, 38). Our experience is too rich, too complex, too textured and many-sided to be adequately represented in abstract categories. "Reality, life, experience, concreteness, immediacy, use what word you will, exceeds our logic, overflows and surrounds it" (*PU*, 96).

Attention must be given here to an ambiguity in this "immediate experience" to which James so frequently refers and from which he wishes to draw so much. Some crucial implications of this ambiguity will appear when we consider James's claim that we are "part and parcel of a wider self." Let me begin by suggesting that James came to realize that not everything in immediate experience was "immediate." I think we must distinguish immediate or concrete experience from "pure immediacy." The latter would refer only to what is in conscious focus, including the conscious margins; the former would include "virtualities" and "other" relations that may be or may not be brought to consciousness at a later time. Since these are constituents of the concrete experience, we might say that they are experienced subconsciously.

Several of James's late notes, combined with his views on the subliminal self (to be treated later), support the distinction here suggested. On November 26, 1905, James wonders whether he might be omitting something vital in his effort "to run things by pure immediacy." For the world to run as it should, "*an other than* the immediate" seems to be required. He goes on to ask whether it would be possible to "treat this other as equivalent to *subconscious* dynamic operations between the parts of experience, distinct from the *conscious* relations which the popular term 'experience' connotes" (*TC*, II:753). Some months later (June 8, 1906), James writes:

> The "cosmic omnibus" around about experience, is the "being" of the experiences and what not *immediately* experienced relations they may stand in. All these facts are *virtually* experience or matters of later experience, however. . . . Not all that an experience virtually "is" is content of its immediacy. . . . The cosmic omnibus for any given experience would thus seem to be only other correlated experiences. (*TC*, II:758)[11]

In exploring any experience, then, it would seem that we are obliged to range much more widely than the realm of "pure immediacy." This is why such exploration is open-ended and ongoing; why it must involve hypotheses, speculations, and extrapolations if, paradoxically, we are to move more deeply into "immediate experience."

These same characteristics of process and relation that I have repeatedly stressed become more explicit as James realizes how much "staticality" has remained in his articulation of experience. As late as September of 1906, he asks: "May not my whole trouble be due to the fact that I am still treating what is really a living dynamic situation by logical and statical categories?" He goes on to say that he ought to have the courage to postulate activity, to introduce agents—in short, to "vivify the mechanism of change!" (*TC*, II:760). But more than a year later (February 1908) he still wonders whether part of the difficulty is due to "a retention of staticality in the notion of 'that' and 'is.'" This is the period, however, during which James is writing what will later be published as *A Pluralistic Universe*, and so he has seen the necessity for surrendering logic if we are to enter into the depth and thickness of living experience. He now realizes that the problem is to *state* without paradox the intuitive or live constitution of the active life. This can be done "only by approximation, awakening sympathy with it rather than assuming logically to define it; for logic makes all things static." It is the processive-pluralistic-relational character of the universe that James is now stressing: "Be the universe as much of a unit as you like, plurality has once for all broken out within it." What the universe *effectively* manifests are "centres of reference and action . . . and these centres disperse each other's rays." Thus, James tells us, no living "*it* is a stark numerical unit. They all radiate and coruscate in many directions; and the manyness is due to the plurality round them." What all this adds up to is that "neither the world nor things are finished, but in process; and that process means *more's* that are continuous yet novel. This last involves the whole paradox of an *it* whose modes are alternate and exclusive of each other, the same and not-same interpenetrating" (*TC*, II:763–64).[12]

CON AND EX

When we come to focus more directly on self-compounding consciousness, we shall see that this involves "the same and not-same interpenetrating." First, however, it is necessary to consider an allied question, which takes the form of a series of what might be designated *con* (*co*) and *ex* problems—how individual realities can be both with and without each other. The most crucial of these problems for my purposes is how human persons can be *con* God and *ex* God; both continuous and discontinuous with God; both present to and absent from God.

James's approach, of course, is to give a hypothetical or speculative response to this question after having shown the *con* and *ex* characteristics of all concrete experiences. On intellectualist grounds, he says, this is impossible: "The intellectualist statement is that *esse* and *sentiri* are the same, a state of mind *is* what it is realized as. If *M* is realized as *con a*, then it *is con a*, and to be identical with its own self must always be *con a;* whatever else it may be *con* with, it can never be *ex a*. That *M* must permanently carry *a* along with it" (*TC*, II:763). But as we have already seen and will further see, "the immediate experience of life solves the problems which so baffle our conceptual intelligence" (*PU*, 116). We have also already seen and will further see that given the processive-relational or field character of experience, every "bit of experience" is *con* and *ex* other bits. Further, since these fields are continually shifting, gaining, and losing, other fields that were *ex* will become *con* and vice versa.[13]

Using Bergsonian language, James describes this processive-relational world as "an endosmosis or conflux of the same with the different: they compenetrate and telescope" (*PU*, 114). In such a telescopic and endosmotic world "there is no reason why A might not be *co*- and *ex*-B, i.e., continuous in any direction with something else." This would be a universe in which nothing "is absolutely cut off from anything else, and nothing is absolutely *solidaire*" (*TC*, II:762).[14] This is a *dynamically* continuous world rather than one of discontinuous "plural solipsisms" (*TC*, II:757). The experiences constituting this world change in such fashion that there is a continuous overlap of the earlier and the later. The *view* that emerges is never an absolutely novel creation following a complete annihilation; rather, "there is partial decay and partial growth, and all the while a nucleus of relative constancy from which what decays drops off, and which takes into itself whatever is grafted on, until at length something wholly different has taken place." The universe is continuous, then, without being one throughout. "Its members interdigitate with their next neighbors in manifold directions, and there are no clean cuts between them anywhere" (*PU*, 115).[15] While logical distinctions are insulators, "in life distinct things can and do commune together every moment" (*PU*, 116).[16] The logically distinct experiences diffuse, and connections are made; for this reason, reality cannot be penned in; "its structure is to spread, and *affect*" (*TC*, II:762).[17] Unlike our concepts, our concrete pulses of experience are not pent in by definite limits. "You feel none of them as inwardly simple, and no two as wholly without confluence where they touch." Interrelatedness, then, is essentially characteristic of all realities. "The gist of the matter is always the same—something ever goes indissolubly with something else. You cannot separate the same from its other, except by abandoning the real altogether and taking to the conceptual system" (*PU*, 127, 128).

In the light of all this, James contends that the old objection against the self-compounding of states of consciousness—that it was impossible for purely logical reasons—"is unfounded in principle." I think that James might have more accurately said, "unfounded in fact or concrete experience," for he never does explain, nor does he claim to, *how* states of consciousness can be compounded. As early as 1895, to the question as to whether we can account for complex facts "being–known–together," he responded: "The general *nature* of it we can probably never account for, or tell how such a unity in manyness can be, for it seems to be the ultimate essence of experience, and anything less than it apparently cannot be at all" (*EP*, 78).[18] If we cannot explain, at least by means of concepts, the unity in diversity that characterizes all experiences, we can point and describe, however inadequately. Again the distinction of James lies in his having brought so brilliantly to our awareness the details of the flux of experience. When we focus on the concrete, we become aware of the overlapping complex of fields peculiar to the tiniest bit of experience as well as to the largest. "Every smallest state of consciousness, concretely taken, overflows its own definition. Only concepts are self-identical; only 'reason' deals with closed equations; nature is but a name for excess; every point in her opens out and runs into the more" (*PU*, 129).[19] As for mental facts compounding themselves, James maintains that in spite of what he said in his *Principles of Psychology*, they "can . . . if you take them concretely and livingly, as possessed of various functions. They can count variously, figure in different constellations, without ceasing to be 'themselves'" (*TC*, II:765).

It is clear that if we are to speak of the self as the "passing Thought," as James did earlier, we must understand this "passing Thought" in terms of James's later metaphysics of experience. By doing so, we are presented with a self immeasurably richer than an epiphenomenalist or behavioristic self. The self is always the self of the "passing moment," but we have seen that every passing moment radiates outward and consists of numerous and diverse overlapping fields, many if not most of which are not in conscious focus. "There are countless *co's* that are immediately undiscerned as such, unanalyzed." These include the continual *co* of our organic sensations, the sense of the immediate past, of outlying space, of the background of interest, and the like: "All these are so ready to be distinctively experienced, that we deem them experienced *subconsciously* all the while." James then asks us to "suppose that total conflux, possible or actual, is really the 'bottom' fact, suppose it actual 'subconsciously,'—then the problem is that of the conditions of insulation" (*TC*, II:757). This, as James notes, is the problem of his 1897 Ingersoll lecture, published as *Human Immortality*—the problem of individual human consciousnesses being immersed in a wider consciousness of which they are only sporadically aware.

Before turning to that problem, we can conclude this section by presenting again that text which, along with another cited earlier,[20] constitutes perhaps the most succinct and significant statement by James as to the character of the self. This text can serve as a summation of what has just preceded, and as an anticipation and experiential ground for the more speculative and extrapolative considerations to follow.

My present field of consciousness is a centre surrounded by a fringe that shades insensibly into a subconscious more. I use three separate terms here to describe this fact; but I might as well use three-hundred, for the fact is all shades and no boundaries. Which part of it properly is in my consciousness, which out? If I name what is out, it already has come in. The centre works in one way while the margins work in another, and presently overpower the centre and are central themselves. What we conceptually identify ourselves with and say we are thinking of at any time is the centre; but our *full* self is the whole field, with all those indefinitely radiating subconscious possibilities of increase that we can only feel without conceiving, and can hardly begin to analyze. The collective and disruptive ways of being coexist here, for each part functions distinctly, makes connexion with its own peculiar region in the still wider rest of experience and tends to draw us into that line, and yet the whole is somehow felt as one pulse of our life,—not conceived so, but felt so. (*PU*, 130)

WIDER CONSCIOUSNESS

The ground we have just covered, which led us to James's description of the "full self," can profitably be explored—or reexplored—by focusing our attention more directly on the reality, or at least the possibility, of a wider consciousness with which individual human consciousnesses are in touch by way of their subconscious or subliminal selves. As Perry has noted, "The idea of consciousness 'beyond the margin' or 'below the threshold' was a metaphysical hypothesis of the first importance. This hypothesis afforded an experimental approach to religion, and constituted the only hopeful possibility of giving scientific support to supernaturalistic faith" (*TC*, II:160). In a letter to Bergson, James himself expressed the view "that the indispensable hypothesis in a philosophy of pure experience is that many kinds of other experience than ours, that the question of [co-consciousness / conscious synthesis] (its conditions, etc.) becomes a most urgent question" (*TC*, II:610).

Tentatively, we might distinguish four groups of experiential data or experiential claims, varying in degrees of immediacy and acceptance, which are involved in the extrapolation of a wider self or wider consciousness. The first group would be made up of those fields of experience that include but are not restricted to the fields of our special senses (auditory, visual, tactile). These were described in the previous section, and I stressed their constitution as processes and relations having centers and margins or fringes in a continually shifting relationship. They, of course, have the highest degree of immediacy and acceptability. The second group would consist of the subconscious or unconscious evidenced in psychotherapeutic situations and articulated in psychological theories. Here the immediacy would be less compelling, but the successful results, real or believed, consequent upon presupposing unconscious factors have led to a fairly widespread acceptability.[21] The third group would include all those experiential claims or phenomena that are referred to as psychical or parapsychological. James, as is well known, was most interested in and sympathetic to these experiential claims; for many years he supported and to a limited degree participated in psychical research. Nevertheless, one year before his death, after noting in the "Final Impressions of a Psychical Researcher" that he had been in touch with psychical research literature for twenty-five years, he confessed: "Yet I am theoretically no 'further' than I was at the beginning" (*MS*, 175).[22]

I am going to label the fourth group of experiences involved in the extrapolation of a wider self "mystical experiences." These are the most important experiences or experiential claims for my purposes, and I am deliberately distinguishing them more sharply from parapsychological claims than did James. He tended to use the term "mystical" more widely that I will do, but the difference is more functional or methodological than substantive. I would admit that *if* the parapsychological claims are authentic, then they are evidence of that wider consciousness manifest in mystical experiences if *they* are authentic. My justification for this distinction is James's own pragmatic one—the "fruits" that have apparently been forthcoming in one case and absent in the other. Those whom we usually think of as great mystics appear to have brought forth both in their own lives and in those touched by them a deepening, an illumination and enrichment. Such fruits are decidedly less evident in the lives of those usually classed as "psychics" or "spiritualists." James himself rather reluctantly and sadly concluded that "the spirit-hypothesis exhibits a vacancy, triviality and incoherence of mind painful to think of as the state of the departed" (*CER*, 438–39).[23] I am not suggesting, nor did James, that mystical experiences could be employed to "prove" the existence of God or the immortality of the self. Following James, however, I am maintaining that mystical experiences are the strongest experiential grounds upon which we can base any extrapolation concerning a more encompassing reality.

James was desirous of bringing forth a hypothesis that would cover the phenomena in all of the groups I have roughly delineated. It was his hypothesis, variously expressed, of the "wider self" that he believed did so most successfully—although even in *The Varieties of Religious Experience* and *A Pluralistic Universe*, we are given at most a sketch and suggestive hypothesis. Before considering these works, let us look briefly at some of the other texts in which James expresses his views concerning a "wider consciousness."

To begin with, I would like to note that James's position on this matter cannot be separated from his long-standing religious belief to the effect that we are engaged in a process not adequately accounted for in traditional restrictive materialistic or naturalistic terms. In one of his talks to teachers, James stated: "No one believes more strongly than I do that what our senses know as 'this world' is only one portion of our mind's total environment and object."[24] And several years earlier, in "Is Life Worth Living?" (1895), he had expressed the view that "whatever else be certain, this at least is certain,—that the world of our present natural knowledge *is* enveloped in a larger world of *some* sort of whose residual properties we at present can frame no positive idea" (*WB*, 50). But even years before these texts were written, James's general course was set, for whatever the important and specific differences he had with his father, he never wavered in his belief that the world of his father's religious concerns was the deeper world. James's "scientific" bent, combined with his religious sensibility, gave rise to what at times appears to be almost a schizophrenia. But he never accepted the conflicts between religion and science as permanent and irresolvable.

James's continuing concern was to show that one could acknowledge the achievements of science without surrendering a religious belief in realities and dimensions of human experience that must ever elude science. Although he never systematically reconciled his scientific and religious proclivities and at times seemed to assume irreconcilable positions, I believe that as his metaphysics slowly took form, a more harmonious relation between science and religion was increasingly suggested. This direction is indicated in Perry's text cited above, but note that he says James's metaphysics offers the "possibility of giving scientific *support* to supernaturalistic faith" (*TC*, II:160; emphasis added) not scientific *proof*. Both in our moral life and in our religious life—indeed, even to a degree in our scientific life—James insisted upon the necessity of beliefs or faith commitments, to whatever extent such acts might be reinforced by rational or scientific investigations.

EXCURSUS: FREEDOM AS POSTULATE AND
METAPHYSICAL PRINCIPLE

A brief look at the phenomenon of "freedom" will serve to illustrate how James's later metaphysics came to lend support to, but not prove, his long-standing beliefs. In an oft-cited text from his 1870 diary, in describing how he pulled back from the brink of self-destruction, he stated: "My first act of free will shall be to believe in free will" (*LWJ*, I:147).[25] Fourteen years later, in "The Dilemma of Determinism," James expressed this same point: "Our first act of freedom, if we are free, ought in all inward propriety to be to affirm that we are free" (*WB*, 115). Again, in *The Principles of Psychology*, we are told that "freedom's first deed should be to affirm itself." At this time, James has not yet broken free of dualism, at least as a methodological postulate, and thus he can only juxtapose "the great scientific postulate that the world must be one unbroken fact" alongside "a *moral* postulate about the Universe, the postulate that *what ought to be can be*" (*PP*, II:1177).

James begins, then, with freedom as a moral postulate or an act of faith, and there is a sense in which it remains so to the end. Any alleged proof or rational demonstration would be inimical to the radical character of freedom. If we are rationally coerced to affirm freedom, then we are deprived of a significant dimension of freedom—the freedom to affirm freedom. Yet while James never denies a faith dimension to human freedom, it becomes less and less a "blind" faith as he grows more confident of his metaphysics. What began as a desperate act of faith and a moral postulate is gradually transformed by being organically incorporated within a metaphysics. A pluralistic-processive-relational world, an "open" and "unfinished universe" characterized by chance and novelty, is one that does not reduce freedom to a subjectivistic or psychological juxtaposition at best and an aberration at worst. As noted earlier, the particular kind of world affirmed by James is one in which there are "original commencements of series of phenomena, whose realization excludes other series which were previously possible" (*CER*, 31).[26] In one of his last writings, James insists that the difference between monism and pluralism rests on the reality or unreality of novelty. He goes on to say that "the doctrine of free will" is "that we ourselves may be authors of genuine novelty" (*SPP*, 75).

James no longer posits dualism, even methodologically, for he no longer thinks in terms of an "objective" determined world that is the concern of science and a "subjective" undetermined world that grounds morality and religion. There is one world, he says, however pluralistic and diverse it may be; and chance, novelty, and self-origination in some sense characterize this world in all its dimensions. A metaphysics of experience that overcomes ontological dualism is, of course, a crucial and indispensable factor in any effort to bring about greater harmony between science and religion. An experience which, in its most immediate and tiniest bits, involves dimensions that escape a mechanistic-materialistic reductionism is open to beliefs in realities "thicker" and more extensive than those portrayed by the customary category of "sense-data." These realities, while not encompassed or exhausted by the more immediate and sensible experience of the moment, are nevertheless viewed as continuous with these momentary experiences, thereby obviating the necessity to posit a radically discontinuous "other" or "spiritual" world beyond "this world."

WIDER CONSCIOUSNESS: DIVERSE MANIFESTATIONS

As with "freedom," James was aware of and affirmed a mode of "wider consciousness" some years before his metaphysics crystallized sufficiently to account for it rather than simply juxtapose it to the physical world. In his early psychical research as well as in *Human Immortality*, dualism is still presupposed. in *The Varieties of Religious Experience*, it is implicitly overcome; in *Essays in Radical Empiricism*, *A Pluralistic Universe*, and *Some Problems of Philosophy*, it is formally and explicitly rejected. By considering how James viewed and employed this "wider consciousness," we can best understand its nature and importance as well as its utility for a belief in personal immortality.

Let us begin with the role assigned a "larger consciousness" in James's *Human Immortality*, in which he responds to two objections against personal immortality. The second objection, which is of secondary importance for the question of a "wider consciousness," might be labeled the "logistical objection"—how could God possibly maintain in existence the billions of people who have existed and who will come to exist? James's response, in brief, is that we cannot judge God's capacity in terms of our finite limitations: "God, we can say, has so inexhaustible a capacity for love that his call and need is for a literally endless accumulation of created lives" (*HI*, 42).

The first objection, and the one directly relevant to our present concern, is that if "*thought is a function of the brain*," consciousness cannot survive the brain's dissolution. James accepts the postulate of thought as a function of the brain, but he suggests that there are two different kinds of function, both of which are possible but only one of which excludes personal immortality. First, there is the "productive function," whereby the brain would produce consciousness as the electric current produces light or the teakettle produces steam. If this is the function of the brain, then of course consciousness can have no reality apart from the brain. But there is another possibility: namely, the "transmissive function" by which the brain serves merely to transmit consciousness whose source is located outside the brain, as a stained-glass window transmits light (*HI*, 10–14). Obviously, if consciousness is only transmitted rather than produced by the brain, there is no necessity for consciousness to cease to exist when the brain does. "The sphere of being that supplied the consciousness would still be intact; and in that more real world with which, even whilst here, it was continuous, the consciousness might, in ways unknown to us, continue still" (*HI*, 18).

According to James, both production and transmission are hypotheses polemically on a par, for "in strict science, we can only write down the bare fact of concomitance." But considered in a wider way, the transmission theory has "positive superiorities." To begin with, it is not necessary to generate consciousness anew in a vast number of places; "it exists already, behind the scenes, coeval with the world." Further there is a whole class of experiences better accounted for by the transmission theory: "such phenomena, namely, as religious conversions, providential leadings in answer to prayer, instantaneous healings, premonitions, apparitions at the time of death, clairvoyant visions or impressions, and the whole range of mediumistic capacities." The production theory has a hard time explaining how such phenomena can be produced by our sense organs, whereas for the transmission theory, "they don't have to be 'produced.'" Instead, "they exist ready-made in the transcendental world, and all that is needed is an abnormal lowering of the brain-threshold to let them through" (*HI*, 20–27).

In describing our relation to this larger consciousness, James speaks of "the continuity of our consciousness with a mother-sea" (*HI*, 27). In his preface to the second edition of the book, James notes that this led some critics to accuse him of allowing only for the continued existence of the larger consciousness, our finite persons having expired with the brain. In reply, he maintained that the transmission theory allows one to "*conceive the mental world behind the veil in as individualistic a form as one pleases.*" If one takes the extreme individualistic view, then one's "finite mundane consciousness would be an abstract from one's larger, truer personality, the latter having even now some sort of reality behind the scenes" (*HI*, vi–vii).

In spite of James's explicit support of the possibility of personal immortality in this essay, I think this support should be received with some caution. It is true, as Perry noted, that "the transmission theory was clearly an anticipation of the hypothesis developed in his later metaphysics and philosophy of religion, in which the mystical and similar experiences were interpreted as an overflow of superhuman mentality through a lowering of the normal threshold" (*TC*, II:133). Nevertheless, much in this theory as it is presented in *Human Immortality* is in conflict with what I believe are the richer and more fruitful features of James's metaphysics. It is clear, for example, that James places his theory against the background of a dualistic reality, as is evidenced in his asking us to "suppose . . . that the whole universe of material things—the furniture of earth and choir of heaven—should turn out to be a mere surface-veil of phenomena, hiding and keeping back the world of genuine realities" (*HI*, 15). This sounds frightfully close to that rationalistic world with which the experiential James never ceased to struggle. Further, it is a world essentially static and peopled by human beings who are passive transmitters of a higher reality. This would seem to hold whether that "higher reality" is understood in a pantheistic or individualistic sense. In the latter case, persons would be reduced to instruments gathering experiences and memories for some "larger, truer personality" whose real world is elsewhere. Absent in all of this are those real continuities and real individual agents that James at his best did so much to illuminate. Whether it is possible to extrapolate a plausible mode of personal immortality depends on whether an experiential self fashioned along Jamesian lines can affirm the richness and significance of our personal lives "here and now" while remaining open to a continuing existence.

I would like to consider next an essay written some six months before James died—"A Suggestion about Mysticism" (*EP*, 157–65). Based on several experiences that took place after 1905, this essay presents, perhaps in its sharpest form, both the experiential *and* ambiguous character of this wider consciousness with which James had been concerned for so many years.[27]

In each of three experiences, James tells us, there was a very sudden and incomprehensible enlargement of the conscious field, accompanied by "a curious sense of cognition of real fact." Each experience lasted less than two minutes, and in each instance it "broke in abruptly upon a perfectly commonplace situation."

> What happened each time was that I seemed all at once to be reminded of a past experience; and this reminiscence, ere I could conceive or name it distinctly, developed into something further that belonged with it, this in turn into something further still, and so on, until the process faded out, leaving me amazed at the sudden vision of increasing ranges of distant fact of which I could give no articulate account. The mode of consciousness was perceptual, not conceptual—the field expanding so fast that there seemed no time for conception or identification to get in its work. . . . The feeling—I won't call it belief—that I had had a sudden *opening*, had seen through a window, as it were, distant realities that incomprehensibly belonged with my own life, was so acute that I cannot shake it off to-day. (*EP*, 159–60)

What suggestion or hypothesis does James offer to account for these and other "mystical" experiences? To grasp his hypothesis, it is first necessary to describe what he means by "field of consciousness" as well as the "threshold" metaphor he employs.

> The field is composed at all times of a mass of present sensation, in a cloud of memories, emotions, concepts, etc. Yet these ingredients, which have to be named separately, are not separate, as the conscious field contains them. Its form is that of a much-at-once, in the unity of which the sensations, memories, concepts, impulses etc., coalesce and are dissolved. The present field as a whole came continuously out of its predecessor and will melt into its successor continuously again, one sensation-mass passing into another sensation-mass giving the character of a gradually changing *present* to the experience, while the memories and concepts carry time-coefficients which place whatever is present in a temporal perspective more or less vast. (*EP*, 158)

Now it is important, here, to distinguish the succeeding masses of sensation from the memories, concepts, and conational states that also enter into the "field of consciousness." We do not know how far we are "marginally" conscious of these latter constituents; in any event there is no definite boundary "between what is central and what is marginal in consciousness," nor does the margin itself have a definite boundary. Let us imagine the field of consciousness in the form of a wave or inverted "U" with a horizontal line designated the "threshold" running through it. The closed end of the wave above the threshold is "ordinary consciousness," and the open-ended segment below the threshold is marginal or transmarginal consciousness or subconsciousness. Just as the slightest movement of the eye will bring into the field of vision objects that had always been there, so, James hypothesizes,

> a movement of the threshold downwards will similarly bring a mass of subconscious memories, conceptions, emotional feelings, and perceptions of relation, etc., into view all at once; and . . . if this enlargement of the nimbus that surrounds the sensational present is vast enough, while no one of the items it contains attracts our attention singly, we shall have the conditions fulfilled for a kind of consciousness in all essential respects like that termed mystical. It will be transient, if the change of the threshold is transient. It will be of reality, enlargement, and illumination, possibly rapturously so. It will be of unification, for the present coalesces in it with ranges of the remote quite out of its reach under ordinary circumstances; and the sense of *relation* will be greatly enhanced. (*EP*, 159)

James concludes by noting, as he did in describing his own experiences, that the form is intuitive or perceptual, not conceptual. All of this leads to the "suggestion . . . that states of mystical intuition may be only very sudden and great extensions of the ordinary 'field of consciousness.' "

This is, of course, a most ambiguous suggestion as regards the "wider consciousness," which is apparently realized in mystical experiences. D. C. Mathur, concerned to stress the "naturalistic" currents in James's thought, interprets it as apparently "giving a 'naturalistic' description of 'mystical states.' "[28] I believe this is a possible interpretation which is not as at variance with James's treatment of mystical states in *The Varieties of Religious Experience* as Mathur suggests it is. Even in those texts in which James is drawing out "religious" or "super-naturalistic" possibilities, he never denies that the phenomena, as such, cannot "prove" the reality of any consciousness beyond the human. As we shall see, the affirmation of such reality or realities is an extrapolation or overbelief, which must involve not only the bare phemomena of "mystical states" but also other human needs and experiences.

The *Varieties* was written some years before James underwent the experiences just described. Thus, while this work is a treasure trove of descriptions of personal experiences, they are, with one notable exception,[29] presented by James secondhand; from the enjoyment of mystical experiences, he tells us, he was almost entirely excluded by his own constitution.[30] But it is the mass and universality of experiences variously called religious, mystical, psychical, or hallucinatory that impressed James and that he chided science for ignoring.[31] The bulk of the *Varieties* consists of descriptions of experiences that James feels have not been adequately accounted for in the usual scientific language. Having presented these experiences, he attempts to distill from them shared characteristics and then suggest how they might be accounted for in both psychological and religious terms, which, while distinct, are not necessarily opposed.

There is a plethora of human experiences—philosophical, religious, psychological—that testify, correctly or incorrectly, to the "reality of the unseen." Their range and multiplicity lead James to suggest that "it is as if there were in the human consciousness a *sense of reality, a feeling of objective presence, a perception* of what we may call '*something there*,' more deep and more general than any of the special and particular 'senses' by which the current psychology supposes existent realities to be originally revealed" (*VRE*, 55).[32] For many of those in the religious sphere, the objects of their belief are presented to them "in the form of quasi-sensible realities directly apprehended." For those who have them, such experiences are as convincing "as any direct sensible experiences can be" and usually "much more convincing than the results established by mere logic ever are" (*VRE*, 59, 66).

In his phenomenological consideration of "conversion," James describes it as involving "forces seemingly outside of the conscious individual that bring redemption to his life." Psychology and religion are in agreement on the reality of such forces while disagreeing as to their ultimate locus. For psychology they are "subconscious" and do not "transcend the individual's personality"; religion, at least Christianity, "insists that they are direct supernatural operations of the Deity" (*VRE*, 174). James will eventually endeavor to incorporate both these perspectives, and the medium by which he will do so is the self regarded as a "field of consciousness." Again, James describes how our mental fields continually succeed each other and how their centers and margins are ever shifting. Further, "some fields are narrow fields and some are wide fields." We rejoice when our fields of consciousness are wide, for "we then see masses of truth together, and often get glimpses of relations which we divine rather than see." On the other hand, when we are drowsy or ill or fatigued "our fields may narrow almost to a point" (*VRE*, 188–89).

James maintains that "the most important fact which this 'field' formula commemorates is the indetermination of the margin." Since "ordinary psychology" is not able adequately to account for this margin, James holds that the discovery, "first made in 1886," of the subconscious (or the subliminal self) is the most important step forward in psychology since he began studying it. The claim made, initially by Frederick Myers, is that, "in certain subjects at least, there is not only the consciousness of the ordinary field, with its usual centre and margin, but an addition thereto in the shape of a set of memories, thoughts, and feelings which are extra-marginal and outside of the primary consciousness altogether, but yet must be classed as conscious facts of some sort, able to reveal their presence by unmistakable signs" (*VRE*, 190).[33] A self so constituted, of course, is subject to incursions from what might be called an unknown, open-ended source. While this source may be the more hidden aspects of one's own personality, it may also be a reality actively present to the individual field but having a life extending far beyond it.[34] That is a question which, as already noted, cannot be settled—if it can be "settled" at all—solely on the basis of the reality of a subconscious or subliminal self. In a note, James states: "It is thus 'scientific' to interpret all otherwise unaccountable invasive alterations of consciousness as results of the tension of subliminal memories reaching the bursting-point. But candor obliges me to confess that there are occasional bursts into consciousness of results of which it is not easy to demonstrate any prolonged subconscious incubation" (*VRE*, 192n.).

Throughout the *Varieties,* James wishes to describe the self in such fashion as not to foreclose its continuity with a "higher reality," yet at the same time not to confuse a possibility with a certainty. Just as in *Human Immortality* he endeavored to show that viewing thought as a function of the brain did not exclude the possibility of personal immortality, so here he insists that the reference of a phenomenon to a subliminal self does not altogether "exclude the notion of the direct presence of the Deity": "It is logically conceivable that *if there be* higher spiritual agencies that can directly touch us, the psychological condition of their doing so *might be* our possession of a subconscious region which alone should yield access to them. . . . If there be higher powers able to impress us, they may get access to us only through the subliminal door" (*VRE*, 197–98).[35]

If the reality of the subconscious or subliminal self does not foreclose the possibility of a divine reality, neither does the existence of mystical states guarantee such reality. "The fact is that the mystical feeling of enlargement, union, and emancipation has no specific intellectual content whatever of its own." While such states wield no authority "due simply to their being mystical states," they do overthrow "the pretension of non-mystical states to be the sole and ultimate dictators of what we may believe." That is why "it must always remain an open question whether mystical states may not possibly be . . . superior points of view, windows through which the mind looks out upon a more extensive and inclusive world" (*VRE*, 337–39).

Before considering the "wider self" as it is apparently manifest in religious experience, let me briefly focus on an allied notion as presented in a key metaphysical essay, "The Experience of Activity." James tells us that when discussing the ultimate character of our activity experiences, we should remember "that each of them is but a portion of a wider world, one link in the vast chain of processes of experience out of which history is made." Every particular process, then, is part of a larger process in the same way, as I earlier suggested, that every particular field is encompassed by a larger field. "Each partial process, to him who lives through it, defines itself by its origin and goal; but to an observer with a wider mind-span who should live outside of it, the goal would appear but as a provisional halting-place, and the subjectively felt activity would be seen to continue into objective activities that led far beyond." James goes on to say that we become habituated to defining activity experiences by their relation to something more. Thus there arises a question as to what kind of and whose activity it is. While we think we are doing one thing, we may in reality be doing something quite different, something of which we are unaware. "For instance, you think you are but drinking this glass; but you are really creating the liver-cirrhosis that will end your days" (*ERE*, 87–88).

Eventually the question "Whose is the real activity?" is tantamount to the question "What will be the actual results?" According to James, this is merely a version of the old dispute between *materialism* ("elementary short-span actions summing themselves 'blindly' ") and *teleology* ("far foreseen ideals coming with effort into act"). James distinguishes three philosophical accounts of the ultimate ground or real agent or agents of activity: a "consciousness of wider time-span than ours," "ideas," and "nerve-cells." The pragmatic difference in meaning is vastly different and significant, reducing, as just indicated, to materialism or teleology. While James is not claiming to prove which is the correct account, his sympathies clearly rest with the hypothesis of teleology and a wider thinker. "Naively we believe, and humanly and dramatically we like to believe, that activities both of wider and narrower span are at work in life together, that both are real, and that the long-span tendencies yoke the others in their service, encouraging them in the right direction; and damping them when they tend in other ways." Just how this steering of small tendencies by large ones is accomplished remains a question to be pondered by metaphysical thinkers "for many years to come" (*ERE*, 90–91). While James will not reach a solution to this question, in *A Pluralistic Universe*—written some four years later—there is a sense in which he is more confident, as we shall shortly see, of his belief that we can retain our individuality and agency even if we are encompassed by, or co-conscious and confluent with a larger consciousness. That James was already reaching toward such a view in his earlier essay, however, is clearly indicated in the description given there of the pragmatic meaning of a wider thinker:

> If we assume a wider thinker, it is evident that his purposes envelope mine. I am really lecturing *for* him; and altho I cannot surely know to what end, yet if I take him religiously, I can trust it to be a good end, and willingly connive. I can be happy in thinking that my activity transmits his impulse, and that his ends prolong my own. So long as I take him religiously, in short, he does not de-realize my activities. He tends rather to corroborate the reality of them, so long as I believe both them and him to be good. (*ERE*, 89)

"PART AND PARCEL OF A WIDER SELF"

Let me return now to *A Pluralistic Universe*, in which, combined with *The Varieties of Religious Experience*, we find some of the richest texts for the construction of a field model of the self. It is, as has been repeatedly under-lined, James's field-self that most adequately accounts for flowing, concrete experience while remaining open to those dimensions of reality affirmed by speculative and faith activity. We earlier saw that after establishing the reality of self-compounding consciousnesses—overlapping consciousnesses—James reached the conclusion that since our states or fields of consciousness overlap both successively and simultaneously, the "*full* self" is nothing less than the "whole field." But here we enter upon a key speculative or extrapolative path, one that leads to the heart of any effort to construct a model of the self open to personal immortality. "Every bit of us at every moment is part and parcel of a wider self, it quivers along various radii like the wind-rose on a compass, and the actual in it is continuously one with possibles not yet in our present sight" (*PU*, 131). This text, combined with the earlier cited "full self" one, while not necessarily in essential conflict with the presentation of the self in *The Principles of Psychology*, is nevertheless significantly beyond it.

We earlier saw that a materialistic interpretation of James's doctrine of self seemed plausible, particularly if such statements as the following were taken in isolation: "*The 'Self of selves,' when carefully examined, is found to consist mainly of the collection of these peculiar motions in the head or between the head and the throat*" (*PP*, I:288). I suggested that even texts such as this one are better understood when placed within a field model of the self and that the later James would bear out such a reading; the same is true of those difficult "body-texts" in which James appeared to identify the individualized self with the body. A particularly unsettling one—"The world experienced (otherwise called the 'field of consciousness') comes at all times with our body as its centre, centre of vision, centre of action, centre of interest" (*ERE*, 86n.)—was presented in a long note in "The Experience of Activity," and I think it interesting that a note to the "part and parcel of a wider self" text should both clarify that text and support the field-self doctrine being suggested:

> The conscious self of the moment, the central self, is probably determined to this privileged position by its functional connexion with the body's imminent or present acts. It is the present *acting* self. Tho the more that surrounds it may be "subconscious" to us, yet if in its "collective capacity" it also exerts an active function, it may be conscious in a wider way, conscious, as it were, over heads. (*PU,* 131n.)[36]

Again we are confronted with that ambiguous, vague, and elusive "more" that we have been feverishly pursuing through the labyrinth of consciousness. Let us assault it again, this time from James's description of religious experience. This experience, he says, despite a multitude of diverse expressions, has a common nucleus with two parts or stages: a felt uneasiness and a solution or salvation through removal of this uneasiness. The uneasiness takes the form of a sense of wrongness, and insofar as the individual suffers from and criticizes this wrongness, he is already beyond it and possibly in touch with something higher. The religious person, then, is aware of comprising a wrong part and—at least in germinal form—a better part. When the solution or salvific stage is reached, the person identifies his real being with the germinal higher part of himself: "*He becomes conscious that this higher part is conterminous and continuous with a* more *of the same quality, which is operative in the universe outside of him, and which he can keep in working touch with, and in a fashion get on board of and save himself when all his lower being has gone to pieces in the wreck*" (*VRE,* 400). Several years later, in *A Pluralistic Universe,* James repeats this description in very similar terms:

> The believer finds that the tenderer parts of his personal life are continuous with a *more* of the same quality which is operative in the universe outside of him and which he can keep in touch with, and in a fashion get on board and save himself, when all his lower being has gone to pieces in the wreck. In a word, the believer is continuous, to his own consciousness, at any rate, with a wider self from which saving experiences flow in. (*PU,* 139)

To this point, James has given a vivid description of the way in which numerous individuals have experienced profound personal transformation. The obvious question, of course, is whether their experiential claims are simply projections of their own subjective psyches or whether indeed they are manifestations of the touch of a higher power. In short, is this "more" merely their own notion, or does it really exist? and if so, in what shape? and is it also active? Here speculative and theoretic categories in all religions come into play, as well as significant divergencies of interpretation. That the "more" really exists and acts is widely agreed upon, whereas there are great differences as regards its shape (personal god, gods, nature, Being) and the mode of "union" with it. James now wades in with his own hypothesis, which he hopes will be acceptable to science while remaining open to the claims of religious experience. The mediating term, James feels, might be the *subconscious self,* which has become an acceptable psychological entity. Prescinding from any religious considerations, "there is actually and literally more life in our total soul than we are at any time aware of" (*VRE,* 402). In a text from Frederick Myers, which James now makes his own, this depth dimension of the human self is succinctly and convincingly expressed:

> Each of us is in reality an abiding psychical entity far more extensive than he knows—an individuality which can never express itself completely through any corporeal manifestation. The Self manifests through the organism; but there is always some part of the Self unmanifested; and always, as it seems, some power of organic expression held in abeyance or reserve. (*VRE,* 403)[37]

Given the reality, then, of a self whose life and reality extend far beyond what its state of consciousness may be at a particular moment, James is now equipped to fashion his mediating hypothesis: "Whatever it may be on its *farther* side, the 'more' with which in religious experience we feel ourselves connected is on its *hither* side the subconscious continuation of our conscious life." What James appears to be saying is that in the first instance the "higher" power experienced in the religious life is "primarily the higher faculties of our hidden mind." Hence, "the sense of union with the power beyond us is a sense of something not merely apparently, but literally true" (*VRE,* 403). Without reference to any overbeliefs, according to James, we can posit as a fact "*that the conscious person is continuous with a wider self through which saving experiences come.*" This gives us a "positive content of religious experience which . . . *is literally and objectively true as far as it goes*" (*VRE,* 405). Of course, the qualification "as far as it goes" is James's mediating phrase, for it obligates the psychologists to take religious experience seriously on his terms, while not closing off the "*farther* side" of the "more" from reflective living, speculation, and overbelief.

A fuller treatment of this "*farther* side of the 'more' " and the extrapolations and overbeliefs relating to it must await our later consideration of "God" as fashioned along Jamesian lines. We must here, however, follow James as he suggests the plausibility of the continuity of our individual human consciousness with some superhuman consciousness or consciousnesses. Having established as a "certain fact" that smaller, more accessible portions of our mind can self-compound, James contends that we must consider as a legitimate hypothesis "the speculative assumption of a similar but wider compounding in remoter regions." Inasmuch as mental facts function both singly and together, "we finite minds may simultaneously be co-conscious with one another in a superhuman intelligence" (*PU,* 132). Further, in describing the makeup of the "full self" with its shifting margins, we see that we are at every moment co-conscious with our own momentary margin. Is it not possible, then, that "we ourselves form the margin of some really central self in things which is co-conscious with the whole of us? May not you and I be confluent in a higher consciousness and confluently active there, tho we know it not?" (*PU*, 131).

James was aware of the fact that this was an area in which one must dare to hypothesize in the wildest and most imaginative fashion if one hoped to realize even a glimmer of illumination concerning its character. Analogies and hypotheses suggested by and consistent with the smaller versions of our experience—not strict formal logical deduction—are the only tools available for some understanding of that vast region of reality with which we are in "ordinary" experience only marginally related. This is why the views of the psychophysicist Gustave Fechner were attractive to James and why he devoted an entire chapter in *A Pluralistic Universe* to an exposition of those views.

Fechner posited a hierarchy of overlapping souls or consciousnesses from God down through an earth-soul to unobservable subconscious states.[38] The aspect of Fechner's hypothesis with which James is most concerned, and the one most relevant to the world of overlapping fields suggested throughout this essay, "is the belief that the more inclusive forms of consciousness are in part constituted by the more limited forms" without being "the mere sum of the more limited forms." There might, then, be a wider field with purposes and forms which are unable to be known by our narrower fields. Thus, while we are closed against its world, that world might be open to us. That larger world might be a great reservoir, pooling and preserving human memories, and when the threshold lowers in exceptional individuals, information not available to ordinary consciousness may leak in (*PU*, 78, 135).

One can immediately see the attractiveness of this hypothesis for anyone attempting to suggest the plausibility of personal immortality. If we are here and now constituted in part by and partly constituting a consciousness of immeasurably wider, perhaps everlasting, life, then a postdeath continuing relation with such a consciousness cannot be immediately and with certainty ruled out. We may, unknown to us, be already living "within" this larger life, and certain of those fields now constituting the individual self may already be playing a role in and in a sense constituting this larger life. Hence, when *some* of the fields or relations now constituting personal selves dissolve, it is possible that other presently constituting fields might be continued in existence through the activity of this larger self.[39] The description James gives of Fechner's view of our relation to the earth's soul is along such lines:

> Fechner likens our individual persons on the earth unto so many sense-organs of the earth's soul. We add to its perceptive life so long as our own life lasts. It absorbs our perceptions, just as they occur, into its larger sphere of knowledge, and combines them with other data there. When one of us dies, it is as if an eye of the world were closed, for all *perceptive* contributions from that particular quarter cease. But the memories and conceptual relations that have

spun themselves round the perceptions of that person remain in the larger earth-life as distinct as ever, and form new relations and grow and develope throughout all the future, in the same way in which our own distinct objects of thought, once stored in memory, form new relations and develope throughout our whole finite life. (*PU,* 79)

In a fascinating, if somewhat obscure, passage at the end of his short essay "How Two Minds Can Know One Thing," James maintains that the character of "pure experience" is such that "speculations like Fechner's of an Earth-soul, of wider spans of consciousness enveloping narrow ones throughout the cosmos are . . . philosophically quite in order." These words immediately follow a passage that appears almost whimsical, given the context in which James introduces it. It emerges within the context of his effort to show that a pure experience—"pen," for example—is in itself neither physical nor mental but becomes one or the other depending on the context or relations into which it enters. I have already expressed my difficulties with this doctrine and with James's conclusion that "pure experiences . . . are, in themselves considered, so many little absolutes." Immediately following this conclusion is a passage as elusive as it is tantalizingly attractive for my purposes:

> A pure experience can be postulated with any amount whatever of span or field. If it exert the retrospective and appropriate function on any other piece of experience, the latter thereby enters into its own conscious stream. And in this operation time intervals make no essential difference. After sleeping, my retrospection is as perfect as it is between two successive waking moments of my time. Accordingly, if millions of years later, a similarly retrospective experience should anyhow come to birth, my present thought would form a genuine portion of its long-span conscious life. "Form a portion," I say, but not in the sense that the two things can be entitively or substantively one—they cannot, for they are numerically discrete facts—but only in the sense that the *functions* of my present thought, its knowledge, its purpose, its content and "consciousness," in short, being inherited, would be continued practically unchanged. (*ERE,* 66–67)

James goes on to insist that if we are to accept the hypothesis of wider spans of consciousness enveloping narrower ones, the functional and entitative points of view must be distinguished. He apparently wishes to avoid a static notion of identity between the wider and narrower, which is what would follow if the minor consciousnesses were treated "as a kind of standing material of which the wider ones *consist*" (*ERE,* 67).

"CONTINUUM OF COSMIC CONSCIOUSNESS"

In his later writings and with increasing confidence, James expressed the view, already present in his earliest reflective experiences, that we are not alone in the universe, that we are not the highest conscious beings: "I firmly disbelieve, myself, that our human experience is the highest form of experience extant in the universe" (*P*, 143). There are many worlds of consciousness of which our present consciousness is only one, and these other worlds must contain experiences that have meaning for our life. While, for the most part, our world is insulated from these other worlds, they do "become continuous at certain points, and higher energies filter in" (*VRE*, 408).[40] James felt, then, that the evidence was strongly moving us "towards the belief in some form of superhuman life with which we may be in the universe as dogs and cats are in our libraries, seeing and hearing the conversation, but having no inkling of the meaning of it all" (*PU*, 140).[41] Thus, despite his doubt and uneasiness concerning the various "psychic" claims, he tells us in "Final Impressions of a Psychical Researcher" that from his experience "one fixed conclusion dogmatically emerges":

> We with our lives are like islands in the sea, or like trees in the forest. . . . There is a continuum of cosmic consciousness, against which our individuality builds but accidental fences, and into which our several minds plunge as into a mother-sea or reservoir. Our "normal" consciousness is circumscribed for adaptation to our external earthly environment, but the fence is weak in spots, and fitful influences from beyond leak in showing the otherwise unverifiable connection. Not only psychic research, but metaphysical philosophy, and speculative biology are led in their own ways to look with favor on some such "panpsychic" view of the universe as this. (*MS*, 204)[42]

This passage, of course, is reminiscent of the transmission theory encountered in *Human Immortality*, reprising as it does the "mother-sea" metaphor. The crucial difference, however, is the metaphysical framework within which the metaphor is now suggested. To begin with, the dualism presupposed in *Human Immortality* is no longer operative in a metaphysics of experience that differentiates physical and mental on the basis of functions and relations rather than ultimately different modes of being. In his discussion of Fechner, James notes that for his own purposes, Fechner's most important condition was "that the constitution of the world is identical throughout" (*PU*, 72). Needless to say, as indicated by the title *A Pluralistic Universe*, James does not mean "identical" in any monistic sense, either materialistic or idealistic. But how can reality be "identical throughout" and pluralistic at the same time? Only, I believe, if we recognize that the multiplicity of experiences constituting reality are "fields" or processive-relational complexes, constituting and constituted by other fields, continually changing and shifting and transacting in various modes of exchange. We have followed James in his later writings as he described this world of "fields within fields within fields . . ." in terms of continuous and overlapping conscious fields characterized by co-constitution, self-compounding, narrower enveloped within wider. If we remember that all fields are "centers of activity," we also avoid the danger attached to the transmission theory, as presented in *Human Immortality*, of making human fields the merely passive instruments of a larger consciousness or consciousnesses. Continuous transaction is a determining characteristic of *all* fields, wider and narrower, higher and lower, which enter into the constitution of reality.[43] In a review essay James wrote in 1903, just such a field metaphysics is expressed rather strikingly:

> The only fully complete concrete data are, however, the successive moments of our own several histories taken with their subjective personal aspect, as well as with their "objective" deliverance or "context." After the analogy of these moments of experiences must all complete reality be conceived. Radical empiricism thus leads to the assumption of a collectivism of personal lives (which may be of any grade of complication, and superhuman or infrahuman as well as human), variously cognitive of each other, variously conative and impulsive, genuinely evolving and changing by effort and trial, and by their interaction and cumulative achievements making up the world. (*CER*, 443–44)[44]

FIELD-SELF AS "SUBSTANTIVE-SELF"

Before shifting our focus to the "wider self" extrapolated as "God," I would like to indicate the propriety of designating the field-self we have been describing as a "substantive-self." Recall that the central purpose of my concern with the "self" is to show that it is possible to construct a model of the self which, while faithful to the flow of experience, is nevertheless open to a continuing existence after the cessation of some of the particular spatiotemporal fields by which it is presently constituted. I believe that the more fully developed doctrine of the self suggested here avoids both the classical Soul Substance theory and the classical empiricist or phenomenist one. The former posits a permanent principle ontologically different from and underlying or "behind" the experienced appearances or phenomena. The latter identifies the self as a "bundle" of discrete appearances or phenomena streaming into and immediately out of existence.

We have already noted that James's doctrine of the self as the passing or perishing Thought undoubtedly lends itself to a phenomenistic interpretation. When, however, this "passing Thought" is seen as related to or continuous with or enveloped by a "more"—that is, a wider self or consciousness—at every moment, however brief, of its existence, a phenomenistic interpretation is ruled out. At the same time the experiential character of the "passing Thought" is retained, and there is no relapse into a substantialist perspective positing a shadow principle "behind" our experiences. To say, however, that there is nothing "behind" our experienced activities is not to say that these activities, as we are at any moment aware of them, exhaust the full reality of the self. For example, Freud's "unconscious" is not "behind" or "underneath" consciousness; rather it is an alleged present-acting process "outside" the present margin of consciousness. The self at any moment, as has been repeatedly claimed, is constituted by a variety of fields or relational processes, most of which are not in "focus" but are on or "beyond" the margin or fringe of consciousness. Some can be brought within focus; others can be discovered only indirectly, as in the case of cells or organs. Mystics claim that a self or consciousness of which we are ordinarily unaware has come into focus—moved from the margin, or beyond, of consciousness to the center.

James maintained in his *Principles of Psychology* that he could dispense with the Soul Substance theory because his theory of the "passing Thought" accounted for such features of the self as unity, identity, continuity—which had traditionally been the justification for positing the reality of the "soul." But James never held that the notion of "substance" was a totally empty or useless one, for in his earliest and last writings he insisted that the category of substance expressed an indispensable feature not only of the self but of reality. "To say that phenomena inhere in a Substance," he tells us, in the *Principles*, "is at bottom only to record one's protest against the notion that the bare existence of the phenomena is the total truth. A phenomenon would not itself be, we insist, unless there were something *more* than the phenomenon" (*PP*, II:328). But even earlier, in an unpublished essay written probably around 1874, James affirms the utility of "substance." This essay, "Against Nihilism," was a critique of Chauncey Wright's positivism, which reduced the world "to an assemblage of particular phenomena having no ulterior connections—ideal, substantial or dynamic." According to Perry, James viewed such positivism as a "sort of philosophical 'nihilism,' affirming that beyond the particular phenomena there is 'nothing' " (*TC*, I:524). The central criticism of "nihilism" and the primary justification for the category of substance is that the former denies "continuity," while the latter recognizes it. The test of substantial reality, according to James, is "dynamic connection with other existences." Which is to say that "a thing only has being at all as it enters in some way into the being of other things, or constitutes part of a universe or organism. . . . As to their *being*, things are continuous, and so far as this is what people mean when they affirm a substance, substance must be held to exist." James is aware that something more than this is usually meant, such as "an other and a primordial *thing* on a plane behind that of the phenomena, but numerically additional to them." But James insists that all he means by "substance" is the "unity which comes from the phenomena being continuous with each other" (*TC*, I:525).[45]

The emphasis upon continuity, as we have already seen, did not diminish but intensified as James's metaphysics matured. While "substance" does not become a central term in his metaphysical writings it is significant that in his last work, *Some Problems of Philosophy*, he touches again upon the theme of "Against Nihilism":

> What difference in practical experience is it supposed to make that we have each a personal substantial principle? This difference, that we can remember and appropriate our past, calling it "mine." What difference that in this book there is a substantial principle? This, that certain optical and tactile sensations cling permanently together in a cluster. The fact that *certain perceptual experiences do seem to belong together* is thus all that the word substance means. (*SPP*, 66)

James then goes on to "inquire whether instead of being a principle, the 'oneness' affirmed may not merely be a name like 'substance,' descriptive of the fact that certain *specific and verifiable connections* are found among the parts of the experiential flux" (*SPP*, 66).

In keeping with the pragmatic evaluation of all concepts, then, the designation of the self or reality as "substantive" is important only insofar as it keeps us aware of or avoids closing us off from important dimensions of experience. This is why in any Jamesian consideration of personal immortality, it is important to insist on the substantive character of the self while rejecting the traditional Soul Substance theory. We have earlier seen that in his critique of the soul theory, James rejects the argument that the soul is of practical importance because its alleged simplicity and substantiality are the grounds for inferring immortality. In a passage already cited, James on "practical" grounds rejects this argument:

> The Soul, however, when closely scrutinized, guarantees no immortality of a sort *we care for*. The enjoyment of the atom-like simplicity of their substance *in saecula saeculorum* would not to most people seem a consummation devoutly to be wished. The substance must give rise to a stream of consciousness continuous with the present stream, in order to arouse our hope, but of this the persistence of substance *per se* offers no guarantee. (*PP*, I:330)

It is, of course, this "stream of consciousness continuous with the present stream" that has been stressed in the doctrine of a flowing field-self, and it is this characteristic that is the experiential ground for any pragmatic extrapolation of personal immortality.

In *The Principles of Psychology*, James is polemically engaged with the rationalists and hence concerned to underline the limitations of a substance view of the self. In the essay "The Sentiment of Rationality," however, he chides the antisubstantialist empiricists for failing to recognize an extremely important function of "Substance": namely, to fulfill the "demands of expectancy." Consider "the notion of immortality. . . . What is this but a way of saying that the determination of expectancy is the essential factor of rationality?" He agrees with Mill and the other empiricists that nothing is, or need be, added to the description of past sensational facts by positing an inexperienced *substratum*. "But with regard to the facts yet to come the case is different. It does not follow that if substance may be dropped from our conception of the irrecoverably past, it need be an equally empty complication to our notions of the future." James is insisting here that "desire to have expectancy defined" is so deep and central to human life "that no philosophy will definitively triumph which in an emphatic manner denies the possibility of gratifying this need" (*WB*, 69–70). He does not develop this point further in this essay, but it is clear here and elsewhere that belief in personal immortality is one—though by no means the only—expression of this expectancy. In an example not given by James, we might suggest that any one who struggles for the realization or fulfillment of a future goal or purpose—achieving a degree, writing a book, painting a picture—manifests such expectancy. Every person so engaged firmly believes that however much he or she may change in the interim and however long the interim, the person who experiences the realization will be "substantively" the same as the person who initiated the process or processes that led to it.[46]

A comparison of the soul theory with the substantive field-self theory reveals obvious similarities and significant differences. Both claim to account for unity, continuity, identity, endurance, individuality, and interiority. The substantive-self, however, unlike the soul, is not a principle in itself; it is not a nonempirical principle belonging to an ontologically different order of being; and it has no reality-in-itself apart from its constituting fields. The implications for immortality are again similar but different. While personal immortality is possible for both, it is a "positive" possibility for the soul. The most that can be claimed for the substantive-self is that it has a "negative" possibility; that is, it does not positively exclude the possibility. Since the soul is allegedly simple, it is "naturally" incorruptible; and though it could be annihilated by God, we can logically and rationally infer its immortality. Since the substantive-self is an ever changing field dependent for its reality at every moment upon the fields that constitute it, there is no logical necessity for it to continue upon the cessation of those constituting fields most evident to our experience. Inasmuch as one of its here-and-now constituting relations is with a wider field or consciousness, however, the possibility cannot be ruled out that this wider field will maintain the human self after the cessation of other constituting fields. It is not legitimate to logically infer such continuing existence, because such existence depends upon the unknown purposes of this wider consciousness, which may or may not include the continuing existence of those narrower fields that are now constitutive with it. If there are other experiential grounds, however, for believing that these narrower fields, along with their ideals, purposes, strivings and the like, are included within the purposes of the wider consciousness, then the substantive field-self as herein described presents no logical or experiential obstacle to the realization of such purposes.

CHAPTER 6

James: Self and God

> But life, life as such, he protested inwardly—it
> was not enough. How could one be content with
> the namelessness of mere energy, with the less
> than individuality of a power, that for all its
> mysterious divineness, was yet unconscious,
> beneath good and evil?
> —Aldous Huxley
> *Eyeless in Gaza*

> Nothing is more reasonable than to suppose that
> if there be anything *personal* at the bottom of
> things, the way we behave to it *must* affect the
> way it behaves to us.
> —F. C. S. Schiller
> "Axioms as Postulates"

The general hypothesis governing this essay is that a plausible belief in personal immortality depends upon a self open to continuing existence beyond the spatial and temporal parameters of what is usually referred to as the "present life." A key step in the direction of supporting this hypothesis has been taken through the establishment of a field-self that participates in and is constituted by a range of fields, some of which can be designated "wider" in relation to the identifying "center" of the individual self. Following James, I have described these wider fields in terms of a superhuman consciousness or consciousnesses, delaying till now a more detailed specification of such wider consciousnesses. This brings us, of course, into the thorny and to some extent impossible question of "God." However tentative and minimalist a philosophy of God may emerge, there is no avoiding some consideration of this question, inasmuch as I wish to argue that the possibility of an immortal self depends upon the graciousness of God.

For many—if not most—believers in personal immortality, it is sufficient to believe in a divine promise of eternal life, avoiding any and all unsettling difficulties or questions by taking refuge in the "mystery" of God. To some degree, of course, all God-believers must take refuge in mystery. But in an essay in philosophical theology, it is incumbent upon me, as a minimum, to indicate a view of God that is reasonably consistent with my controlling metaphysical assumptions, as well as with the view of the self already presented.

In this effort to construct a God-hypothesis, I will continue to utilize James's ideas and approach without claiming to present James's definitive doctrine of God. Rather, I would like to suggest what might be more accurately described as a "Jamesian" God. In doing so, I will draw directly on James where I deem him useful, explicating points that may be only implicit in his expressed doctrine and extrapolating a view of God from a view of reality and experience fundamentally consistent but not totally identical with that of James. While I may incidentally allude to some of the difficulties and technical problems attached to James's doctrine of God, I will for the most part bypass them in an attempt to construct a God-hypothesis that allows for and is supportive of a belief in personal immortality.

Historically, all doctrines of God have emerged from and been bound up with a particular view of reality having profound implications for the way in which life ought to be lived. Thus, as one commentator has correctly noted:

> For James, the mere question as to whether to believe in God has momentous practical bearings, regardless of whether the believer is a practicing Christian, Jew, or whatever. This is necessarily so because the question of God is not just a question about the existence of another being; it is a question concerning the nature of the universe, not only taken as a whole, but taken as its individual parts as well.[1]

As noted earlier, I am presupposing metaphysical assumptions significantly different from those of classical philosophy, and any view of God consistent with the metaphysical assumptions of pragmatism will be significantly, though not totally, different from the view of God drawn from the metaphysical assumptions of classical thought. More specifically, as I shall later indicate, a radically processive-relational world such as that presupposed by pragmatism is not congenial to the traditional view of God as immutable, omniscient, and omnipotent.

I am further assuming that all language, including God-language, is historically, culturally, and perspectivally conditioned. A crucial corollary of this assumption is the rejection of any simple correspondence or representative view of language; hence, there can be no claim to describe God as he is in himself. All God-language is symbolic in the Tillichian sense of pointing "beyond itself while participating in that to which it points."[2] We cannot evaluate our symbols, then, on the basis of some alleged correspondence with "objective reality" but only on their serviceability for human life. This does not mean, however, that what is being suggested is an unqualified subjectivism. The pragmatic perspective rejects *both* classical objectivism and modern subjectivism[3] when the former is understood as claiming that our language represents an object (God) as it is in itself, independently of the human knower, and the latter is understood as reducing the reality of God to nothing but a projection of the human psyche.[4]

James has frequently been misunderstood as presenting a subjectivistic view of God. As Ralph Barton Perry notes, however, James "insisted upon retaining not only the ideality but also the *actuality* of God—as a conscious power beyond, with which one may come into beneficent contact."[5] James himself argued, in a letter to Charles A. Strong, that God could be *both* existent and ideal: "I do not believe it to be healthy minded to nurse the notion that ideals are self-sufficient and require no actualization to make us content. . . . Ideals ought to aim at the *transformation of reality*—no less!" (*LWJ*, II:269–70).

Perry points out that James was not "prepared to abandon the objectivity of God," however much he emphasized the vital, personal, and pragmatic features of religion (*TC*, II:348). Thus when James says, "I myself believe that the evidence for God lies primarily in inner personal experiences" (*P*, 56), he is not to be understood as reducing the reality of God to human experience. Nevertheless, he does hold that any claims made about God must be grounded in and ultimately evaluated in terms of human experience. Given the ambiguity in James's use of "immediate experience" such that not everything in immediate experience is "immediate," however, the exploration of experience takes us beyond the realm of "pure immediacy." Throughout this essay I have designated such exploratory activity "extrapolation," which is neither intuition nor inference, neither immediate awareness nor deduced conclusion, but may incorporate characteristics of both these modes of activity. Remember, extrapolation is a speculative or imaginative endeavor that must proceed from data given in experience, and the extrapolated conclusion must be reasonably consistent with and potentially enriching of the experience from which it began.

While James does not formally speak of extrapolation, I feel that the approach he makes to the God-question is best described as such. "God," for James, is affirmed by a belief or overbelief, and the obvious question is what these have to do with any extrapolating. I would suggest that just as thinkers within the classical tradition were not content simply to affirm a belief in God but attempted to construct rational arguments for God's existence, so one making a pragmatic approach must attempt to show the "reasonableness" of God belief by means of extrapolation. Thus, extrapolation would seem to fall somewhere between a blind, emotive faith and an absolutely compelling logical argument. The rejection of rational arguments for the existence of God, therefore, is not to be equated with a radical exclusion of "reason" from the sphere of faith. Reflective believers must attempt to show that faith in God is grounded in experience and that anything we can legitimately say about this God must not be in fundamental conflict with this experience but must have the possibility of expanding and deepening it. Further, faith in God must be demonstrably in harmony with other experiential claims. "The truth of 'God,'" James maintains, "has to run the gaunt-let of all our other truths. It is on trial by them and they on trial by it" (*P*, 56).[6]

James is in the broad Kantian tradition that denies the possibility of prov-ing or disproving the existence of God, while leaving the door open for belief or faith in God. It is not that James patronizes or scoffs at efforts to construct absolutely certain arguments for God's existence. Nor does he consider it necessary to "discredit philosophy by laborious criticism of its arguments," since as a matter of history it fails to prove its pretension to be "'objectively' convincing" or universally valid. Philosophers do what all humans do—attempt to find arguments for their convictions, "for indeed it [philosophy] *has* to find them." In brief, then, the arguments serve to con-firm the beliefs of believers but are useless for atheists (*VRE*, 344).

Of course, James's reasons for rejecting the classical arguments go much deeper than simply noting that they lack universal acceptance. The meta-physics and epistemology to which he is committed exclude the possibility of any absolute proofs, including those relating to God. All arguments for the existence of God—explicitly, the "design argument"—presuppose, as-sume, or consider self-evident that we live in an essentially ordered world, whereas James views order and disorder as "purely human conventions." Moreover, he contends, "there are in reality infinitely more things 'un-adapted' to each other in this world than there are things 'adapted'; infinitely more things with irregular relations than with regular relations between them. But we look for the regular kind of thing exclusively, and ingeniously discover and preserve it in our memory" (*VRE*, 346n.). Rationalism, then, is just as inadequate when arguing for God and religion as when arguing against them. This is in keeping, of course, with James's contention that the whole of our mental life exceeds that part accounted for by rationalism. "If you have intuitions at all," he tells us, "they come from a deeper level of your nature than the loquacious level which rationalism inhabits" (*VRE*, 67).

I have already cited James to the effect that the "evidence for God lies primarily in inner personal experiences" (*P*, 56).[7] It is important, however, to indicate the character of that evidence so as to avoid any interpretation that would lead to a claim that experience, even mystical experience, "proves" the existence of God. I have also called attention to James's conten-tion that a range and variety of experiences suggest a "*sense of reality*" present to human consciousness that is deeper and more general than any reality revealed by the special and particular senses (*VRE*, 55, 58–59). Among such experiences are distinctively religious experiences within which, for those who have them, the objects of their belief are present in "the form of quasi-sensible realities directly apprehended" rather than in "the form of mere conceptions which their intellect accepts as true" (*VRE*, 59). The most heightened form of such experiences are those reported by mystics, but respectful as James is of mystical experience, he explicitly denies that it can be employed to draw conclusions binding upon all reflective and reasonable persons. For the individual who has the experience, it is sufficient. If the mystic can live by it, and his or her life manifests fruitful consequences flowing from it, no one has a right to denigrate this experience. At the same time, the mystic is not entitled to claim that others, lacking such experiences, must accept the mystic's interpretation (*VRE*, 336): "Mystical states indeed wield no authority due simply to their being mystical states. But the higher ones among them point in directions to which the religious sentiments even of non-mystical men incline. They tell of the supremacy of the ideal, of vastness, of union, of safety, and of rest. They offer us *hypotheses*, hypotheses which we may voluntarily ignore, but which we as thinkers cannot possibly upset" (*VRE*, 339).

I wish to suggest that it is the richness of the experience of those who get singled out as mystics and the "germ of mysticism" in all of us that serve as the ground and stimulus for extrapolating the reality of God. It is the task of philosophical extrapolation to winnow out those features of mystical experience that offer the greatest possibilities for human life. This is, of course, a never ending process whose conclusions will always be tentative and in need of further development and refinement. It means a continuing evaluation of the fruits of our own experiences as well as those of others. While we cannot avoid employing "some sort of a standard of theological probability of our own whenever we assume to estimate the fruits of other men's religion, yet this very standard has been begotten out of the drift of common life" (*VRE*, 265). Elsewhere, James noted that the "gold-dust" of religious experiences must be extricated from the "quartz-sand" ("superstitions and wild-growing over-beliefs of all sorts"). Yet he cautions against trying to short-circuit this process of extrication, for the historical results of such short-circuiting are "thin inferior abstractions" such as "the hollow unreal god of scholastic theology, or the unintelligible pantheistic monster" of Absolute Idealism (*PU*, 142–43). Philosophy has the task of eliminating through comparison the "local and accidental" features that inevitably accompany all "spontaneous religious constructions." Historic incrustations can be removed from both dogma and worship; by utilizing "the results of natural science, philosophy can also eliminate doctrines that are now known to be scientifically absurd or incongruous"; and "sifting out in this way unworthy formulations, she [philosophy] can leave a residuum of conceptions that at least are possible. With these she can deal as *hypotheses*, testing them in all the manners, whether negative or positive, by which hypotheses are ever tested" (*VRE*, 359).

Now it must be made clear that in calling for extricating, sifting out, and refining our God-reflections, James is not suggesting—even as an ideal—that we should strive to formulate one definition of God to which all humans ought to subscribe. Nowhere is James's pluralism more in evidence than in his denial "that the lives of all men should show identical religious elements." He insists:

The divine can mean no single quality, it must mean a group of qualities, by being champions of which in alternation, different men may all find worthy missions. Each attitude being a syllable in human nature's total message, it takes the whole of us to spell the meaning out completely. . . . We must frankly recognize the fact that we live in partial systems, and that the parts are not interchangeable in the spiritual life. (*VRE*, 384)[8]

The field model employed throughout this essay is, I believe, eminently congenial to this pluralistic view of the divine. It involves diverse and over-lapping fields, thereby allowing for various modes of mutual participation no one of which exhausts any field, wide or narrow. The divine life, under-stood as the widest field, enriches and is enriched by the variety of fields with which it is related. Thus, the plurality of religions may not be a neces-sary evil to be endured until the one true religion is formed; rather this plurality may be the necessary and only means by which the richness of the divine life can be lived and communicated. Needless to say, this does not diminish the need for and importance of abolishing those features of partic-ular religions that lead to destructive relations with those belonging to other communities. The point being advanced, however, is that plurality in re-ligion is no more destructive in itself than is plurality in art, literature, or music.[9]

A variation on James's doctrine that the evidence for God is found in our inner experience is that belief in God is a response to inner needs: our belief in God "is not due to our logic, but to our emotional wants" (*TC*, I:493). It would seem that there are at least five distinct kinds of needs—logical, mor-al, esthetic, practical, and religious.[10] Ideally, perhaps, a fully realized per-sonal life should incorporate all of these, but one that does so is a very rare phenomenon; the more usual situation is that there is a decided difference, at least as to which is primary, in needs among individuals. In his essay "*Is Life Worth Living?*" James argues that science is a response to a need every bit as much as morality or religion is. Without claiming to know the ultimate origin of such needs, James nevertheless insists that there is hardly a scien-tific law or fact "which was not first sought after . . . to gratify an inner need." He goes on to say, "The inner need of believing that this world of nature is a sign of something more spiritual and eternal than itself is just as strong and authoritative in those who feel it, as the inner need of uniform laws of causation ever can be in a professionally scientific head" (*WB*, 51).

While James never claims that the need for God is sufficient to establish God's existence, he does maintain that such a need at least suggests the pos-sibility of such a reality, for "if needs of ours outrun the visible universe, why *may* not that be a sign that an invisible universe is there?" (*WB*, 51). Further, James contends that the only determination we can make concern-ing the nature of God depends upon the kind of beings we are. In an early essay, "Reflex Action and Theism," James argues for a correlation between God and the human mind. He first notes that many writers were currently arguing that the doctrine of reflex action had given "the *coup de grâce* to the superstition of a God," while in an earlier time "reflex action and all other harmonies between the organism and the world were held to prove God." Sidestepping the issue of proof or disproof, James limits himself to

> showing that a God, whether existent or not, is at all events the kind of being which, if he did exist, would form *the most adequate possible object* for minds framed like our own to conceive as lying at the root of the universe. My thesis . . . is this: that *some* outward reality of a nature defined as God's nature must be defined, is the only ultimate object that is at the same time rational and possible for the human mind's contemplation. *Anything short of God is not rational, anything more than God is not possible,* if the human mind be in truth the triadic structure of impression, reflection, and reaction which we at the outset allowed. (*WB,* 93)

Though James in his later writings refines his view of the human mind, he continues to the end to speak of God only in terms of human needs. In *The Varieties of Religious Experience,* he states: "The gods we stand by are the gods we need and can use, the gods whose demands on us are reinforcements of our demands on ourselves and on one another" (*VRE,* 266). Further, as we change, so will our conceptions of God, for "when we cease to admire or approve what the definition of a deity implies, we end by deeming that deity incredible" (*VRE,* 264–65).

In a later section I will develop more fully this point of the relation between human change and change in conceptions of God, and perhaps in God himself. For the moment, let me say a word about an obvious objection to James's tying our faith in God to our concrete needs: is he not, one might ask, simply reflecting the historical and cultural conditions of the Victorian age in which he lived? While a description of the psychological needs of James and his brother and sister Victorians would more often than not involve a need for some kind of reality beyond the ordinary, how can we be sure that at a later time such needs will not be nonexistent?

The first part of the response to the objection, of course, is that neither James nor anyone else can "be sure" that these needs will always be present. But if a situation should emerge (as it already has emerged for some) in which such needs generally are *not* present, then there would no longer be even a question of the existence or nonexistence of God. This, however, would only confirm James's view that faith in God is inseparably bound up with concrete, specific human needs. The abstract possibility of the disappearance of such needs would not be, for James, the decisive issue. While conceding, of course, that *all* conceptions, including those of science, are historically and culturally conditioned, James does not accept that this entails a passive skepticism or a destructive relativism. There are good grounds, though never absolutely certain ones, for *believing* that certain features of the human condition will continue to exist in some form as long as humans exist. James would contend that the history of religions indicates something of those features, however vaguely and inadequately. Further, he believes, and can supply "justifying reasons" for his belief, that religious needs and the efforts to satisfy them have profoundly enriched and deepened human life.[11] It is possible that these needs and efforts will disappear in the future, but if they do—James would confidently hold—the result will be a radically diminished human situation. It might be argued, analogously, that we cannot be absolutely certain that in a future world the long-standing, so far universal, and pervasive need for art in its various forms will also disappear. Is it possible for anyone to positively conceive of such a world as other than radically impoverished?

Whatever difficulties attach to religious claims, James is insistent upon the important difference they introduce into the world. The difference, of course, is most significant in the modes of living to which they give rise which, were they fundamentally the same as those brought forth by naturalism, would be rendered worthless.

> The whole defense of religious faith hinges upon action. If the action required or inspired by the religious hypothesis is in no way different from that dictated by the naturalistic hypothesis, then religious faith is a pure superfluity, better pruned away, and controversy about its legitimacy is a piece of idle trifling, unworthy of serious minds. I myself believe, of course, that the religious hypothesis gives to the world an expression which specifically determines our reactions, and makes them in a large part unlike what they may be on a purely naturalistic scheme of belief. (*WB*, 32n.)[12]

Committed as James was to modern science and Darwinism, he nevertheless was unsympathetic to the antireligious conclusions that many were drawing from them. He saw the human community, if devoid of religion, as faced with a deenergizing anxiety bordering on despair, which could be confronted at best only with a kind of stoic resignation:

> For naturalism, fed on recent cosmological speculations, mankind is in a position similar to that of a set of people living on a frozen lake, surrounded by cliffs over which there is no escape, yet knowing that little by little the ice is melting, and the inevitable day drawing near when the last film of it will disappear, and to be drowned ignominiously will be the human creature's portion. The merrier the skating, the warmer and more sparkling the sun by day, and the ruddier the bonfires at night, the more poignant the sadness which one must take in the meaning of the total situation. (*VRE*, 120)[13]

Religious experiences must ultimately be judged on the basis of "that element or quality in them which we can meet nowhere else" (*VRE*, 44). If the universal message of religion were to be expressed in a single phrase it would be: "All is *not* vanity in this Universe, whatever the appearances may suggest" (*VRE*, 38–39). The empiricist may well sneer at this "as being empty through its universality." We may be unable to meet the empiricist's demand that we "cash it by its concrete filling . . . for nothing can well be harder." James goes on to say, however, that "as a practical fact its meaning is so distinct that when used as a premiss in a life, a whole character may be imparted to the life by it. It, like so many universal concepts, is a truth of orientation, serving not to define an end, but to determine a direction" (*TC*, I:503; also *TC*, II:448).

It would be a grave misunderstanding of James's position to view it as restricting the implications of religion to human experience with no consequences for the larger world. When the world is interpreted religiously, it is not the "materialistic world over again, with an altered expression"; it must be a differently constituted world such that "different events can be expected in it, different conduct must be required" (*VRE*, 408). Hence, James considers the view of Absolute Idealism— "refined supernaturalism"—incredible because it claims that the existence of God in no way alters the complexion of any of the concrete particulars of experience (*VRE*, 411). A God who would make no difference in such experiences or who would make a difference only at the end of the world would be meaningless and merely verbal. Insofar, however, as our conceptions of God "do involve such definite experiences, God means something for us, and may be real" (*CER*, 425).

When asked where the differences due to God's existence are in fact to be found, James confesses that he has "no hypothesis to offer beyond what the phenomenon of 'prayerful communion' . . . immediately suggests." Here he refers again to that "wider world of being" and the subliminal self that were discussed in the last chapter. God can be viewed as the symbol for those "transmundane energies" that seem to produce immediate effects in the natural world with which our experience is continuous (*VRE*, 411–12). James notes that petitional prayer is only one mode of prayer and a narrow one at that. Prayer in the "wider sense as meaning every kind of inward communion or conversation with the power recognized as divine" remains untouched by scientific criticism and "is the very soul and essence of religion." James concedes that if nothing is transacted through such prayer, "if the world is in no whit different for its having taken place," then religion is the delusion that "materialists and atheists have always said it was" (*VRE*, 365–67).[14]

Religion, then, stands or falls "by the persuasion that effects of some sort genuinely do occur" (*VRE*, 367). According to James, the instinctive belief of mankind is that "God is real since he produces real effects." Hence, "we and God have business with each other; and in opening ourselves to his influence our deepest destiny is fulfilled. The universe, at those parts of it which our personal being constitutes, takes a turn for the worse or for the better in proportion as each of us fulfills or evades God's demands" (*VRE*, 406–7). Inasmuch as it produces real effects, James feels that we are not philosophically justified in designating the "unseen or mystical world unreal." Communion with this world results in work being done upon our finite personalities that turns us into new human beings, and consequences in the way of conduct ensue in the "natural world upon our regenerative change" (*VRE*, 406).

Faith in God, therefore, cannot be restricted to a claim about and effects upon the individual believer or even upon human experience. Only when faith says something about reality, such as "God's existence is the guarantee of an ideal order that shall be permanently preserved," does faith "get wholly free from the first immediate subjective experience, and bring a *real hypothesis* into play." James contends that a good scientific hypothesis, in order to be sufficiently prolific, must include properties other "than those of the phenomenon it is immediately invoked to explain." For this reason, "God, meaning only what enters into the religious man's experience of union, falls short of being an hypothesis of this more useful order. He needs to enter into wider cosmic relations in order to justify the subject's absolute confidence and peace" (*VRE*, 407).[15]

Before attempting to spell out a bit more fully the characteristics of a Jamesian God, I would like to touch briefly upon a complex and sensitive issue: the question of whether religion supplies something more than morality. The radical question of life, for James, is "whether this be at bottom a moral or an unmoral universe" (*WB*, 84). James, of course, opts for its being a moral universe, and its being so does *not* depend on there being a God:

> Whether a God exist, or whether no God exist . . . we form at any rate an ethical republic. . . . And the first reflection which this leads to is that ethics have as genuine and real a foothold in a universe where the highest consciousness is human, as in a universe where there is a God as well. "The religion of humanity" affords a basis for ethics as well as theism does. (*WB*, 150)

Yet though faith in God does not constitute the difference between morality and no morality, it does make a difference between moralities. A solely humanistic morality does not have the potential for energizing human beings to their fullest: "In a merely human world without a God, the appeal to our moral energy falls short of its maximal stimulating power" (*WB*, 160). According to James, it is the difference between the easygoing and the strenuous mood that makes the deepest practical difference in the moral life of humans (*WB*, 159). Unfortunately, he weakens his case by implying that the strenuous mood is found only among religious believers, leaving himself open to the objection "that neither James nor anybody else has ever offered empirical evidence for the assertion that unbelievers lead less active or strenuous lives than believers."[16] James admits that "the capacity for the strenuous mood probably lies slumbering in every man," but he goes on to suggest that without belief in God this capacity will remain unfulfilled (*WB*, 160–61). In my opinion, his case would have been stronger had he made a weaker claim: that is, that the overwhelming number of those who have manifested and are manifesting the strenuous mood are energized by a religious belief involving either God or a God-surrogate such as art, science, or posterity. More speculatively, and as an expression of faith, he could then have argued that these surrogates are not likely, in the long run, to continue to energize any substantial segment of the human community unless they are related directly or indirectly to a reality more encompassing and enduring than that manifest by the quotidian world.

James expresses the inadequacy of any naturalistic or humanistic ideal strikingly, if a bit harshly, in the following passage:

> Many of us . . . would openly laugh at the very idea of the strenuous mood being awakened in us by those claims of remote posterity which constitute the last appeal of the religion of humanity. We do not love these men of the future keenly enough; and we love them less the more we hear of their evolutionized perfection, their high average longevity and education, their freedom from war and crime, their relative immunity from pain and zymotic disease, and all their other negative superiorities. This is all too finite, we say; we see too well the vacuum beyond. It lacks the note of infinitude and mystery, and may all be dealt with in the don't-care mood. (*WB*, 160)

I will touch upon this theme of posterity-immortality in a later section, but we must first consider the kind of God which, on Jamesian terms, would be adequate to energize humans to their fullest potential.

Recall my controlling metaphysical assumption that all realities are structured after the fashion of a "field" and, further, that fields are processive-relational realities; hence, the divine field, like all fields, is continually changing in its relations to other fields. This in no way suggests that the character and mode of this change is identical with those of any or all the fields designated nondivine. At the same time, however different the divine reality is from human reality, it cannot be totally different. The grounds for extrapolating the distinct character of the divine field must be found in the human field. Following James, I would insist that any God in which we can properly believe must be a God we can *live* with, and "live" must be understood actively rather than passively. In keeping with the pragmatic perspective, any speculative or extrapolative expression of God will be evaluated in terms of its enhancement, enrichment, and stimulation of human life—actual or potential. Hence, a God who leaves nothing significant for human beings to do, who absorbs human individuality, who trivializes human freedom, is neither consistent with James's metaphysical assumptions nor worthy of human belief and effort.

If one takes seriously the development of human consciousness and experience, one cannot remain content with the view of God that served an earlier moment of human history. As James puts it, perhaps a bit too simply:

> What with science, idealism, and democracy, our own imagination has grown to need a God of an entirely different temperament from that Being interested exclusively in dealing out personal favors, with whom our ancestors were so contented. Smitten as we are with the vision of social righteousness, a God indifferent to everything but adulation, and full of partiality for his individual favorites, lacks an essential element of largeness; and even the best professional

sainthood of former centuries, pent in as it is to such a conception, seems to us curiously shallow and unedifying. (*VRE*, 277)

Now neither James nor I in any way deny that indispensable insights concerning the divine have been realized in earlier moments of human experience, and continue to orient and energize us. Consider, for instance, the long, rich, and varied tradition concerning the priority of the "eternal." Of course, it is not possible to affirm the radical processive character of reality, and the pervasive feature of time *and* the metaphysical dualism between the temporal and the eternal. Still, what is needed is not a simplistic substitution of a nonnuanced temporal for a static eternal; rather, a way must be found or created to deepen our grasp of both the temporal and eternal such that both will be enriched. "A nameless *unheimlichkeit*," James maintains, "comes over us at the thought of there being nothing eternal in our final purposes, in the objects of our loves and aspirations which are our deepest energies" (*WB*, 71).

While not pretending to do it here, I wish to stress that the traditional attribute of the eternity of God must be accounted for within any viable pragmatic-processive philosophy of God. It is quite evident that a God who could possibly cease to be would be radically inadequate with reference to that human need for the "eternal." This kind of "temporal" God would render impossible that trust and confidence which has characterized the relation of the human to the divine in the deepest and richest moments of religious experience. Indeed, with such a God it would be frivolous to speak of "salvation," for a God who cannot save himself can hardly save others. Thus the only kind of God who would meet a profound human need and in whom humans can believe must be one who is eternal or everlasting.

It does not follow, however, that God must be eternally or everlastingly the same. Divine love, for example, is eternal, but its eternality does not exclude its expansion and enrichment. For these, however, God needs other beings who do not share his eternality but who come to be as a consequence—in part, at least—of the ever growing divine love. This touches upon the essential relational character of God, which is particularly important for any personal immortality extrapolations. But before considering this feature, I must explore James's "pluralistic pantheism."

PLURALISTIC PANTHEISM

There would appear to be three general versions of God and the world, with numerous variations. The oldest and most persistent, of course, views God as eternal and self-sufficient. In the West, at least, this has taken two forms—traditional theism in which God creates the world *ex nihilo,* and post-Kantian absolutism in which God or the Absolute is the fully realized, all-knowing ground of the world. A second view, greatly influenced by the growing evidence that all reality is evolving, speculates that God is evolving or emerging out of the eternal world processes. While this view has attracted a few sophisticated philosophers, for obvious reasons it has not been attractive to those with explicit religious concerns. The third general view, also greatly influenced by evolutionary theories and modern and contemporary science, extrapolates a God as coeternal but not identical with a plurality of processes that are in part constituted by and constitute the divine. Since the relation between God and these world processes is ever changing, God also is ever changing. The divine change, however, does not exclude such eternal aims as love, harmony, and unity. These aims, it is important to note, cannot be realized by God alone but depend in part for their realization upon the cooperative endeavor of at least some of the processes coexisting with God. The most systematically developed mode of this third general view is found in those process theologies whose dominant influence is Alfred North Whitehead. It should be evident, and I hope will become more so, that a Jamesian philosophy of God is also a variant of this view.

It is in his *Pluralistic Universe* that the metaphysical ground for James's version of God is most explicitly developed. This work was originally delivered as a series of lectures at Manchester College, Oxford, in 1907. While the principal target of the lectures was the philosophical absolutism that dominated late nineteenth- and early twentieth-century philosophy, Richard Bernstein quite correctly notes that James gives us "nothing less than a critique of Western philosophic thought" (*PU*, xxiv). Some of the more specific and semitechnical criticisms are somewhat dated, inasmuch as the "Absolute" is no longer at the center of the philosophical stage; nevertheless, a brief review of James's arguments is useful for my purposes because they orient us in relation to the crucial elements that must be incorporated into the Jamesian philosophy of God, elements that I hold indispensable for a viable belief in personal immortality.

As a recent insightful commentator has noted, "Intimacy was the principle of order in James's hierarchy of universes from 1904 on."[17] Nowhere is the importance and centrality of "intimacy" more evident than in *A Pluralistic Universe*.[18] James first distinguishes materialistic from spiritualistic philosophies, giving short shrift to the former because it defines the world in such a way as to leave the human "as a sort of outside passenger or alien" (*PU*, 16). He then differentiates two species of spiritualism—dualistic theism and monistic pantheism. While not denying all intimacy to dualistic theism, James maintains that a "higher reach of intimacy" is suggested by pantheistic idealism insofar as it makes "us entitatively one with God" (*PU*, 16). He faults dualistic theism because,

> picturing God and his creation as entities distinct from each other, [it] still leaves the human subject outside of the deepest reality in the universe. God is from eternity complete, it says, and sufficient unto himself; he throws off the world by a free act and as an extraneous substance, and he throws off man as a third substance, extraneous to both the world and himself. (*PU*, 16–17)

Such a view renders us foreigners—outsiders, as it were—in relation to God. What James finds lacking here is the "strictly social relation" of reciprocity, since while God's action can affect us, "he can never be affected by our reaction" (*PU,* 17). The "theological machinery" of our ancestors is no longer serviceable for a human imagination formed by "the vaster vistas which scientific evolutionism has opened and the rising tide of social democratic ideals." The "older monarchical theism" has been rendered obsolete; "the place of the divine in the world must be more organic and intimate" (*PU,* 18).

As always for James, any speculative claim must be evaluated in terms of its consequences for concrete living. Thus the pragmatic "difference between living against a background of foreignness and one of intimacy means the difference between a general habit of wariness and one of trust." James suggests that this is really a social difference, "for after all, the common *socius* of us all is the great universe whose children we are." If we are materialistic, "we must be suspicious of this socius, cautious, tense, on guard. If spiritualistic, we may give way, embrace, and keep no ultimate fear" (*PU,* 19). Insofar, then, as the spiritualistic interpretations of reality give our life and actions a depth and richness absent in materialism, he opts for the former. By the same token, he rejects dualistic theism in favor of the "pantheistic field of vision, the vision of God as the indwelling divine rather than the external creator, and of human life as part and parcel of that deep reality" (*PU,* 19).

James is convinced that only "some kind of an immanent or pantheistic deity working *in* things rather than above them" is congenial to our contemporary imagination (*P,* 39). But that is not the full story, for the brand of pantheism current at the time was monistic or absolutistic pantheism, features of which clashed at least as strongly with specific needs and James's metaphysical principles as did dualistic theism. "*As such,* the absolute neither acts nor suffers, nor loves, nor hates; it has no needs, desires or aspirations, no failures or successes, friends or enemies, victories or defeats" (*PU,* 27). Quite obviously, an Absolute or a God so devoid of all the characteristics that James discovers in life and experience could only be viewed by him as the acme of irrelevance. While the "Absolute Mind" as the substitute for God is allegedly the "rational presupposition of all particulars of fact . . . it remains supremely indifferent to what the particular facts in our world actually are." James compares the Absolute to the "sick lion in Esop's fable, all footprints lead into his den, but *nulla vestigia retrorsum.*" The Absolute then maintains no connection with the concreteness of life, and while we are assured that all is eternally well with him, he leaves us to be saved by our own temporal devices (*P,* 40).

It is significant, I believe, that while James in his later works is critical of the Absolute for doing nothing to aid our salvation, in an early essay, "Reflex Action and Theism" (1881), he was critical of the Calvinistic God for doing everything: "A God who gives so little scope to love, a predestination which takes from endeavor all its zest with all its fruit, are irrational conceptions, because they say to our most cherished powers, There is no object for you" (*WB*, 100). Yet there is no inconsistency between these texts, nor is there any essential shift in James's doctrine. Early and late he affirmed a religious need for a power greater than the natural: "Man is too helpless against the cosmic forces, unless there be a wider Ally" (*TC*, II:383). Similarly, at all stages of his thought he resisted any view that deprived individual human action of significance and efficacy. It is clear, therefore, that the only God consistent with James's long-standing concerns is one who is available to humans in their struggles but who also depends upon human initiative and creativity in order to realize the divine aims.

Those same long-standing concerns led James to reject absolutistic monism in favor of pluralism. A decade before writing *A Pluralistic Universe,* he suggested that "the difference between monism and pluralism is perhaps the most pregnant of all the differences in philosophy" (*WB*, 5). Hence it is not surprising to find him maintaining in the later work that

> pluralism, in exorcizing the absolute, exorcizes the great de-realizer of the only life we are at home in, and thus redeems the nature of reality from essential foreignness. Every end, reason, motive, object of desire or aversion, ground of sorrow or joy that we feel is in the world of finite multifariousness for only in that world does anything really happen, only there do events come to pass. (*PU*, 28)[19]

While affirming a pluralistic mode of pantheism, therefore, James rejects that absolutistic brand which, "reared upon pure logic," spurns the dust of concrete life. As he states in an oft-cited text: "The prince of darkness may be a gentleman, as we are told he is, but whatever the God of earth and heaven is, he can surely be no gentleman. His menial services are needed in the dust of our human trials, even more than his dignity is needed in the empyrean" (*P*, 39–40).

Absolutistic pantheism is repugnant to James, therefore, because it trivializes the change, struggle, and pain that characterize our daily living, rendering them surface appearances of the eternally unchanging ground of reality. In notes for his 1903–1904 seminar, "A Pluralistic Description of the World," James commented, "The essence of my system is that there is really growth." He added that for him "the world exists only once, in one edition, and then just as it seems." For the philosophies in vogue at the time, on the other hand, there was a completed eternal edition devoid of growth and "an inferior, side-show, temporal edition, in which things seem illusorily to be achieving and growing into that perfection which really preexists. . . . Transcendentalism has two editions of the universe—the Absolute being the edition *de luxe*" (*TC*, II:384).

In maintaining that there is only one universe, however, James is not af-

firming a naturalistic reductionism. He is persuaded by mystical phenomena and religious experience "that our normal experience is only a fraction" of experience (*TC*, II:384). Phenomena such as "new ranges of life
succeeding on our most despairing moments" would never have been in-
ferred by reason, since "they are discontinuous with the 'natural' experiences they succeed upon and invert their values." Creation widens to the
view of those undergoing religious experience, leading to the suggestion
that "our natural experience, our strictly moralistic and prudential experience, may be only a fragment of real human experience" (*PU*, 138). This
indispensability and irreplaceability of religious experiences, and the inadequacy of "reason," has been previously noted and cannot be over-
emphasized. In his 1906 address to the Unitarian Club of San Francisco,
James points out the ambiguity of "facts": while there are both moral and
physical facts supporting the righteousness, order, and beauty of reality,
there are also "contrary facts in abundance," and the "rational" conclusion
reached will depend on which facts have been singled out. Indeed, if the
decision is left to "reason" alone, James is of the opinion that it would be
bad news for religion:

> If your reason tries to be impartial, if she resorts to statistical comparison and
> asks which class of facts tip the balance, and which way tends the drift, she
> must, it seems to me, conclude for irreligion, *unless you give her some more
> specific religious experiences to go by,* for the last word everywhere, according to
> naturalistic science, is the word of Death, the death sentence passed by Nature
> on plant and beast, and man and tribe, and earth and sun and everything that
> she has made.[20]

Returning to the question of monism versus pluralism, it must first be
noted that James rejects both in their absolute modes. The world is both one
and many—"one just so far as its parts hang together by any definite connexion" and "many just so far as any definite connexion fails to obtain" (*P*,
76). The pluralism James affirms, therefore, rejects both a world that is already completely or essentially unified and one that is totally chaotic. Pluralism has no need of that dogmatic rigoristic temper displayed by those
who maintain that "absolute unity brooks no degrees." All James's pluralism asks is that one grant "*some* separation among things, some free play
of parts, some real novelty or chance, however minute." Given this, "she is
amply satisfied and will allow you any amount, however great, of real
union" (*P*, 78).

Radical empiricism and pluralism, according to James, stand for the legitimacy of *some*. James here touches upon "the great question as to whether
'external' relations can exist" (*PU*, 40–41). The dominant view of the absolutism he is criticizing is that they could not. The doctrine of internal relations holding that everything is *essentially* included in and *essentially* related
to everything else, leading inevitably to the Absolute as the only truly real

being, is the doctrine James challenges. The technical aspects of this controversy need not concern us; for my purposes, the importance of this question
is that in affirming external relations, James is allowing for a plurality of real
beings and excluding any all-inclusive being. This in no way compromises
James's metaphysical relationalism, since all realities are relational but are
not related to all other realities with the same degree of immediacy and
intimacy. What is posited is a "strung-along" rather than an "all-at-once"
universe. It is James's contention that "radical empiricism . . . holding to
the each–form and making of God only one of the eaches, affords the higher
degree of intimacy" (*PU*, 26).

   This view, however, has an important and controversial implication: it
limits the reality of God. "If there be a God, he is no absolute all-experiencer,
but simply the experiencer of widest actual conscious span" (*MT*, 72).[21]
This brings us, of course, to James's doctrine of God as finite.

GOD AS FINITE
While James is willing to jettison the Absolute, he is not willing to dispense
with God or a higher consciousness.

> But if we drop the absolute out of the world, must we then conclude that the
> world contains nothing better in the way of consciousness than our own con-
> sciousness? Is our whole instinctive belief in higher presences, our persistent
> inner turning towards divine companionship to count for nothing? Is it but the
> pathetic illusion of beings with incorrigibly social and imaginative minds?
> (*PU*, 63)

James contends that even if it should prove probable that the Absolute does
not exist, it will not in any way follow "that a God like that of David, Isaiah,
or Jesus may not exist" (*PU*, 54). He finds no logical impediment to believing in "superhuman beings without identifying them with the absolute."
The only thing that the God of the Old and of the New Testament has in
common with the Absolute is "that they are all three greater than man"
(*PU*, 63–64).

   In the previous section, I touched upon James's affirmation of the reality
of "external relations." Put very simply, this doctrine maintains that not all
real relations are included in the essence of a being. For example, to say that
the "book is *on* the table" does not seem to imply that the book is implicated
or involved in the inner structure of the table *or vice versa*. For the absolutist
this *appearance* of the externality of relations would result in a chaotic world
of unconnected or unrelated and unrelatable realities. Hence, there must be
an all-inclusive mind in which all appearances of externality are overcome,
and this alone guarantees the rationality of reality. James, of course, never
claims to be able to disprove the reality of the Absolute but he does find the
arguments in favor of it unconvincing and, more important, the notion of
an Absolute as seriously undermining the reality and authenticity of experi-

ence. He finds both absolutism and pluralism to be hypotheses and the latter to be the more plausible one: "What pluralists say is that a universe really connected loosely, after the pattern of our daily experience, is possible, and that for certain reasons it is the hypothesis to be preferred" (*PU*, 39). There is no ground for even suspecting the existence of a reality other than "that distributed and strung-along and flowing sort of reality which we finite beings swim in" (*PU*, 97). Since the "absolute is not forced on our belief by logic," its rival, the "strung-along unfinished world in time," *may* exist just as it seems, not in the shape of an all but rather as a set of eaches (*PU*, 62).

The crucial implication of all this, of course, is that any God consistent with metaphysical pluralism must be finite. Whereas absolutism maintains that God is fully divine only in the form of totality, pluralism is "willing to believe that there may ultimately never be an all-form at all, that the substance of reality may never get totally collected, that some of it may remain outside of the largest combination of it ever made" (*PU*, 20). Thus while we are, for James, "internal parts of God and not external creations," God is himself a "part" rather than the Absolute when conceived pluralistically. The divine functions, then, can be taken as not wholly dissimilar to our own functions. All realities, including the divine reality, have an environment. Since this means that God is in time and working out a history just as we are, "he escapes from the foreignness from all that is human, of the static timeless perfect absolute" (*PU*, 143–44). Pluralism, pragmatically interpreted, simply means that everything, however vast or inclusive, has some sort of genuinely "external" environment. While things are "with" one another in many ways, there is no reality that includes or dominates everything. Hence,

> "ever not quite" has to be said of the best attempts anywhere in the universe at attaining all-inclusiveness. The pluralistic world is thus more like a federal republic than like an empire or kingdom. However much may be collected, however much may report itself as present at any effective centre of consciousness or action, something else is self-governed and absent and unreduced to unity. (*PU*, 145)[22]

James contends that it is precisely the claim that the absolute has absolutely nothing outside of itself that gives rise to those irrationalities and puzzles from which the finite God remains free. He goes on to say that the finite God "may conceivably have *almost* nothing outside of himself." He may indeed have already triumphed over and absorbed "all but the minutest fraction of the universe," but however small that fraction outside him, it reduces God to a "relative being, and in principle the universe is saved from all the irrationalities incidental to absolutism" (*PU*, 61). Thus, whether in theology or philosophy, the line of least resistance is to affirm "that there *is* a God, but that he is finite, either in power or knowledge, or in both at once" (*PU*, 141). Such a God, according to James, is quite compatible with religious experience, which cannot "be cited as unequivocally supporting the infinitist belief." The only unequivocal testimony of religious experience "is that we experience union with *something* larger than ourselves and in that union find our greatest peace." James insists that the practical needs of religious experience are adequately met by this belief in a power at once larger than and continuous with it (*VRE*, 413). We are incurably and inseparably rooted in the temporal and finite point of view (*PU*, 23). Exhortations such as those of Emerson to "lift mine eye up" to the style of the Absolute which is the one true way are fruitless. "I am," James tells us, "finite once for all, and all the categories of my sympathy are knit up with the finite world *as such,* and with things that have a history" (*PU*, 27).

Again we see how James is concerned to safeguard the reality and significance of concrete human experience. Things would be different if we were merely *readers* of the cosmic novel, "but we are not the readers but the very personages of the world-drama" (*PU*, 27). And it is because James also believes that God is one, though not the only one, of the personages in this drama that he refuses to excuse him from the limitations and the obstacles that confront *all* the participants. An omniscient and omnipotent God would, of course, escape all this, but the existence of such a God would imply that the battles that seem so real and important to us are but surface events in relation to the "really real." On the contrary, James tells us, "the facts of struggle seem too deeply characteristic of the whole frame of things for me not to suspect that hindrance and experiment go all the way through" (*TC*, II:379). Elsewhere, he asserts:

> God himself, in short, may draw vital strength and increase of very being from our fidelity. For my own part, I do not know what the sweat and blood and tragedy of this life mean, if they mean anything short of this. If this life be not a real fight, in which something is eternally gained for the universe by success, it is no better than a game of private theatricals from which one may withdraw at will. But it *feels* like a real fight—as if there were something really wild in the universe which we, with all our idealities and faithfulnesses, are needed to redeem. (*WB*, 55)

It is evident, then, that only a finite God can help us and be in *real* need of our help. He must be sufficiently powerful to be able to help us and be worthy of our trust and confidence, but he cannot be so powerful as to find our efforts unnecessary, thereby trivializing them and robbing them of meaning and significance.[23] Something of this is captured by Perry: "Thus pluralism means a finite God, who evokes a passionate allegiance because he is in some measure hampered by circumstances, and dependent on the aid of others; or because, the evil of the world being external to him, he may be loved without reserve" (*TC*, II:211–12).

From James's perspective, one of the key fruits of the notion of God as finite or having an environment other than himself is that it avoids the classical paradox of how there can be evil in a world created by an infinitely good and all-powerful God. In the final analysis, perhaps, evil is a mystery to be lived with rather than a problem to be solved, whether on James's terms or those of anyone else. Still, we are not entitled to use the mystery of evil as an excuse for not reflecting upon it and attempting, at least, to remove the more egregious contradictions. The resolutions of both absolute idealism and classical theism are unacceptable to James, the former because it denies the reality of evil, and the latter because it involves a dualism rife with the difficulties that we have been detailing. Whatever the shortcomings of James's approach to evil, one thing is clear—evil is real and is incapable of being overcome simply by being subsumed within a higher mind. In his *Varieties of Religious Experience,* James faults the attitude of "healthy-mindedness" because it fails to recognize the evil facts that make up a genuine portion of reality (*VRE*, 136). Elsewhere he states: "Whatever Indian mystics may say about overcoming the bonds of good and evil, for *us* there is no higher synthesis in which the contradiction merges." He goes on to say that we should "admit that, whilst some parts are good, others are bad, and being bad *ought* not to have been . . . possibly *might* not have been" (*TC,* I:638).

This last raises, of course, the thorny metaphysical issue of the origin of evil and suggests a kind of Manichaean account whereby evil originates outside God. While James does little more than hint at such an account, it is consistent with his pluralism. Evil would not need to be essential if we scrap the monistic view and "allow the world to have existed from its origin in a pluralistic form, as an aggregate or collection of higher and lower things and principles." From such a perspective, evil "might be and may always have been, an independent portion that had no rational or absolute right to live with the rest, and which we might conceivably hope to see got rid of at last" (*VRE*, 113).[24] James contends that popular or practical theism has not been upset with a "universe composed of many original principles"; it has only insisted that God be the supreme principle—in which case "God is not necessarily responsible for the existence of evil; he would only be responsible if it were not finally overcome" (*VRE*, 112).

In the final analysis it is evil as a practical, not a speculative, problem that concerns pluralistic metaphysics. "Not why evil should exist at all, but how we can lessen the actual amount of it, is the sole question we need there consider" (*PU*, 60). This concern for the lessening of evil seems to have been paramount in James's mind from his earliest years. In a letter to Thomas Ward in 1868, he wrote: "If we can only bring ourselves to accept evil as an ultimated inscrutable fact, the way may be open towards a great practical reform on earth, as our aims will be clearly defined, and our energies concentrated" (*TC*, I:161).

Thus, it is James's contention that in the religious life of ordinary people, God is not the name of the whole of things. Rather, he is a "superhuman person who calls us to cooperate in his purposes, and who furthers ours if they are worthy. He works in an external environment, has limits, and has enemies." All of this leads James to assert: "I believe that the only God worthy of the name *must* be finite" (*PU,* 60).

One final word concerning the classical and continuing problem of reconciling divine omnipotence with divine goodness. There have been in the past and are in the present some sophisticated and intellectually respectable efforts at such reconciliation, but, following James, I think that they are and will continue to be fatally flawed and unpersuasive. No complex arguments or modes of reasoning are needed to indicate why, for many at least, it is literally *incredible* to suggest that there is a morally good being who has the power to alleviate the pain and suffering of millions of innocent human beings but for reasons known only to himself freely chooses not to do so. Two texts, one from a modern novel and the other from a contemporary theological work, succinctly and sharply delineate the incredibility of such a being.

> How much reverence can you have for a Supreme Being who finds it necessary to include such phenomena as phlegm and tooth decay in His divine system of creation? What in the world was running through that warped, scatological mind of His when He robbed old people of the power to control their bowel movements?[25]

> A God of absolute power who either causes or deliberately permits everything that happens must take full responsibility for it himself. Nothing can take place unless he wills it. That includes Auschwitz and our devastation of Vietnam. Can a God who willingly tolerates such outrageous suffering be called good? Is he not callously indifferent to both the integrity and the welfare of his creatures? A God like that cannot be worshiped by thinking people today. Any man or woman who has a modicum of human decency is morally superior to him.[26]

Any attempt to say anything specific about God, after hundreds of years of arguments and efforts, has about it a decided dimension of foolishness. Nevertheless, it is not possible to believe in God without venturing some suggestion concerning the character of that in which one believes. As H. D. Lewis has expressed it, "No one can expect or believe anything without having *some* idea of what it is that he expects."[27] Let me state what, for me, is a minimalist belief concerning the nature of God: that God is a moral person who is at least as good as the very best human being imaginable. I submit that we would judge any human being morally deficient who failed to exercise all the power he or she possessed to alleviate human suffering, and that we therefore cannot expect less of God. The classical response that God has limited his use of power out of respect for human freedom is profoundly unconvincing. Imagine a parent who, wishing to respect the freedom of the child, allows this child to do something that is disastrous for itself or for another when it is within the power of the parent to prevent it. This is really "unimaginable."

Recall James's contention that "when we cease to admire or approve what the definition of a deity implies, we end by deeming that deity incredible" (*VRE,* 264–65). Hence, if God does nothing when confronted by the profound suffering of millions of innocent human beings, the only possibility for believing in the moral goodness of that God is that he was unable to do anything. As Clark M. Williamson has expressed it, "God does all that God can possibly do for us."[28] In reviewing Williamson's work, John K. Roth criticizes this statement because he questions whether a God of such limited power "is fully worthy of worship." The alternative Roth suggests, however, is rather astounding: "Certainly men and women do not always do the best they can. The Holocaust and its antecedents in the anti-Judaism of the Christian church, however, may testify that God is *not* one who always does the best either."[29] Unless I am missing something here, Roth seems to be saying that it is more possible to worship a God who has unlimited power but does not always exercise it in the *best* way possible. I do not see how such a God could be judged other than morally defective.

We are confronted, then, with two inadequate and not totally satisfying images of the divine: a God who at every moment employs all his limited power, or a God of unlimited power who fails in numerous instances to use this power for what would appear to be very worthwhile ends. Whether able to be worshipped or not, the former is surely a lovable God. As for the latter God, I would not wish to worship him and would find it difficult if not impossible to love him.[30]

RELATIONAL SELF—RELATIONAL GOD
I have been describing reality in terms of a plurality of fields, at least some of which are conscious fields. Further, we have seen that the human field of consciousness is related to and thereby in part constituted by a wider field or superhuman consciousness. The following text from Perry succinctly describes James's view of these relational spans of consciousness:

> Turning to the problem of unity of the world, he explained such degrees and varieties of unity as the world possesses in terms of experienced relations. To avoid subjectivism, he argued for the "conterminousness" of minds, that is their convergence in or towards the same experiences—defending this view against the skeptic on the one hand and the absolutist on the other. Borrowing Peirce's term, he adopted the "tychistic" theory that the ultimate origins of things are both plural and spontaneous. No philosophy, he said, can really avoid the recognition of a sheer datum at some point. But beings of independent and accidental origin can *come into* interaction with one another, through a spreading "consciousness of transition." This notion suggests different "spans" of consciousness, and the possibility of a consciousness such as God with a span far exceeding that of man. . . . It eliminates the problem of evil,

and "goes with empiricism, personalism, democracy and freedom." (*TC*, II:373–74)[31]

I have been speaking of this wider field of consciousness specifically as "God" or "divine," and have indicated why this reality must be wider and more powerful than the human, but not necessarily all-inclusive or all-powerful. Further, following James, I have insisted on the significance and efficacy of human initiative and activity, thereby rejecting any versions of God that deny or radically diminish this efficacy. Though not referring specifically to James, Ian Barbour has described a view of agency which is completely consistent with that of James.

> God's relation to other agents seems to require a social or interpersonal analogy in which a plurality of centers of initiative are present. The biblical model of Father, after all, allowed for the presence of many agents, rather than concentrating on the divine agent alone. . . . In the process model more than one agent may influence a given event, so that both God's action and that of other agents can be represented.[32]

There is, of course, a much wider consensus concerning the relational character of the human self than there is concerning the claim that one of those constituting relations, indeed the central one, is the relation to a superhuman consciousness designated "God." The most that I have claimed throughout this essay is that the field-self, which is widely manifest in the diverse modes of experience and reasonably confirmed by a number of intellectual disciplines, is open to a relation to a field that can be called divine. Recall just how the self as field is characterized by such openness: as a "field," the boundary of the self is open, indefinite, and continually shifting such that other fields are continually leaking in and leaking out. There is, however, sufficient stability and difference in the rates of shifting among selves and all other fields to allow us to speak of individual fields. The individuality of all fields, but preeminently self-fields, is relational, hence relative in the sense that inasmuch as its constituting fields are continually changing, so is the individual. Further, individual entities, including selves, are characterized by being, and can exist only so long as they are, centers of activity. Since these centers are constituted by their transactions with other centers, they are independent. The most crucial question, for my purposes, is whether the human self has, as one of its constituting relations and transactions, a relation to a wider and more powerful consciousness, which consciousness is able to maintain its constituting relation to the self even in the absence of other relations that may now also partially constitute it. The possibility of personal immortality, as I have repeatedly insisted, depends upon the reality of such a relation.

What is needed, of course, is a model of an emergent self that is consistent with the best philosophical and scientific evidence concerning the self and, as a minimum, does not exclude the possibility of such a superhuman constituting relation. Such a model would have to be constructed along the following lines. The human self emerges from fields designated "physical," but this self is neither identical with nor reducible to the physical fields from which it emerges and on which it presently depends. The grounds for this claim would, of course, be the fact that the self performs activities that are *really* different from the distinguishing activities of physical fields. While we may be unable to answer *why* such a distinct field emerges or even to describe precisely *how* or exactly *when* it emerges, there would appear to be rather compelling evidence *that* such a self does emerge. There are both "subjective" and "objective" data in support of this contention. Subjectively, there is the *felt* awareness of identity, continuity, freedom, and the like. Objectively, we are able to describe behavior that is neither identical with nor reducible to the behavior of other entities, such as plants, animals, cells, or atoms.

An "emerged" self has access to and is able to act upon, participate in, and transform other real fields, including self-fields, in a distinctive fashion. Thus the individual self is a more encompassing field than those from which it emerged and which are still involved in its constitution. Further, this self is able to participate in fields more encompassing than itself, such as linguistic, cultural, and social fields; and it does so in a manner not available to its own subfields when they are isolated from it. It would seem legitimate to suggest that the self now takes on characteristics of those wider fields so as to give it a reality "beyond" the fields from which it has emerged and upon which it still depends. All of this seems phenomenologically verifiable, quite apart from the question of the divine field. If so, this becomes the experiential ground which, when combined with religious experience, allows for extrapolating the reality of God.

Assuming this extrapolation along the lines previously described, it may be useful here to underline a few key aspects of the relation between the divine and the human fields. In keeping with the metaphysical pluralism discussed earlier, I wish to stress that while all things are connected, they are not all connected to all others with a relation of immediacy. Hence, though God is connected to all things, and though his connections of immediacy are the greatest in existence, even God is not connected *immediately* to all things. More, there are degrees of immediacy even between God and those beings with whom he is immediately related.

Suppose we characterize the human on the basis of its immediacy to the divine. There would be a wide range and difference in the degree of this immediacy even within the human species, a species distinguished as such on the basis of the potential of its individual members for a relation of immediacy with God. Both individually and collectively, however, human beings would have to strive, whether consciously or unconsciously, directly or indirectly, to realize and increase this relation. The mystical might serve as the paradigm of the relation of immediacy between the divine and the human, but it would be neither the exclusive nor the complete mode of immediacy. The long and arduous evolutionary and historical process would seem almost frivolous if the highest mode possible of immediacy between God and the world had already been or is now realized in the experience of even one mystic.[33] Hence, this relation of immediacy must be a growing one, and its realizations both past and present cannot be restricted to explicit mystical or religious experiences. Great poets, scientists, artists, composers, statesmen—indeed all truly great human beings, whether publicly recognized or not—can be viewed as manifesting modes of immediate relations to a wider and richer reality. Quite obviously not everyone is led to articulate this relationship explicitly, and even among those who do, it will be variously described. Some might express the experience of a reality "beyond" that of their narrowly "personal" reality in terms of poetry, painting, music, nature, or science. A few have, of course, described it in terms of a personal being, traditionally referred to as God.

It is this personal relationship between the individual and that wider, superhuman consciousness designated "God" that is the necessary presupposition for any belief in personal immortality. Unless belief in a personal God is possible and plausible, there is no point in even considering the possibility of a belief in personal immortality.[34] Whatever difficulties James had with traditional theism, he never seemed to surrender that personalistic character of God that was so essential to it. Negative evidence for this can be found in James's lecture notes for a course called "The Philosophy of Evolution," given some half-dozen times in the years 1879–96. Much of the course was taken up with criticizing Herbert Spencer's "evolutionism," in particular rejecting its claim that the "unknowable" could serve as a suitable object for religious faith. Not so, according to James: "Mere existence commands no reverence whatever, or any other emotion until its quality is specified. Neither does mere cosmic 'power,' unless it 'makes for' something which can claim kinship from our sympathies." He concludes that we might as well "speak of being irreverent to Space or disrespectful of the Equator" (*TC*, I:486).

A more positive expression of theism's God as personal is found in "Reflex Action and Theism." The two essential features of theism are that "God be conceived as the deepest power in the universe" and that he be conceived "under the form of a mental personality." James goes on to say that "God's personality is to be regarded, like any other personality, as something lying outside of my own and other than me." Finally, whatever the differences between the divine and human personalities, they "both have purposes for which they care, and each can hear the other's call" (*WB*, 97–98).[35] Elsewhere, James notes that our religions represent the "more perfect and eternal aspect of the universe . . . as having a personal form." He goes on to say that if we are religious, "the universe is no longer a mere *It* to us, but a *Thou*," and hence we are able to have any relation with it that we are able to have with another person (*WB*, 31).

In his *Varieties of Religious Experience,* James contends that religious individuals see their personal concerns as the grounds on which they encounter and are encountered by God (*VRE,* 387). Hence, "the pivot round which the religious life . . . revolves, is the interest of the individual in his private personal destiny" (*VRE,* 387). This personal God witnessed to by religious experience is contrasted with the God recognized by science. The latter is a "God of universal laws exclusively, a God who does a wholesale, not a retail business. He cannot accommodate his processes to the convenience of individuals" (*VRE,* 390). That God was explicitly affirmed by Albert Einstein when he said that he believed "in Spinoza's God who reveals himself in the orderly harmony of what exists, not in a God who concerns himself with the fates and actions of human beings."[36]

In spite of James's assertion that "religion . . . is a monumental chapter in the history of human egotism" (*VRE,* 387), it would be grossly misleading to understand his stress on the individual and personal dimension of religious experience in terms of an atomistic individualism or an isolating egotism. The whole drift of James's relational metaphysics, as we have repeatedly seen, goes against such a narrowing and empty individualism. Less than a year before his death, he wrote a letter to his friend and fellow-pragmatist, F. C. S. Schiller, chiding him for failing to adequately recognize the social dimension of the human situation:

> It seems to me really fantastically formal to ignore *that* much of the truth that is already established, namely, that men do think in social situations. . . . *I simply assume the social situation,* and I am sorry that . . . you balk at it so much. It is not assumed merely tactically, for those are the terms in which I genuinely think the matter. (*TC,* II:510)

James's language has undoubtedly at times been misleading, and his fervent desire to affirm the reality of the individual perhaps led him to fail to emphasize sufficiently those social relations that were so stressed by Karl Marx and John Dewey. The charge that James was a supporter of "rugged individualism," however, is simply without merit. He explicitly called for philosophers of all stripes to join in combatting "the practical, conventionally thinking man, to whom . . . nothing has true seriousness but personal interests" (*CER,* 24–25). Henry Levinson is right on the mark when he contends that James "did not pit the personal and the private against the social experience—on James' grounds both individuals and their religions were inevitably social. James pits the sociality of persuasion—the sociality of friends and compatriots—against the sociality of coercion—the sociality of sovereigns and subjects" (*RIWJ,* 132). One might add that by the same token, James pits the individuality of persons (the individuality that is constructed and developed by transactions with other persons) against the individuality of egotism (the individuality that isolates and impoverishes itself by turning toward that imaginary unrelational center which is in truth "nothing").

The self as essentially social or relational is a doctrine that has appeared in many forms in contemporary thought—not only in pragmatism but also in Marxism, existentialism, and phenomenology, as well as in certain psychologies, sociologies, and anthropologies.[37] Ralph Harper gives an existentialist version strikingly similar to that of James. "No one," he tells us, "can become a 'true self' without the encouragement of others. Identity depends on presence, on being singled out." Harper adds that "to be a person is to look for a person, first to confirm one's own reality and identity and next to set up a relationship of mutual fulfillment."[38] In the *Principles,* James suggests that "*a man has as many social selves as there are individuals who recognize* and carry an image of him in their mind" (*PP,* I:281–82). He later claims that of all our more potential selves, *the potential social self* is the most interesting, in virtue of "its connection with our moral and religious life." When I act contrary to the wishes and judgments of my friends or family or "set," and thereby experience a diminution of my actual social self, I am strengthened by the thought that there are "other and better *possible* social judges." Even if I have no hope of realizing the ideal social self during my lifetime or expectation that future generations will know anything about me, I am still called to pursue an ideal social self—one "that is at least *worthy* of approving recognition by the highest *possible* judging companion, if such companion there be." James adds that "this self is the true, the intimate, the ultimate, the permanent Me which I seek. This judge is God, the Absolute Mind, the 'Great Companion' " This accounts for the impulse to pray, which is a "necessary consequence of the fact that whilst the innermost of the empirical selves of a man is a Self of the *social* sort, yet it can find its only adequate *Socius* in an ideal world" (*PP,* I:300–301).

Needless to say, James is only claiming here to give a phenomenological or psychological description of distinctive human experience. It is interesting to note that Dewey recognizes this same phenomenon: "One no sooner establishes his private and subjective self than he demands it be recognized and acknowledged by others, even if he has to invent an imaginary audience or an Absolute Self to satisfy the demand."[39] Of course, where Dewey will remain or become convinced that this higher self is merely "imaginary," or at least not "real" in any sense which might be called "objective," James insisted on the right to believe that this higher self—God—has a reality not reducible to human or "natural" reality.

Concerning the possibility and plausibility of any belief in personal immortality, then, it is inseparably bound up with our belief in a "Great Companion" who cares for us and will bring to realization that in us which is worthy of realization. In a late essay, James makes an observation about those who are beset with a secondary personality; I believe that it can be applied, properly qualified, to all human beings: "What *they* want in the awful drift of their being out of its customary self, is any principle of steadfastness to hold on to. We ought to assure them and reassure them that we will stand by them, and recognize the true self in them to the end" (*CER*, 508–9). Is not something very like this what we ask of God, whom alone we believe to be capable and desirous of recognizing our true selves and keeping them from sinking into that abyss of nothingness from which they have emerged and which remains a continuing threat to the integrity and the very reality of our lives? I must explore this crucial point later; for the moment I wish simply to emphasize our radical dependence upon God for any hope of a life that does not, in spite of our greatest efforts and the efforts of our human lovers, dissolve into a nothingness ultimately indistinguishable from a life that has never been.

It is this individual and personal relationship with God that has always been at the center of any belief in a continuing life. According to R. H. Charles, "Jeremiah was the first to conceive religion as the Communion of the individual soul with God. . . . Thus through Jeremiah the foundation of a true individualism was laid, and the law of individual retribution proclaimed. The further development of these ideas led inevitably to the conception of a blessed life beyond the grave."[40] I have been suggesting throughout this section that because we can believe we are here and now in part constituted by and in transactional relation with God, we can believe and hope that God will maintain and continue this constituting relation even after other relations that now make up our being have been terminated.[41] It would seem to be a life-sustaining relation such as this of which Luke joyfully tells us: "Now he is God, not of the dead, but of the living; for to him all men are in fact alive."[42]

The key to life, present or future, would seem to be "love." Essential to any love worthy of the name would seem to be a care, concern, and desire that the one loved realize to the fullest his or her aims and ideals insofar as this realization brings enrichment and enhancement of life not only to the beloved but also to the others with whom the beloved is life-related. Whereas God's life is essentially love, endeavoring at every moment to enable those loved by him to realize their life potential, all nondivine beings—humans in particular—can fall short of their love for God and those toward whom God's love is directed. This, of course, is saying neither more nor less than that loving God is inseparable from loving those whom God loves. One cannot truly love God unless one loves those who are loved by God, since not to do so would be in essential conflict with the aims and desires of the beloved.

As for belief in personal immortality, it is evident that everything comes down to the possibility of there being a loving God capable of sustaining a relationship of value that has come into being within the creative process. That we are invited to participate in this process and are *promised* a share in its fruits would seem to be at the center of Christian faith. We cannot, of course, *know* or *feel guaranteed* that we will personally share in eternal life, but by the same token, we cannot exclude the possibility that our mode of sharing will be personal. In the final analysis, perhaps, our love and trust in the divine must be such that we here and now accept whatever mode of sharing is possible for God without in any way lessening our dedication to those goals, values, and ideals that enhance life. Our primary focus must be on contributing to the realization of the very best features of the creative process and thereby to an enrichment of both human and divine life. In such endeavors, we must be willing to act in spite of our ignorance as to the precise form the ultimate fruits of our actions will take. In the final analysis, Christians and many others *believe* that they live and move and *achieve* their being within a process richer and more encompassing than can be known, one suffused with a mystery of promise and vitality.

CODA BY WAY OF AN OBJECTION

A formidable objection to a central claim of this chapter—and indeed to the entire essay—must be acknowledged, though I have no fully satisfying response to it. I have advanced as plausible and believable a God whose power is limited as regards the evils of experience, yet who is powerful enough to save us from complete annihilation. The obvious objection is that, on the face of it, more power would seem necessary to overcome the absoluteness of death than to overcome most earthly evils. Both the immediate and the reflective response to this objection can only be that we are here confronted with an irreducible and insuperable mystery.

Every reflection upon God must at some point take refuge in "mystery," but much depends on where the mystery is located. The traditional view, positing an omnipotent God, must say that it is a mystery why such an all-good God does not use his power to alleviate suffering and obviate death. My view, positing a good but finite God, must say that it is mystery how God's power is insufficient to protect us from suffering and death but sufficient to save us from total annihilation. That God does *not* protect us from suffering and death is a matter of indubitable experience; that he *may* save us from annihilation is a matter of faith. On this there is no significant disagreement. What is in dispute is the kind of God who is *credible*. The traditional God, in possession of an eternally fulfilled and self-sufficient life, desires out of his goodness to share this life with his creatures and freely opts to do so by submitting them to suffering and death. A God understood along the lines suggested in this essay would be one whose ever developing life, characterized by an intrinsic desire *and* need to share this life, slowly and processively brings forth diverse and distinct expressions of the divine life. At a particular stage in this process there is realized a mode of life that is preciously close but still immeasurably distant from the center of the divine life. God, desiring a more intimate union with those individual bearers of this mode of life, chooses to bring this union about in the *only* way possible by submitting himself and them to the transformative experiences of suffering and death. Thus, in a life process that is everlastingly bringing forth new and richer modes of life by means of transformation of itself, death may be a necessary characteristic, both in the divine and nondivine modes of the process. If death, proportional to the mode of life, is the *only* means by which *new* life can come forth, whether in God or his creatures, then the goodness of God is in no way compromised by the suffering and death which these creatures must endure and which in some way are shared by God himself. This does not remove the mystery, but it does relocate it to the center of the divine life itself.

PART II

Personal Immortality: Desirability and Efficacy

CHAPTER 7

Immortality: Hope or Hindrance?

> If the hope we have learned to repose in Christ
> belongs to this world only, then we are unhappy
> beyond all other men.
> — 1 Corinthians 15:19

> Looking down into my father's
> dead face
> for the last time
> my mother said without
> tears, without smiles
> without regrets
> but with *civility*
> "Good night, Willie Lee, I'll see you
> in the morning."
> — Alice Walker
> "Good night Willie Lee,
> I'll See You in the Morning"

In recent years philosophers and theologians have done dying to death, and death to nowhere in particular after the occurrence of that catastrophic event. "Whether we are to live in a future state," Bishop Joseph Butler said some two hundred and fifty years ago, "as it is the most important question which can be asked, so it is the most intelligible one which can be expressed in language."[1] A few contemporary thinkers consider immortality an important question; none to my knowledge argues that it is the "most intelligible." Among the wider population, in America at least, the majority that claim to believe in immortality seem to consider that belief peripheral to faith and life. Whether we are to live in a future state seems to have become a question intellectually and existentially irrelevant.[2] It is surely "an undeniable fact," as Hans Jonas has noted, "that the modern temper is uncongenial to the idea of immortality."[3] When faced with the direct question, "Do you believe in a life after death?" comments Hans Küng, "even theologians are embarrassed."[4] Something of this embarrassment is reflected in an essay by the Roman Catholic thinker Joseph Blenkinsopp, who, after acknowledging that "it is no longer easy to speak both theologically and honestly about life after death," goes on to say that "the subject conveys at least for the developed con-

165

sciousness of Western man, a sense of unreality and an absence of existential concern."[5] The process theologian Schubert M. Ogden goes further: "What I must refuse to accept, precisely as a Christian theologian, is that belief in our subjective existence after death is in some way a necessary article of Christian belief."[6]

Within the contemporary intellectual and cultural ambience, then, the most judicious response to the immortality question would appear to be silence. "If one is asked abruptly," says William Earnest Hocking, "'What do you think about death? or of the immortality of man? or of the total sense of life?' assuredly one's first impulse is silence."[7] And in the famous text with which Ludwig Wittgenstein closes his *Tractatus,* we are admonished: "What we cannot speak about we must pass over in silence."[8] Add to all of this the observation of Jonas that "in more than two thousand years probably everything has been said there is to say" (*PL,* 263), coupled with the comment of Hocking that "there is an aroma of triviality attending most argument about immortality" (*MI,* 20), and the case for silence seems almost ironclad.

Almost—but not quite. The question still touches too many open wounds, superficially covered over by intellectual and emotional band-aids, to allow us the luxury of total exclusion from our reflections. What some of these wounds are will become evident later in this chapter, but one "topical" comment is perhaps in order at this point. The fierce resurgence of uncritical religious emotivism, East and West, from the relatively benign to the positively destructive, from evangelicals and charismatics to theological terrorists and mind-destroying cults—such phenomena, as a minimum, indicate the continued presence of a need for meaning that is not being met. Even if it were evident that these movements are but manifestations of atavistic or primitive longing, of infantile nostalgia, of a "failure of nerve," all attached to an illusionary or delusionary desire and hope for another life, it would still be worthwhile to explore such desire and hope.

But strikingly, in the last two decades it has become increasingly evident that we are no more confident of and satisfied with our simplistic psychological and sociological explanations for these human activities than we are with simplistic theological explanations. The need to move beyond such inadequate accounts of the human condition is as important as it is evident. Even if we cannot at this stage of human history make any significant new movements, it might still be helpful to understand why we cannot. Reflection upon and clarification of the possibilities available to us, at least, would seem to be worthy of consideration. "Thus," as Jonas states, "an examination at this hour will be as much an examination of ourselves as an examination of the issue of immortality; and even if it should throw no new light on the latter . . . it may yet throw some light on the present state of our mortal condition" (*PL,* 263).

PRAGMATISM AND FAITH

It was Kant, along with Hume, who initiated a decisive shift within Western culture in the approach to the questions of God, freedom, and immortality. Kant tells us that he "found it necessary to deny *knowledge,* in order to make room for *faith.*" For the more positivistically minded, the Kantian exclusion of God, freedom, and immortality from the hallowed halls of science radically diminished the importance of such concerns and confined them to the realms of subjectivity and emotion. Others, those religiously inclined, saw in the Kantian critique what Kant evidently intended—a way of saving religion without placing it in fruitless competition with science. The long, complex, and often contentious history of the post-Kantian dispute concerning science and religion is not of concern here except to locate my pragmatic perspective. I believe it defensible to place pragmatism within the broad Kantian tradition insofar as it rejects all claims to absolute certainty or absolute knowledge[9] but does not exclude, indeed insists upon, the necessity of faith. It is important to recall the processive world being assumed, for faith within such a world takes on a more crucial role than does faith within a world whose structure and values are already essentially realized. Faith within a world-in-process is not merely a guess as to the way things are that are not yet known; rather, it is a creative process playing a role in the very making of the world—in its structure, goals, and values. While enhancing the importance of faith, a processive world also increases the risk, personal and collective, that accompanies all beliefs or faiths.[10]

It goes without saying that from the pragmatic perspective, no faith, including the Christian faith, is exempt from these faith conditions. The need for a reflective or critical faith has been present since well before the time of early Christianity; a segment of the Christian community (as well as of other religious communities) has always felt obliged to reconcile the best fruits of secular culture and experience with its beliefs and faith.[11] That such reconciliation remains a necessity is widely recognized. Less widely acknowledged, however, is that the efforts to bring Christianity or any other religion into harmony with contemporary thinking, experience, and sensibility is immeasurably more complicated and religiously dangerous than were earlier efforts. If we are to avoid "bad faith" or self-deception, we cannot pursue critical inquiry protected by the absolute assurance that the beliefs investigated will remain fundamentally unchanged or even that they will survive such inquiry.[12] The more conservative members of religious communities—Christian and other—have always been highly sensitive to the threat that critical inquiry poses to traditional doctrines, and they have no difficulty in marshaling mountains of data in support of their views. It is disingenuous, therefore, to pretend that critical reflection upon one's faith can serve only to deepen and refine it. If one is asked, "Can you assure me that if I subject my belief in the resurrection and eternal life—beliefs that are the life-blood of my spirit and the ground of meaning in my life—to the withering gaze of critical consciousness, I will not have my faith demolished?" the only honest response must be No! Would any sane believer, then, run such a risk? Only if he or she also believes that any faith that cannot stand the most severe critical scrutiny is not worthy of a human being.

The advantages for the purposes of a consistent immortality belief offered by some mode of classical metaphysics must be readily conceded. It was noted above that a mind/body dualism is most congenial to and consistent with the *possibility* of immortality. Similarly, a metaphysical dualism that posits an essential bifurcation between the temporal and the eternal has relatively little difficulty in showing that belief in immortality is worthwhile, significant, and reasonable—in short, desirable. "This world," the temporal world, is a kind of moral arena within which we are given the opportunity to prove by the moral quality of our lives that we merit union with the Eternal. The many and varied modes of this view, in their diverse Eastern and Western forms, share the judgment that the Eternal is alone that which gives value and meaning. The temporal is of value only insofar as it is a reflection of or participation in the Eternal or a stepping-stone to this higher reality. The purpose of "this world," therefore, is to give us an opportunity of so living that we are liberated from it. The *meaning* of this world is merely located in the "other" world.

Given such a world view, it makes sense to govern and direct our lives on the basis or belief in immortality. This belief gives us our fundamental goal and meaning, as well as our basic moral criterion: whatever contributes to the saving of my soul is good; whatever obstructs this salvation is bad. Of course, there are both crude and sophisticated versions of such a belief structure. I have no intention of patronizing this world view, nor of pretending that I have disproved or that anyone can disprove it. It is a long, honorable, and in many respects immeasurably rich tradition, and I firmly believe that it incorporates insights and qualities that can be ignored by any alternative world view only at the peril of trivialization. It would be rash as well as potentially false to claim that the world view presented here adequately achieves such incorporation. The most that can be claimed is that this is the intention; it will remain more implicit than explicit and for the most part unrealized in what follows.

Recall that the task set for this essay is to determine whether a belief in immortality is "reasonable," given the assumptions of pragmatism's world view. It should be noted that there is no pretense of arguing for the stronger hypothesis that immortality belief is the only "reasonable," life-enhancing, meaning-giving belief. I propose a much weaker hypothesis for exploration: namely, that such belief is *a* reasonable or plausible one. To support this hypothesis, it will be necessary to show not only that immortality belief is not an obstacle to life-affirmation but that it contributes, or at least has the possibility of contributing, distinctive insights and qualities to human life.

But how does a pragmatist go about showing that either this or any other belief is a worthy one? The short answer, as already given, is one must observe whether the experiential consequences and quality of life that follow from this belief are worthy. Recall the key points made in the Introduction concerning pragmatic evaluation. First, all conclusions of any argument are for the pragmatist always tentative and subject to modification or jettisoning in the light of new evidence. Second, a pragmatic evaluation of a question such as the one under consideration must be as responsive as possible to the overwhelming mass of cumulative experience; hence, it must be responsive to the data from all areas of experience as well as from history and the sciences. Third, pragmatism is not restricted to description—even assuming that such description could be more complete than it ever is—since it also includes a speculative or extrapolative component whereby it suggests possibilities for a future course of action. Put simply, on the basis of the way things are and have been, the pragmatist ventures a guess as to how they might be.

IMMORTALITY: ITS DESIRABILITY

Is immortality desirable? The words can be viewed as two different questions, distinct though not completely separate. The first addresses itself to the "state of immortality" and asks whether it is desirable. Everything here depends on so describing this state that our response would be, "Whether or not such a state is possible, I do not know, but I would like it to be." Few would dispute that a life from which disease had been banished is desirable, and that is a life both imaginable and reasonably possible, if not probable, in the future. But what about a life from which death has been banished, an unending, limitless life?

One of the most repugnant pictures of such interminable life is found in *Gulliver's Travels*.[13] While visiting the *Luggnuggians,* Gulliver is asked if he has yet seen any "*Struldbruggs,* or *Immortals.*" He is informed that "these Productions were not peculiar to any family, but a mere Effect of Chance." Gulliver's initial enthusiasm for immortality is quickly extinguished once the lives of those "Immortals" is described and observed: "They commonly acted like Mortals, till about Thirty Years old, after which by Degrees they grew melancholy and dejected, increasing in both till they came to Fourscore." Lacking any significant memory and devoid of curiosity, they were also physically monstrous: "Besides the usual Deformities in extreme old age, they acquired an additional Ghastliness in Proportion to their Number of Years, which is not to be described." Little wonder, then, that Gulliver's "keen Appetite for Perpetuity of Life was much abated."

The British analytical philosopher Bernard Williams presents us with an equally depressing though less graphic picture of life without death in his oft-cited essay, "The Makropulos case: reflections on the tedium of immortality."[14] Williams argues that "death is not necessarily an evil." Death can be a misfortune; hence, we are justified in our anti-Lucretian hope for a longer rather than a shorter life. But does it follow that we are "committed to wanting to be immortal?" No, for an endless life would be endlessly boring. Williams cites the case of Elina Makropulos, a character in a play by Karel Čapek. In the sixteenth century, she had received an elixir of life from her father, a court physician.

> At the time of the action she is aged 342. Her unending life has come to a state of boredom, indifference and coldness. Everything is joyless: "in the end it is the same," she says, "singing and silence." She refuses to take the elixir again; she dies; and the formula is deliberately destroyed by a young woman among the protests of some older men. (*PS*, 82)

Boredom, Williams argues, is not a contingent fact of life for Elina Makropulos but is inseparable from an endless human life. He considers several alternative models to that of Elina—among them "serial and disjoint lives" and "an after-life sufficiently unlike this life"—but finds no convincing ground for excluding boredom: "Nothing less will do for eternity than something that makes boredom *unthinkable*." This question of how "thinkable" a future life must be in order to be credible is crucial and must eventually be considered. For the moment, let me simply underline the "profound difficulty," noted by Williams, "of providing any model of an unending, supposedly satisfying, state or activity which would not rightly prove boring to anyone who remained conscious of himself and who had acquired a character, interests, tastes and impatience in the course of living, already, a finite life" (*PS*, 94–95).

Though James would reach, or at least incline toward, a different conclusion concerning immortality, he passionately described the boredom and longing to escape that overcome us when confronted with "the painting of any paradise or utopia, in heaven or on earth."

> The white-robed harp-playing heaven of our sabbath-schools and the ladylike tea-table elysium represented in Mr. Spencer's *Data of Ethics,* as the final consummation of progress, are exactly on a par in this respect—lubberlands, pure and simple, one and all. We look upon them from this delicious mess of insanities and realities, strivings and deadnesses, hopes and fears, agonies and exultations, which forms our present state, and *tedium vitae* is the only sentiment they awaken in our breasts. To our crepuscular natures, born for the conflict, the Rembrandtesque moral chiaroscuro, the shifting struggle of the sunbeam in the gloom, such pictures of light upon light are vacuous and expressionless, and neither to be enjoyed or understood. If *this* be the fruit of the victory, we say; if the generations of mankind suffered and laid down their lives; if the prophets confessed and martyrs sang in the fire, and all the sacred tears were shed for no other end than that a race of creatures of such unex-

ampled insipidity should succeed, and protract *in saecula saeculorum* their contented and inoffensive lives,—why, at such a rate, better lose than win the battle, or at all events better ring down the curtain before the last act of the play, so that a business that began so importantly may be saved from so singularly flat a winding-up. (*WB*, 130)

Depressing descriptions of a future life, as James makes clear, are not confined to a future life in another world; Spencer's evolutionary Elysium has all the tediousness of Milton's regained paradise. This raises the question of whether hope for a future life is possible only if we can describe it in detail. Perhaps not. But I think that those who believe in such a life must at least offer a rough sketch of what it ought to involve. In the next chapter, I will suggest by way of extrapolation some characteristics of a "desirable" state of immortality.

First, however, I would like to consider a more important meaning of the question: Is immortality desirable? This second meaning focuses on the here and now, and asks whether belief in immortality is worthy of the best in human beings. Is this belief life-enhancing? Does it give depth, scope, and meaning to human existence? Does it, or at least can it, release or create possibilities that otherwise would be lost or diminished? In short, is belief in immortality energizing or deenergizing? An adequate response must show that not only is such belief not an obstacle to life-affirmation but that it does (or can) contribute distinctive insights and qualities to human life.

Corliss Lamont has stated: "The general pragmatic effects, for good or ill, of belief in a future existence are writ large in the history of the race, whether we examine the practices of ancient tribes or modern civilized nations."[15] Because these effects are *both* good *and* bad, and because they are so numerous and complex, any simple judgment based on the consequences is precluded. Yet individually and collectively, we do take positions on questions such as immortality, and in the absence of anything approaching mathematical proof. There remains a division on the worth of belief in immortality or in God because to this point in human history the data embody considerable ambiguity. Of course, this itself is a judgment on which individual pragmatists disagree. Dewey saw little or no ambiguity; the evidence, he increasingly came to hold, pointed to the need to rid ourselves of life-obstructing religious beliefs. James, on the other hand, read the cumulative record of human experience differently and continued to the end to see positive possibilities in these beliefs.

Whether belief in immortality has a future is at best debatable. We can be reasonably sure, however, that unless an effort is made to confront the charge that it is antilife, it will continue only as a nostalgic or superstitious relic even among those who give it nominal consent. Note that I say "confront," not "refute," for the scope and depth of this charge are such that at best it might be neutralized, thereby leaving the door open for the entry of more positive possibilities. There are Marxian, Freudian, existentialist, humanist, and pragmatic expressions of the charge that belief in immortality is both essentially and historically destructive of the fullness of life. Whatever their differences, all such expressions view this belief as escapist, as a betrayal of the earth, and as sapping the human community of energies needed for the continuing struggle to ameliorate the evils attending the human condition and to create new potential for human development. "Of belief in immortality," Dewey states, "more than any other element of historic religions it holds good, I believe, that 'religion is the opium of the peoples'" (*II,* xiii).

BELIEF AND COUNTERBELIEF—AN EXISTENTIAL DIALECTIC

An acceptable mode of immortality belief cannot be simply and unequivocally opposed to its counterbelief. Abstractly or conceptually they are opposed—either we are immortal or we are not—but what we must try to describe is an existential situation that eludes such a conceptualistic either/or.[16] Can those different but not necessarily contradictory ways of thinking and believing be located within the same individual? If we take "believing" and "thinking" existentially, as modes of life rather than as abstract systems of concepts, I think they can. Indeed, I wish to suggest that this is increasingly the case for reflective believers—whether in God or in humanity. Abstractly, belief and doubt exclude each other; concretely, they coexist in an ever changing existential dialectic.[17]

Let me try to relate this to the belief in personal immortality. In his readable and suggestive book *Death and Beyond,* Andrew Greeley concludes that "one must choose between meaning and absurdity."[18] Now for many, perhaps most, people this is an understandable choice, but for others it does not appear to be so. There are those who experience meaning and absurdity not as things that one chooses but as structural characteristics of the human condition that should be freely affirmed and acknowledged. Meaning and absurdity do not exclude each other but confront us inseparably bound up with each other. The question is this: is it possible to "live" a life suffused by *both* meaning *and* absurdity? May it not be the task, if not the destiny, of at least some to refuse the dichotomy?[19] The hope is that a richer mode of human life might thus emerge—a mode which, though it cannot yet be conceived and is at most vaguely felt, can be hoped and worked for.[20]

Just as meaning and absurdity resist conceptual reconciliation, so too do immortality and tragedy. Again we confront an abstract either/or. Either we are immortal and the human situation is not tragic, or it is tragic because we are not immortal. Thus Julius Seelye Bixler sees the alternative as "either belief in immortality or a more tragic view of life."[21] Now it may be that the denial of immortality involves a *more* tragic view of life than its affirmation, but I would insist that such affirmation *ought not* to be a means for avoiding the essentially tragic dimension of human life.[22] This is perhaps the most sensitive aspect of the immortality question for anyone attempting to affirm personal immortality while remaining faithful to the human condition in some of its deepest and most serious features. Modern and contemporary experience have intensified the tragic aspect. Those who have lived constructively and creatively with a conscious belief in the eventual annihilation not only of themselves and those they personally loved but of all human beings have displayed a profound and admirable courage. Even if we were able to show that no one has lived or is able to live with the belief in such a total annihilation—that in spite of their manifest beliefs, they have been motivated by surrogate immortality beliefs such as immortality through fame or posterity—even so, there is no doubt that they have lived with the acceptance of the cessation of their own personal mode of being. At the very least, those who do not share their belief cannot but be edified by their dedicated disinterestedness. But this is not enough; a defensible belief in immortality will share the tragic experience occasioned by the reality of death. Belief in immortality without tragedy risks moral cowardice.

Many charge—and I find it unsettling—that the Christian faith in resurrection or eternal life manifests a "failure of nerve." Because of metaphysical and moral cowardice, it is alleged, Christians lack the courage to face the fact and finality of death; they palliate the pain of finitude by sugarcoating it with an illusory doctrine of future life. Let me say at once that I am unaware of any completely satisfying response to this charge, and the present effort is no exception. Without a response, however, Christianity will become either a revered relic of the past or an emotional crutch in the present. One unsatisfactory response, which ironically draws upon twentieth-century critiques of attempts to establish absolute certainty, is to point out that since immortality is impossible to prove or disprove, we are free to believe in it. It is naive to suggest that we can dismiss Marxian, Nietzschean, Freudian, and allied critiques because they have not produced watertight arguments proving the nonexistence of God or the impossibility of immortality. We are not, of course, obliged to accept slavishly the conclusions of these critiques, but we cannot use our faith to shield us from those features of the human condition that many serious and sensitive contemporary thinkers and artists have brilliantly and disturbingly illuminated. Hence, it is not enough to say that while I believe in a future or new life, I acknowledge the abstract possibility that this belief may be an illusion. The possibility of illusion must be existential, lived, experiential. Instead of being juxtaposed, it must permeate belief in immortality. But even this is not enough. The immortality-believer may not escape or be excused from confrontation with the reality of finitude and death. Hans Jonas, in describing the "modern temper," says: "We do not wish to forgo the pang and poignancy of finitude; we insist on facing nothingness and having the strength to live with it" (*PL,* 267–68). Lael Wertenbaker, in describing how her husband faced death, recalls a line from Jean Giraudoux's *Amphitryon 38* in which Jupiter says of the gods: "But we miss something, Mercury—the poignance of the transient—the intimation of mortality—that sweet sadness of grasping at something you cannot hold."[23]

It may be a combination of monumental self-deception, sloppy sentimentality, and philosophical absurdity to claim that one can simultaneously believe in immortality or resurrection and still experience the "pang and poignancy of finitude," "the poignance of the transient." The issue cannot be engaged if we remain at the psychological level, however, for the very belief in immortality may give rise to an intemperate and unworthy fear of death.[24] The task is to show with some reasonable consistency that belief in immortality neither avoids the pain of finitude nor undialectically juxtaposes two antithetical experiences.[25] There is no question here of constructing a conceptual model in which these two experiences are perfectly reconciled. At the same time we must strive to indicate how they might be in a dialectical relationship that transforms but does not obliterate the reality of both experiences. Recall that the question posed from the outset is whether it is possible to believe in immortality or resurrection while participating in that contemporary sensibility which is to such a great extent the consequence of the "death of God" and the denial of personal immortality. The task is to suggest how the experiences of a contemporary believer in and a contemporary denier of immortality might *significantly* overlap. It is important to avoid both making the distance between the two so great that their sharing is peripheral and superficial, and affirming a similarity so close that, pragmatically, there is no difference between them.

What follows are notes toward the construction of a more developed though never final conceptual model. I begin by drawing directly on William James, on whose work my own reflections are to a great extent a gloss. More important, in his person and in his philosophy, James embodied an uneasy tension between theism and humanism, a tension still felt by those striving to be faithful to both these traditions.

Consider two texts from James:

> Where God is, tragedy is only provisional and partial, and shipwreck and dissolution are not the absolutely final things. (*VRE*, 407)

> Pluralism . . . is neither optimistic nor pessimistic, but *melioristic,* rather. The world, it thinks, *may* be saved, *on condition that its parts do their best.* But shipwreck in detail, or even on the whole, is among the open possibilities. (*SPP,* 73)

When reflecting on these texts, it is important to recall James's metaphysical presuppositions. We live in a processive-relational world, an "unfinished universe," a "world in the making." As "personal centres of energy," we are related to a wider, more encompassing processive field of energy by which we live and to whose reality we contribute through our creative activities. Finally, as a matter of belief—or "over-belief," as James would call it—we may designate the wider reality that is present to us as "God." In the two texts under consideration, we seem at first to have two conflicting views concerning tragedy: the first sees tragedy as "only provisional and partial"; the second affirms the possibility of total tragedy. The first rejects the finality of "shipwreck"; the second does not. An apparently simple way of removing inconsistency between the texts is to see the first as an expression of belief or faith, the second as a philosophical statement. Though not completely inaccurate, such an interpretation is more misleading than helpful, however, since James held that the base of every philosophy is an act of faith.

How then might these two texts be reconciled so that they are seen as expressing a healthy and creative tension rather than either an irrational opposition or a mere existential juxtaposition? The key, I believe, rests in James's own designation of his pragmatic-pluralistic philosophy as "melioristic" rather than "optimistic" or "pessimistic." Describing these viewpoints in terms of world salvation, "optimism" maintains that the world is already saved; "pessimism," that the world is not and cannot be saved; and "meliorism," or "pragmatism," that the world *may* be saved. It can be argued that the faith of the meliorist or pragmatist, though existentially and conceptually distinct from that of either the optimist or the pessimist, shares experiences with both of them.

Let us first compare the pragmatist and the pessimist. To begin with, it is important to stress that in comparing the view that the world may be saved with the view that it cannot, we are making a comparison not between belief and unbelief but between two belief or faith structures. A crucial presupposition here is that the human situation is characterized by metaphysical ambiguity. In their fundamental faith both the pessimist and the pragmatist commit themselves to an interpretation of this ambiguity. When the pragmatist believes that "where God is, tragedy is only provisional and partial," he neither has nor believes that he has removed the ambiguous character from the existential situation. Unless he continues to share certain experiences with the pessimist, he cannot simultaneously believe in the nonfinality of tragedy while possessing a lived awareness of its possible finality.

Now this is more than an abstract consideration of two possibilities. The pragmatist believes that tragedy is only provisional and hence commits himself—stakes his life, as it were—on this belief. As a belief, however, it offers no guarantee and involves profound risk. More important for my purpose, it does not obliterate those experiences that are shared with the pessimist and that give rise to the awareness that "shipwreck in detail, or even on the whole, is among the open possibilities." The pragmatist and pessimist have overlapping experiences but differ profoundly in interpreting many of the data of these experiences. The pragmatist, because of an essential characteristic of his faith, can claim neither to have resolved the pessimist's questions or problems nor to have eliminated those experiences that give rise to the pessimist's faith. The pragmatist who allowed his faith to dilute or mask such experiences and the ever present threat of nihilism they embody would be guilty of "bad faith." Unless the abyss brought to consciousness in contemporary thought and experience remains a constant possibility, faith is an escape and a means to a *superficial* consolation.

In the concluding chapter of *Pragmatism,* James contrasts the faith of "religious optimism" with that of his own pragmatism. He makes it quite clear that the faith to which at least some pragmatists give assent is not escapist, is not such that the seriousness and sorrows of human life are hidden or attenuated.

> May not religious optimism be too idyllic? Must *all* be saved? Is *no* price to be paid for the work of salvation? Is the last word sweet? Is all "yes, yes" in the universe? Doesn't the fact of "no" stand at the very core of life? Doesn't the very "seriousness" that we attribute to life mean that ineluctable noes and losses form a part of it, that there are genuine sacrifices somewhere, and that something permanently drastic and bitter always remains at the bottom of its cup? (*P,* 141)

James goes on to say that he is "willing to take the universe to be really dangerous and adventurous, without therefore backing out and crying 'no play.'" And then in lines that can be related directly, I believe, to the question of personal immortality, he says, "I am willing that there should be real losses and real losers . . . even tho the lost element might be one's self." Finally, James maintains that the "genuine pragmatist . . . is willing to live on a scheme of uncertified possibilities which he trusts; willing to pay with his own person, if need be, for the realization of the ideals which he frames" (*P,* 142–43).

James insists that the negative and painful features of human experience are constituents of the world process; they are not removed by the salvation process, though we can believe that they are being transformed thereby. Further, while not excluding the possibility of a personal share in the fruits of this work, it does not make such reward a condition of our participation. Paradoxically, only by attending to the tasks at hand "for their own sakes" can we legitimately hope for the *gift* of sharing in whatever future life might result. A model of personal immortality developed along these lines would go a long way toward meeting objections that such belief is both escapist and egotistic. A sketch of such a model will be presented in the next chapter. First, however, it will be useful to amplify the existential dialectic related to belief in personal immortality by considering several thinkers who are highly critical of any such belief.

NIETZSCHE: IMMORTALITY BELIEF AS ANTILIFE

Despite an occasional shrillness, it is Friedrich Nietzsche who presents us with the most searing and brutal critique of God, religion, and immortality. It is not a critique that can be refuted or gone around. Whether it can be gone through without consuming those who dare the journey remains an open question. What emerges from Nietzsche's critique is not an abstract question but a Nietzschean one—existential and experimental—one that must be lived rather than merely conceptualized and, short of the grave or perhaps madness, admits of no *final* resting place or answer.

It is a commonplace among the more perceptive commentators to note that there is no shortcut to Nietzsche's thought. Excerpts can be both brilliant and trivial when removed from Nietzsche's vital and experimental context. It might be said that Nietzsche proves nothing but illuminates everything. Though something of an overstatement, the quip does caution us against seeking proofs or arguments in the usual form and, finding none, assuming that nothing of worth has been said.[26] What is it, then, that Nietzsche has illuminated? Nothing less than the human situation loosed from both its philosophical and religious underpinnings. Nietzsche's notorious parable of the "death of God" signals the collapse of Western civilization and the death of humanity as it has hitherto been and been known to itself. Nevertheless Nietzsche refuses to accept nihilism as the last word. Nihilism, on pain of self-deception, must be gone through; but, at the risk of self-dissolution, we must endeavor to go beyond it. In his doctrines of will to power, revaluation, the overman, and eternal recurrence, Nietzsche strives to avoid the abyss.

The extent to which he succeeded and/or failed is not my concern here. Suffice it for my purposes to say that his is perhaps the most radical effort ever made to live in a totally immanental world. God, the immortal soul, platonic forms, eternal values, absolute unchanging essences, immutable scientific laws—all are for Nietzsche cowardly attempts to persuade ourselves that we live in a rational, purposeful, meaningful world. More important, such beliefs serve to obstruct the emergence of the only life worthy of human beings—one in which we courageously accept responsibility for the creation of our values and ourselves. For Nietzsche, the only truly authentic life is one strong enough to create meaning in a fundamentally meaningless world. To place our faith and hope in any kind of transcendent reality is to trade our human birthright for a mess of otherwordly pottage. Inasmuch as there is no "beyond," any transcendent belief is an expression of the worst and most truly destructive mode of nihilism. In *The Antichrist,* written in the last year of his sane life, Nietzsche expresses his view trenchantly and powerfully:

> When one places life's center of gravity not in life but in the "beyond"—*in nothingness*—one deprives life of its center of gravity altogether. The great lie of personal immortality destroys all reason, everything natural in the instincts—whatever in the instincts is beneficent and life-promoting or guarantees a future now arouses mistrust. To live so, that there is no longer any *sense* in living, *that* now becomes the "sense" of life. Why communal sense, why any further gratitude for descent and ancestors, why cooperate, trust, promote, and envisage any common welfare?[27]

Nietzsche, then, wishes to overcome nihilism but insists that this can be done only in a highly qualified sense.[28] He tells us that nihilism is *ambiguous,* manifesting itself in *active* and *passive* modes. It is the latter, represented by all "otherworldly" philosophies and religions, that he denounces in such passionate terms and describes as "decline and recession of the power of the spirit." "*Active* nihilism," on the other hand, is celebrated and pursued, for it is "a sign of increased power of the spirit."[29] The neatness of this distinction, however, masks the depths and terrors of nihilism which Nietzsche experienced in his own life and which he saw as the forthcoming fate of humanity.[30] He did not take lightly, therefore, the "death of God," and some of his strongest criticism was directed against "those who do not believe in God," since they have not faced up to the radically threatening consequences of the loss of religious belief. Nietzsche feared that when the generality of human beings became fully conscious of the collapse of the foundations of their individual and cultural lives, they would lose all zest for living. This, then, is the existential paradox manifest in the "death of God": We live in a world *without* a goal, purpose, or meaning, but we cannot *live* without a goal, purpose, or meaning. In other terms, the task Nietzsche sets himself is to evoke "hope" in a world that is essentially "hopeless," to say "yes" to life in the face of the pervasive threat and inevitable realization of "nothingness."

However elusive their meaning and whatever the conceptual difficulties to which they give rise, Nietzsche intends his doctrines of "the overman" and "eternal recurrence" to be life-affirming. The overman must replace God as the ground of meaning and hope: "The overman is the meaning of the earth. Let your will say: the overman *shall be* the meaning of the earth! I beseech you, my brothers, *remain faithful to the earth,* and do not believe those who speak to you of otherworldly hopes."[31] The overman will be the one (or ones) strong enough to accept the responsibility for legislating values, a role previously assigned to God. In addition, the overman will be strong enough to make of the doctrine of eternal recurrence not an abstract affirmation but a lived affirmation. The affirmation and experience of eternal recurrence will characterize the inner structure of the overman's being.[32] Whatever else it might connote—and the range and diversity of interpretations suggests that it connotes much more—the doctrine of eternal recurrence was *experienced* by Nietzsche as his most radical affirmation of the worth of life. I would note only two features of this affirmation. First, against the threat of all escapist eternalisms and narrow temporal hedonisms, he insists upon an eternity that is not opposed to or separable from time but is the depth of time.[33] Each temporal moment has an eternal depth that lends to this life a significance denied by the eternalist and missed by the hedonist.[34] A second and perhaps more crucial aspect of the doctrine of eternal recurrence is that it expresses Nietzsche's effort to refuse to mask—or to hold out any hope for removing—the suffering and terror that are permanent and inevitable characteristics of life, and still say a joyful "yes" to this life.[35] For Nietzsche, it is the belief in eternal recurrence that makes tolerable, for those who have the spiritual strength, an intolerable situation. It does so by testing the extent to which they really affirm life. Only those who can love life with all its pain and meaninglessness are true lovers of life and not escapists into some illusory world.

There is perhaps no one today who could accept literally Nietzsche's doctrines of the overman and eternal recurrence. Nevertheless, anyone who seriously reflects on the questions with which they are concerned cannot, or at least ought not, avoid them—particularly anyone sympathetic to the perspective presented in this essay. Those dimensions of human reality so dramatically described by Nietzsche cannot be avoided in experience, and no attempt should be made to avoid them in thought.

AMELIORATION: YES! SALVATION: NO!

Over twenty years ago, in an essay entitled "The American Angle of Vision," John J. McDermott wrote: "Over against the doctrine of obsolescence in which the history of man waits patiently for a paradisiacal *Deus ex machina,* the American temper points to a temporalized eschatology in which the Spirit manifests itself generation by generation and all counts to the end."[36] In a subsequent series of perceptive and provocative essays, McDermott has developed, directly and indirectly, the notion of a "temporalized eschatology."[37] Increasingly, his position tends to exclude belief in God and immortality. Since we share so many metaphysical and epistemological assumptions, and since my own reflections have been so deeply influenced by him, it is important to call attention to the divergence between us on the question of God and immortality.

The simplest way to describe the difference might be to say that on this question McDermott's tilt is Deweyan, whereas mine is Jamesian. While an epistemological agnosticism characterizes both perspectives, *belief* in God and immortality is viewed more sympathetically by one than by the other. Dewey felt that religious experience—in any way involving God and immortality, at least—had for the most part exhausted itself, while James to the end of his life viewed the positive possibilities of religious experience as indispensable for the growth and development of the human community. Despite the fact that McDermott is one of the most insightful and imaginative contemporary interpreters of James, I read him as increasingly siding with Dewey as regards religious experience. McDermott does not absolutely rule out the possibility of God and immortality, of course, but he effectively does so for the purposes of his reflective existential life. For him, this belief is no longer, in James's sense, a "live hypothesis": that is, "one which appeals as a real possibility to him" (*WB,* 14). If McDermott has not totally excluded belief in God and immortality from his reflections, he has most certainly removed it from the vital center to the periphery of his reflective life. In so doing, I think that he has sharpened and deepened the force and bite of his positive insights. This is most in evidence in his essay "The

Inevitability of Our Own Death: The Celebration of Time as a Prelude to Disaster" (*SE,* 157–68). While McDermott disavows any "final knowledge" concerning immortality claims, the tone of the essay clearly diminishes the seriousness and viability of any and all such claims. We are told that "over-belief in some form of salvation or immortality" is "a major way in which many persons shun the trauma of death." Further, "many of us cling to the existence of one or more of these solutions, as a redoubt, a trump card or a last-minute reprieve from the overwhelming evidence that we are terminal" (*SE,* 162).

McDermott is underlining that self-deception which Marx, Nietzsche, Freud, and others have maintained is at the root of all belief in God and immortality. I will touch upon this a bit more fully later, but the obvious question I will raise then, as I raise it now, is whether this is the whole story—has the entirety of religious experience been accounted for by the revelation that self-deception is perhaps to some degree a characteristic of all religious experience? First, however, I would like to consider a few more aspects of McDermott's doctrine in order to illuminate a hypothesis that I consider real and formidable but, as the fundamental thrust of this essay indicates, not fully persuasive.

I wish to stress at the outset the extent to which I share with McDermott a Jamesian view of the self, a self which, in McDermott's words, "is self-creating in its transactions with the environment" (*SE,* 45), and which "risks belief in hypotheses so as to elicit data unavailable were an agnostic position adopted" (*SE,* 49). Where our perspectives diverge is in the scope of the "environment" and the range of available "data." In the chapters "James: Full Self and Wider Fields" and "James: Self and God," I have argued, with James, the plausibility of believing that we are continuous "with a wider self from which saving experiences flow in" (*PU,* 139). McDermott, on the other hand, with Dewey, "acknowledges no forces at work, neither Dionysian nor Divine, other than the constitutive transactions of human life with the affairs of nature and the world" (*SE,* 167). Both hypotheses presuppose experience as transactional, but one suggests a personal transcendent pole, while the other effectively denies it.

The divergence is indicated by the different interpretation or emphasis that McDermott and I would give to the following text of James:

> If we survey the field of history and ask what feature all great periods of revival, of expansion of the human mind, display in common, we shall find, I think, simply this: that each and all of them have said to the human being, "The inmost nature of reality is congenial to *powers* which you possess." (*WB,* 73)

McDermott comments: "In this text of James, the fundamental dialectic of our situation is laid bare in one trenchant sentence. Reality has its givenness, its obduracy, its nature" (*SE,* 106). To which I would add: its mystery and more encompassing dimensions, which possibly are manifestations of a creative principle struggling to incarnate itself and in part dependent upon us to do so. I share with McDermott his desire to affirm a human future that "does not await some natural or divine *deus ex machina*" (*SE*, 96). Whether it is possible to construct a God-hypothesis that allows for and indeed necessitates human effort is the burden of the previous chapter. I have repeatedly maintained that the possibility of any immortality belief depends on the plausibility of such a God-hypothesis. It is my sympathy for this hypothesis that leads me to diverge from McDermott on the meaning of the future, time, and salvation.

In the late 1960s—the era of the "counterculture"—the young were often said to fear that they had no future. To the extent that this was true, perhaps the young were going proxy for all those who, in the wake of the searing modern critiques of philosophy and religion and the more recent disillusionment with the salvific possibilities of science, feared that *humanity* had no future. It was Nietzsche who most dramatically explored this possibility, and McDermott shares with him the effort to say "Yes" to life and to strive to build a future in the absence of those self-deceptive beliefs upon which an earlier "sense of the future" depended. Both thinkers desire a future without illusions. In McDermott's language, "The fundamental question is whether there is a median way between the self-deception of immortality, on the one hand, and the radical commitment to the moment, on the other hand" (*SE*, 164). The task, as he sees it, is to avoid the "twin pitfalls of the humdrum, ennui, and boredom, and the equally dehumanizing attempt to escape the rhythm of time on behalf of a sterile and probably self-deceptive eternal resolution" (*SE*, 168).

Concerning the possibility of a human future, the terminality-believer and the immortality-believer are confronted with contrasting problems. Paradoxically, both beliefs threaten to impoverish the present. Terminality belief threatens the depth of the present by emptying it of any significance beyond the moment, inasmuch as eventually all dimensions of the moment come to nothing. Immortality belief, on the other hand, tends to view the present as at best a mere means, something to be escaped and overcome in a future life. Thus the task of the terminality-believer is to show that the present has a life and role beyond the moment in spite of the absence of any absolute or eternal future: hence McDermott's "temporalized eschatology." The immortality-believer, in contrast, must show that the only nonmagical, nonescapist future life is one so organically bound up with the present that the quality of that life is in part, at least, dependent on the way in which the present is lived, the only access to a significant future being an intensely lived present.

From either perspective, there is a recognition that the present is enhanced, deepened, expanded when viewed and lived in relation to a future. Historically, no community has ever been energized except insofar as its members believed that their efforts were contributing to some future life, either for themselves or their heirs. A serious doubt can be raised, therefore, that humans—either individually or collectively—would continue to sacrifice and struggle if any and all belief in a future life were surrendered. Pragmatically speaking, then, there is no question of the fruitfulness of such belief. What is in question is the character of that future life. Will those individuals who are at present striving to build it participate in it directly and personally, or merely indirectly and symbolically?

Inseparably related to the question of the future is the question of "time." For McDermott, "time" must be rescued from both the classical perspective, in which it is but a surface that must be penetrated and escaped in order to realize refuge in the permanent, eternal depth, and from those contemporary perspectives in which the entire significance of time is exhausted in the thin pleasure and pain of the moment. Time stands in need of redemption, but it can be redeemed, if at all, only by human effort. In one of his more touching passages, McDermott writes: "I believe that time is sacred. It is not sacred, however, because it has been endowed by God or by the Gods, or by nature, or by any other extra or intra force. I believe that time is sacred because human history has so endowed it, with our sufferings, our commitments and with our anticipations" (*SE,* 167). In asserting its sacredness, McDermott in no way intends to sugarcoat the destructive and dissolving features of time. Living as we do "within the bowels of the temporal process," McDermott believes "that we should experience our lives in the context of being permanently afflicted, that is, of being terminal" (*SE,* 164). He here joins with a number of other contemporary thinkers who insist that unless we can accept and to some degree affirm the finality of our own death, we cannot live truly human lives. It is the understandable but enervating and somewhat unworthy fear of death that leads humans to believe in and hope for an illusory immortality. "Time is the tooth that gnaws," Dewey tells us. "It is the root of what is sometimes called the instinctive belief in immortality. Everything perishes but men are unable to believe that perishing is the last word."[38]

Both Dewey and McDermott recognize death as "the last word," but neither will accept it as the *only* word. While McDermott insists that we should experience ourselves as terminal, he also insists that we can "live a creative, probing, building life." It is not sufficient to say that we *can* live this way; rather "it is only in this way that we can live a distinctively human life" (*SE,* 164). The very possibility of growth is stimulated by recognition of our terminality, since "hanging back, while waiting to be rescued ultimately, from the flow, will not generate growth" (*SE,* 166–67).[39] It appears to me that McDermott is saying we can live a creative life in spite of death rather than because of it. Influenced as he has been for many years by the work of Norman O. Brown,[40] he nevertheless refuses to join in Brown's Dionysian death-dance. In McDermott's judgment, Brown "asks us to marry our own death" (*SE,* 163). Unlike Brown or Nietzsche, McDermott hopes for a mode of living available to more than a few isolated, idiosyncratic, and heroic individuals. In a relatively early essay, he asks:

> How can human life, collectively understood, sustain such a vision, such a lonely vigilance on behalf of human values, stripped of their guarantee and lighted only by their human quality? I speak not of this person nor that person, not of Camus, nor of William James, nor of John Dewey, nor of Hannah Arendt, but rather of those who gather together without such insight and live in and off the "everyday." We cannot, after all, in Buber's phrase, live only with the "spasmodic breakthroughs of the glowing deeds of solitary spirits." (*CE,* 64)

In the tradition of James and Dewey, McDermott is dedicated to forging a philosophy that is of service not only to the specialist but in some way to the widest range of persons possible. He must act on the belief that not just the few but the many can come to terms with the absence of salvation and bend their energies to ameliorating the human condition. Nietzsche said, "Those who cannot bear the sentence, There is no salvation, *ought* to perish!"[41] While McDermott would not accept the harsh "*ought* to perish," he does imply, as we have seen, that the surrender of the hope for salvation is essential to living a distinctively human life and contributing to whatever amelioration of the human situation is possible.

I have presented McDermott's view at such length because in addition to its emerging from the same metaphysical assumptions as does mine, it poses a serious and strong hypothesis in sharp conflict on key points with my own. The fundamental, and I believe decisive, divergence between us, as already indicated, has to do with the role of the God-hypothesis in our respective doctrines. I would like to consider a few "sticking points" for me, but within the framework of the "existential dialectic," in the mode of questioning responses rather than alleged refutations.

To begin with, McDermott's assertion of "the overwhelming evidence that we are terminal" would seem in need of much fuller exposition. That we are "terminal" in some sense, that we "die," is of course beyond question. The dispute has to do with whether we are *absolutely* terminal, whether "death comes as the end." Much depends on what is to count as evidence, and here it would seem that reasonable men and women are divided. What seems to drop out of McDermott's picture is that vast ambiguous body of religious experience considered so important by James which is central to my hypothesis. At the same time, there is no denying—as I have acknowledged from the first—that the overwhelming number of the most creative thinkers and artists in the modern and contemporary world seem to live and act within a belief framework that takes the absolute cessation of personal life for granted. But at least at this moment in human evolution, there remain, even in the West, large numbers of dedicated people—individuals voluntarily living with and serving the poor, families adopting disabled children, and the like—who believe that neither their lives nor the lives of those they serve are exhausted in their momentary existence within the visible world.

Another claim of McDermott's that I consider open to question is that immortality belief is an obstacle to growth and creative activity, whereas terminality belief is a stimulus. It would seem that there is no compelling evidence either way. Immortality belief does deenergize some, becoming an obstacle to their participation in the "building of the earth." Yet the same belief spurs others to engage in a variety of modes of creative activity. Here I will cite no less an authority than McDermott himself. Some years ago, in an essay in which he argued for the nonobsolescence of the Puritan experience, he stated: "The history of Calvinist doctrine in the hands of the American Puritans is a revealing instance of the transmutation of theological assertions for purposes of grounding a more extensive society while there is still commitment to the fundamental Christian concern for redemption" (*CE,* 77–78). And just as immortality belief can lead to engagement or disengagement with the task of the human community, so terminality belief can lead either to the courageous building of a constructive life or to a debilitating despair or destructive narcissistic hedonism.

In urging us to live creative lives while experiencing ourselves as terminal, McDermott also urges us to ask "for no guarantees and for no ultimate significance to be attributed to our endeavor" (*SE,* 164). This last phrase would seem to conflate two quite different questions: that of "guarantees" and that of "ultimate significance." There is no doubt that for many, faith and hope have been accompanied by claims of certitude and guarantee. I share with McDermott the Jamesian view of belief or faith as risk-laden and devoid of any guarantees, but whether such faith necessarily excludes a *hope* that our efforts have ultimate significance is quite another question. McDermott is not as clear on this point as he might be. After questioning the overbelief of salvation or immortality, he quickly adds:

> I do not refer here to a *hope* that somehow, somewhere, somewhen, all will go well for all of us who are, have been or will be. Certainly, such a hope is a legitimate and understandable human aspiration. To convert this hope into a commitment, a knowledge, a conviction, is to participate in an illegitimate move from possibility to actuality. It is understandable that we wish to escape from peril, but it is unacceptable to translate that desire into a belief that we have so escaped. (*SE,* 162)

I find this passage perfectly acceptable insofar as it quite properly distinguishes hope from knowledge and possibility from actuality. What I do not understand is what the first two sentences mean for McDermott, given his terminality belief. How is it possible to "*hope* that somehow, somewhere, somewhen, all will go well for all of us" if one believes that each and every one of us is destined for absolute annihilation?[42] I am not, of course, suggesting that McDermott claims certainty concerning our annihilation anymore than I claim certainty as regards our salvation. While his view, then, does not exclude the abstract possibility of hope for salvation, I am questioning the existential efficacy of such hope within the framework of terminality belief.

There are two other passages in McDermott's essay in which he appears to me to soften the harsh consequences of his terminality belief. "Memories," he tells us, "save the loss of places and the loss of persons from total disappearance" (*SE,* 166). But do they? For a time, of course, yes—but only "for a time," and a very short time at that. If human memory is the sole source of protection against "total disappearance," then the overwhelming number of the billions of human beings who have existed have already and irrevocably disappeared, and "in time" *all* humans and all traces of humans are likely to disappear as the cosmos returns to the preorganic state out of which human life emerged for its brief, fleeting moment—"troubling the endless reverie."

McDermott concludes his essay by citing one of Rilke's elegies:

> . . . Just once,
> everything, only for once. Once and no more. And we too,
> once. And never again. But this
> having been once, though only once,
> having been once on earth—can it ever be cancelled?[43]

To which McDermott responds: "Indeed, can it, we, ever be cancelled? I think not. Celebrate" (*SE,* 168). Here I may be missing some subtlety in both the poet and the philosopher, but I cannot resist asking, what does it mean to be terminal if it does not mean to be canceled? For me, the strength of McDermott's essay is its insistent celebration of human lives *in spite of* their inevitable termination *and* cancellation.

GOD: YES! IMMORTALITY: NO!

An effort to show that the cessation of the lives of individual persons is both a necessary and a constructive characteristic of reality is found in the thought of Charles Hartshorne. "The basic reason for mortality," he tells us, "is simple and clear, in my opinion, and it is aesthetic. Life is interesting because of birth and death, not in spite of them. . . . They give life form, and without form there is no satisfaction and no value. I really believe it is as simple as that."[44] Hartshorne is neither alone nor particularly original in comparing individual lives to works of art and finding an unending life as repugnant and defective as an unending play or novel.[45] More distinct, however, if not unique, is that Hartshorne locates our individual dramas within a cosmic one. It would seem that for him, only insofar as our lives have a transcendent reference can they be said to have meaning. Hence, he offers the doctrine of "contributionism" as a solution to the problem of death. While we cannot, after our death, benefit from "having lived well," there must be supposed some life that does benefit: "Only if we can believe in a superhuman and in some strict sense divine form of life, to which our lives make contributions proportional to their goodness or beauty, only then is the permanence of our contributions clearly implied." Hartshorne adds that "this does solve the basic question about death, which is how the meaning of life can survive its termination."[46]

It is God, then, who saves our lives from total extinction by receiving the fruits of these lives and incorporating them within his own. Hartshorne does not hesitate to refer to God as "the Cosmic organism" and to assert that "we are as cells in the divine organism." It follows that "we serve God . . . by furnishing prospering, happy cells to contribute to his own joy, to the aesthetic goodness and richness of his life" (*PAT* II:88–89).

In spite of Hartshorne's prodigious intellectual powers, I find it difficult to avoid a response characterized by both repugnance and frivolity. He softens the picture somewhat by maintaining that we "will serve God, not as puppets in his hands, but as, in humble measure, co-creators with Him" (*PAT* II:87). The bottom line, however, is still that we are to act in such a way as to make life interesting and enjoyable for the divine spectator-participant. Hartshorne's view seems close to one described, though not shared, by Miguel de Unamuno:

> Before this terrible mystery of mortality . . . man adopts different attitudes and seeks in various ways to console himself for having been born. And now it occurs to him to take it as a diversion and he says to himself with Renan that this universe is a spectacle that God presents to Himself, and that it behooves us to carry out the intentions of the great Stage-Manager and contribute to make the spectacle the most brilliant and the most varied that may be. (*TSL*, 51)

It is difficult to understand why we should be particularly motivated to put on a "good show," even for such a distinguished audience. Despite the many and suggestive comparisons between life and a stage, most of us tend to believe that "real life" embodies a depth and meaning that forbid us to reduce it to mere "play-acting."

In "Immortality and the Modern Temper" (*PL*, 262–81), Hans Jonas presents a doctrine of immortality strikingly similar to Hartshorne's but more consciously tentative and permeated by a moral rather than aesthetic overtone. Jonas suggests a metaphysical myth, within which his view on immortality is developed: "In the beginning, for unknowable reasons, the ground of being, or the Divine, chose to give itself over to the chance and risk and endless variety of becoming." Jonas insists that the Divine gave itself without remainder; "on this unconditional immanence the modern temper insists" (*PL*, 275). It would seem that for Jonas, God has sunk himself completely in the evolutionary process; subsequently, its mode of being will be totally dependent upon what burgeons forth from this process. Every stage of the cosmic process is an instance of "God's trying out his hidden essence and discovering himself through the surprises of the world-adventure" (*PL*, 276). With the appearance of life, but particularly human life, we have "a hesitant emergence of transcendence from the opaqueness of immanence" (*PL*, 275).

A price must be paid, however, for the emergence of individual life, and that price is death: "Mortality is the very condition of the separate self-hood . . . so highly prized throughout the organic world" (*PL*, 276). As in Hartshorne's view, God is the chief beneficiary of this mortality, since through births and deaths, sufferings and joys, love and even cruelty, "the Godhead reconstitutes itself." Hence, "this side of the good and evil, God cannot lose in the great evolutionary game" (*PL*, 277). Are we humans, then, to have no share in the fruits of our efforts; is human life completely devoid of any immortal character? It is consequences such as these that Jonas strives to avoid. Since the individual, in particular the person, is "by nature temporal and not eternal," there is no possibility of personal survival (*PL*, 278). This is not the whole story, however, for Jonas suggests that as experiments of eternity, we may achieve immortality through our deeds. "Not the agents, which must ever pass, but their acts enter into the becoming godhead. . . . and in this awesome impact of his deeds on God's destiny, on the very complexion of eternal being, lies the immortality of man" (*PL*, 274, 277).[47]

Jonas draws two crucial ethical conclusions from his metaphysical myth: first, our deeds and how we live our lives takes on a "transcendent importance"; second, through our deeds and our lives "we can nourish and we can starve divinity, we can perfect and we can disfigure its image" (*PL*, 278). Hence, "we literally hold in our faltering hands the future of the divine adventure," for inasmuch as he has "given himself whole to the becoming world, God has no more to give: it is man's now to give to him" (*PL*, 281, 279). As to our stake in the future, "although the hereafter is not ours, nor eternal recurrence of the here, we can have immortality at heart when in our brief span we serve our threatened mortal affairs and help the suffering immortal God" (*PL*, 281).

The positions of Hartshorne and Jonas are akin to that of Whitehead. Unlike them, however, Whitehead does not positively exclude the possibility of personal immortality—"subjective immortality," in Whiteheadian language; the significant similarity is evident in his doctrine of "objective immortality." No doctrine of Whitehead's is easy to summarize, but his view on the matter under consideration is something like the following. Reality is best described as a multiplicity of related processes, the basic units of which are designated actual entities or actual occasions. Actual entities are submicroscopic centers of activity, which come to be through acts that are at least partially self-creative and that perish almost instantly. "Perpetual perishing," which characterizes all actual entities with the exception of God, is not a total perishing. While actual entities cease to be as regards their subjective immediacy, they continue to be—are "immortal"—insofar as they are appropriated and enter into the constitution of new actual entities. The relatedness that characterizes actual entities is, Whitehead tells us, "wholly concerned with the appropriation of the dead by the living—that is to say, with 'objective immortality' whereby what is divested of its own living immediacy becomes a real component in other living immediacies of becoming."[48]

In the concluding chapter of *Process and Reality* Whitehead attempts to show that "the objective immortality of actual occasions requires the primordial permanence of God" (*PR*, 527). In so doing, he is endeavoring, perhaps, to give a metaphysical justification for a rather strong claim he made a few years earlier (1925): "The fact of the religious vision, and its history of persistent expansion, is our one ground for optimism. Apart from it, human life is a flash of occasional enjoyments lighting up a mass of pain and misery, a bagatelle of transient experience."[49] In the later work, Whitehead insists that "objective immortality within the temporal world does not solve the problem set by the penetration of the finer religious intention. 'Everlastingness' has been lost; and 'everlastingness' is the content of that vision upon which the finer religions are built" (*PR*, 527).

Whitehead goes on in a series of what might be called dialectical paradoxes to affirm essential interdependence and interpenetration (but not identity) between God and the world. All temporal occasions embody God and are embodied in God. "Each actuality has its present life and its immediate passage into novelty; but its passage is not its death. This final phase of passage in God's nature is ever enlarging itself. . . . Each actuality in the temporal world has its reception into God's nature" (*PR*, 528–31). What remains unclear, however, is whether the unique individuality characterizing those societies of actual entities called "persons," has its "reception into God's nature."

From my perspective, the philosophies of immortality expressed by Hartshorne, Jonas, and Whitehead realize a number of admirable insights, some version of which must be included in any reasonably satisfactory model of immortality. To begin with, they present an immortality far superior to and humanly richer than the one so beloved of the Greeks and still so prevalent, if only implicitly, in the contemporary world—namely, fame-immortality,[50] whose limitations and moral shortcomings have become increasingly evident to reflective persons, however strong the desire for fame may continue to be in most achievers. "How soon they forget" might be the lament of all but a very few of the billions who have populated the earth. Further, with the end of the earth and the human race a distinct possibility, if not certainty, it becomes increasingly likely that in the long run we will all be forgotten. We need not, however, project so far ahead to recognize the moral inadequacy of any immortality through fame. It too often happens that those who might well be deemed worthy of fame pass unnoticed, while the more reprehensible achieve a fame that keeps them in the minds of posterity: given a fame-immortality perspective, as Jonas laments, "the Hitlers and the Stalins of our era would have succeeded to extract immortality from the extinction of their nameless victims" (*PL,* 265).

Another merit of the kind of immortality suggested by these three thinkers is that it immeasurably enhances the significance of human acts, individual and collective. Pragmatically speaking, an account of human actions that sees them as not only having an intrinsic meaning but also contributing to the enrichment and advance of an eternal process is far superior to the many modes of what might be called passive Platonism: that is, superior to any view that posits essences, values, or forms as eternally complete and fully realized, thereby restricting human action to mere imitation. Something close to such "passive Platonism" is conveyed, I believe, by Santayana: "He who lives in the ideal and leaves it expressed in society or in art enjoys a double immortality. The eternal has absorbed him while he lived, and when he is dead his influence brings others to the same absorption."[51]

Finally, Hartshorne, Jonas, and Whitehead, each in a somewhat distinctive fashion, have made formidable efforts to be faithful to that radical immanentism which has been so widely and diversely advanced by contemporary thinkers. At the same time they have striven to avoid the smothering and suffocating character of such immanentism, which too often can give rise to the feeling of being locked in a cosmic madhouse. Jonas, after noting the reality and pervasiveness of time, adds: "And yet—we feel, temporality cannot be the whole story, because in man it has an inherently self-surpassing quality, of which the very fact and fumbling of our idea of eternity is a cryptic signal" (*PL,* 268).

It may well be that for some time to come, the best that reflective thinkers can do is call attention to the "cryptic signal" or the "rumor of angels." The efforts of the Hartshornes, Jonases, Whiteheads, and their like to affirm an eternal, a transcendent, a God that does not serve as a refuge or an escape from the scratchings and sufferings of human agents, are as needed as they are likely to fall short. Whatever the shortcomings of such attempts from the point of view of systematic conceptualization, their direction, I feel confident, is the one that offers the most hope and the richest possibilities for both the deepening and expansion of our present life and the contribution toward significant human life in the future. The modest criticisms and tentative proposals that follow are to a great extent but a variation and a gloss on the ideas of such thinkers.

It is important to stress that while no pretense is made of anything approaching "proof" or refutation, there is a necessity for at least attempting to move beyond any sentimental posture which holds that both the immortality belief and its counterbelief can be reconciled with neither pain nor loss. Nevertheless, as already noted, we are obliged to listen to these and other counterclaims and their accompanying arguments with an "existential ear." A pragmatist, while not excused from attending to the signs of argument and the need for systematic conceptualization, must continually remain sensitive to those lived liabilities and possibilities that ever elude argument and conceptualization. Finally, the need for continuing critical evaluation does not exclude the necessity for a simultaneous commitment. Evaluation and commitment experiments must persist in an unending dialectical relation that excludes both *final* evaluation and *closed* commitment.

My chief objection to the views of Hartshorne, Jonas, and the dominant version of Whitehead is that within their perspectives the priority and centrality of the individual person tends to become subordinated to some higher value.[52] I have already suggested that the gain or loss in relation to immortality is directly proportional to the worth of the individual person and that no surrogates can serve to alleviate the pain of loss. It seems quite well established that belief in some kind of immortality preceded both belief in a personal God and belief in the unique value of the individual person. But as John Hick notes, "what is important is the fact that the idea of a desirable immortality, as distinguished from that of an undesired because pointless and joyless survival [for example, in the Greek Hades or the Hebrew Sheol], arose with the emergence of individual self-consciousness and as a correlate of faith in a higher reality which was the source of value." Hence, "the belief in a desirable immortality depends, logically and historically, upon the notion of *value* both of the human individual and in a higher reality which is superior even to the power of death."[53] Of course, it does not follow that the reverse is true—that the value of the person depends upon immortality—but that is not my claim. What I am contending is, first, that there was and is a reasonableness in relating immortality to the value of such realities as human persons; and second and more evidently, that the annihilation of such valuable entities involves a profound and irreparable loss.

"*Person* signifies," according to Aquinas, "what is most perfect in all nature—that is, a subsistent individual of a rational nature."[54] Whatever the shifts in the meaning and metaphysics of persons, it is safe to say that, if anything, the value of persons has increased in the contemporary world. An eminently supportable claim and a decent argument might be made to the effect that individual persons are, among all the realities of our experience, the most valuable. Without here attempting to prove that claim, let me simply assert that in theory and intent, if not in practice, persons are so regarded. To illustrate this assertion, let us imagine the following situation: I am in a room occupied also by the most precious art object ever produced and a child. There ensues a fire such that I have the time and the ability to save either the art object or the child. Would not the overwhelming number of human beings in such a situation—learned or no—make the painful choice to save the child?[55]

The person as supreme value might be and has been challenged by those who make that claim for eternal or timeless or absolute values. Wherever one comes down on this long-standing dispute concerning the nature, possibility, and reality of such values, I think most would agree that many human beings have lived lives rich in consequence both for themselves and others in the light or pursuit of "truth," "goodness," "justice," and the like. It may be that these values have a reality in themselves apart from human experience, but surely the most compelling evidence for believing that they are in any way "real" is found in the lives of individual persons who believe in them. Further, apart from their incarnation in individuals and communities, these values are always in danger of becoming empty and lifeless abstractions. Finally, even granting the supremacy of "timeless values," the human person takes on a very high value in virtue of the ability to grasp, share in, or live by such values.

If individual death, as in Hegel, serves the universal or absolute Spirit, or, as in Hartshorne and Jonas, serves the development and enrichment of divine life, then there is a meaning to individual lives and a propriety to their cessation. Such perspectives, however, cannot avoid reducing human beings to the status of a "means," thus placing these perspectives in opposition to the principle advanced by others, most notably Kant, that a human being may never be used as a means but must always be regarded and treated as an "end-in-itself." There is no dispute concerning the unacceptability of any individual's or group's use of other individuals and groups as a means to an end from which those so used are excluded. When the user becomes Nature, or Spirit, or God, or Mankind, the issue is less clear and the consensus less than total; nevertheless, I would insist that using humans, whether individually or collectively, as a "means" to some end or life outside themselves is just as repugnant in the latter instance as in the former. John Hick quite forcefully rejects both religious and humanistic justification for human suffering. Religious justification is exemplified in St. Paul's text: "Will what is moulded say to its moulder, 'why have you made me thus?' Has the potter no right over the clay?"[56] The humanistic justification posits "a more real humanity or superhumanity in the future which will have evolved out of the painful process of human life as we know it." Hick finds both unacceptable because "they imply a view of the individual human personality not only as expendable in the sense that he can be allowed to pass out of existence but, more importantly, as exploitable in the sense that he can be subjected to any extent and degree of physical pain and mental suffering for a future end in which he cannot participate and of which he knows nothing" (*DEL,* 158–59).

Assuming, then, that human persons are precious, if not the most precious, realizations of nature or the cosmic process, the failure to maintain these persons in that mode upon which their preciousness depends can hardly be viewed as grounds for celebration. At the same time, I do not believe it possible to argue from the value of human individuals to the rational necessity of their immortality. In his Ingersoll Lecture, Julius Seelye Bixler made a simple but telling point against such an argument: "If the universe is rational or just, they say, it cannot ruthlessly stamp out its fairest product, personal life. The argument is not convincing, however, because we know so little of what rationality as applied to the universe can be" (*IPM*, 30). Bixler, of course, is still presupposing that some mode of rationality belongs to the universe. In the wake of powerful Nietzschean and existentialist critiques, however, the possibility of an "absurd" rather than "rational" universe cannot be ruled out. These critiques have rendered questionable, at least, *all* claims concerning "rationality." While it is not possible to "prove" that we live in an absurd world any more than we can "prove" that we live in a rational one, still the specter of absurdity hovers over and touches all our undertakings.[57]

Another effort to establish the rationality of immortality has been based on the evolutionary process. The argument here is that since human beings are the highest specimens produced by the long evolutionary process, it would be irrational for this process now to allow its finest achievements to completely disappear. Corliss Lamont justifiably criticizes those advancing this argument, noting that at one time the dinosaurs "were the highest form of terrestrial life" and, had they been capable of thought, would have made the same claims as does the immortalist (*II*, 185). Of course, we can never be certain that we are not grist for the evolutionary mills just as previous species have been, and hence fated for the same extinction. As already indicated, however, immortality is a question not of certainty but of credibility, and the credibility of immortality is intimately bound up with another question of credibility: namely, whether we can believe with some degree of justification that through the evolutionary process there has emerged a species whose individuals have the possibility of achieving a distinct, personal relation to the divine.

Even if we admit God into the picture, there is no obvious rational necessity for personal immortality, as the writings of Hartshorne and Jonas illustrate. There is, however, an important difference in the nature and quality of reflective inquiry when a shift is made from an impersonal nature or cosmic process to a personal, loving God.[58] As a minimum, such a shift lends a certain poignancy to the situation. Let us presuppose a God who is existentially related to human persons such that we can speak of this relation as an essential constituent of human personhood. Further, let us posit with Whitehead a divine activity characterized by "a tender care that nothing be lost . . . a tenderness which loses nothing that can be saved" (*PR*, 525). Assuming, with Hartshorne, Jonas, and most Whiteheadians, that individual persons are not among that which "can be saved" and hence must, in spite of God's "tender care," be judged lost, what follows? Surely sadness, not only human but, more important, divine.[59] Granting that no simple identity can be made between human and divine love, it is still hard if not impossible to imagine the character of a personal love in which one of the participants in the relationship was not sorely grieved by the loss of the other.

It may well be, as some serious and formidable thinkers assure us, that keeping us in mind is the very best God can do, but that can hardly be said to be something for us to look forward to. Just as it is good for humans to remember loved ones, so it may be good for God to do so, but in neither case—if that is all there is—can it be said to be good for the loved ones. Here one must agree with Epicurus and Lucretius that the nonexistent can be neither harmed nor benefited. If it makes sense to say that for human beings it is immeasurably better to sustain loved ones in reality rather than merely in memory, why does it not make sense to say the same about God, even if we must reluctantly conclude that he possesses no more such power than we, beyond a certain point?

Nowhere, perhaps, is the effort to give individual lives some meaning beyond the fleeting moment more touchingly portrayed than when Hans Jonas discusses "the gassed and burnt children of Auschwitz" and the "numberless victims of the other man-made holocausts of our time." Forbidden by his principles to accord them personal immortality, Jonas nevertheless refuses to believe that they are "debarred from an immortality which even their tormentors and murderers obtain because they could act— abominably, yet accountably, thus leaving their sinister mark on eternity's face." Instead, he asks, "should we not believe that the immense chorus of such cries that has risen up in our lifetime now hangs over our world as a dark and accusing cloud? That eternity looks down upon us with a frown, wounded and perturbed in its depths?" Jonas will say no more than that it would be fitting if, on the account of the slaughtered, "a great effort were asked of those alive to lift the shadow from our brow and gain for those after us a new chance of serenity by restoring it to the invisible world" (*PL*, 279– 80).

When confronted with evil of the magnitude of that manifest in the Holocaust and allied horrors, the only relatively appropriate human response would seem to be *silence*—a "silence" not only in the Wittgensteinian sense, which is due to the lack of any language adequate to such events, but more important, in the sense of what might be called a "silence of the spirit." This latter mode of silence brings us as close as possible to an experience of the unexperienceable abyss of nothingness; it is an evocation of that radical emptiness which accompanies not all experiences of death but all experiences of the death of a beloved whose being had been joined with our own in a mode of metaphysical intimacy. Against the background of such silence, *all* explanations or accounts of the meaning of death have a character of superficiality and triviality. Yet silence cannot be the total and exhaustive response, as has been evidenced from the dawn of civilization in the plethora of religious rites, symbols, practices, philosophical explanations, biological justifications, and literary and artistic expressions.[60] Yet while we must speak, we must do so against a background of silence such that we never cease to be aware of the radical inadequacy of our language.

BELIEF IN IMMORTALITY: ESSENTIAL OR DISPENSABLE FOR CHRISTIANITY?

Belief in immortality is not inseparable from religion in general. The Eastern religions, for the most part, hold no immortality doctrines, though I find suggestive the persistence of reincarnation as a belief in all segments—learned and unlearned—of Eastern religious communities, including those accepting nontheistic forms of Buddhism. In spite of the differences—and they are numerous, subtle, and important—among doctrines of immortality, resurrection, and reincarnation, all seem to reject the total annihilation of whatever is understood as my "authentic" or "true" self.

When we turn to the Western mode of religion, in particular Christianity, there can be little doubt that belief in personal survival has been a central characteristic. As James pointed out, "religion, in fact, for the great majority of our race *means* immortality, and nothing else. God is the producer of immortality; and whoever has doubts of immortality is written down as an atheist" (*VRE*, 412). John Herman Randall, Jr., maintains that belief in personal survival was the first of "the old religious doctrines" to become a casualty of the critiques stemming from the advent of modern science. He quickly adds, however, that "immortality was a far more vital belief than that in God" and that "there persisted a deep yearning for immortality, even if vicarious"—a yearning by no means confined to the unsophisticated and the conservative, though the immortality of the race often replaced immortality of the person: "In giving up its hope of personal survival, religious faith, even of the modernists and liberals, had staked everything on the immortality of mankind. Even eighteenth-century materialism had assumed the permanence of the universe as it is, and with the promise of an unlimited social progress" (*PAD*, 19).

That immortality or resurrection-belief has been a central and significant feature of Western religion is one thing; whether it *must* and *should* continue to be so is, of course, quite a different matter. Unamuno's response is unequivocal: "Once again I must repeat that the longing for the immortality of the soul, for the permanence, in some form or another, of our personal and individual consciousness, is as much of the essence of religion as is the longing that there may be a God" (*TSL*, 221). But Unamuno's voice is by no means representative of contemporary thinkers. Many, though sympathetic to religion, contend that it can be purified only by surrendering any and all belief in immortality. Bixler, for example, insists that "the religious requirement that life be made worth while, and that values be achieved for their own sake, has all the more force when the hope for a final adjustment is removed" (*IPM*, 40).[61]

A more formidable obstacle for the Christian who wishes to retain a belief in some mode of personal survival is the argument "that the Christian
hope of resurrection is . . . misinterpreted as survival of death." The contemporary theological scholar Joseph Blenkinsopp advances this viewpoint
in a sensitive essay in which he endeavors, by means of a hermeneutical
effort, "to get inside traditional (and this, of course, includes biblical) statements about resurrection and life after death in order to grasp the experience
and the immediacy from which they spring and to discover whether such
experience is still available to modern man, whether it can speak to his experience of himself and the world in which he lives" (*IR*, 116). Without going
into the details of his argument, let me cite Blenkinsopp's conclusion, which
to my nonhermeneutical eye does not follow from the biblical evidence
presented.

> While we will recognize the popular idea of the resurrection—a new body
> waiting for us "on the other side" like a new suit ready to put on—as a rather
> ridiculous caricature, it is still difficult even for a sophisticated Western Chris-
> tian to think of it in anything but individualistic terms. Hence it must be
> stressed that the resurrection of the dead is *not* the guarantee of personal sur-
> vival after death. If we wish to remain faithful to the biblical testimony, we
> must not separate the destiny of the individual from that of the community—
> the body of Christ—and of the entire created order. The resurrection of the
> body expresses primarily and essentially the destiny of the new community,
> the eucharistic body, the body of the risen Christ, which is the nucleus of a
> world-wide community. (*IR*, 125–26)

I am aware that hermeneutical theology strives to relate the earlier experience and articulations of the Christian community to present-day life. It
does not try to describe the psychological consciousness of earlier Christians
but to uncover through subtle reading of received texts the still vital core of
lived experience and meaning-structure. I admire without claiming to fully
understand Blenkinsopp's hermeneutical effort. Nevertheless, the results
raise a number of questions.

My initial reaction to the passage quoted above was, "What in heaven's
name could he possibly be trying to say?" To which it might be replied,
"You'll find out only when and if you get to heaven." But since such a
heavenly destiny seems very unlikely on Blenkinsopp's terms, it is necessary
to make a few mundane comments. To begin with, if, in calling the idea of a
new body awaiting us like a new suit of clothes a caricature, Blenkinsopp is
cautioning against any attempt to picture the resurrection, then there can be
little dispute. His criticism appears much stronger, however; he states that
"the Christian hope of resurrection is also often misinterpreted as survival
of death" (*IR*, 119). Now there is no difficulty in understanding this—
though there may be in accepting it—if Blenkinsopp means that death terminates our personal existence and hence any "hope of resurrection" must
pertain to a "here and now" existential transformation. Such a reading,

however, is not easy to reconcile with another passage that refers to "determining the precise form of the Christian hope for *life after death*" (*IR*, 116; italics added).

Blenkinsopp stresses "that the resurrection of the dead is *not* the guarantee of personal survival after death." Note that the term "not" rather than "guarantee" is italicized. Were it the other way around, we might conclude that what is being rejected, quite properly, is any effort to "prove" that we survive, using such belief as a hedge against the terrors of life. Such a view would not only be similar to the one advanced earlier in this essay but also concur with Blenkinsopp's previous statement: "To speak in terms of a rational certitude threatens to void of meaning both death and the Christian promise of new life from death." But Blenkinsopp would not seem to be stressing the *faith* character of the resurrection. Instead, he appears to be denying "personal survival" while affirming "new life from death." Perhaps the apparent conflict between these passages is overcome through the notion that "the resurrection of the body expresses primarily and essentially the destiny of the new community"? (*IR*, 119, 126). As we saw above, Blenkinsopp insists that "we must not separate the destiny of the individual from that of the community" and he further identifies this "new community" as "the eucharistic body, the body of the risen Christ, which is the nucleus of a world-wide community." Two simple questions, which are really one question, must be asked concerning this new community. First, granted that it is improper to "separate the destiny of the individual from that of the community," is it permissible to separate the destiny of the community from that of the individual?[62] Second, does (or can) this new community include as constituent members those individual persons, past and present, who have been invited to join in and who have worked for its coming?[63]

My final question concerning Blenkinsopp's provocative article is far from simple. It requires, indeed, a digression in the form of an apology. Any effort of religious reconstruction has the difficult task of showing how interpretations of Christianity greatly influenced by modern thought and experience maintain significant continuity with the earlier faith experiences of the community. Those who undertake such a task dare not overlook the possibility that they may contribute to the demise of the very community they strive to serve. At best, an interpretation that diverges from the dominant mode of understanding—as, for example, that God is changing—will have a tentative, hypothetical character and must be submitted to long-range testing through reflection and action. There are two premature and immature responses to such innovative interpretations: unquestioning acceptance and unhesitating rejection.

And so, to my final question: Does not any interpretation of resurrection belief that excludes the possibility of some mode of personal postdeath participation in the divine life radically undermine the justification for the continued existence of this belief?

Let us assume that theology will increasingly hold, with Blenkinsopp, that to believe in personal survival of death is to misinterpret the doctrine of resurrection. I believe it can be shown that belief in personal resurrection has played a role in the life of the Christian community comparable to and inseparable from God belief. Not only have the overwhelming number of Christians in all stations of life, and from the earliest moments of the community life, believed that some mode of personal survival is embodied in the divine promise of eternal life, but it has inspired and energized liturgy and ritual, poetry and painting, philosophy and theology, meditation and practice.[64] I am not ruling out, a priori, a case for continued allegiance to Christian tradition in the absence of belief in personal immortality or personal resurrection, but that case has not yet been made. Nor do I see what Christianity devoid of such belief is able to achieve or contribute that cannot be realized on other faith grounds, grounds much less problematic and burdensome than those of Christianity.

The pragmatic perspective honors no difference in ideas or ideals that does not make a difference in experience. With reference to religious faith, James has stated the issue succinctly:

> The whole defense of religious faith hinges upon action. If the action required or inspired by the religious hypothesis is in no way different from that dictated by the naturalistic hypothesis, then religious faith is pure superfluity, better pruned away, and controversy about its legitimacy is a piece of idle trifling, unworthy of serious minds. (*WB*, 32)

This raises a complicated issue. Reflective Christians, it seems to me, must ask themselves and each other whether the existence and continuance of Christianity makes a difference. Suppose whatever is of value in Christianity can be envisioned or realized by other means. It might then make sense to maintain membership in this venerable community for psychological and sociological reasons, but the necessity and seriousness of membership would be immeasurably diminished.

Let us pose the question of whether Christianity makes a difference in terms of a belief in God to the exclusion of personal survival of death. Unamuno recounts an incident in which he proposed to a peasant "the hypothesis that there might indeed be a God who governs heaven and earth, a Consciousness of the Universe, but for all that the soul of every man may not be immortal in the traditional and concrete sense. He replied: 'Then wherefore God?'" (*TSL*, 5). Near the conclusion of his *Tragic Sense of Life*, Unamuno addresses himself directly and dramatically to the relation between God and immortality: "We do not need God in order that he may teach us the truth of things, or the beauty of them, or in order that he may safeguard morality by a system of penalties and punishments, but in order that He may save us, in order that He may not let us die utterly" (*TSL*, 319).[65]

Now while it is evident that a God who does "not let us die utterly" makes a difference, it does not follow that this is the only kind of God who would make a difference. It might be suggested that belief in God and symbolic resurrection directs and energizes us toward personal transformation and self-realization, toward a respect and concern for our fellow human beings, toward a removal of the inequities and injustices that plague the world, and toward a new community in which love would be the determining and controlling quality. All these goals and others that might be mentioned are eminently worthwhile, but what is not evident is that these goals need God, much less symbolic resurrection, for either their conception or their realization. Even if it could be shown that historically they all entered human consciousness within a religious context, it does not follow that they can now be pursued *only* within such a context. Indeed, these goals and values are affirmed by many enlightened secular humanists.

If, then, there is no experiential difference—either in actuality or possibility—between an enlightened theist and an enlightened atheist, the pragmatist insists that there is no significant difference. The consequence, as James noted, is that the "religious faith is pure superfluity, better pruned away." I suggest that a Christianity emptied of any vital belief in the possibility of some mode of personal survival is irrelevant at best, and obstructive and burdensome at worst. Applying a version of the principle of parsimony, the contention is that the enormous baggage belonging to religion in general and Christianity in particular should not continue to be carried if what it attempts to affirm and realize can be achieved more simply. If fundamentally the same values can be realized through the faith of secular humanism, then the monumental energies employed to sustain Christianity are criminally wasted.

Think, for example, of the dedication and effort of those theologians striving to interpret and purify and develop Christian doctrine. If the goal of their efforts is not different from that of the humanist, is it not a grave misdirection of human energy, when there are so many concrete human problems that cry out for attention and imaginative response? It might be legitimate to continue to study the religious experience of humankind, past and present, in order to distill from it insights for incorporation into the effort to alleviate the human condition. But the maintenance of religious institutions and the theological as well as personal defense of the beliefs and practices of religious communities would seem to be both unduly burdensome and pointless if the best fruits of such efforts can be otherwise achieved. The negative features of religions, including Christianity, are well known and well documented. The record of religion, past and present, discloses inhumanities ranging from the petty to the petrifying. The continuing struggle to overcome the debilitating and dehumanizing characteristics of religion through the purification of religious experience and the transformation of its forms and institutions can be justified only if at least some positive possibilities with which religion is concerned are available in no other way.

One such possibility would be expressed in the belief that we are *here and now* participating in a process more encompassing than what is *ordinarily* available to consciousness and one in which we can hope for a continuing participation in a new life. Such belief might give human life a depth, scope, and vitality which, while not in conflict with the best features of humanism, would nevertheless be significantly different.

IMMORTALITY: HOPE OR HINDRANCE?
It is evident that my response to the title question of this chapter is "both." I have already suggested and will continue to suggest that the need is for an existential dialectic whereby immortality belief engenders and deepens hope without masking those aspects of such belief that hinder responsible living. Aspects of hindrance are inevitably and existentially intertwined with the hope to which belief in personal immortality gives rise, and these hindering elements must be continually and honestly faced, and efforts made to lessen if not completely eradicate them. I want to stress, however, that a mixture of hopeful and hindering aspects in relation to the meaning of human life is not a characteristic only of those who believe in personal immortality; it is an inescapable dimension of the human condition, and there will be as many different combinations of hope and hindrance as there are individual faiths and lives. The distinctive mix will be the result, at least in part, of the creative effort of each person. Immortality belief, then, is not an exception *from* the human condition but a specification of it.

CHAPTER 8

Immortality: A Pragmatic-Processive Model

I am the resurrection and the life. If anyone
believes in me, even though he dies he will live,
and whoever lives and believes in me will never
die. Do you believe this?
                              —John 11:25–26

Leap, life
Leap and dance.
Dance out of death.
  Leap.
  Dance.
  Life,
          sun-filled, touch
          the phoenix self
          of death to life.

          Death to life:
          all death
          to life
          in flame.
              —William Birmingham
              "The Phoenix"

Just as it is unacceptable to advance a belief in God without venturing some
guess as to the character of the divine, so it would be fruitless to present a
belief in immortality that did not—however tentatively and sketchily—suggest what a new life would, or at least *ought to,* involve. As John Hick has
noted: "A doctrine which can mean anything means nothing. So long, then,
as we refrain from spelling out our faith it remains empty."[1] In the same
vein, H. D. Lewis contends that "no one can expect or believe anything
without having *some* idea of what it is that he expects."[2] The task of this
chapter, then, is to suggest a model of the cosmic process that would justify
belief in immortality as attractive and as life-enhancing. In keeping with the
experiential character and this-worldly focus of the pragmatism I espouse,
any acceptable model will have to offer possibilities for the enhancement and
enrichment of life. It will be unacceptable to the extent that it is an escape

200

from life as we here and now experience it.[3] It will be acceptable to the extent that it is an invitation to enter more deeply and fully into such life. Readers might be aided by mentally placing the term "this life" in quotation marks, because the nature and scope of human life is precisely what has been and will likely continue to be a matter of intense dispute among reflective human beings. A crucial aspect of the dispute centers on what ought to be the relationship between the present and future characteristics of this life. Apart from a superficial "eat, drink, and be merry" mode of hedonism, most reflective efforts have involved some vision or philosophy of the future. For example, no thinkers have been more passionately opposed to any philosophical or religious positing of any other world than Marx and Nietzsche. In its eschatological dimensions, Marxism invokes a dedication to the present in virtue of a belief that one is thereby contributing to a future utopian state. Nietzsche, despite his radical individualism and fierce attacks on religion, manifests a profound concern for the future. However variously they may be interpreted, his doctrines of revaluation, the overman, and eternal return are calls to move beyond the present situation and bring forth a mode of life more creative and fulfilling.

There is, I believe, a rather wide consensus among contemporary thinkers to shun both a view of the present devoid of a significant future and a view of the future that reduces the present to a sheer means. Two texts from John Dewey express a mode of this present-future dialectic:

> We always live at the time we live and not at some other time, and only by extracting at each present time the full meaning of each present experience are we prepared for doing the same thing in the future. This is the only preparation which in the long run amounts to anything.
>
> The ideal of using the present simply to get ready for the future contradicts itself.[4]

Albert Camus expresses a similar sentiment when he notes that "real generosity toward the future lies in giving all to the present."[5] William Ernest Hocking, who is as sympathetically inclined toward belief in immortality as Dewey and Camus are opposed, asserts: "To be able to give oneself wholeheartedly to the present one must be persistently aware that it is *not all*. One must rather be able to treat the present moment as if it were engaged in the business allotted to it by that total life which stretches indefinitely beyond" (*MI*, 155). At the same time he rejects—quite properly, in my view—any notion of the future that would give meaning to a presently meaningless life:

> Unless there is an immediately felt meaning there is no meaning at all; no future meaning could compensate for a complete absence of meaning in the present moment; and whatever meaning life may come to possess hereafter must be simply the ampler interpretation of the meaning which it now has. (*MI*, 159)

Christopher Mooney makes an allied point in somewhat different language: "Christian hope in resurrection will have meaning for us only to the extent that we have some inkling of resurrection now, some experience of fullness of life, of self-discovery, love or creativity."[6] Finally, H. D. Lewis considers it

> a great travesty of Christian truth to suppose that we should think of our salvation solely in terms of some destiny to be achieved later. It is a present reality, and the full realization of this is essential to the appreciation of Christian claims and the impact they can have on our present attitudes. But however important this emphasis may be, and however necessary in the commendation of Christianity today, it would be odd, to say the least, if the peculiar relationship established between God and men in the coming of Christ were concerned wholly with the present life. It must surely be understood in the context of an abiding fellowship. (*SI*, 207–8)

These latter texts suggest that an adequate model of the creative process demands the most intense living in the present, at the same time remaining open to the possibility of participating in transcendent and future modes of existence. To argue in favor of belief in immortality, it is not necessary to claim that such belief is needed to avoid a superficial presentism or hedonism; it is sufficient to show that there is nothing intrinsic to this belief that leads to diverting energies from the tasks at hand. One can readily concede that it is possible for individuals to work in the present to build a future life in which they believe they will have no personal share; it does not follow, however, that a belief that we *shall* be personal participants in this future life is a deterrent or an obstacle to our living fully at the present moment. After all, few would claim that it is either unreasonable or unworthy of young persons to believe and to be taught that the efforts they are making at the moment will affect the quality of their lives as adults. Indeed, the significance and depth of youth would seem to be immeasurably increased by the belief that young persons are participating in a process in which the future depends upon the present.

PRAGMATIC-PROCESSIVE MODEL

The general features of pragmatism's model of the cosmic process have already been touched upon in my earlier discussion of metaphysics and the self. Keeping in mind the mode of pragmatic extrapolation employed throughout this essay, it remains now to explore this model with specific reference to immortality or the possibility of new life consequent upon death. Recall that for the pragmatist the world is characterized by processes and relations that can be expressed metaphysically in terms of ever changing "fields within fields." Thus the world or reality can be described as a processive-relational continuum or field embodying and bringing forth a plurality of subfields, each with a unique focus but dependent upon, overlapping with, and shading into other fields.

From the pragmatic perspective, reality is pluralistic rather than monistic. Hence, it is a bit misleading to speak, as I have spoken, of *a* or *the* cosmic or creative process. It is more accurate to speak of a plurality of processes with a variety of relations and interrelations. Though such a perspective does not exclude the possibility that one of these processes is wider and more encompassing than all others, it does exclude the conception of this process as absolute, with the narrower processes absorbed by it. Moreover, to affirm a plurality of processes is not to affirm chaos—nor is it to deny some kind of unity. This unity cannot be an essentially completed or finished unity, however, nor can it be one that excludes plurality or makes plurality peripheral or accidental. Whatever unity belongs to the collectivity of processes must, to be consistent with pragmatism's pluralistic universe, be constituted by these processes. The contributions these processes makes to this unity are not necessarily equal; it is permissible to believe that some make significantly greater contributions than others. Unity so viewed is itself a process: reality is at every moment "one," and is at every moment "becoming one." Thus the unity that pragmatism affirms does not exclude disunity. Indeed, if our extrapolation retains experiential rootedness, it must include both unity and disunity as characteristics of reality. None of this, however, excludes a belief in and a working toward increasing the unity and diminishing the disunity, toward a world of ever increasing harmony.

This model allows, then, for the highest and most intense mode of interrelationship and participation without losing the distinctiveness and independence of the participating processes. Since all these processes, according to the specific quality or character of each, are contributing to the development and enhancement of the collective whole, one can speak with reasonable consistency of their living or acting "for their own sakes" while simultaneously contributing to other processes—narrower and wider. Hence, in the language of present and future, we can plausibly live fully for the present while contributing to the emerging life of the future.

This model is quite obviously evolutionary, and in suggesting an evolutionary process in which there emerge individuals capable of sharing in life beyond death, it is hardly unique. Interesting and fruitful comparison could be made with the models described by Henri Bergson, Pierre Teilhard de Chardin, and Sri Aurobindo.[7] One similarity worth mentioning is that they all in some way affirm a continuity between our experienced life and any wider or future life.[8] This means that our present acts are here and now contributing to a process or processes far more extensive than is evident to our ordinary consciousness. Our actions have present and future consequences for the character and quality of those processes which can at best be only vaguely grasped. "It may be true," James tells us, "that work is still doing in the world-process, and that we are called to bear our share. The character of the world's results may in part depend upon our acts" (*SPP*, 112). Elsewhere, James confesses that he does not see "why the very existence of an invisible world may not in part depend on the personal response which any one of us may make to the religious appeal. God himself, in short, may draw vital strength and increase of very being from our fidelity. For my own part, I do not know what the sweat and blood and tragedy of this life mean, if they mean anything short of this. If this life be not a real fight, in which something is eternally gained for the universe by success, it is no better than a game of private theatricals from which one may withdraw at will" (*WB,* 55).

This, of course, is an expression of a hope, but so is the humanist or Marxist claim that our present actions have a bearing, for better and for worse, upon the future condition of humanity. The depth and scope of the process needed for a plausible belief in immortality is admittedly greater, but all such claims share a commitment to the present based at least partly on a belief in consequences, many of which will be realized, if ever, only in a distant future.

Although I am certainly not suggesting that these views are substantially the same, the model I am arguing for is both like and unlike humanistic and traditional "religious" approaches. Later I will maintain that a transforma-tionist character is essential to any new life, and this moves my model in the direction of more traditional beliefs concerning an afterlife. The point here under consideration is closer to the humanistic emphasis upon the signifi-cance of present acts. Since "work is still doing in the world-process," our actions have consequences radiating far beyond the bounds of a narrowly conceived spatio-temporal present. Feeding the poor, caring for a child, tending the sick, creating works of art, solving scientific problems—all these and many other human activities must be seen as in some way advanc-ing and deepening the quality of the world-processes, just as our negative actions must be seen as impeding and diminishing them.

The pragmatic model contrasts sharply with one that would picture this life as a test which, if successfully endured, will deliver us from the tem-poral process into the eternal world. Pragmatism rejects the classical du-alism between the temporal and the eternal. Since pragmatism affirms con-tinuity between the narrower and more immediate fields of our experience with the wider and more encompassing ones, our everyday activities take on greater significance than in traditional religious or humanistic views. Historical and cosmic processes—known and unknown—are not processes from which we are striving to escape, nor are they tales "told by an idiot, signifying nothing." However mysterious the deeper and more ultimate characteristics of these processes are, a pragmatic perspective allows for a belief and a hope that transcend, without negating or diminishing, the more immediately accessible fruits and consequences of these processes. Time is not something to be gone through or gotten beyond; it is itself reality inso-far as it brings forth novelty and growth as well as loss and diminution.[9] Since chance is one characteristic of creative processes, their outcome is neither preset nor totally determined, even by the divine participant. The character and quality of the processes that constitute reality, present and future, will be determined by the free creative acts of all the participants, only a few of which, perhaps, are actually known to us at the moment.[10]

Any model of the creative processes that allows for immortality must account not only for the relation of the present world to some future world but also to dimensions of the present world to which we do not usually attend. Further, no model of reality would serve belief in immortality if it allowed only for the emergence at some future time of persons capable of participating endlessly in the divine life. This would exclude a possible immortality for all human persons involved in the evolutionary process save those who had the good fortune to emerge in its final stage.[11]

THIS WORLD—OTHER WORLD

Whether we may think of those lengthy and at times tortuous theological speculations concerning immediate judgment and final judgment, the state of souls prior to the resurrection, and the like, they were concerned with a question that no immortality extrapolation can avoid: namely, the continuing existence of those persons who die prior to the eschaton. Though the detailed mode of such existence may be almost completely beyond our imaginative powers, the belief in such an existence is plausible only if it is also plausible to extrapolate an other world distinct but not separate from this one. But will this not be an escape into that otherworldiness that has been so soundly criticized in the modern era? Perhaps, but there are indications that this question has not been as decisively settled as many on both sides imagine.

The difficulty rests in the not-so-evident meaning or meanings attached to the phrases "this world" and "other world." The question involved is somewhat analogous to that concerning "natural" and "supernatural." When there was a consensus on the nontranscendent meaning of nature, affirmation of transcendence meant that the theist posited some kind of supernatural, which the secularist denied. But when nature is taken as provisional, processive, and open-ended, the question is transformed: we now seek to understand the various dimensions of nature or reality, and the supernatural is either relativized (as is nature) or irrelevant. Similarly, when "this world" was understood in a more restricted materialistic-mechanistic sense, or in the Greek-Medieval sense of a closed and finished republic of natures, then affirmation of an "other world" was indispensable to avoid cutting off important human possibilities. Now that this dialectic appears to have run its course, a new model is called for, one that will avoid an escapist otherworldliness and a superficial this-worldliness.

There are, to begin with, good grounds for extrapolating worlds other than those more commonly recognized. For example, it is quite evident that any reference to "this world" is relative and perspectival.[12] Remaining close to ordinary experience, we can see that at every moment and at different moments we are engaged in a plurality of "worlds." We speak, for example, of the "workaday world," the "world of art," the "scientific world," the "world of common sense." We do not designate one of these the "real world" and call the rest "subjective" or "imaginary." Each is real insofar as it bears upon the concrete presence and continuing development of life. If the mystical world or the divine world meet this criterion of vital presence, and that is the claim and belief of many, then these worlds are no more and no less "other" than, say, the world of art or the world of science. I do not claim for them the same kind or degree of evidence, but I do argue that the reality of an other world cannot be rejected solely because it is not identical with some alleged "this world."

Of course, for the pragmatist, such other worlds are always matters of belief, but at least one pragmatist—William James—maintained that such belief, or overbelief, was neither alien nor opposed to experience. "If needs of ours outrun the visible universe," James argues, "why *may* not that be a sign that an invisible universe is there?" (*WB*, 51).[13] Two texts show how seriously James entertained the notion that we participate in worlds of which we are unaware or only vaguely aware.

> The whole drift of my education goes to persuade me that the world of our present consciousness is only one out of many worlds of consciousness that exist, and that those other worlds must contain experiences which have a meaning for our life also; and that although in the main their experiences and those of this world keep discrete, yet the two become continuous at certain points, and higher energies filter in. (*VRE*, 408)

> In spite of rationalism's disdain for the particular, the personal, and the unwholesome, the drift of all the evidence we have seems to me to sweep us very strongly towards the belief in some form of superhuman life with which we may, unknown to ourselves, be co-conscious. We may be in the universe as dogs and cats are in our libraries, seeing the books and hearing the conversation, but having no inkling of the meaning of it all. (*PU*, 140)[14]

I find that last sentence the experiential base for the extrapolation of other worlds.[15] It is important to recall that an extrapolation is not constructed in air but must be an imaginative construct suggested by data given in experience.[16] Moreover, successful acts of imagination enrich and enhance experience and reality, often in ways not immediately evident.[17] We could add to the situation cited by James innumerable instances in which organisms are totally unaware of processes which at every moment contribute to the constitution of their being. Focusing on human experience, we have evidence of what might be called "unaware participation." To what extent are most human beings aware of their involvement in social and historical worlds, processes that have a reality not simply reducible to the consciousnesses of their constituent members? Nietzsche's genealogical inquiries, Freud's psychoanalytic techniques, Marxist and structuralist analyses all claim to reveal the underlying structures of morality or the psyche or history or language. These are imaginative efforts to bring to light worlds that are operative in human life but not attended to consciously.

Of course, the most significant data pointing toward the reality of a world or worlds other than or beyond the customary one are the claims of those we call mystics. From the pragmatic perspective, these claims do not prove the reality of such worlds but, as James argued in *The Varieties of Religious Experience,* they may not be lightly dismissed. The pragmatist would insist that despite the mystic's claim to direct experience of God or the One or the Absolute, there is still a faith or interpretive dimension to these experiences. The issue here, however, is not whether the mystic is correct in describing his or her experience as intuition or higher knowledge or enlightenment. Whatever the description, we have an enormous number of individuals distributed over the length of human history and a variety of cultures who make experiential claims which, to say the least, remain decisively unaccounted for within a narrow space-time framework. Such data, combined with other factors, contribute to the plausibility of extrapolating as real some dimensions that transcend the narrow confines of our conventional world. Such data will, of course, fail to persuade someone who has not had at least an experiential inkling of what the mystic points toward. Unless one has, minimally, a vague sense of something "more" to life than that which constitutes our quotidian experience, the extrapolation I propose will lack meaning and validity.[18]

CONTINUITY BETWEEN PRESENT LIFE AND NEW LIFE

Granting the plausibility of extrapolating the reality of an other world, what characteristics would make a new life in it desirable? Bernard Williams, who rejects the desirability of immortality, nevertheless lists some of those characteristics. The first is "that it should clearly be *me* who lives forever." I have already stressed at some length that personal survival is crucial to any significant immortality.[19] Williams's second condition is "that the state in which I survive should be one which, to me looking forward, will be adequately related, in the life it presents, to those aims which I now have in wanting to survive at all."[20]

A process model along the lines suggested allows for this effective continuity between our present life and any new life. It does so in its insistence that we act in the belief that we are contributing to a process or processes wider in scope and longer than those of which we are immediately aware. While not limiting any future participation to the exact mode in which we are now participating, we must believe that those aims, goals, and ideals that now energize us will remain in some way operative in any new life.

Any adequate model of the creative process and extrapolated immortality will have to take account of the eternal. Even Nietzsche, though ready to surrender God and immortality, is unwilling to part with "eternity." Zarathustra sings a hymn proclaiming that "all joy wants eternity / Wants deep, wants deep eternity."[21] Nietzsche wants an eternity located neither in some distant future nor in some other world presently inaccessible to human experience. An important element of the Christian tradition also insists, despite differences, on the possibility—indeed the necessity—of here-and-now participation in the eternal. Friedrich Schleiermacher insists that just such participation is the authentic mode of immortality.

> The goal and the character of the religious life is not the immortality desired and believed in by many. . . . It is not the immortality that is outside of time, behind it, or rather after it, and which still is in time. It is the immortality which we can now have in this temporal life; it is the problem in the solution of which we are forever to be engaged. In the midst of finitude to be one with the Infinite and in every moment to be eternal is the immortality of religion.[22]

Though with a slightly different emphasis, Soren Kierkegaard makes much the same point: "Immortality cannot be a final alteration that crept in, so to speak, at the moment of death as the final stage. On the contrary, it is a changelessness that is not altered by the passage of the years."[23]

Though the pragmatic model of reality would not employ the language of Schleiermacher and Kierkegaard, and in particular would not accept any literal meaning of "changeless," it remains open to the depth of experience they call for. What it would need is an account allowing for, even insisting upon, a relation to God or the divine or the eternal that is everlasting without being everlastingly the same. In such an account, "changeless" might be accepted as a symbol of the constancy or trustworthiness of divine love but would not exclude some kind of change in both the divine and the human relata.

To shift the focus a bit—it is exactly everlastingness that is questioned as to whether it is humanly desirable by many who reject personal immortality. At stake here is whether duration is a value that makes an endlessly enduring life desirable. Williams, who argues against Lucretius that "more days may give us more than one day," nevertheless denies that unending life would give us anything over and above what can be realized in a life that ends: "There is no desirable or significant property which life would have more of, or have more unqualifiedly, if we lasted forever" (*PS*, 89).

The counterview is expressed by Hocking: "*Duration is a dimension of value.*" George Santayana maintains that "length of things is vanity, only their height is joy."[24] But according to Hocking, "it is the normal destiny of experience to be prolonged in proportion to its height, not inversely"; hence, "life is objectively worth more as a continued than as a closed affair" (*MI*, 68–69).[25]

NEW LIFE: DURATION AND TRANSFORMATION

The attractiveness or unattractiveness of duration will depend upon how it is to be understood. Bergson, finding it attractive, describes it as "the continuous progress of the past which gnaws into the future and which swells as it advances."[26] On the other hand, those who find endless duration unattractive presuppose that it involves an unending continuance of fundamentally the same mode of life. Thus Williams, in citing the Makropulos case as evidence that one would become bored by an immortal life, describes a life that had really not changed for some three hundred years, a life devoid of significant growth and real novelty. This same presupposition, that a life of unending duration would be merely an indefinite extension of human life in the same mode as it now exists, undergirds the views of those who distinguish it from the eternal life of Christian tradition. "Eternal life," we are told by Stewart Sutherland, "is not to be equated with endless life."[27] We are not told, however, just what the difference is between the two, and while conceding that any new life cannot be identical with our present one, I confess that I am completely unable to grasp what an eternal life would be that excluded the characteristic of everlastingness. The distinguished American philosopher John Smith has expressed a view similar to those being challenged; though more understandable, it retains the presupposition of unending sameness. Smith considers "historically inaccurate" the "belief that the Judaeo-Christian tradition espouses a doctrine of 'immortality.' On the contrary, the symbol of 'eternal life' expresses a new dimension or new quality of life and in no sense implies merely the endless continuation of the same."[28] While I question, in part, his interpretation of Judaeo-Christian tradition, I can understand Smith's existential interpretation of eternal life. I have already expressed strong reservations concerning the efficacy of any such interpretation; my concern here, however, is with his assertion that everlastingness is to be understood as "forever more of the same." Much closer to the mark, in my opinion, is John Baillie's view that "the soul's hope has not been for more of the same, but for something altogether higher and better."[29]

What we need is a doctrine of transformation that enables us to acknowledge both continuity and difference between the present life and any new life that might be hoped for. That transformationist views are congenial to those reflecting within a Christian framework is evidenced in the following texts from E. J. Fortmann and William Frost:

> Does the end of the world mean its annihilation (and re-creation) or merely its transformation? . . . Today the second view, transformation and not annihilation, seems to be growing stronger and stronger. Those who hold it think that the biblical passages should be construed as "change-passages," not as "annihilation-passages," if they are taken in a fuller biblical context.[30]

> This theology of hope places imagination in a Christian context. Christ, the Messiah, is portrayed as one who does not simply take the facts of life for

granted. In his unique contribution to the human race he encourages us to work and labor for the transformation of things so that the kingdom may become a reality. . . . This emphasis on transformation of reality in the name of life's promises and expectations culminates in the narratives of Christ's resurrection. Thus Christians receive the promise of a life beyond the grave.[31]

Any process model of reality is and must be transformationist, but whether this is a help or a hindrance to belief in personal immortality is a much more complicated question. Any evolutionary theory that extrapolates some mode of new being or new consciousness must confront a dilemma: if the changes in human nature are such that this nature remains basically as we now know it, then there is no possibility for the kind of divine community projected by the best visionary thinkers; if, on the other hand, such a community is made possible by a total transformation of human nature, then we no longer have human nature as we now know it. Because the available evolutionary data are ambiguous, it is possible to make two very different extrapolations of the future: one in which humanity continues to exist, though in a profoundly transformed manner; another in which humanity disappears and a new species emerges. Initially, this second interpretation would seem to be more consistent with our present knowledge of the evolutionary process. After all, the revolutionary and, for many, threatening aspect of Darwinism was that it posited the "transformation of species." The crucial consequence of evolution would seem to be that just as the human emerged as a new species from a species no longer in existence, in the distinct future there will be such a transformation of the human species that it will become extinct.

While this is surely a plausible extrapolation, it is not strictly entailed by the evidence. To begin with, we are not compelled to assume that the way in which evolution will continue to take place is identical with the way in which it has taken place. Indeed, such an assumption would seem to be contrary to one of the more exciting features of evolution—the emergence of the radically new. Hence, while up to this point the transformation of species appears to have resulted in a loss of fundamental identity between the old and the new, we cannot definitively rule out a change in the evolutionary process itself whereby future transformation—whether in "this world" or in an "other world"—will result in enrichment without the loss of identity.

I suggest that there are already some grounds for such an extrapolation in both individual and collective development. The transformation of a fertilized egg into a relatively helpless, speechless, instinctive infant and then into an adult capable of wondrous feats of creativity would not seem to be qualitatively less significant than the transformation of a fish into a reptile. Yet there is a mode of identity present in the former transformation that is absent in the latter. Further, we now recognize that the earlier stages of individual human lives have a value and meaning in themselves while simultaneously contributing, positively or negatively, to the transformed later stages in which identity continues, however profoundly transformed.

Shifting our focus to the human collectivity, we are able to detect further grounds for affirming great transformative development without simple loss of identity. Consider the evolution of *Homo*, which began with *Homo habilis* about two and a half million years ago, was transformed into *Homo erectus* about one and a half million years ago, and became *Homo sapiens* some three hundred thousand years ago. Although anthropologists are not in complete agreement as to how "close" *Homo habilis* was to the present-day *Homo sapiens*, they do seem to be making two judgments. First, they are distinguishing the earliest *Homo* from that species of which *it* was a transformation. Second, they are affirming a mode of "identity" between that original *Homo* and the present-day one. Since no one would deny the profound changes that have taken place within humanity over those two and a half million years—or even over the three hundred thousand years of *Homo sapiens*—transformation and identity cannot be asserted as mutually exclusive. Some modes of transformation do result in loss of identity, but others result in transformed identity.

Further, it might be suggested, as Teilhard de Chardin apparently has,[32] that a new quality or mode of life has already emerged from the evolutionary process, one that allows for an even greater transformation without loss of identity than in the previous stages of evolution. Hence, one might now extrapolate a new level of *human* existence that will be inconceivably different from but nevertheless fundamentally continuous with our present mode of life. The alternative extrapolation, which has already been criticized, is to view humanity as a means or preparation for the emergence of a new species (whether in "this world" or in any "other world") that will retain the human only in the way in which we now retain the subhuman from which we have evolved.

There is a formidable difficulty with the mode of extrapolation I favor, and it must be faced, though I do not know how to resolve it even to my own satisfaction. It can be objected that I am conflating two distinct time-space continua by extrapolating from the evident time-space continuum available to science to the not-so-evident time-space continuum to an other world. Thus, even if one were to concede that there will be a future transformation of the human species along the lines I have suggested, this is radically different from some future or new life entered into by all humans— past and present as well as future—on the occasion of their individual deaths. The most serious threat to the perspective here advanced is that a claim that such a new life is already available to those who die renders the long evolutionary process irrelevant. One way out is to say that the purpose of evolution, or at least a consequence of it, was to bring forth a species whose individuals are so constituted that death henceforth has the possibility of transformation rather than obliteration. While something such as this must be held if my claims for personal immortality are to stand, it still leaves unsettled the questions of why evolution should be continuing and why we should be working here and now to bring about a future transformation of the human community.

In response, I must revert to the contention that our actions and their consequences are not confined within those processes available to ordinary and scientific consciousness. My entire case depends upon a belief such as that which we have already heard expressed by James:

> The world of our present consciousness is only one out of many worlds of consciousness that exist, and . . . those other worlds must contain experiences which have a meaning for our life also; and . . . although in the main their experiences and those of this world keep discrete, yet the two become continuous at certain points, and higher energies filter in. (*VRE*, 408)

Given such an overlapping and interpenetration of processes and worlds, it makes sense to exert our fullest efforts toward transforming the world or worlds most immediately accessible to us, spurred on by the belief that these efforts bear fruit we are unable to perceive clearly at this moment. The evolutionary process, therefore, is multidimensional, and human participation—past, present, and future—is not restricted to the most immediately conscious dimension.[33] Incidentally, an evolutionary model such as this is congenial, I believe, to a reconstruction of the traditional doctrine of the communion of saints and the practice of praying for and to the dead.

NEW LIFE: POSITIVE CHARACTERISTICS

However radical the transformation that brings about a new life would be, it cannot be such as to obliterate all trace of those characteristics that presently constitute human life. Prominent among the characteristics of human life that seem inseparable from it are creative action, growth, self-development, love, joy, laughter, community, suffering, struggle, and loss. If we are to extrapolate these as also belonging to any new life, it cannot be too strongly stressed that by such extrapolation we are able to know as much and as little about the new life mode of these characteristics as we can about them when they are extrapolated as belonging to God. The same possibilities and limitations that attach to talking *about* God would attach to talking *about* any new life. The most obvious limitation attending any "new life" extrapolation concerns the "new" aspect, of which little or nothing can be said positively. That a future life such as the one here suggested and hoped for must be new in an inconceivable and unimaginable way seems both congenial to and mandated by faith *and* reason. The "newness" characterizing the risen Christ is a belief of long standing. As one commentator succinctly expressed it, "The Resurrection was not merely a coming back to life, but a birth into a new life which Christ did not have in his bodily humanity."[34] The evidence from reason for the necessity of newness is quite simply the dissolution which, in our experience, accompanies all living beings. Unless there is a "new" character realized through death and the saving grace of God, there is no possibility of a life without dissolution—without death. Let me now briefly discuss the necessity that the positive characteristics of human life continue in some way in any new life. It is quite obvious that since pragmatism's process metaphysics denies any absolute permanency or status, it cannot consistently allow for any new life from which process or change is completely absent. But a central feature of process or change is that at its best it brings about growth. Hence, a pragmatist could not extrapolate any divine or new human life that would exclude the possibility of growth. There is a growing consensus, despite metaphysical and theological differences, that any new life must be a growing or processive one. "A certain growth," Piet Schoonenberg tells us, "also remains possible in the final fulfillment. Otherwise we would perhaps cease to be human."[35] Ignace Lepp maintains that "the idea of progress is in fact so intimately related to that of life that we can only conceive of eternal life as eternal growth."[36] Similarly, John Shea rejects the notion of a static heaven, noting that "many people cannot conceive of human happiness except in terms of growth" (HH, 86).[37]

Growth, whether human, cosmic, or divine, is possible only insofar as the participative realities or beings have the power of creative action. Diverse as the activities may be, all realities—from electrons to God—are real in virtue of and to the extent that they are centers of activity. It follows, then, that our extrapolation of a new life will include the possibility of proportionate creative activity for the participants in such a life. "It is the yearning after continued action," according to Bergson, "that has led to the belief in an after-life."[38] And Goethe in a letter to J. P. Eckermann asserted: "To me the eternal existence of my soul is proved by my idea of activity."[39]

The creative activity performed by those entities designated selves is directly or indirectly bound up with self-development or self-realization. Pragmatism shares the view of those who insist that the self is a project or task, not a fully realized given. It is the task of self-creativity begun in this life that must be extrapolated as continuing in any new life. John Shea makes clear that such a viewpoint is not restricted to a pragmatic extrapolation: "When time and history are not viewed as terrors but as mediums of human development, heaven will not be viewed as external and static perfection. Heaven will be a time for continued growth and moral progress. The project of each man's life which is begun in this world demands more time to develop" (HH, 86). Similarly, Hocking contends that there can be no sense to a continuing life unless "the reflective self is concrete and active, carrying on that questioning which is the identity of its life here" (MI, 66).[40]

In his "justification" of the desire for immortality, Ralph Barton Perry notes that "there is always some unfinished business." Further, "the desire for more life springs from the belief that life on the whole is good, and to ask for more time is to have some affirmative reason for its use."[41] Perry was in all likelihood influenced in this matter by his mentor, William James. Perry tells us:

> As James grew older he came to *believe* in immortality. In 1904 he had acquired a feeling of its "probability." Although he did not feel a "rational need" of it, he felt a growing "practical need." What was this practical motive? In explaining why he was now, late in life, acquiring the belief for the first time, he said, "Because I am just getting fit to live." . . . With his temperamental love of the living, his affectionate sympathies, and his glowing moral admirations, he had come more and more to feel that death was a wanton and unintelligible negation of goodness. (*TC*, II:356)[42]

None of this, of course, in any way proves that we are immortal. The most that can be claimed is that it indicates a certain *meaning* and *propriety* that would accompany a new life in which the projects and tasks—including the task of self-creation—that have been begun and that death *always* leaves unfinished, would be continued and brought to fuller realization.[43]

The activity which above all other human activities seems to cry out for a continuance without end is, of course, love. "The surest warrant for immortality," according to James, "is the yearning of our bowels for our dear ones" (*PP*, II:937). Mooney points out that "human love . . . is quite shameless in hoping for immortality and believes against all evidence that it will not be affected by death" (*PAT*, II:146).[44] George Maloney suggests that "our love relations here and now determine the true, future direction of our psychic powers and the degree that they will be realized" (*PAT*, I:147).

Whether or not love is a sign of a continuing life, there seems to be no question that it is the human experience most painfully frustrated by the event of death. The love relation has an enduring character that the present conditions make difficult if not impossible to realize. The love relation is continually strained and ravaged by a multiplicity of factors, but those loves that endure seem to express most adequately the essence of love. One of the painful features of our present mode of existence is that some loves do end, or become incapable of being maintained in their richest mode and greatest intensity. Nevertheless, it appears to be humanly impossible to love and simultaneously accept without pain that love will end absolutely and without remainder, as death seems to indicate. The death of a loved one is almost beyond question the most tragic experience human beings undergo.

This tragic antithesis between love and death is poignantly expressed by Thomas Hardy in his *Tess of the D'Urbervilles*. As Tess is leaving her husband, Angel Clare, shortly before she is to be hanged, the following exchange takes place:

> "Tell me now, Angel, do you think that we shall meet again after we are dead? I want to know."
> He kissed her to avoid a reply at such a time.

"Oh, Angel—I fear that means no!" said she with a suppressed sob. "And I wanted so to see you again—so much, so much! What—not even you and I, Angel, who love each other so well?"[45]

Tess does not fear death; what she finds intolerable is that the love between herself and Angel will end with her death—and it will end except as a memory for Angel if she ceases to be. It would seem that if death is the annihilation of the individual, one cannot really be said to love someone who has died. If love involves the touching of two relational centers, the cessation of one of these centers necessitates the cessation of love. It would not seem possible to really love a nonexistent, a nothing. Of course, it might be argued that love is maintained through a memory, but unless the memory involves some kind of "presence" of the other, it is short-lived, as experience repeatedly shows. Gabriel Marcel has sensitively and perceptively explored the role of "presence" in the relationship between love and death. "Fidelity truly exists," he maintains, "only when it defies absence, when it triumphs over absence, and in particular, over that absence which we hold to be—mistakenly no doubt—absolute, and which we call death."[46]

Love, then, is the experience that gives the deepest ground for and greatest impetus to extrapolating a life that is not absolutely terminated by death. Further, any desirable new life must be such that the love relations so haltingly and imperfectly begun here, including those interrupted or diverted, will have an opportunity for reconciliation, renewal, and fuller realization.

A central feature of pragmatism, as was seen earlier, is that human individuals are constituted by their social or communal relationships. This view, of course, is not peculiar to pragmatism but is shared by a range of thinkers in the twentieth century.[47] An immediate corollary of the communal nature of humans is the need to construct communities or a community that will enrich and expand the actualities and possibilities of human life. There is a consensus that to this point in history the communities that have emerged are radically deficient in terms of enabling their members to reach the fullness of their potential. There follows, then, if not a consensus, a widely shared notion that human efforts ought to be directed to creating a truly human community free from those features that now limit and destroy so many. Whether in Utopian, Marxian, or Deweyan form, the call for such a community involves an extrapolation from past and present experience to future experience. Any suggestion of a desirable immortality must include an extrapolation similar to though obviously not identical with such future community extrapolations. It will share with these "secularist" extrapolations the notion that we are "here and now" striving to create a better community that will, we hope, be realized in the future. At the same time it will not restrict the parameters of this community, either in its present struggling form or its future realized form, to a narrowly conceived "this world."

Further, and most important, the kind of extrapolation called for will not restrict membership in the "new community" to those individuals who had the good fortune to come into existence concurrent with the fruitful realization of the often powerful efforts of so many other individuals.[48]

NEW LIFE: NEGATIVE CHARACTERISTICS
To this point the extrapolation of a desirable immortality has focused on what might be called the positive aspects of any new life that might be forthcoming after death. If we are to avoid a kind of self-deception or "bad faith," however, we cannot ignore certain negative aspects that properly should be extrapolated as likely to accompany this new life. Let me mention three such aspects—struggle, suffering, and loss—and indicate why and how they should be incorporated into a developed extrapolation of immortality.

The evolutionary process at all levels and stages gives no evidence of taking place without the seemingly essential character of "struggle."[49] An extrapolated life totally devoid of struggle would seem to involve a discontinuity, which has been previously ruled out, between the present life and the new life. The more encompassing process extrapolated from the more immediate processes of our experience has been described as continuous with these processes. In other terms, that divine life in which any new life would be a participation is already in a real relation to and hence in some way a participation in the world of immediate experience, just as human life is really related to and already participating in the divine life. It follows that God is a participant in the evolutionary struggle.[50] How then could we properly extrapolate a new life that would be transformed participation in the divine life, while excluding from such new life that struggle which even the divine does not escape? No, the struggle that is inseparable from human life appears to be related to one that is cosmic and even in a sense "trans-cosmic."[51]

This, of course, touches upon that deepest of mysteries, the mystery of evil. With no pretense to resolving the irresolvable, let me simply indicate a response consistent with pragmatism. First, pragmatism, as we saw in the chapter "Self and God," strongly objects to any view of evil that sees it either as incorporated within the eternal plan of an omniscient, omnipotent God or as preserved but overcome within the Whole or the Absolute. The only philosophical account of evil congenial to pragmatism is one that energizes human beings in their struggle to lessen and overcome it. Hence, any pragmatic immortality belief will be in part motivated by the hope and desire of having new opportunities for continuing the struggle against evil in which humans are presently engaged.

An almost inevitable accompaniment of the evolutionary struggle, particularly as manifest in the human species, is suffering. It is significant, I believe, that more and more efforts have been made to show that a God intimately involved in the creative process must be a "suffering God."[52] Again, therefore, any extrapolated new life cannot exclude the possibility of suffering in some form.

There remains the question of "loss" as it might pertain to any new life. Perhaps the most crucial aspect of this question has to do with the loss of everlasting union with the divine. Since I have already extrapolated a continuing struggle after death, it would follow that the achievement of everlasting union with the divine may depend on actions that are not restricted to "this life." It is because it is increasingly hard to believe that the actions of most human beings in the time allotted them in this life are of such a nature as to merit them either eternal life or eternal damnation that thinkers such as John Hick suggest a succession of lives, whereby a continuing purification will take place such that there will emerge individuals worthy of the most intimate union with God. Elsewhere, I have expressed my reservations about Hick's successive lives theory[53]—he fails, in my judgment, to safeguard that individuality which I consider essential to significant personal immortality. Here I wish to take issue with another aspect of his philosophical theology: namely, his affirmation of "universal salvation."[54] Finding the idea of hell or eternal suffering repugnant, Hick argues that the divine love is such that all will eventually be saved, though some may have to undergo a succession of a greater number of lives than others in order to achieve adequate self-purification.

The question that must be raised here is whether the doctrine of universal salvation, highly motivated though it may be, does not diminish the "seriousness" of human experience. While I do not think that hellfire and eternal torment ought to be presented even as a possibility, I am not sure that in order to avoid them we must assert that all human beings will necessarily be united with God in a union of joyful immediacy. At stake here, of course, is the nature and scope of human freedom. Without even touching upon the numerous subtle issues related to this freedom, let me simply suggest that there is a profound difference between a human freedom whose exercise *must* lead to union with God and one that allows for the possibility of eternal separation from God. This in no way rules out the possibility that all humans will eventually be united with each other within the depths of the divine life—indeed, this should be our hope. It would seem, however, that a world in which there can only be winners is a less serious world than one in which the possibility of the deepest loss is real. From a perspective such as Hick's, the goal is assured; the only question is how long an individual will take to reach it—as if God has said to us, "You're going to keep doing it till you get it right." Hence, while I think that Hick has advanced a very suggestive and supportable hypothesis—namely, that the process of creating ourselves and thereby moving closer to God must continue beyond "this life"—he has unnecessarily weakened and softened it by asserting that the final goal is preset and certain to be reached. Hell—understood as the everlasting separation of the individual from the divine center of love—must remain a live option for radically free human beings.

Concluding
Reflections

No, I shall not die, I shall live
   to recite the deeds of Yahweh;
though Yahweh has punished me often,
   he has not abandoned me to Death.
                              —Psalm 118:17–18

Some suppose that this post-natal life
where all we have is time, is fetal life,
is where as we bounce and flex in time
our years of moons change us
into beings viable not here
but somewhere attentive. Suppose,
borne down on, we are birthed
into a universe where love's not crazy;
and that split out of time is
death into a medium where
love is the element we cry out to breathe,
big love, general as air here,
specific as breath.
                    —Marie Ponsot
                    "The Great Dead, Why
                    Not, May Know"

From the available evidence, it would appear that immortality belief and terminality belief have been present in varying degrees of explicitness and with shifting degrees of dominance from the dawn of human consciousness.[1] It is interesting to note that in some of the earliest religious literature, it is death rather than immortal life which is seen as the destiny of human beings. In response to Gilgamesh's poignant but fruitless search for immortality, the Ale-wife informs him:

> The life thou pursuest thou shalt not find.
> When the gods created mankind,
> Death for mankind they set aside,
> Life in their own hands retaining.[2]

Her advice to him is echoed later in Ecclesiastes, where we are told:

> This, then, is my conclusion: the right happiness for man is to eat and drink and be content with all the work he has to do under the sun, during the few days God has given him to live, since this is the lot assigned him. . . . Whatever work you propose to do, do it while you can, for there is neither achievement, nor planning, nor knowledge, nor wisdom in Sheol where you are going.[3]

Contemporary expressions of such sentiments are numerous, of course, but what distinguishes them, perhaps, is that they emerge out of and over against a culture that for more than two thousand years was saturated with the belief that "this life" was the pathway to another life and that the way in which individuals lived "here and now" would determine the quality of their lives "hereafter." This belief was articulated in both the philosophical and religious traditions in such fashion that both the "rationality" and the existential meaning of human life were organically bound up with a belief in and a hope for some mode of its continuance beyond the grave. It is this belief and perspective which, as was noted at the outset, has been rendered radically problematic by modern and contemporary thought and experi-

221

ence. Moreover, the reality of death has taken on a much more terrifying dimension as the intimate continuity of human beings with nature has diminished, tribal and communal supports have lessened, and individual consciousness has acquired a more isolating identity. Death has become intensely personal, and a corresponding fading of belief in personal immortality has heightened the anxiety evoked by the encroachment of nothingness. Contemporary literature abounds in expressions of the metaphysical pain that is bound up with the ephemerality of human existence, but few, if any, surpass Samuel Beckett's play *Waiting for Godot,* the starkest lines of which, for me, are these:

> One day we were born, one day we shall die, the same day, the same second, is that enough for you? They give birth astride of a grave, the light gleams an instant then it's night once more.[4]

The efforts to find surrogates for the loss of personal immortality and the threatened loss of meaning are widespread, ranging from politics, art, and science to frenetic sex, auto racing, and drugs. Whether any of them will suffice for any length of time, and for more than an isolated few, cannot be determined at the present with any degree of confidence. Regardless of whether one opts for some mode of personal immortality or one of its surrogates, reflective consciousness cannot completely exclude the possibility that both for the individual and the collective, they will all fail. A character in a recent novel expressed this fear quite vividly: "Some people use bullfights, some the Mass, some art in order to ritualize or transform death into life or at least into meaning. But my terror is that life itself is a ritual transforming everything into death."[5]

Finally, it is Sigmund Freud who in one brief sentence conflates the ancient "wisdom" of Gilgamesh and Ecclesiastes with the claims of modern "knowledge"—"*The aim of all life is death.*"[6]

I have already suggested that an immortality-believer is not or at least should not be exempt from those terrifying dimensions of human experience that so many modern and contemporary thinkers and artists have so vividly portrayed. There is no possibility of or propriety in attempting to "answer" or "refute" such portrayals, yet it is necessary to "respond" to those who, on the basis of such portrayals, formulate a terminality belief or hypothesis. I have insisted that both the affirmation of life as continuing beyond and the certitude that it terminates in the grave are beliefs or faiths. In Jamesian language, a belief or "faith is synonymous with a working hypothesis." James goes on to say that "while some hypotheses can be refuted in five minutes, others may defy ages," and those dealing with God or immortality are such that "corroboration or repudiation by the nature of things may be deferred until the day of judgment" (*WB,* 79). Of course, a central point of pragmatism is that regardless of whether we believe in immortality or terminality, we must live *without* corroboration, the only tentative mode of corroboration being the quality of life, actual and possible, brought forth by our belief.

The personal, existential option for either belief, of course, involves a multiplicity of factors—temperamental, historical, cultural, and others—which in the case of every person constitute a gestalt that defies definitive, clear, and distinct analysis. In spite of the dimension of tentativeness, however, that ought to accompany both immortality belief and terminality belief, partisans of each are obliged to present as strongly as possible the justifying reasons for their own belief and the shortcomings of the one they reject. The mode of exchange, of course, should be reflective dialogue rather than debilitating debate. The danger in all such disputes is always the trivilization of the rejected hypothesis; open-minded dialogue, particularly on sensitive issues, is more easily honored than practiced. Nevertheless, every effort should be made to illuminate all relevant aspects of the question and the existential situation rather than simply to establish the erroneousness of the position opposed. One must mask neither the weaknesses of one's own view nor the strengths of the other's. Within such a framework, sharp criticism—even overstatements of the hypothesis being rejected—are proper and perhaps inevitable; however, these should never be isolated, closed claims but rather thought-experiments, which take place within an existential situation always richer, more ambiguous, and more suffused with mystery than even the most refined and sophisticated argument can ever adequately express. The most that either immortality-believers or terminality-believers can claim with any degree of confidence is that "on the whole," the fruits—present and to come—of their belief significantly outweigh the fruits of the belief they are rejecting.[7]

SELF-DECEPTION AND ESCAPISM: TWO-EDGED SWORDS

No immortality-believer who is even minimally aware of the thought and experience of the last two hundred years can avoid the real possibility that her or his belief is grounded in self-deception. When one encounters descriptions by Nietzsche, Marx, Freud, and others of the modes of self-deception suffusing religious belief, one cannot help recognizing that a certain degree of rightness characterizes those descriptions. That religious experience is often a weakness masking its will to power, a manifestation of the oppressed seeking consolation for their miserable state, or a wishful yearning for a protective father would no longer seem to be in serious dispute. But notice the qualifying words, "a certain degree" and "often." What still remains for some an open question is whether either separately or collectively these accounts exhaust the phenomenon of religious experience. For those for whom they do, of course, religion is no longer a live option. The situation for the others is more complicated. A reflective God- or immortality-believer must risk the likely presence of at least a degree of self-deception in order to realize those somewhat tenuous aspects of religious experience that seem not to be covered by self-deception.

While I concede that the danger of self-deception appears to be greater for the religious believer, I strongly reject any suggestion that self-deception is exclusively a feature of religious belief. Rather, the evidence would seem to indicate that it is a characteristic of the human condition in a variety of its modes. Is it so clear that Nietzsche with his doctrine of the overman, Marx with his prediction of a near-Utopian millennium, and Freud with his hopes for psychoanalysis were completely free of self-deception? If it is possibly self-deception to believe that our lives may not be totally extinguished at death, is it not also possibly self-deception—wishful thinking, an illusion—to believe that we can build a world in which humans will lead contented, fulfilled lives, fully aware that they will absolutely cease to be after a brief, fleeting moment of existence?

Self-deception, then, might properly be called a "two-edged sword," and anyone reflecting on immortality or terminality must constantly keep both edges in mind. A few brief examples will serve to concretize this point. The religious believer, who quite correctly notes the extent to which many of the best values of human culture are derived from religious experience, is tempted to argue, incorrectly, that religion is the only logical and existential ground for these values. Those who reject religion will concede that historically these values were associated with religion, but will contend that they could be maintained without fear of loss if religion were to disappear. Hence, the possibility that we are still living off the "fat" of religion is not seriously entertained. But it ought to be, for as one thinker trenchantly expressed it: "Perhaps all of us . . . are like children of rich men who live unknowingly off a still sumptuous inheritance (while we think it already exhausted). Perhaps we are going to leave our descendants a misery far deeper than we can imagine."[8]

Or consider the all too accurate charge that immortality belief is an unedifying effort to escape the harsh reality of death,[9] and as a consequence our responsibilities for the present state of the human condition are greatly diminished. On the other hand, the belief that death is absolutely final has an escapist dimension as well, as Hamlet suggests:

> To die—to sleep—
> No more; and by a sleep to say we end
> The heart-ache and the thousand natural shocks
> That flesh is heir to,—'tis a consummation
> Devoutly to be wish'd. (*Hamlet* 3.1)

If immortality belief has its mode of consolation, cannot the belief that our responsibility ceases totally with our death carry with it a consolation of its own? The belief that our life is not completely terminated at the grave does not in itself assure or exclude responsibility; hence, we might reasonably claim the possibility of its deepening this responsibility. The grounds for such an extrapolation are located in the experiential fact that responsibility for our actions usually extends beyond the moment—we are responsible for the future consequences of our acts as well as for our past actions. Is it not plausible, then, that we might be responsible in some new life for the way in which we are now living, and would not such consciousness lend a depth and significance to our present actions?[10]

NEEDS AND VALUES

We have considered James's insistence on taking seriously those needs in response to which religions have emerged. There is no claim, of course, that a felt need for salvation or immortality "proves" the reality or even the possibility of salvation or immortality. The most that is claimed is that a need or needs that have been widespread and persistent cannot be dismissed out of hand. If, of course, one is persuaded that those needs which have from the earliest moments of human consciousness to the present been expressed in various modes of religion—ranging then and now from benign to destructive, from insightful to frivolous, from humanizing to de-humanizing—that those needs are nothing but modes of self-deception, then every effort should be made to expose them as such and to replace them with more constructive needs. If, however, one believes that such needs, in spite of their often horrendous manifestations, are expressive of that dimension of the human self which opens it to the deepest resonances of reality, then one must bend one's efforts toward the redirection of those needs and the reconstruction of the modes in which they are expressed.

We may not be as confident today as James was that "immortality is one of the great spiritual needs of man" (HI, 2), but neither can we be certain that it is not. Having surrendered certainty either way, I have been attempting to suggest that such belief is a worthy, desirable, and hence "reasonable" belief. It is a reasonable belief if it does not involve the loss of important values and has the possibility of realizing some values that otherwise would be lost.[11] If one avoids or minimizes the escapist temptation that often accompanies belief in immortality, it is hard to see just what important values would be lost through such belief. I have suggested that quite possibly immortality-believers might be spurred to work harder even for those values that are at the center of the lives of secular humanists—more humane political, economic, and social structures, for example.

Detailing the distinctive values that might be gained by immortality belief is more difficult. Perhaps the most that can be claimed, and it is not a modest claim, is that all the values associated with human life thereby take on a greater depth and richness. And perhaps the most crucial value is that of the human person. A central feature of this essay has been the construction of a model of the human person constituted in part by its relation to a transcendent person, God. I have maintained that a view of the person as open to the possibility of a life continuous with everlasting divine life is a richer view than one that restricts the reality of the person to visible spatio-temporal parameters.

The key value gained by immortality belief, then, is inseparable from that transcendent dimension of reality traditionally symbolized as "God." Experientially, James maintains, the reality of God means "the presence of 'promise' in the world. 'God or no God?' means 'promise or no promise?' " (*MT*, 6). Elsewhere, he suggests that belief in God "changes the dead blank *it* of the world into a living *thou*, with whom the whole man may have dealings" (*WB*, 101). Now I am not arguing that the values related to belief in the divine are logically inseparable from immortality belief, but I am suggesting that those values take on a distinctive dimension when we believe that we have more than a momentary role to play in their realization. Take the value of "love," for example. Of course, this may be nothing more than a human emotion or activity that emerges from human experience and is restricted in its meaning and reality to this experience. Let us assume, however, that human love is a continuation and specification of a more encompassing principle which, given our processive world, is endeavoring increasingly to incarnate itself. Now immortality belief is not necessary for believing participation in this principle of love—indeed, I will shortly suggest that, paradoxically, the most fruitful participation would seem to exclude undue focusing on personal immortality. Nevertheless, the possibility that our participation in this everlasting principle of love is more than momentary does tend to distinguish it from participation in which the lasting fruits of all love activity are retained by this principle alone.

One of the most important fruits associated with the belief in personal immortality is that of a moral universe. Note, I say "moral universe," not "moral order," and with this distinction I am diverging somewhat from James's usage for, as we saw earlier, James maintained that ethics has "as genuine and real a foothold in a universe where the highest consciousness is human, as in a universe where there is a God as well" (*WB*, 150). Nevertheless, James contended that in the absence of faith in God, human beings will not be energized to their full potential. There is no question, then, that James recognizes a significant difference between a universe in which God and personal immortality are realities and one from which they are excluded. Following James, in part, I wish to acknowledge the possibility of morality within the second kind of universe but insist that it will be restricted to a dimension of this universe, whereas in the first kind of universe, morality would in some sense flow from its depth and center. Given this real difference, I think it proper to describe a universe involving God and personal immortality as a "moral universe." A universe in which these realities were absent could quite probably be said to *involve* a "moral order" but not to *be* a "moral universe." It is quite possible that morality is solely a creation of human beings and that it takes place within a nonmoral universe.

One of the controlling assumptions of this essay has been that the classical claim that reality is rational has been radically undermined by the thought and events of the modern and contemporary world. The world, as Nietzsche, Sartre, Camus, and others contend, may be essentially meaningless and absurd so that our incorrigible longings for justice, peace, harmony, and life are doomed to utter frustration. Pragmatism, as has been indicated, strives to form an alternative position—one which denies that a world of finished rationality and one of irredeemable absurdity are the only alternatives. Hence, we may *believe* that the world is becoming rational, moral, and that the all too evident feature of absurdity may eventually be overcome. As has been stressed, however, at this moment of human evolution it is not possible to claim that these are more than possibilities. Thus there can be no decisive refutation of either the classical view that the underlying structure of the world is finished and rational or the contemporary view that the world is to its core, and eternally, absurd.

JUSTICE AND COMPENSATION
One of the earliest spurs to belief in personal immortality was the evident fact of injustice in the world. If death ends all, then there can be no question of "justice" in the very basic sense of each individual's receiving his or her due. As noted in Ecclesiastes, "This is the evil that inheres in all that is done under the sun: that one fate comes to all." Yet one of the long-standing contentions of much of philosophy and religion is that "one fate" does not await us all.[12] It is a deep-seated, almost instinctive repugnance for such a view that has led philosophers in the name of rationality, moralists in the name of morality, and theologians in the name of God to argue for the reality of a life in which a more equitable participation in the goods of reality would be realized.

It is not being suggested, of course, that belief in personal immortality "proves" that we live in a moral universe. It is suggested that belief in personal immortality is bound up with belief in a moral universe. Surely, the overwhelming number of human beings now living and the billions who have lived can hardly be said to reflect in their allotted lives anything approaching justice. Even if those of us who have been more fortunate can say that in spite of everything we have been treated justly, it would surely be rash if not arrogant for us to suggest that the same holds for others. In the absence of personal immortality, then, there is no avoiding the existentialist's contention that the world is absurd and that morality is a characteristic—and a most tenuous one—of a small part of reality. Now whether or not we live in a moral universe, one in which justice will ultimately prevail, the desire for such a world is a worthy one and—absent compelling evidence that such a world is impossible—a reasonable one. Thus, if personal immortality is necessary to a moral universe, then it too is a worthy and reasonable belief.[13]

Having said this, and believing it to be true in some sense, I remain un-easy—it seems too simple, too neat, too "reasonable" when reflected against the dark underside of human experience. If there is a deep repug-nance to the notion that there is no ultimate justice, there has also emerged, particularly in the modern era, a repugnance to the notion that the poor and oppressed will be "compensated" for their sufferings in another life. Here again we are confronted with an instance of that existential dialectic de-scribed earlier. Immortality belief should not eradicate those experiential absurdities that its adherents share with the terminality-believers, in spite of the conflicting concepts, interpretations, and beliefs that arise from this shared experience.

There is a *sense* in which there are sufferings and evils that cannot be compensated for, here or hereafter. Consider the suffering of innocent chil-dren—what "divine plan" could ever justify such suffering? Why do we feel offended, why do we feel that their sufferings have been trivialized, when we hear someone glibly say, "It's all right; they are in heaven now"? Yet are we any less offended, do their sufferings seem any less trivialized, when we hear it said that "things will be better for future humanity"? As noted ear-lier, there is a sense in which *silence* seems to be the only appropriate re-sponse to some deeds, but neither the terminality-believer nor the immor-tality-believer can rest content permanently with silence. We must respond, undoubtedly in "fear and trembling," but we must respond, and the diver-sity of responses gives rise to our divergent concepts and beliefs.[14]

Let me hint at the direction I think a response consistent with the assump-tions and concerns of this essay might take. How might we acknowledge that some sufferings defy "compensation" and at the same time avoid ren-dering them completely meaningless? Suppose we are involved and incor-porated within a growth process along the lines I have described. The strug-gles and sufferings of everyone involved help to move the process to an even higher and richer process; as we are all contributors to the growth of this process, we share in both its sufferings and its joys—though not all equally nor simultaneously, since we enter in an indefinite number of different mo-ments and develop at widely varying rates. Suffering and loss, then, are the prices all participants pay, including God, for the creating of the world.[15] How, then, is this not "compensation" for our sufferings? Well, of course, in a sense it is, but we might call it "creative compensation" to distinguish it from "extrinsic compensation."

What might this mean? I am, needless to say, reaching here, but I am attempting to extrapolate a possible mode of life, however transformed, from available experience. For example, supposing some young man's legs are horribly burned in a theater fire for which the building's owner was responsible. The owner pays this young man a large sum of money, com-pensates him. The young man or someone close to him might say, "No amount of money can ever compensate for the pain and suffering he has undergone." Let us call this "extrinsic compensation." Now imagine that the young man is determined to overcome his handicap, and through persistent effort he is not only able to regain the use of his legs but in so doing develops into a world-class runner.[16] I would call this "creative compensation" and view it as the experiential ground for the extrapolation of the way in which sufferings, irreducibly absurd and meaningless in themselves, may possibly acquire meaning by their role in the creative process.[17]

Now one might object at this point that if this is the best argument that can be constructed for "creative compensation," it highlights the poverty of arguments for personal immortality when faced with the enormity of human suffering. I would not for a moment deny this, but what are our alternatives? Suppose the totality of the lives of those who have undergone profound and undeserved suffering are absolutely terminated with their deaths. Is this any more palatable, any more "just," than if somehow there were a God able to "save" their personal centers so that their horrible suffering would not have been the *whole* of their life? I have already expressed my view that what would be scandalous would be a God who had the power to save them without their having undergone such suffering but for whatever reasons failed to alleviate their pain. But a suffering God who is intimately bound up with the suffering of humans, who is "saving" them in the *only* way possible, is another matter. Of course, no such God may exist, and our faith may be a deceptive illusion—this possibility has been repeatedly conceded. If such a God did exist, however, he would hardly be reprehensible; hence, one's faith would not be morally repugnant, nor would the hope that those who have endured such intense and "senseless" suffering might in some mysterious way be "compensated" through a transformed mode of existence within the divine life.

Allied to the compensation objection to belief in personal immortality is the contention that such belief offers an unacceptable consolation for the pain and suffering that inevitably accompanies human life. I earlier dodged this objection by rejecting any faith that serves as a "means to *superficial* consolation." It seems foolish, however, and patently untrue to experience, to deny that even the kind of rigorous faith for which I am calling may give rise to some mode of consolation. The only point I would insist upon is that consolation may never be directly sought, that faith must never be a deliberate or conscious means to achieve the end of consolation. If consolation does accompany faith, it must come as a grace. As such, of course, it is not inevitable, and one may indeed believe yet receive little or no consolation. Indeed, I would suggest that nothing should make the believer more wary of the authenticity of his or her faith than an excess of consolation.

Another charge against the propriety of immortality belief must be acknowledged—a charge prevalent at least since the Enlightenment—that to believe in personal immortality is to be mired in an outmoded, primitive rewards-and-punishments version of morality that is demeaning to and unworthy of mature human beings. This charge has both secular and religious expressions: the first is encapsulated in the maxim "Virtue is its own reward," and the second in "God must be loved for his own sake." In both perspectives the implication is that to love God or serve our fellow beings *because* such actions will redound to our credit manifests a crass and superficial egotism. Since a crucial claim of the later part of this essay has been that immortality belief is pragmatically efficacious, I must again take refuge in paradox—a paradox, however, which is at the heart of all religious experience.

Prescinding from the psychological complexity, perhaps impossibility, involved, I would insist that believers in personal immortality should not love and serve God or their fellow beings *because* they will be rewarded, here or hereafter, for such love and service.[18] This would seem to be the insight at the heart of "losing one's soul in order to find it." A simplistic means-end relation appears inadequate to what is being counseled. If we seem compelled to recognize a dimension of unworthiness attached to serving others *in order that* we be personally rewarded—secularly or religiously—we also seem compelled to recognize that an enhanced quality of life often does result from disinterested service to others. The lesson the immortality-believer must draw is that thoughts of a new life ought not to be the primary focus of and motivation for their actions.[19] God and our fellow beings *ought* to be loved for their own sakes and not for any benefits that might accrue to us personally. The dedicated terminality-believer, therefore, will serve as a challenge to the authenticity of the immortality-believer's life and in a sense may even be a model for it. Immortality-believers must not make their dedication and contribution to the bettering of the human community and the world dependent upon their assurance of immortality. Their trust in the divine benevolence must be such that if their egos are the price to be paid for the advancement of the Spirit, so be it. This, of course, does not exclude their believing and hoping that the goodness of God is such that all will be graciously enabled to share in the fruits of the Spirit to whose life all have contributed.

An allied paradox is that while belief in personal immortality gives meaning to our lives, we should not so believe in order to give meaning to a meaningless life. Belief in personal immortality should not be the source or cause of a meaningful life; rather, the experienced worthwhileness and meaningfulness of life itself should give rise to the hope for continuing life. It is not because this life is so bad that we must seek meaning for it in another life. It is because life is so good that we desire to extend, deepen, and enrich it without limit.[20]

The ambiguous, clouded character of the human condition at the moment is such that, at best, both immortality belief and terminality belief are modes of a holding action until "the gods return." The humanistic immortality-believers cannot but acknowledge the poverty of their articulations, and the elusiveness and ambiguity of the experiences from which these articulations emerge. The humanistic terminality-believers cannot but acknowledge the gap between the idealized humanity of the Enlightenment—whether in its subsequent Nietzschean, Marxian, or Deweyan expressions—and the generality of human beings. Both must believe and hope that we are in transition to a new mode of human consciousness. The former will believe that this new mode will make the divine dimension of reality more evident and vital. The latter will believe and hope that the new mode of consciousness will achieve enough self-sufficiency to effectively overcome the long-standing need for transcendence. Both must live to the fullest in accordance with their respective beliefs and interpretations of their needs. Neither, of course, will believe that these are merely their individual or group needs, and they will therefore strive to persuade the others that the best of what these others seek is found in the opposing belief framework. Each group living so will test out their beliefs so that, over the long run, what is worthy of survival will survive. The terminality-believers might come to an awareness of a depth and reality accompanying their experience that is no longer adequately accounted for in mere human terms. The immortality-believers might come to realize that their belief in an encompassing personal reality with which their lives are continuous was but a primitive projection of the best in the human community and that the positive possibilities of such belief can now be lived without the early symbols by which it was expressed.

REPRISE

We have seen that the classic criticism of belief in immortality is its alleged deenergizing character, its turning individuals away from the difficult tasks at hand and focusing their attention and energies in an illusory "other world."[21] I believe that a pragmatic extrapolation along the lines suggested offers an alternative to such a life-denying immortality belief. It does so because, if consistently acted upon, it intensifies the present efforts to transform the world in which we find ourselves. Further, any future participation in the "new" human community will be significantly, though not necessarily exclusively, determined by the way we live and act in our present span of life. Hence, such belief in immortality does not divert our energies from "this life"; rather, it intensifies them by awakening us to the depth, scope, and seriousness belonging to "this life." Since a new community or new world or new reality is "here and now" in the process of being created, and since we are important—though not necessarily the only—participants in this creative process, the value of our present efforts is immeasurably increased. Inasmuch as the *sole* pathway to any new life is through "this life," any escapist beliefs or activities that fantasize an already realized and completed paradise to which we will leap are profoundly antithetical to authentic belief in immortality.

In the final analysis, of course, the pragmatic perspective assumed throughout this essay insists that belief or faith is not knowledge, and there is no guarantee that immortality-belief, or any other belief, is not illusory. The risk of belief is inevitable, and no reflective person can avoid it or transfer it to a surrogate, whether that surrogate is called tradition, the Church, the Bible, or God. The emphasis upon personal responsibility is only fitting, given that what is at stake is personal immortality. But since the person is relational or communal as well as individual, there is no suggestion here of any isolated, self-enclosed, egotistic, and merely mental belief activity. Indeed, unless belief in immortality gives rise to some evident existential fruits for both the individual and the community, pragmatic evaluation would be compelled to conclude that this belief is merely notional—a hollow relic left over from an earlier age.

Inasmuch as living belief never occurs within a historical and cultural vacuum, we may not minimize the formidable obstacles to belief in immortality within our present context. But neither should we succumb to them because we are unable to fashion arguments that will completely neutralize these obstacles. Fashion arguments we must, but they should reinforce, deepen, and enrich rather than substitute for other human activities. Paradoxically, the best arguments produced by any believing community, including perhaps the scientific community, have always led to mystery rather than demystification, expanding our sense of awe and wonder instead of explaining it away. Even the best arguments, however, never initiate or create life or belief. Only where there is a community already energized by vital belief stemming from a mysterious and irreducible experiential depth have there emerged those whose reflections have served to support, to modify, to expand, and at times to trivialize or destroy the originating belief or faith. Those who choose the path of reflective believing cannot know, a priori, which of these may result from their reflections. All we can know with some degree of confidence is that a belief in immortality which lacks *either* personal and communal fruits *or* reflective support has already lost its very reason for being—the deepening and expansion of life.

One last point. Belief in immortality should not isolate those who espouse it from others who also *believe* in the need to work toward the creation of a richer and more humane community. These latter would include a variety of Marxist and humanistic believers who also maintain that no significant and desirable future is possible unless a continuing effort on the part of an increasing number of human beings is made to "change the world" as it is presently constituted. Though the belief structures that energize those endeavoring to create a better world will involve important differences, which ought not be minimized, they should not be in superficial competition with each other. Only by a shared effort to realize convergent goals and values will an atmosphere emerge for a more fruitful dialogue concerning divergent beliefs—beliefs of such magnitude and scope that what is at stake is literally a matter of death *and* life.[22]

*Notes
and
Index*

NOTES

INTRODUCTION

1. John Herman Randall, Jr., *The Role of Knowledge in Western Religion* (Boston: Starr King Press, 1958), 140. See also Randall's *Nature and Historical Experience* (New York: Columbia University Press, 1958), 269–70 (hereafter, *NHE*): "Intellectual consistency between 'scientific' and 'religious' beliefs—if the latter are taken as giving an intellectual explanation of anything—is a very great value. But it is an intellectual and philosophical value, not a 'religious' value. . . . In any event, there is a basic distinction between religious beliefs that are 'fundamental,' and perform a religious function—that are religious symbols—and those that give intellectual understanding, that construe and interpret religious insight in terms of some particular philosophy, and adjust it to the rest of man's knowledge and experience. The latter beliefs are the basis of a 'rational' or 'philosophical' theology."

2. Cf. *SPP*, 30: "The question of being is the darkest in all philosophy. All of us are beggars here, and no school can speak disdainfully of another or give itself superior airs. For all of us alike, Fact forms a datum, gift, or *vorgefundenes*, which we cannot burrow under, explain or get behind. It makes itself somehow, and our business is far more with its *what* than with its *whence* or *why*."

3. John Dewey, "The Need for a Recovery in Philosophy," *On Experience, Nature, and Freedom*, ed. Richard J. Bernstein (New York: Liberal Arts Press, 1960), 23.

4. The hyphen instead of "and" as the connective here is deliberate and important, since it emphasizes the distinctive version of pragmatism's "experience" as a transaction between two poles of reality rather than an interaction between two essentially complete and separate entities.

5. *The Philosophy of Alfred North Whitehead*, ed. Paul Arthur Schilpp (New York: Tudor, 1941), 645, 647–48.

6. A. N. Whitehead, *Process and Reality* (New York: Humanities Press, 1955), 6.

7. A. N. Whitehead, *Adventures of Ideas* (New York: Free Press/Macmillan, 1967), 228. This is a reissue of the 1933 edition.

8. Cf. *PU*, 123: "All the whats as well as the thats of reality, relational as well as terminal, are in the end contents of immediate concrete perception."

235

9. Ralph Barton Perry, *The Thought and Character of William James,* 2 vols. (Boston: Little, Brown, 1935), II:257 (hereafter *TC*).

10. See also *VRE,* 72–73: "If you have intuitions at all they come from a deeper level of your nature than the loquacious level which rationalism inhabits."

11. Cf. Richard Stevens, *James and Husserl: The Foundations of Meaning* (The Hague: Martinus Nijhoff 1974), 37 (hereafter *JH*): "The task of achieving a fully coherent network of meaning is never finished, for even the most elaborate conceptual system always gives meaning only from a certain perspective, or from a limited number of perspectives."

12. Cf. Hans Küng, *Eternal Life?* trans. Edward Quinn (New York: Doubleday, 1984), 73–74: "A responsible decision of faith thus presupposes not a blind but a justified belief in an eternal life; the person is then not mentally overpowered but convinced with the aid of good reasons." See also, the penultimate paragraph of John Smith's fine Introduction to James's *Varieties of Religious Experience*: "The book stands as a necessary corrective to the fideistic tendency manifested in the religious thinking of recent decades, which has resulted in the encapsulation of religion within the walls of sheer faith, where it is divorced from any form of knowledge. James did not accept that bifurcation" (p. li).

13. Cf. Ian G. Barbour, *Myths, Models, and Paradigms* (New York: Harper & Row, 1976), 124 (hereafter *MMP*): "One cannot prove one's most fundamental beliefs, but one can try to show how they function in the interpretation of experience." See also Arthur O. Lovejoy, *The Revolt Against Dualism* (La Salle, Ill.: Open Court Publishing, 1960), 398: "Since our knowing is characteristically concerned with beyonds, we know by faith. But not all beyonds of which we can frame ideas are the objects of faiths for which we have motives equally persuasive, urgent, or irrepressible, equally deeply rooted in our cognitive constitution, and equally reconcilable with one another and with what—through our primary faiths in the reality of remembrance and in the existence of other knowers—we believe to have been the constant and common course of experience." It is worth noting that neither of these thinkers considers himself a pragmatist.

14. Ian G. Barbour, theologian and physicist, has developed an exceptionally accessible viewpoint on the relation between science and religion. Though more conceptually refined and developed, Barbour's views are strikingly similar to those found within the pragmatic tradition. See in particular his *MMP* and *Issues in Science and Religion* (New York: Harper Torchbooks, 1971).

15. The impossibility of rationally grounding first principles is widely held by twentieth-century thinkers. Gödel's incompleteness theorem is often cited in this regard. Hans Jonas, no friend of irrationalism, has made the point in somewhat less technical language: "If there is a 'life of reason' for man (as distinct from the mere use of reason), it can be chosen only nonrationally, as all ends must be chosen nonrationally (if they can be chosen at all). This reason has no jurisdiction even over the choice of itself as a means. But use of reason as a means, is compatible with any end, no matter how irrational. This is the nihilistic implication in man's losing a 'being' transcending the flux of becoming" (*The Phenomenon of Life* [New York: Dell, 1966], 47).

16. In "The Applicability of Logic to Existence," Dewey maintained that "existence apart from that of reflection is logic*able,* but not logic*ized*" (*Dewey and His Critics,* ed. Sidney Morgenbesser [New York: The Journal of Philosophy, 1977],

519). It first appeared in the *Journal of Philosophy* 27, no. 7 (1930). For a similar point made within a very different philosophical context, see Friedrich Nietzsche, *The Will to Power,* trans. W. Kaufmann and R. J. Hollingdale, ed. W. Kaufmann (New York: Vintage Books, 1967), 283: "The world seems logical to us because we have made it logical."

17. Cf. John Dewey, *The Influence of Darwin on Philosophy* (Bloomington: Indiana University Press, 1965), 13 (hereafter *ID*): "Philosophy forswears inquiry after absolute origins and absolute finalities in order to explore specific values and the specific conditions that generate them."

18. Cf. John Wild, *The Radical Empiricism of William James* (New York: Doubleday, Anchor Books, 1970), 388–89: "In such facts there is an element of opacity and 'mystery,' as James calls it. No matter how far his knowledge of existence may reach, there will be further depths beyond. Hence the radical empiricist should recognize that in these concrete investigations, he is not concerned with problems that can ever be solved once and for all. He is concerned rather with mysteries into which he may penetrate in various degrees, but which he will never be able to exhaust. This means that he will put forth his own conclusions in a tentative way, attempting at all costs to maintain that openness of mind which is so characteristic of James."

19. For similar notions by thinkers outside the pragmatic tradition, cf. John Hick, "Biology and the Soul," in *Language, Metaphysics, and Death,* ed. John Donnelly (New York: Fordham University Press, 1978), 159: "We are not here in the realm of strict proof and disproof but of an informal process of probing in search of a more adequate conceptualization of the data." See also Ralph Harper, *The Existential Experience* (Baltimore, Md.: Johns Hopkins University Press, 1972), 6: "It would be wise to think of existential thinking always as exploratory and provisional."

20. Dewey, *ID,* 194.

21. Cf. James, cited in *TC,* II:350: "The truth is what will survive the sifting— sifting by successive generations and 'on the whole.' "

22. John Dewey, *Experience and Nature* (New York: Dover, 1958), 7. Cf. *WB,* 112: "The thinker starts from some experience of the practical world, and asks its meaning. He launches himself upon the speculative sea, and makes a voyage long or short. He ascends into the empyrean, and communes with the eternal essences. But whatever his achievements and discoveries be while gone, the utmost result they can issue in is some new practical maxim or resolve, or the denial of some old one, with which inevitably he is sooner or later washed ashore on the *terra firma* of concrete life again."

23. Elizabeth Flower and Murray G. Murphey, *A History of Philosophy in America,* 2 vols. (New York: Putnam, 1977), II:682.

24. Ralph Barton Perry, *In the Spirit of William James* (New Haven, Conn.: Yale University Press, 1938), 203.

25. In a letter to Arthur Lovejoy in 1907, James made the following concession: "Consequences of true ideas *per se,* and consequences of ideas *qua believed by us,* are logically different consequences, and the whole 'will to believe' business has got to be re-edited with explicit uses made of the distinction" (cited in *TC,* II:481).

26. See also *P,* 143: "On pragmatistic principles, if the hypothesis of God works satisfactorily in the widest sense of the word, it is true. Now whatever its residual difficulties may be, experience shows that it certainly does work, and that the problem is to build it out and determine it, so that it will combine satisfactorily with all

the other working truths." Cf. Morton White, *Science & Sentiment in America* (New York: Oxford University Press, 1973), 205: "A holistic . . . conception of science . . . emerges in those parts of *Pragmatism* in which he [James] describes the establishment of belief as a process in which we do not test opinions in isolation but rather as parts of a whole stock of opinions."

27. Louis Dupré, *Transcendent Selfhood* (New York: Seabury Press, 1976), 80.

28. Cf. Randall, *NHE*, 198: "We never encounter *the* Universe, we never act toward experience or feel being or existence as 'a whole.'" See also Karl Jaspers, *Way to Wisdom*, trans. Ralph Manheim (New Haven, Conn.: Yale University Press, 1960), 43: "The world as a whole is not an object, because we are always in it and we never confront the world as a whole. Hence we can not, from the existence of the world as a whole, infer the existence of something other than the world. But this notion takes on a new meaning when it is no longer regarded as a proof. Then metaphorically, in the form of an inference, it expresses awareness of the mystery inherent in the existence of the world and of ourselves in it."

29. Eugene Fontinell, "John Hick's 'After-Life': A Critical Comment," *Cross Currents*, Fall 1978, pp. 315–16.

30. It is important to stress that pragmatic extrapolation is rational, and while any extrapolation, such as the one relating to immortality, may be unsuccessful and fall as a result of critical analysis, it cannot be dismissed out of hand simply because it points us beyond the bounds of present experience or strict inferential reasoning. Pragmatic extrapolation does not have the dimension of irrationalism apparent in an affirmation of immortality such as Miguel de Unamuno's. The similarities and contrasts between the two approaches cannot here be delineated, but one crucial difference is that the faith-reason relation in pragmatism does not have the fierce oppositional character that it has in Unamuno. See his *Tragic Sense of Life*, trans. J. E. Crawford Flitch (New York: Dover, 1954), 114: "To believe in the immortality of the soul is to wish that the soul may be immortal, but to wish it with such force that this volition shall trample reason underfoot and pass beyond it."

31. Barbour makes one further point supportive of the kind of pluralism espoused by pragmatism: "In place of the absolutism of exclusive claims of finality, an ecumenical spirit would acknowledge a plurality of significant religious models without lapsing into a complete relativism which would undercut all concern for truth" (*MMP*, 8).

32. Plato scholar Henry G. Wolz has given what I would call a near pragmatic description of extrapolation: "The outcome of an extrapolation can, therefore, be said to be empirical in its *origin*, transempirical in its *nature*, and, in as much as it may serve as a norm or means of elucidation, once more empirical, namely, in its *function*" (*Plato and Heidegger: In Search of Selfhood* [Lewisburg, Pa.: Bucknell University Press, 1981], 132).

33. Whether an extrapolation is so "beyond" experience as to be invalidly discontinuous with is one of the matters not able to be decided in isolation from a range and diversity of factors. Nietzsche, for example, concedes that his notion of the overman is as much a conjecture as is the notion of God, but he considers the former a valid conjecture, the latter invalid: "God is a conjecture; but I desire that your conjectures should not reach beyond your creative will. Could you *create* a god? Then do not speak to me of any gods. But you could well create the overman" (*Thus Spoke Zarathustra*, in *The Portable Nietzsche*, ed. and trans. Walter Kaufmann [New York: Viking, 1968], 197).

34. Throughout this essay, I will use the terms "immortality" and "resurrection" interchangeably. In another context it would be important to differentiate them, but it is not crucial from my perspective. I agree with John Hick that "if we posit the reality of God, the difference between immortality and resurrection, as variations within a theistic picture, becomes secondary" (*Death and Eternal Life* [New York: Harper & Row, 1976], 181).

35. This classification is but a variation of that given by Robert Jay Lifton in *Boundaries* (New York: Vintage Books, 1970), 21ff., and *The Life of the Self* (New York: Simon & Schuster, 1976), 32–34. For an earlier and similar version, see Corliss Lamont, *The Illusion of Immortality* (New York: Frederick Ungar, 1965), 22–23 (hereafter *II*).

36. For a biting dismissal of what he calls "those shabby pseudoimmortalities that atheists and pantheists are forever proffering as substitutes for the real thing," which is "personal immortality," see Martin Gardner, "Immortality: Why I Am Not Resigned," in *The Whys of a Philosophical Scrivener* (New York: Quill, 1983), 280.

37. Cf. Lamont, *II*, 251. After describing a number of such "symbolic interpretation[s]" of immortality and resurrection and conceding that for him they contain "the only truth that immortality ideas ever had," Lamont adds that these "abstruse redefinitions of immortality and the resurrection cannot be expected to have much emotional efficacy or religious value. They will appeal here and there to certain esoteric religious, philosophic and esthetic groups, but for the great masses of men they will have little significance."

38. Bertrand Russell, *Mysticism and Logic* (London: Longmans, Green, 1921), 47–48.

39. W. B. Yeats, "The Song of the Happy Shepherd," in *The Collected Poems of W. B. Yeats* (New York: Macmillan, 1956), 7.

40. Fyodor Dostoevsky, *The Brothers Karamazov*, trans. Constance Garnett (New York: Modern Library, n.d.), 253.

41. Cited by Jacques Choron in *Death and Modern Man* (New York: Collier Books, 1972), 15.

42. Ralph Harper, *The Existential Experience* (Baltimore, Md.: Johns Hopkins University Press, 1972), 69.

CHAPTER 1

1. John J. McDermott, ed., *The Writings of William James* (Chicago: University of Chicago Press, 1977), xlv (hereafter *WWJ*).

2. These notes are reproduced in Ralph Barton Perry, *The Thought and Character of William James*, 2 vols. (Boston: Little, Brown, 1935), II:365ff. (hereafter *TC*). Needless to say, there is no suggestion here that James originated the notion of "fields." Mary Hesse locates one source of field theory in physics in the work of the eighteenth-century cosmologist Ruggiero Boscovich:

> For Boscovich, "matter" is reduced to point particles having inertia but interacting by distance forces of attraction and repulsion, whose magnitude depends on the distance between the particles. . . . If attention is concentrated on the forces that are exerted in space between the point masses, it is possible to regard these as in some way constituting a medium, thus "substantializing" the force field itself and reducing the point masses to mere singularities in this field. This was essentially the step taken by Michael Faraday in transforming Boscovich's theory into field

theory as it is understood in both classical and modern physics. ("Action at a Distance and Field Theory," in *The Encyclopedia of Philosophy,* 8 vols., ed. Paul Edwards, [New York: Free Press/Macmillan, 1967], I:11–12). Since its origination in physics, the "field" concept has been employed in a variety of disciplines. The most notable and developed instance, perhaps, is found in the work of Kurt Lewin, who produced a highly technical social-psychological field theory. For an insightful and suggestive use of a field metaphor, drawn from physics, to illuminate the nature of poetic and religious ecstasy, see Justus George Lawler, "Ecstasy: Towards a General Field Theory," *Journal of the American Academy of Religion,* Dec. 1974, 605–13.

3. Cf. Richard Stevens, *James and Husserl: The Foundations of Meaning* (The Hague: Martinus Nijhoff, 1974), 129 (hereafter, *JH*): "James discovered that the most primitive data of the stream of consciousness are 'sensible totals,' i.e., ensembles of sense data which always present themselves in a focus-fringe pattern." Stevens is here discussing James's description of experience as it is presented in *The Principles of Psychology.* I think it evident that these "sensible totals" are an early version of "fields." The following text from Stevens suggests a similar congeniality between James's field language and his doctrine of pure experience: "The primordial field of pure experience is a vaguely pre-structured flow of loosely-linked 'sensible totals.' No totality is ever complete or self-enclosed. On this fundamental level, there is no precise line of demarcation which separates one sensible totality from another" (*JH,* 24).

4. For an allied notion, cf. A. N. Whitehead *Adventures of Ideas* (New York: Free Press/Macmillan, 1967), 206: "The universe achieves its values by reason of its coordination into societies of societies, and into societies of societies of societies."

5. John Herman Randall, Jr., *Nature and Historical Experience* (New York: Columbia University Press, 1958), 133, 146n. (hereafter *NHE*).

6. Robert Pollock, "James: Pragmatism," in *The Great Books,* 4 vols., ed. Harold Gardiner (New York: Devon-Adair, 1953), IV:197, 191.

7. A. N. Whitehead, *Process and Reality* (New York: Humanities Press, 1955), 53 (hereafter *PR*).

8. A. N. Whitehead, *Modes of Thought* (New York: Capricorn Books, 1958), 221. Whitehead later adds: "We have to construe the world in terms of the bodily society, and the bodily society in terms of the general functionings of the world. Thus, as disclosed in the fundamental essence of our experience, the togetherness of things involves some doctrine of mutual immanence. In some sense or other, this community of the actualities of the world means that each happening is a factor in the nature of every other happening. . . . We are in the world and the world is in us" (pp. 225, 227).

9. John Dewey, *Experience and Nature* (New York: Dover, 1958), 208 (hereafter *EN*). Cf. Randall, *NHE,* 245: "It is not merely organisms that can be said to 'respond to stimuli,' that is, to respond to particulars as instances of ways rather than as mere particulars."

10. John Dewey, "Experience, Knowledge and Value," in *The Philosophy of John Dewey,* ed. Paul Arthur Schilpp (New York: Tudor, 1951), 544.

11. John Dewey, "In Defense of the Theory of Inquiry," in *On Experience, Nature, and Freedom,* ed. Richard Bernstein (New York: Liberal Arts Press, 1960), 135 (hereafter *ENF*).

12. John Dewey, *Logic* (New York: Henry Holt, 1938), 66–67 (hereafter *L*).

13. John Dewey and Arthur F. Bentley, *Knowing and the Known* (Boston: Beacon Press, 1960), e.g., 67–69 (hereafter *KK*).

14. Bernstein, Introduction, *ENF*, xl. See also Bernstein's *John Dewey* (New York: Washington Square Press, 1967), 83: "From a transactional perspective, an 'element' is a functional unit that gains its specific character from the role that it plays in the transaction. . . . A transaction does not occur with an aggregate or combination of elements that have independent existence. On the contrary, what counts as an 'element' is dependent on its function within a transaction." That this radical character of "internal" change is not restricted to macroscopic realities is suggested by the following: "Thus twentieth-century science has revolutionized many fundamental ideas of the nineteenth century; the atom is not only much more complex than Dalton [the founder of chemical atomic theory] thought; it is also much more dynamic. . . . The main mistake of Dalton and other advocates of essentially mechanistic theories lay in the conviction that atoms did not undergo any internal change" (Andrew G. M. van Melsen, "Atomism," *Encyclopedia of Philosophy*, I:197).

15. George R. Geiger, *John Dewey* (New York: Oxford University Press, 1958), 17.

16. See also John Dewey, *Experience and Education* (New York: Macmillan, 1956), 41 (hereafter *EE*): "The statement that individuals live in a world means, in the concrete, that they live in a series of situations. And when it is said that they live *in* these situations, the meaning of the word 'in' is different from its meaning when it is said that pennies are 'in' a pocket or paint is 'in' a can." For a useful comparison of Dewey's "environment" and Alfred Schutz's version of the *Lebenswelt*, see Rodman B. Webb, *The Presence of the Past* (Gainesville: University Presses of Florida, 1975), 40ff.

17. John Dewey, *Democracy and Education* (New York: Macmillan, 1961), 47.

18. John Dewey, *Human Nature and Conduct* (New York: Modern Library, 1930), 14, 16. For what can properly be considered a field view related to James and particularly Dewey, see Randall's "Substance as a Cooperation of Processes," in *NHE*, 142–94. Randall notes that what he calls "Substance" can be called "the Field" (p. 149n). He later states: "Substance is what we today call 'process.' . . . More precisely, Substance is encountered and known as a complex of interacting and cooperating processes, each exhibiting its own determinate ways of cooperating, or Structure" (p. 152).

Given the rather broad sense in which I am understanding "field metaphysics," one could maintain that Whitehead has constructed the most systematic field metaphysics to date. His *Process and Reality* is, needless to say, a thoroughly processive-relational view of reality. Two texts from his more accessible *Modes of Thought* indicate the deep congeniality between Whitehead and James and Dewey on the central theme of reality as "fields": "The whole spatial universe is a field of force, or in other words, a field of incessant activity" (p. 186). "The notion of self-sufficient isolation is not exemplified in modern physics. There are no essentially self-contained activities within limited regions. These passive geometrical relationships between substrata passively occupying regions have passed out of the picture. Nature is a theatre for the inter-relations of activities" (p. 191).

19. Cf. Elizabeth Flower and Murray G. Murphey, *A History of Philosophy in America*, 2 vols. (New York: Capricorn Books, 1977), II:666: "Alternately it [pure experience] can be read as an ontological formulation of what there is, or as a phenomenological field where ontological interpretation is suspended. Again, it could

simply be used, in a technical way, as the experience-matrix out of which objects of knowledge are constructed. It even has affinities with Dewey's 'experience' and it gave James as much trouble as it afterward made for Dewey." As Perry shows, James had no illusions that he had realized a definitive and finished theory. What James said concerning the mind-body question is applicable to his more general theory: "The only surely false theory would be a perfectly clear and final one" (*TC*, II:386). While James did not deny the importance and utility of clarity and consistency, in the final analysis, as Perry notes, "he was much more afraid of thinness than he was of inconsistency" (*TC*, II:668).

20. Cf. *TC*, II:367: "In the main . . . he was preoccupied with the 'pure experience hypothesis'—in a determined effort to resolve certain *entitative* differences of traditional thought into *relational* or *functional* differences." See also Stevens, *JH*, 15: "Thus, the traditional problem of an unbridgeable chasm between radically different entities, thoughts and things, is seen as a false question, when entitative differences are replaced by relational or *functional* differences within a common sphere of pure experiences."

21. Cf. Charlene Haddock Seigfried, *Chaos and Context* (Athens: Ohio University Press, 1978), 43–44 (hereafter, *CC*). Seigfried convincingly shows the inadequacy of this passage: "All the criteria for physical things beg the question," since

> as criteria *for* the physical he gives physical descriptions which would themselves have to have other criteria for being physical. For instance, he says that the physical can be distinguished from the mental if it is recognized as entering into "relations of physical influence." But it is precisely the problem of providing a rule to identify the physical that is at issue. The recognition of a relation as physical does not tell us why it is physical and not mental. Furthermore, the criteria for the mental world are not exclusive and would apply equally well to the physical world. The physical world is as transitory as the mental field, changing all the while we ourselves change, and the appeal to its "physical inertness" again begs the question.

Of course, the difficulty of finding definitive, clear-cut characteristics to distinguish the physical from the psychical is what leads both materialists and idealists to deny that there are any. For an example from the side of idealism, see Josiah Royce, *The Spirit of Modern Philosophy* (Boston and New York: Houghton, Mifflin, 1892), 350ff.

22. Bruce Wilshire correctly, I believe, notes that James places an excessive burden on a "pure experience" when he "conceives of a single pure experience as being both the knower and the known. This is exceedingly spare substantively, and it puts a great theoretical load on pure experience; a single pure experience must be perceiver, perception, and perceived" (*William James and Phenomenology* [New York: AMS Press, 1979], 170; hereafter *WJP*).

23. A. J. Ayer, *The Origins of Pragmatism* (San Francisco: Freeman, Cooper, 1968), 292.

24. This sentence concludes: "the philosophy of pure experience being only a more comminuted *Identitatsphilosophie*." Wilshire, concerned to expose the phenomenological tendencies of James's thought, relates this text to James's effort to overcome dualism by coming "to the point of saying that thought and thought's object are in some fundamental way *identical*" (*WJP*, 14–15). Cf. *ERE*, 263: "Can we say, then, that the psychical and the physical are absolutely heterogeneous? On the contrary, they are so little heterogeneous that if we adopt the commonsense point of view, if we disregard all explanatory inventions—molecules and ether waves, for

example, which at bottom are metaphysical entities—if, in short, we take reality naively, as it is given, an immediate, then this sensible reality on which our vital interests rest and from which all our actions proceed, this sensible reality and the sensation which we have of it are absolutely identical one with the other at the time the sensation occurs. Reality is apperception itself."

25. John Wild, *The Radical Empiricism of William James* (New York: Doubleday Anchor Books, 1970), 361 (hereafter *REWJ*). Wilshire expresses a similar view in describing why he finds a certain richness in *PP* which is lacking in *ERE*. In the former work, James "does not confront us *ab ovo* with a set of discrete pure experiences, but rather with a whole lived-world of experience which is experienced by a person *as* lived by himself. He takes the first steps toward a direct linking of modes of experiencing and modes of the experienced, and so conceives experience that it never takes place outside a context. Indeed, the founding level of meaning is a context" (*WJP*, 171). It is just this fundamental contextual character of experience that is acknowledged and safeguarded by the use of "field" or "fields" as the primary metaphysical metaphor.

26. Flower and Murphey, *History of Philosophy*, II:666.

27. Actually, the ambiguity to which Stevens refers is already present in *PP*; a few lines before James describes the personal character of thought or consciousness, he says: "*The first fact for us, then, as psychologists, is that thinking of some sort goes on.* . . . If we could say in English 'it thinks,' as we say 'it rains' or 'it blows,' we should be stating the fact most simply and with the minimum of assumption. As we cannot, we must simply say that *thought goes on*" (*PP*, I:219–20).

28. Wild contends that James's desire to make room in experience for both the subjective and the objective gives rise to two quite different interpretations. The first, and acceptable, one holds that "experience may have an overarching structure that is neither purely subjective nor purely objective but with a place for both of these phenomena." On the other hand, since pure experience "has room for both the subjective and the objective, it is easy to infer that in itself, as pure experience, it must be neither the one nor the other, and in itself neutral." This in turn leads to the view that "pure experience itself is composed of units which are themselves neither one nor the other, but neutral to the whole distinction." Wild comments that "the dualism of mind and body needs to be overcome but this is too high a price to pay" (*REWJ*, 355–56).

29. Cf. Wilshire, *WJP*, 200: "It is in this sense of an overabounding world, too rich and fluid to be contained by any set of concepts—as truthful as that set might be—which sets James off from Husserl and which places him nearer to Heidegger and Merleau-Ponty."

30. See also Stevens, *JH*, 177: "The givenness of the perceptual field is absolute in two senses: it is the absolute source from which consciousness derives the entire fabric of reality and the absolute standard of truth for all meaning."

31. Both Stevens and Seigfried stress the fact that, for James, we never encounter a chaotic flux of pure heterogeneity. See Stevens, *JH*, 20: "James insists on the fact that the original flow of experience is not a manifold of totally heterogeneous impressions without structure or continuity. But it is, nonetheless, relatively unstructured by comparison with the ulterior patterns of organization imposed by intellectual activity. Thus the return to pure experience refers simply to the uncovering of a world of primary perceptions, considered in abstraction from the selective organiza-

tion of conception." See also Seigfried, *CC*, 53: "Relations in pure experience are quasi-chaotic in that they have not yet been hardened into specific identifiable relations which are attributable to a chosen context."

32. Cf. James, *TC*, II:381: "All that is is experiences, possible or actual. Immediate experience carries a *sense of more*. . . . the 'more' develops, harmoniously or inharmoniously; and terminates in fulfillment or check. . . . The problem is to describe the universe in these terms."

33. The following James text could, I believe, be accommodated within this kind of field perspective: "The paper seen and the seeing of it are only two names for one indivisible fact which, properly named, is *the datum, the phenomenon, or the experience.* The paper is in the mind and the mind is around the paper, because paper and mind are only two names that are given later to the one experience, when, taken in a larger world of which it forms a part, its connections are traced in different directions. *To know immediately, then, or intuitively, is for mental content and object to be identical*" (*MT*, 36).

34. Perry includes a selection from these notes as an appendix under the heading "The Miller-Bode Objections" (*TC*, II:750–65).

35. Cf. the frequently cited text of James: "Life is in the transitions as much as in the terms connected; often, indeed, it seems to be there more emphatically" (*ERE*, 42).

36. Bruce Kuklick, *The Rise of American Philosophy* (New Haven, Conn.: Yale University Press, 1977), 333 (hereafter *RAP*). Kuklick cites James's reference to "a pluralistic panpsychic view of the universe" (*PU*, 141). While James does say that this view is the "great empirical movement . . . into which our generation has been drawn" (*PU*, 141–42), he does not unequivocally make it his own, here or elsewhere in his writings. Thus the commentators are divided on whether James was a panpsychist, with the majority inclining toward the negative. For a subtle and insightful argument that James's later metaphysics was a mode of process panpsychism, see Marcus Peter Ford, *William James's Philosophy* (Amherst: University of Massachusetts Press, 1982), esp. 75–89, the chapter entitled "Pure Experience and Panpsychism."

CHAPTER 2

1. Ralph Harper, *The Existential Experience* (Baltimore, Md.: Johns Hopkins University Press, 1972), 87.

2. Cf. John Wild, *The Radical Empiricism of William James* (New York: Doubleday Anchor Books, 1970), 27: "Thus before 1890 and probably before 1885, James clearly recognized that human consciousness is not enclosed within a subjective container, but is rather stretched out towards objects of various kinds in the manner called *intentional* by later phenomenologists." Cf. also, Bruce Wilshire, *William James and Phenomenology* (New York: AMS Press, 1979), 125: "The self is not a sealed container full of intrinsically private thoughts. It is as if the self were blasted open and distributed across the face of the lived-world."

3. John Herman Randall, Jr., *Nature and Historical Experience* (New York: Columbia University Press, 1958), 173 (hereafter *NHE*). In a sense the characteristic of not being enclosed within the envelope of the skin is not peculiar to human selves as the following text from Dewey indicates: "The thing essential to bear in mind is that

living as an empirical affair is not something which goes on below the skin-surface of an organism: it is always an inclusive affair involving connection, interaction of what is within the organic body and what lies outside in space and time, and with higher organisms far outside" (*Experience and Nature* [New York: Dover, 1958], 282 (hereafter *EN*). See also John Dewey, *Art as Experience* (New York: Capricorn Books, 1958), 58–59: "The epidermis is only in the most superficial way an indication of where an organism ends and its environment begins. . . . the need that is manifest in the urgent impulsions that demand completion through what the environment— and it alone—can supply, is a dynamic acknowledgment of this dependence of the self for wholeness upon its surroundings." Cf. A. E. Bentley, "The Human Skin: Philosophy's Last Line of Defense," *Philosophy of Science* 8 (1941): 1–19. See also Whitehead's *Adventures of Ideas* (New York: Free Press/Macmillan, 1967), 225, and his *Modes of Thought* (New York: Capricorn Books, 1958), 221. For a somewhat similar view from within a different perspective, see Ralph Wendell Burhoe, "Religion's Role in Human Evolution: The Missing Link Between Ape-Man's Selfish Genes and Civilized Altruism," in *Zygon* 14, no. 2: "Biological patterns and behaviors are not limited to determination by genes alone. . . . organic structure and behavior are products of the interaction of the genetic information with a particular set of environing circumstances, including culture and other non-random and enduring factors, which properly have been called 'paragenetic' information by such a veteran biological and evolutionary theorist as C. H. Waddington."

4. Terence Penelhum in his essay on "Personal Identity" (*The Encyclopedia of Philosophy*, 8 vols., ed. Paul Edwards [New York: Free Press/Macmillan, 1967], VI:96.) states: "The use of the word 'self,' however, has the effect of confining the question to the unity of the mind and of preventing the answer from relying on the temporal persistence of the body." Quite obviously, I intend no such restrictive use of the term. On the contrary, it is the neutrality of the term "self" in relation to mind *and* body that commends it.

5. One might note increasing evidence that some religious thinkers reject traditional dualism. See John Shea, *What a Modern Catholic Believes about Heaven and Hell* (Chicago: Thomas More Press, 1972), 47: "This dualistic view of man, so long the ally of Christian faith, does not correspond with either modern or biblical anthropology. Modern science envisions man as a psychosomatic unity. . . . The biblical view of man closely parallels the modern. For both Old and New Testament man is an indivisible whole. In biblical literature there are abundant references to body, soul, spirit, and heart but these are not parts into which man may be divided. Each of these words refers fundamentally to the whole man, although each does so in a special manner." E. J. Fortmann, after acknowledging the nondualistic views of Karl Rahner and John Shea, proceeds to argue in favor of a mode of dualism, drawing upon science, psychology, and parapsychology as well as scripture and the magisterium. See his *Everlasting Life after Death* (New York: Abba House, 1976), 41–68, ch. 2, "Is Man Naturally Immortal?"

6. James, who struggled long and hard to find a viable alternative to dualism, was not unaware of the possibility that it was a fruitless endeavor. In one of his notes he was led to ask: "Doesn't it seem like the wrigglings of a worm on the hook, this attempt to escape the dualism of common sense?" (cited in Ralph Barton Perry, *The Thought and Character of William James,* 2 vols. [Boston: Little, Brown, 1935], II:369; hereafter *TC*).

7. While some form of materialism is the dominant intellectual perspective in a variety of disciplines, including the social sciences, Harold J. Morowitz has called attention to an interesting anomaly: "What has happened is that biologists, who once postulated a privileged role for the human mind in nature's hierarchy, have been moving relentlessly toward the hard-core materialism that characterized nineteenth-century physics. At the same time, physicists, faced with compelling experimental evidence, have been moving away from strictly mechanical models of the universe to a view that sees the mind as playing an integral role in all physical events" ("Rediscovering the Mind," in *The Mind's I*, ed. Douglas R. Hofstadter and Daniel C. Dennett [New York: Basic Books, 1981], 34; reprinted from *Psychology Today*, Aug. 1980).

8. It is the James of the *Principles of Psychology*, primarily though not exclusively, who is often described as a materialist. Charles Sanders Peirce's review of this work calls James "materialistic to the core—that is to say, in a methodical sense, but not religiously, since he does not deny a separable soul nor a future life" (cited in *TC*, II:105). See also, George Santayana's review in *Atlantic Monthly* 67 (1891): 555: "Professor James. . . . has here outdone the materialists themselves. He has applied the principle of the total and immediate dependence of mind on matter to several fields in which we are all accustomed only to metaphysical or psychological hypotheses" (cited by Gerald E. Myers, Introduction, *PP*, I:xxxvii–xxxviii).

9. As an example of how fluid and controversial the claims of materialism can be, the essays in *The Mind's I* and the comments of its editors are most instructive. Hofstadter and Dennett themselves label their perspective as materialism but, significantly, describe minds as kinds of patterns or "sophisticated representational systems." They go on to say: "Minds exist in brains and may come to exist in programmed machines. If and when such machines come about, their causal powers will derive not from the substances they are made of, but from their design and the programs that run in them" (p. 382). In his essay "Minds, Brains, and Programs," reprinted in the same volume, John R. Searle calls such a doctrine "strong AI" [artificial intelligence]—that is, "the computer is not merely a tool in the study of the mind; rather the appropriately programmed computer really *is* a mind" (p. 353)—and maintains that it is a "residual form of dualism" (p. 371):

> Unless you accept some form of dualism, the strong AI project hasn't got a chance. The project is to reproduce and explain the mental by designing programs, but unless the mind is not only conceptually but empirically independent of the brain you couldn't carry out the project, for the program is completely independent of any realization. . . . If mental operations consist in computational operations on formal symbols, then it follows that they have no interesting connection with the brain; the only connection would be that the brain just happens to be one of the indefinitely many types of machines capable of instantiating the program. This form of dualism is not the traditional Cartesian variety that claims that there are two sorts of *substances*, but it is Cartesian in the sense that what is specifically mental about the mind has no intrinsic connection with the actual properties of the brain." (pp. 371–72)

10. Stanislaw Lem, "The Seventh Sally," in *The Cyberiad*, trans. Michael Kandel, in *The Mind's I*, 291.

11. Two thinkers who might be mentioned are Michael Polanyi and Ervin Lazlo. For an expression of the fundamental shortcomings of any reductionism, see Thomas Nagel's essay "What Is It Like to Be a Bat?" In *The Mind's I*, 392–93: "Any

reductionist program has to be based on an analysis of what is to be reduced. If the analysis leaves something out, the problem will be falsely posed. It is useless to base the defense of materialism on any analysis of mental phenomena that fails to deal explicitly with their subjective character."

12. Cf. also Randall, *NHE*, 224: "But the activities of the so-called 'subject' are clearly as 'real,' as 'objective,' as any other processes involved in the total coopera-tion. They have just as valid a claim to a legitimate ontological status in Substance." Remember we previously noted that for Randall, that "Substance" can also be called "the Field."

13. Cf. Gabriel Marcel, *Metaphysical Journal*, trans. Bernard Wall (Chicago: Henry Regnery, 1952), 241: "Can we believe that death is the real cessation of personal life without implicitly recognizing the truth of materialism?"

14. John Dewey, "Experience, Knowledge and Value," in *The Philosophy of John Dewey*, ed. Paul Arthur Schilpp (New York: Tudor, 1951), 604 (hereafter *EKV*).

15. It would be more accurate, perhaps, to say that this text "clearly expresses Dewey's *desire* to reject reductionism," for other texts raise some doubt as to whether he succeeded. See, e.g., *EN*, 253–54: "The difference between the animate plants and the inanimate iron molecule is not that the former has something in addition to physico-chemical energy; it lies in the *way* in which the physico-chemical energies are interconnected and operate, whence different *consequences* mark inanimate and animate activity respectively." Dewey's awareness of a kind of inconclusiveness and ambiguity accompanying this question is indicated, I believe, in *EN*, 262: "While the theory that life, feeling and thought are never independent of physical events may be deemed materialism, it may also be considered just the opposite. For it is reasonable to believe that the most adequate definition of the basic traits of natural existence can be had only when its properties are most fully displayed—a condition which is met in the degree of the scope and intimacy of interactions realized." See also *EN*, 255.

It is clear that Dewey, along with many other twentieth-century thinkers, wishes to present a doctrine of mind and matter that avoids *both* ontological dualism and reductionism. It can safely be said, I believe, that to this day there remains a formida-ble gap between the wish and the realization. In a note appended to "What Is It Like to Be a Bat?" (*The Mind's I*, 403n.), Nagel touches upon one reason for this gap:

I have not defined the term "physical." Obviously, it does not apply just to what can be described by the concepts of contemporary physics, since we expect further developments. Some may think there is nothing to prevent mental phenomena from eventually being recognized as physical in their own right. But whatever else may be said of the physical, it has to be objective. So if our idea of the physical ever expands to include mental phenomena, it will have to assign them an objective character—whether or not this is done by analyzing them in terms of other phe-nomena already regarded as physical. It seems to me more likely, however, that mental-physical relations will eventually be expressed in a theory whose funda-mental terms cannot be placed in either category.

See also p. 392: "Without consciousness the mind-body problem would be much less interesting. With consciousness it seems hopeless. The most important and char-acteristic feature of conscious mental phenomena is very poorly understood. Most reductionist theories do not even try to explain it. And careful examination will show that no currently available concept of reduction is applicable to it. Perhaps a new theoretical form can be devised for the purpose, but such a solution, if it exists, lies in the distant intellectual future."

I believe that it can be said of both James's doctrine of "pure experience" and Dewey's metaphysics of "natural events" that they were attempting to construct "a theory whose fundamental terms cannot be placed in either category."

16. *EN* is "metaphysical" in the descriptive rather than speculative sense of the term; that is, Dewey's aim was to describe the "universal generic traits of existence" rather than arrive at the "ultimate" principles of reality. This distinction should be kept in mind in what follows.

17. Cf. Dewey, *EN*, xii: "The *intrinsic* nature of events is revealed in experience as the immediately felt qualities of things." All events have "qualities" that characterize them, and it is the quality of an event that is immediately experienced. For a clear, concise exposition of "qualities" as understood by Dewey, see Richard Bernstein, *John Dewey* (New York: Washington Square Press, 1969), 89–101, ch. 7, "Qualitative Immediacy." What we "know," according to Dewey, are "objects" not "events." Cf. *EN*, 318: "When it is denied that we are conscious of *events* as such it does not mean that we are not aware of *objects*. Objects are precisely what we are aware of. For objects are events *with* meanings; tables, the milky way, chairs, stars, cats, dogs, electrons, ghosts, centaurs, historic epochs and all the multifarious subject-matter of discourse designable by common nouns, verbs and their qualifiers."

18. The event character of reality as Dewey understands it presents a formidable obstacle to belief in the kind of enduring self I will pose. One text expresses Dewey's view in a rather touching manner:

A thing may endure *secula seculorum* and yet not be everlasting; it will crumble before the gnawing tooth of time, as it exceeds a certain measure. Every existence is an event.

The fact is nothing at which to repine and nothing to gloat over. It is something to be noted and used. If it is discomforting when applied to good things, to our friends, possessions and precious selves, it is consoling also to know that no evil endures forever; that the longest lane turns sometime, and that the memory and loss of nearest and dearest grows dim in time. (*EN*, 71)

19. The slow rate of change, imperceptible to the ancients, was probably one reason why they were led to posit an unchanging reality.

20. Cf. James, *ERE*, 39: "On the principles which I am defending a 'mind' or 'personal consciousness' is the name for a series of experiences run together by certain definite transitions, and an objective reality is a series of similar experiences knit together by different transitions."

21. See also *EN*, xiii: "Mind is seen to be a function of social interactions, and to be a genuine character of natural events when these attain the stage of the widest and most complex interaction with one another." See also *EN*, 267–68, where Dewey, speaking of the correspondence of the "physical" and "psychical," contends that "the one-to-one agreement is intelligible only as a correspondence of properties and relations in one and the same world which is first taken upon a narrower and more external level of interaction, and then upon a more inclusive and intimate level." See also *EN*, 285: "In the hyphenated phrase body-mind, 'body' designates the continued and conserved, the registered and cumulative operation of factors continuous with the rest of nature, inanimate as well as animate; while 'mind' designates the characters and consequences which are differential, indicative of features which emerge when 'body' is engaged in a wider more complex and interdependent situation."

22. See also *EN,* 284: "To explain is to employ one thing to elucidate, clear, shed light upon, put in a better order, because in a wider context, another thing. It is thus subordinate to more adequate discourse, which, applied to space-time affairs, assumes the style of narration and description. Speaking in terms of captions familiar in rhetoric, exposition and argument are always subordinate to a descriptive narration, and exist for the sake of making the latter clearer, more coherent and more significant."

23. This "integration of organic-environmental connections" is, of course, preeminently present in that organic activity designated mind. Cf. Randall, *NHE,* 220–21, for an explicit expression of this Deweyan point:

> Mind as we encounter it in "the mental situation" is rather a complex set of powers of cooperating in that mental functioning. . . . Strictly speaking, Mind in this personal sense is a power, not of operating, but of *co*operating with other powers. Mind is thus, like all powers, a relational power. . . . Hence, if we take Mind as a power to act in certain ways, we must not forget that this power belongs to what is encountered as well as to the encounterer, the so-called human "agent" in thinking. . . . Mind as a power belongs to the *process* of encountering. . . . consequently, the question, "What is it that thinks?" becomes the question, "What are the different powers that cooperate in the process of thinking?"

24. Cf. *PP,* I:277: "The mind is at every stage a theatre of simultaneous possibilities. Consciousness consists in the comparison of these with each other, the selection of some, and the suppression of the rest by the reinforcing and inhibiting agency of attention."

25. Dewey's debt to James concerning such notions as "the vague," "focus," and "fringe" is obvious.

26. John Dewey, *Human Nature and Conduct* (New York: Modern Library, 1930), 61–62.

CHAPTER 3

1. This, at least is the basically persuasive picture presented by Milic Capek's "The Reappearance of the Self in the Last Philosophy of William James," *Philosophical Review* 62 (1953): 526–44. Capek is here rejecting Dewey's claim that James was moving in the direction of a behavioral account of the "self." Cf. "The Vanishing Subject in the Psychology of James," *Journal of Philsophy, Psychology and Scientific Method* 37 (1940): 589–99, reprinted in John Dewey, *Problems of Men* (New York: Philosophical Library, 1946), 396–409 (hereafter *PM*).

2. Cf. James M. Edie, "The Philosophical Anthropology of William James," in *An Invitation to Phenomenology,* ed. James M. Edie (Chicago: Quadrangle Books, 1965), 128: "James is clearest about what he rejects: the theory of the substantial soul, the associationistic theory of Hume, the Transcendental Ego of Kant—all of which are rejected on 'phenomenological' grounds, i.e., as unsatisfactory accounts of our *experience* of self-identity. But on the relationship of the bodily processes to the 'self' which is 'never an object to itself' James gives, in *The Principles,* no clear answer and seems to hesitate between parallelism, epiphenomenalism, and interactionism, depending on his polemical concerns of the moment. He was content to leave the problem open and unsolved."

3. The polemical thrust of much of James's writing on the self must always be kept in mind. In a particular instance he is first of all concerned to expose the inadequacies of one or another "established" position. As Gerald E. Myers says: "James alternated between placing the burden of doubt, now upon the materialist, then upon the spiritualist. In his discussion of emotion and the consciousness of self he placed that burden upon the latter. In his theorizing about attention and will, on the other hand, it is placed upon the materialist" (*PP*, I:xxxiv).

4. Cf. Edie, *Invitation,* 128: "But here again, he does not overcome the original ambiguity; he can be read as an 'egologist' or as a 'non-egologist' (though I believe the egological interpretation is more consonant with the tenor of his philosophy as a whole particularly since he continues to speak of the *experiencing ego* as a unified 'self' up to the end of his life)."

5. Ralph Barton Perry, *The Thought and Character of William James,* 2 vols. (Boston: Little, Brown, 1935), II:668 (hereafter *TC*).

6. There is a sense in which "feeling" is wider than "perceptual experience" and can be applied also to "conceptual experience." It can be said that for James, all concepts are "feelings" but not all "feelings" are concepts. James was concerned to avoid assigning "feelings" and "concepts" to different orders of being. Something of this is reflected in an early article ("Some Omissions of Introspective Psychology," *Mind,* Jan. 1884) a large excerpt from which is reproduced by James in a long footnote in *PP,* I:451–52. A few lines will indicate the direction of his thought.

> The contrast is really between two *aspects,* in which all mental facts without exception may be taken; their structural aspect, as being subjective, and their functional aspect, as being cognitions. . . . From the cognitive point of view, all mental facts are intellections. From the subjective point of view all are feelings. . . .
>
> The current opposition of Feeling to knowledge is quite a false issue. If every feeling is at the same time a bit of knowledge, we ought no longer to talk of mental states differing by having more or less, in having much fact or little fact for their object. The feeling of a broad scheme of relations is a feeling that knows much; the feeling of a simple quality is a feeling that knows little.

7. Ralph Barton Perry, *In The Spirit of William James* (New Haven, Conn.: Yale University Press, 1938), 82–83 (hereafter, *SWJ*).

8. See also *PP,* I:165: "For the essence of feeling is to be felt, and as a psychic existent *feels,* so it must *be.*" I do not wish to suggest that this claim is unproblemed. As we shall see when we discuss the self-compounding of consciousness, some hold that James finally surrendered it. While he modified a particular interpretation of it, I do not think he ever denied the irreducible character of experience that it expresses; in fact, he repeated it in a work he was writing at the time of his death (Cf. *SPP,* 78).

9. See also *PP,* I:591: "*A succession of feelings, in and of itself, is not a feeling of succession.*"

10. Bruce Wilshire comments on this text: "James is thus sharply critical of what we know today as behaviorism which misses these basic tendencies and is, therefore, a psychology which dispenses with the psyche; it is a self-satirizing science" (*William James and Phenomenology* [New York: AMS Press, 1979], 99; hereafter *WJP*). Wilshire goes on to argue that James's "remaining dualistic structure" lands him in difficulties from the perspective of phenomenology (*WJP,* 100). These "difficulties" are not of concern here, since what is being stressed is the irreducible and distinctive character of "feelings of tendency." Concerning the distinctive character of these feelings, Vic-

tor Lowe makes an eminently helpful comparison: "*Whitehead's 'non-sensuous percep-tion' is what James . . . called 'the plain conjunctive experience'*; it has no name in the *Psychology,* but is described under a number of headings such as 'feelings of relation' and 'feelings of tendency'" (*Understanding Whitehead* [Baltimore: Johns Hopkins University Press, 1966], 343).

11. Robert R. Ehman, "William James and the Structure of the Self" in *New Essays in Phenomenology,* ed. James M. Edie (Chicago: Quadrangle Books, 1969), 258 (here-after *NEP*).

12. Recall the previously cited text from Dewey in which he describes "a first-rate test of the value of any philosophy which is offered us: Does it end in conclusions which, when they are referred back to ordinary life-experiences and their predica-ments, render them more significant, more luminous to us, and make our dealings with them more fruitful?" (*Experience and Nature* [New York: Dover, 1958], 7). See also James, *SPP,* 33–34: "The world of common-sense 'things'; the world of mate-rial tasks to be done; the mathematical world of pure forms; the world of ethical propositions; the worlds of logic, of music, etc.—all abstracted and generalized from long–forgotten perceptual instances, from which they have as it were flowered out—return and merge themselves again in the particulars of our present and future perception."

13. Cf. Wilshire, *WJP,* 126: "The general point is that he does not consider the self to be a stable, isolable, and self-identical particular in the sense that a diamond is such a particular."

14. "The Stream of Thought," *PP,* I:219–78. In *PBC,* this chapter is given the title by which it is most widely known, "The Stream of Consciousness."

15. Cf. Dewey, *PM,* 397: "The material of the important chapter on the 'Stream of Consciousness' . . . verbally is probably the most subjectivistic part of the book." Dewey immediately adds: "I say 'verbally' because it is quite possible to translate 'stream of consciousness' into 'course of experience' and retain the substance of the chapter."

16. Cf. Wilshire, *WJP,* 125: "The upshot of Chapter Ten is that the self is not a sealed container full of intrinsically private thoughts. It is as if the self were blasted open and distributed across the face of the lived-world."

17. Cf. Ehman, *NEP,* 264: "In maintaining that our present pulse of conscious life might be selfless, James opens himself to the criticism that his interpretation of the central self as felt bodily movements is indeed reductive."

18. James concedes at least the possibility of the "feeling" that Ehman insists upon. Cf. *PP,* I:323: "The present moment of consciousness is thus, as Mr. Hodgson says, the darkest in the whole series. It may feel its own existence—we have all along admitted the possibility of this, hard as it is by direct introspection to ascertain the fact—but nothing can be known *about* it till it be dead and gone."

19. The previously cited text from James, "*Whenever my introspective glance succeeds in turning round quickly—all it can ever feel distinctly is some bodily process,*" is similar to David Hume's well-known passage in his *Treatise of Human Nature:* "For my part, when I enter most intimately into what I call *myself,* I always stumble on some particular perception or other, of heat or cold, light or shade, love or hatred, pain or pleasure. I never catch *myself* at any time without a perception, and never can observe anything but the perception" (David Hume, *A Treatise of Human Naure,* 2d ed., ed. L. A. Selby-Bigge [Oxford: Clarendon Press, 1978], bk. I, pt. 4, sec. 6, p. 252). I

believe that Roderick Chisholm's critique of Hume is equally applicable to James: "If Hume finds what he says he finds, that is to say, if he finds not only perceptions, but also that *he* finds them and hence that there is *someone* who finds them, how can his premisses be used to establish the conclusion that he never observes anything but perceptions?" ("On the Observability of the Self," in *Language, Metaphysics, and Death*, ed. John Donnelly [New York: Fordham University Press, 1978], 139). See also 144, 146: "'Could it be that a man might be aware of himself as experiencing without thereby being aware of himself?' If what I have suggested is true, then the answer should be negative. For in being aware of ourselves as experiencing, we are, *ipso facto*, aware of the self or person—of the self or person being affected in a certain way. . . . From the fact that we are acquainted with the self as it mainfiests itself as having certain qualities, it follows that we are acquainted with the self as it is in itself."

I have previously noted that a field view of the self rejects any "self as it is in itself" insofar as this suggests that the self has an essential reality independent of its relations and activities. Since there is no "self" independent of the relations or fields (including its activity fields) that constitute it, there is no "self in itself" to be known. Nevertheless, despite terminological differences, my point is not very different from Chisholm's, since I am affirming an awareness of the self in, through, and with those activities and relations *whereby* it is a self.

20. 1 Corinthians 15:35–40.

21. Cf. Maurice Canez, "With What Body Do the Dead Rise Again?" in *Immortality and Resurrection,* ed. Pierre Benoit and Roland Murphy (Herder & Herder, 1970), 93: "For Paul the body cannot be reduced simply to the material component of the animated being which is man. . . . The word 'body' rather describes man in a definite situation, in relation to others, than reduced to himself alone. . . . The body is man responsible for what he does, for how he lives; it is his entire situation, his totality, his personality." See also Joachim Gnilka, "Contemporary Exegetical Understanding of 'The Resurrection of the Body,'" in ibid., 129–141. For a brief description of a number of views on the "risen body," see *Everlasting Life after Death*, E. J. Fortmann, S. J. (New York: Alba House, 1976), 240–50.

To say that there is no simple and unequivocal identity between the "resurrection body" and the present body is not to deny that they must *in some way* be the "same." Cf. Thomas Aquinas, *Summa Theologica,* III (suppl.), Q. 79, Art. 1, trans. Fathers of the English Dominican Province (New York: Benziger Brothers, 1948), III:2890: "We cannot call it resurrection unless the soul return to the same body, since resurrection is a second rising. . . . And consequently if it be not the same body which the soul resumes, it will not be a resurrection, but rather the assuming of a new body." The difference in language and metaphysical assumptions precludes any unqualified incorporation of Aquinas's view within the pragmatic perspective of this essay. Nevertheless, there is a crucial and significant insight here that must be accounted for, as will be evident when I later speculate on the kind of transformation of the self that is necessary if the belief in immortality or resurrection is to have plausibility.

22. Cf. Max Scheler, "Lived Body, Environment, and Ego," in *The Philosophy of the Body,* ed. Stuart F. Spicker (New York: Quadrangle/The New York Times Books, 1970), 159–86, a translation by Manfred S. Frings of an excerpt from Scheler's *Der Formalismus in der Ethik und die materials Werte Ethik,* first published in 1916.

As the translator notes, "Scheler makes a phenomenological distinction between the *lived body* [*Leib*] and *thing-body* [*Korper*]. This distinction, important for the entire phenomenological movement, can be traced back to his essay, 'Die Idole der Sebsterkenntnis,' 1911." (Incidentally, the Spicker volume is an eminently useful collection of essays and excerpts from a variety of thinkers, centering on the theme of the "body" in antidualistic literature.)

23. Jean-Paul Sartre, *Being and Nothingness,* trans. Hazel E. Barnes (New York: Philosophical Library, 1956), 305 (hereafter *BN*).

24. Maurice Merleau-Ponty, *Phenomenology of Perception,* trans. Colin Smith (New York: Humanities Press, 1962), 98, 100. See also p. 139: "We must therefore avoid saying that our body is *in* space, or *in* time. It *inhabits* space and time."

25. Gabriel Marcel, *Mystery of Being,* 2 vols., trans. G. S. Fraser (Chicago: Henry Regnery, 1950), I:100 (hereafter *MB*).

26. Gabriel Marcel, *Metaphysical Journal,* trans. Bernard Wall (Chicago: Henry Regnery, 1952; hereafter, *MJ*).

27. See also Wilshire, *WJP,* 137: "James's talk of movements in the head is an attempt to describe his own body as a phenomenal presentation; it is not an attempt to discover the causal bases of consciousness. . . . It is true that there is a pervasive physiological aura about it all. But perhaps this is the way a physiologist and doctor of medicine sometimes experiences his own body."

28. Richard Stevens, *James and Husserl: The Foundations of Meaning* (The Hague: Martinus Nijhoff, 1974), 72 (hereafter *JH*).

29. See also *JH,* 142–43: after critically analyzing those texts that describe "the interpretation of bodily reaction as automatism, unrelated to the performance of consciousness," Stevens calls attention to other passages in which "James rejects the view of the body as a psychophysical thing whose transformations are automatically provoked by stimuli resulting from physical impressions."

30. John Wild, *The Radical Empiricism of William James* (New York: Doubleday Anchor Books, 1970), 87, 379–80.

31. For a free but accurate expression of James's notion, see Charlene Haddock Seigfried, *Chaos and Context* (Athens: Ohio University Press, 1979), 94: "Sometimes the body is looked upon as a physical object among others, since it can be counted, its metabolic functions tabulated, and its reactions to certain stimuli accurately computed. At other times the body is considered as peculiarly personal, as a center of decision and action and as an arena for spiritual, i.e., private, operations such as memory, desire, dreaming, and thinking."

32. I do not wish to suggest that Wilshire and I are using the "field" metaphor for the same purpose or with the same meaning. He is using it to support his phenomenological reading of the *Principles,* while I am employing it as the metaphysical metaphor that most adequately expresses the metaphysical assumptions of James as well as some other pragmatists. By distinguishing "field-like" and "stream-like" characteristics, Wilshire seems to mean something less intrinsically processive than I do. While I would not insist that *all* fields are processive as well as relational— mathematical fields perhaps are exceptions—I am maintaining that all *existential* fields are processive-relational.

33. Merleau-Ponty, *Phenomenology of Perception,* 98.

34. First published in the *Psychology Review* 12, no. 1 (Jan. 1905); reprinted with "slight verbal revision" in *ERE,* 79–95. All References are to the note on p. 86.

35. Stevens adds: "Husserl remarks that the body, 'reviewed from the inside,' reveals itself as an organism which moves freely and by means of which the subject experiences the external world. From this point of view, it would seem that the body cannot be spatially located alongside of other objects. Rather, the body is experienced as a zero-point, '. . . as a centre around which the rest of the spatial world is oriented.' On the other hand, 'viewed from outside,' the body appears as a thing among others and subject to causal relationships with surrounding objects" (*JH*, 88).

36. The motion of the body as a "center" of relations is not confined to Husserl and James. Cf., for example, Sartre, *BN*, 320, who speaks of "*my body* inasmuch as it is the total center of reference which things indicate." See also Marcel, *MJ*, 334–35, who notes that when he allows "my body" to become an object, "I cease to look on it as *my body*, I deprive it of that absolute priority in virtue of which *my body* is posited as the centre in relation to which my experience and my universe are ordered."

37. Cf. William Ernest Hocking, who, though more sympathetic to philosophical idealism than James, still maintained that "without bodiliness of some sort there can be no personal living. Existence, for a person, implies awareness of events in time—a continuity of particulars, not an absorption in universals or The One" (*The Meaning of Immortality in Human Experience* [New York: Harper, 1957], 188).

38. Cf. Edie, *Invitation,* 122: "By the 'world of sense' James does *not* mean the chaotic mass of dumb 'stimuli' of physiological or 'sensationalistic' psychology, but the concretely experienced 'life-world' to which Merleau-Ponty, for his part, accords 'the primacy of perception.' "

39. This would have to be greatly qualified as regards science in general but particularly as regards contemporary physics: paradoxically, as its language has become more "exact," the reality of "matter" has seemed to dissolve. This has been apparent for some time as the following text written over fifty years ago indicates: "But the physicists themselves have, if the phrase may be allowed, dissolved the materiality of matter. A body is in the last resort, I suppose, now regarded as a complex system of energy" (W. R. Matthews, "The Destiny of the Soul," *Hibbert Journal* 28, no. 2 [Jan. 1930]: 200, cited by Corliss Lamont in *The Illusion of Immortality* [New York: Frederick Ungar, 1965], 53.) More recently R. Mattuck in commenting on interacting particles said: "So, if we are after exact solutions, no bodies at all is already too many" (cited by Douglas R. Hofstader in *The Mind's I*, ed. Douglas R. Hofstader and Daniel C. Dennett [New York: Basic Books, 1981], 145).

40. Cf. Ignace Lepp, *Death and Its Mysteries,* trans. Bernard Murchland (New York: Macmillan, 1968), 158: "I assert unequivocally that a man is truly his body. . . . But a basic intuition, anterior to all rational constructs, teaches us that we are something other, and more than our bodies." There is, for example, a belief present from earliest times and within a variety of cultures and still prevalent today to the effect that what really constitutes us cannot be touched by punishment of our bodies. That the refusal to make a simple identification between ourselves and our bodies is not merely a sentimental residue of more primitive experience is evidenced in the following claim by contemporary analytic philosopher Sydney Shoemaker: "Recent work on the problem of personal identity strongly indicates that the identity conditions for persons are different from those for bodies, in such a way as to make it possible for a person to have different bodies at different times; that persons cannot, therefore be identical with their bodies; and that at any given time in a person's life it is a contingent fact that he has

the body he has instead of some other one" ("Embodiment and Behavior," in *The Identities of Persons,* ed. Amelie Oksenberg Rorty [Berkeley: University of California Press, 1976], 135n.).

41. *The Social Psychology of George Herbert Mead,* ed. Anselm Strauss (Chicago: University of Chicago Press, 1956), 213, 212. See also p. 217: "Persons who believe in immortality, or believe in ghosts, or in the possibility of the self leaving the body, assume a self which is quite distinguishable from the body. How successfully they can hold these conceptions is an open question, but we do, as a fact, separate the self and the organism."

42. Hans Linschoten, *On The Way towards a Phenomenological Psychology: The Psychology of William James,* ed. Amadeo Giorgi (Pittsburgh: Duquesne University Press, 1968), 65.

43. We shall see that in James's later writings he will speak of the self in terms of fields of consciousness rather than the body. Thus the "central self" which, as we have seen, is described in bodily terms in the *Principles* is described in terms of consciousness in *A Pluralistic Universe.* Cf. *PU,* 131n.: "The conscious self of the moment, the central self, is probably determined to this privileged position by its functional connexion with the body's imminent or present acts."

CHAPTER 4

1. The lack of a consensus concerning personal identity—whether it is, and if so in what it consists—has not changed much since James's time. "The Identity of the Self" is the title of the opening chapter of Robert Nozick's widely discussed *Philosophical Explanations* (Cambridge: Harvard University Press, 1981; hereafter *PE*). This chapter focuses on the "metaphysical question" of "personal identity through time," that is, "how, given changes, *can* there be identity of something from one time to another, and in what does this identity consist?" Nozick notes that "so many puzzling examples have been put forth in recent discussions of personal identity that it is difficult to formulate, much less defend, any consistent view of identity and non-identity" (p. 29). Whatever the difficulties, personal identity has not ceased to be a problem of concern to philosophers. Analytic philosophers in particular have contributed to the store of technical arguments in support of the various options—no identity, identity through bodily continuity, identity through psychological continuity, identity through some combination of bodily and psychological continuity, identity through some substantial or transcendental principle—but the options themselves have not significantly increased or decreased though there are continuing shifts in the number of supporters for a particular option. The literature on the question of personal identity is rapidly approaching the category of "vast," but two collections of essays can serve as useful introductions to the "state of the question": *Personal Identity,* ed. John Perry (Berkeley: University of California Press, 1975); *The Identities of Persons,* ed. Amelie Oksenberg Rorty (Berkeley: University of California Press, 1976).

2. Cf. Ralph Barton Perry, *The Thought and Character of William James* (Boston: Little, Brown, 1935), II:72–73 (hereafter *TC*): "Thus 'dualism' was a provisional doctrine by which James the psychologist hoped to eliminate and postpone a question on which James the philosopher had not made up his mind. But this question—namely, of the relation between 'the state of mind' and its 'object'—*refused* to be

eliminated, as James himself realized immediately after the publication of the *Principles,* and more and more strongly as the years passed. . . . James was perpetually being led, despite his profession of dualism and of metaphysical abstinence, to the disclosure of a homogeneous and continuous world."

3. Cf. Robert R. Ehman, "William James and the Structure of the Self," in *New Essays in Phenomenology,* ed. James M. Edie (Chicago: Quadrangle Books, 1969), 257: "The important point to see is that identity for James is not to be regarded as a postulated condition of the flux above or behind it but rather found in an immediate felt continuity and resemblance of the phases of the flux themselves."

4. Roderick Chisholm is a formidable defender of the reality of the Ego-subject. A central notion of his defense involves what he calls "self-presenting" propositions, which I interpret as something akin to feeling. See *Person and Object* (La Salle, Ill.: Open Court, 1976), 112:

> What is a *criterion* of personal identity? It is a statement telling what constitutes evidence of personal identity—what constitutes a good reason for saying of a person *x* that he is, or that he is not, identical with a person *y.* Now there is, after all, a fundamental distinction between the *truth-conditions* of a proposition and the *evidence* we can have for deciding whether or not the proposition is true. The *truth-conditions* for the proposition that Caesar crossed the Rubicon consist of the fact, if it is a fact, that Caesar did cross the Rubicon. The only *evidence* you and I can have of this fact will consist of certain *other* propositions—propositions about records, memories, and traces. It is only in the case of what is self-presenting (that I hope for rain or that I seem to me to have a headache) that the evidence for a proposition conicides with its truth-conditions. In all other cases, the two are logically independent; the one could be true while the other is false.

5. Cf. Gerald E. Myers, *PP,* I:xxxvi: "What makes the identity of a given state of consciousness? Neither James the psychologist nor James the metaphysician could provide the answer. The peculiar identity or unity of a state of consciousness consists of a 'diversity in continuity,' and that can only be *felt.* Such was the verdict of James the mystic." It is true, as we shall see, that James does not claim to "explain" just why experience is as it is. Myers's comment might be misleading, however, if it is understood as suggesting that "James the mystic" emerged after "James the psychologist" and "James the metaphysician" had failed. As already noted and as will be developed more fully later, James insists on taking mysticism seriously precisely because its experiential claims are consistent with his metaphysics of experience.

6. Ralph Barton Perry, *In The Spirit of William James* (New Haven, Conn.: Yale University Press, 1938), 86 (hereafter *SWJ*).

7. "Person and Personality," in *Johnson's Universal Cyclopaedia* (1895), VI:539, cited in Perry, *SWJ,* 86. Cf. *SPP,* 65: "*Experientially,* our personal identity consists, he [Locke] said, in nothing more than the functional and perceptible fact that our later states of mind continue and remember our earlier ones."

8. Though articulated explicitly in *ERE* and *PU,* the seeds of this distinction between perceptual experience of the flux character of reality and conceptualization are already present in *PP.* Here James introduces the metaphor "stream" to denote the changing character of thought while also affirming the unchanging character of our concepts. The issue of the sameness of *meaning* that can be "intended" by a constantly changing mind is too complex to be described in a few sentences. In the chapters "Conception" and "Necessary Truths," James seems to undermine his reputation as a philosopher of process and experience. In the former he states: "Each conception thus

eternally remains what it is, and never can become another. . . . Thus, amid the flux of opinions and of physical things, the world of conceptions, or things intended to be thought about, stands still and immutable, like Plato's Realm of Ideas" (*PP*, I:437). Concerning the dispute between evolutionary empiricists and apriorists over the origin of "necessary truths," James tells us that "on the whole . . . the account which the apriorists give of the *facts* is that which I defend; although I should contend . . . for a naturalistic view of their *cause*" (*PP*, II:1216). James would insist that in both instances he is concerned only with the meaning structures of the mind and is not positing concepts or necessary truths as ontological realities. That the only a priori acceptable to him would have to be a kind of processive a priori is hinted at in the following: "What similarity can there possibly be between human laws imposed *a priori* on all experience as 'legislative,' and human ways of thinking that grow up piecemeal among the details of experience because on the whole they work best?" (letter to Hugo Münsterberg, 1905, cited in *TC*, II:469).

9. Cf. Aron Gurwitsch, "William James' Theory of the 'Transitive Parts' of the Stream of Consciousness," in *Studies in Phenomenology and Psychology* (Evanston, Ill.: Northwestern University Press, 1966), 305n.: "There is another modification emphasized by James himself which takes place when the stream of consciousness is grasped and objectivated instead of being simply experienced. Whereas the stream itself is continuous and is experienced as such, the acts of reflection by which certain moments or phases are grasped are discrete. Behind these discrete markings, however, the stream of experience goes on continuously." Cf. *PU*, 106: "The stages into which you analyze a change are *states,* the change itself goes on between them. It lies along their intervals, inhabits what your definition fails to gather up, and thus eludes conceptual explanation altogether."

10. Thomas Reid, *Essays on the Intellectual Powers of Man,* 1785; cited in Perry, *Personal Identity,* 107.

11. A. N. Whitehead, *Adventures of Ideas* (New York: Free Press/Macmillan, 1967), 186.

12. For a fine exposition of the various expressions of what they call the "de-ontological, or 'no-self,' paradigm," see David Dilworth and Hugh J. Silverman, "A Cross-Cultural Approach to the De-Ontological Paradigm," in *Monist* 61, no. 1 (Jan. 1978): 82–95.

13. Cf. James M. Edie, "The Philosophical Anthropology of William James," in *An Invitation to Phenomenology,* ed. James M. Edie (Chicago: Quadrangle Books, 1965), 128: "He can be read as an 'egologist' or as a 'non-egologist' (though I believe the egological interpretation is more consonant with the tenor of his philosophy as a whole, particularly since he continues to speak elsewhere of the *experiencing ego* as a unified 'self' up to the end of his life)."

14. Cf. ibid., 127: "The more fundamental question involves asking *who* it is who identifies himself in varying degrees with these divers 'empirical' or 'objective' selves. And James here meets one of his most fundamental 'phenomenological' problems: the problem which Sartre faces in 'The Transcendence of the Ego,' which Merleau-Ponty discusses under the 'lived Body,' which Gilbert Ryle puzzles over in his chapter on the 'Systematic elusiveness of the *I*,' and which divides phenomenologists into 'egologists' like Husserl and 'non-egologists' like Gurwitsch."

15. James's statement here cannot be accepted without qualification. The significant difference between his understanding of experience and feeling and that of ear-

lier empiricists prohibits any identification of his philosophy with classical empiricism. This point has already been stressed and will become evident again when we consider James's rejection of the associationist's account of the self.

16. Cf. Milic Capek, "The Reappearance of the Self in the Last Philosophy of William James," *Philosophical Review* 62 (1953): 536: "It would be difficult to contradict oneself more often within a single sentence. Does the 'identifying section' of the stream not belong to the stream itself, that is to 'the totality of things collected'? In what sense is it *superior* to them? How can it collect, survey, own, or disown the past facts, as James claims in the subsequent sentence, while it remains present, that is, *external* to the past already gone?"

17. Robert Nozick attempts to account for identity over time by his "closest continuer theory" which, though less metaphorical, is suggestive of James's hypothesis: "The closest continuer view holds that y at t_2 is the same person as x at t_1 only if, first, y's properties at t_2 stem from, grow out of, are causally dependent on x's properties at t_1 and, second, there is no other z at t_2 that stands in a closer (or as close) relationship to x at t_1 than y at t_2 does" (*PE*, 36–37).

18. Cf. A. N. Whitehead, *Modes of Thought* (New York: Capricorn Books, 1958), 146: "Complete self-identity can never be preserved in any advance to novelty."

19. Cf. Richard Stevens, *James and Husserl: The Foundation of Meaning* (The Hague: Martinus Nijhoff, 1974), 83: "In their attempts to describe the peculiar identity of the pure ego, both Husserl and James reject the model of objective identity within a succession of perceptual perspectives. Both maintain that the permanence of the pure ego must be interpreted in terms of function rather than of content."

20. David Hume, *A Treatise of Human Nature,* 2d. ed., ed. L. A. Selby-Bigge (Oxford: Clarendon Press, 1978), Appendix, p. 636 (cited by James, but without the original italics, *PP,* I:334).

21. Cf. Capek, "Reappearance," 536, where he comments on this passage: "James did not seem to realize that this criticism applied almost *verbatim* to his own notion of 'the core of sameness running through the ingredients of the Self.' " Indebted as I am to Capek's article, I believe that he has missed James here. For James, the "tie" is not "inexplicable" insofar as it is verified in experience. By the same token, inasmuch as experience and/or reality is constituted of "ties" or "connections," there is no need to go *behind* the phenomena to find the substance which does the tying or connecting.

22. Cf. *PP,* I:268: "*There is no manifold of coexisting ideas;* the notion of such a thing is a chimera. *Whatever things are thought in relation are thought from the outset in a unity, in a single pulse of subjectivity, a single psychosis, feeling, or state of mind.*"

23. Capek, "Reappearance," 541.

24. Ibid., 532–33; "The true meaning of the article 'Does Consciousness Exist?' . . . is a denial of the artificial separation of the *act* of consciousness from its *content.* What James denies is a timeless, ghostly, and diaphanous entity, common to all individuals and consequently impersonal."

25. Cf. the previously cited text, *PBC,* 175: "The I, or 'pure ego' . . . is that which at any given moment *is* consciousness, whereas the Me is only one of the things which it is conscious *of.*" This does not, I believe, conflict with my claim that the "I" and the "me" are correlative and that it is not possible to have one without the other. The very possibility of distinguishing me-objects from non-me-objects presupposes, of course, the reality of the "me."

26. Cf. Whitehead, *Modes of Thought,* 227–28: "Descartes' 'Cogito ergo sum' is

wrongly translated, 'I think, therefore I am.' It is never bare thought or bare existence that we are aware of. I find myself as essentially a unity of emotions, enjoyments, hopes, fears, regrets, valuations of alternatives, decisions—all of them subjective reactions to the environment as active in my nature. My unity—which is Descartes' 'I am'—is my process of shaping this welter of material into a consistent pattern of feeling."

27. Cf. Ludwig Wittgenstein, *Notebooks, 1914–1916,* trans. G. E. M. Anscombe (New York: Harper Torchbooks, 1961), 80e:

The I, the I is what is deeply mysterious!

The I is not an object.

I objectively confront every object. But not the I.

So there really is a way in which there can and must be mention of the I in a *non-psychological sense* in philosophy.

28. A simpler example: If it is correct to say that Johnny throws the ball with his arm, it is also correct to say simply that Johnny throws the ball.

29. John Dewey, *Experience and Nature* (New York: Dover, 1958), 208. Cf. *TC,* II:527: Perry cites Dewey's letter to James in which he writes positively of "the whole conception of evolution as . . . reality which changes through centres of behavior which are intrinsic and not merely incident."

30. Cf. A. N. Whitehead, *Process and Reality* (New York: Humanities Press, 1955), 254: "Apart from the experiences of subjects, there is nothing, nothing, nothing, bare nothingness."

31. Cf. Edie, *Invitation,* 130, where he focuses on "*action* as the central category of James' thought."

32. Cf. Ian Barbour, *Myths, Models, and Paradigms* (New York: Harper & Row, 1976), 158, where he describes the "agent model" developed under the influence of the "action" theorists: "An *action* is a succession of activities ordered towards an end. Its unity consists in an intention to realize a goal. . . . an action cannot be specified, then, by any set of bodily movements, but only by its purpose or intent." Cf. also p. 139: "A person is an agent as well as an activity, a centre of thought, intentionality and decision, who can reveal himself to us in deliberate communication."

33. *Mind* 4 (1879): 1–22.

34. Cf. *TC,* II:760, where Perry cites the following note written by James in 1906: "Since work gets undeniably done, and 'we' feel as if 'we' were doing bits of it, why, for Heaven's sake, throw away the *naïf* impression."

35. See also *SPP,* 109: "Meanwhile the concrete perceptual flux, taken just as it comes, offers in our own activity-situations perfectly comprehensible instances of causal agency. The 'transitive' causation in them does not, it is true, stick out as a separate piece of fact for conception to fix upon. Rather does a whole subsequent field grow continuously out of a whole antecedent field because it seems to yield new being of the nature called for, while the feeling of causality–at–work flavors the entire concrete sequence as salt flavors the water in which it is dissolved."

36. Edie, *Invitation,* 131.

CHAPTER 5

1. To get some idea of how thorny, obscure, and frustratingly elusive some of these questions were for James, see "The Miller-Bode Objections," reproduced in part in Ralph Barton Perry, *The Thought and Character of William James* (Boston:

Little, Brown, 1935), II:750–65, Appendix X (hereafter *TC*). This is a selection made by Perry from notes that James kept between 1905 and 1908, dealing with objections to his doctrine of "pure experience." I will draw liberally upon these notes insofar as I think they support the processive-relational or field metaphysics, implicit in James's earliest writing, that becomes most unequivocally evident in *A Pluralistic Universe*.

2. Cf. Milic Capek, "The Reappearance of the Self in the Last Philosophy of William James," *Philosophical Review* 62 (1953): 532: "James thus became a consistent *temporalist* with all the consequences implied in this attitude; temporality does belong, not only to the psychological world of the 'stream of thought,' but also to the whole of reality."

3. Cf. also *PU, 112:* "But if, as metaphysicians, we are more curious about the inner nature of reality or about what really *makes it go,* we must turn our backs upon our winged concepts altogether, and bury ourselves in the thickness of those passing moments over the surface of which they fly, and on particular points of which they occasionally rest and perch."

4. Cf. Gabriel Marcel, *The Mystery of Being,* 2 vols., trans. G. S. Fraser (Chicago: Henry Regnery, 1950, 1951), I:127: "But it is precisely to the degree in which the spectator is more than simply *spectans,* it is to the degree to which he is also *particeps,* that the spectacle is more than a mere spectacle, that it has some inner meaning—and it is, I repeat, to the degree to which it is more than a mere spectacle that it can give rise to contemplation. And our term 'participation', even though it is so far for us not much more than a makeshift, a bridge hastily thrown across certain gaps in our argument, indicates precisely this 'something more' that has to be added to the simple recording of impressions before contemplation can arise."

5. Cf. *VRE,* 341: "I do believe that feeling is the deeper source of religion, and that philosophic and theological formulas are secondary products, like translations of a text into another tongue. . . . In a world in which no religious feeling had ever existed, I doubt whether any philosophic theology could ever have been framed. . . . These speculations must, it seems to me, be classed as over-beliefs, buildings-out performed by the intellect into directions of which feeling originally supplied the hint."

6. Cf. Elizabeth Flower and Murray G. Murphey, *A History of Philosophy in America,* 2 vols. (New York: Capricorn Books, 1977), 671: "If as we expect him [James] to do by this time, one substitutes a continuity over time for an identity of substance, then the conditions of continuity would be satisfied if the experience of the present in some cumulative sense captured past experience. Just as the present state of a plant incorporates its past growth, so the present thought owns or represents all that has gone before."

7. The complex question of continuity-discontinuity cannot be entered into here. While it was a relatively unfinished question in James, Perry suggests that he was working toward a more adequate expression of the senses in which the temporal world is both continuous and discontinuous: "That he would not have left his 'abrupt increments of novelty' unrelieved is clear. One may surmise that he would have described a sequence of happenings in which events occur like strokes or pulses, with a thrust of their own; but in which they would at the same time be continuous—in the sense of conjunction or nextness, rather than in the sense of connection. Their continuity would not consist in the link between them, but in the *absence* of any such intermediary. Being thus in direct contact, they would be subject to 'osmosis' " (*TC,* II:666).

It should be noted that time is not a mathematical continuum for James; rather, it comes in discontinuous "drops" or "pulses." Cf. *SPP*, 80: "On the theory of discontinuity, time, change, etc., would grow by finite buds or drops, either nothing coming at all, or certain units of amount bursting into being 'at a stroke.'" But "discontinuity" is not the whole story, for all experiences also have a dimension of continuity, as is evidenced in James's doctrine of the specious present in which we grasp immediately the receding past and emerging future. "The tiniest feeling we can possibly have comes with an earlier and a later part and with a sense of their continuous procession" (*PU*, 128). Time, then, is continuous insofar as each moment grows immediately (without gap) out of the last moment and will grow immediately into the next. Time is discontinuous insofar as it comes in drops or strokes or pulses—in finite bits.

8. Cf. *PU*, 87n.: "I hold it still as the best description of an enormous number of our higher fields of consciousness. They demonstrably do not *contain* the lower states that know the same objects. Of other fields, however, this is not so true. . . . I frankly withdrew, in principle, my former objection to talking of fields of consciousness being made of simpler 'parts,' leaving the facts to decide the question in each special case."

9. Bruce Kuklick, *The Rise of American Philosophy* (New Haven, Conn.: Yale University Press, 1977), 331.

10. It has been frequently noted that the strictures James attributes to the logic of identity do not hold against the logic of relations developed in the twentieth century. Cf. Marcus Peter Ford, *William James's Philosophy* (Amherst: University of Massachusetts Press, 1982), 106–7:

The logic of identity presupposes that concrete actualities can be defined solely in terms of changeless universals. Consequently, concrete actualities are themselves considered to be changeless. A thing is forever just what it is. Moreover, because concrete things can be defined solely in terms of universals, the relation between one concrete thing and another is not essential to either actuality. Relations are purely accidental. . . . The logic of relations, which includes the logic of identity, affirms what the logic of identity denies, i.e., that a subject may enter into and affect another subject. Because certain kinds of relations are internal to one term and external to the other, subjects may include other subjects. The relations of knowing, loving, or hating include what is known, loved, or hated—knowing x, loving y, hating z. The effect includes the cause, or, more generally stated, the feeling-of-x must include x, otherwise it is merely the feeling-of-.

11. The relevance of all this to the earlier field model of the self as a complex of conscious and nonconscious fields shifting and overlapping is obvious.

12. These passages lend support to interpreting James as a panpsychist. I have already "dodged" this question by suggesting that "panactivism" is a less problemed term for describing James's metaphysics than "panpsychism."

13. Cf. Ford, *James's Philosophy*, 87: "The paradox of something being both *ex* and *co* another actuality is no paradox at all when seen from a process perspective. What was once *ex* may be *co* in a subsequent moment." Cf. also Perry, *TC*, II:664: "But once the logic of identity is abandoned, it is permissible to say that two successive events both are and are not identical: the first develops into the second, the second emerges from the first. There is novelty, but it is a novelty which, when it comes, seems mutual and reasonable, like the fulfillment of a tendency. This notion of a 'really growing world' is the general theme of the latter part of the *Problems of Philosophy*."

14. Cf. James in *TC*, II:757: "I find that I involuntarily think of *co*-ness under the physical image of a sort of lateral suffusion from one thing into another, like a gas or warmth, or light. The *places* involved are fixed, but what fills one place radiates and suffuses into the other by . . . 'endosmosis.' This seems to ally itself with the fact that all consciousness is *positional*, is a 'point of view,' measures things for a *here*, etc. . . ."

15. Cf. *PU*, 121: "The absolute is said to perform its feats by taking up its other into itself. But that is exactly what is done when every individual morsel of the sensational stream takes up the adjacent morsels by coalescing with them. This is just what we mean by the stream's sensible continuity. No element *there* cuts itself off from any other element, as concepts cut themselves from concepts. No part *there* is so small as not to be a place of conflux. No part there is not really *next* its neighbors; which means that there is literally nothing between; which means that no part goes exactly so far and no farther; that no part absolutely excludes another, but that they compenetrate and are cohesive; if you tear out one, its roots bring out more with them; that whatever is real is telescoped and diffused into other reals."

16. Cf. also *PU*, 104: "All *felt* times coexist and overlap or compenetrate each other thus vaguely; but the artifice of plotting them on a common scale helps us to reduce their aboriginal confusion."

17. Cf. Lewis Thomas, *The Medusa and the Snail* (New York: Bantam Books, 1980), 10–12: "If there is life there, you will find consortia, collaborating groups, working parties, all over the place. . . . It is beyond our imagination to conceive of a single form of life that exists alone and independent, unattached to other forms. . . . Everything here is alive thanks to the living of everything else. All the forms of life are connected. . . . We are components in a dense, fantastically complicated system of life, we are enmeshed in the interliving, and we really don't know what we're up to."

18. Cf. Gerald E. Myers, *PP*, I:xxxv–xxxvi: "He confessed that neither he nor anyone else could explain how the peculiar identity and unity of a state of consciousness can result from a combination of elements. In our experience we do find the concept 'diversity and multiplicity in unity' fulfilled, but we cannot explain it. This is because, in the very effort to conceptualize those moments wherein we find unity composed of diversity, we break up the unity; our concepts keep things separated, whereas our experience finds them *together* in a unity and continuity that cannot be conceptualized. Thus, the sort of continuity that pervades a pure experience, that characterizes the diversity of a state of consciousness, that connects human experiences to God's, cannot be described."

I have cited Myers's fine introduction to the *Principles* several times, for, as the citations indicate, he locates the *Principles* within the larger context of James's philosophy with which I am concerned. I regret that his full-length study of James, *William James: His Life and Thought* (New Haven, Conn., 1986), was not available during the period in which my essay was composed. Myers's impressive work is the most comprehensive treatment of James's life and thought yet written, and it is likely to remain so for some time.

19. Cf. Ralph Barton Perry, *The Spirit of William James* (New Haven, Conn.: Yale University Press, 1938), 115–16: Perry points out that James escaped the paradox of one entity being "in some sense both identical and non-identical with another . . . by taking the concrete entity as an integrated complex which by overlapping another

could be both identical with that other as regards their community, and also non-identical as regards their individualities and private remainders."

20. See above, page 104.

21. Cf. *VRE*, 191: "In the wonderful explorations by Binet, Janet, Breuer, Freud, Mason, Prince, and others, of the subliminal consciousness of patients with hysteria, we have revealed to us whole systems of underground life, in the shape of memories of a painful sort which lead a parasitic existence, buried outside the primary fields of consciousness."

22. It is doubtful whether almost three-quarters of a century later we can be said to be much "further" than James. For a more recent consideration of parapsychological claims by one who like James is sympathetic but also reaches a "very open and uncertain" conclusion, see John Hick, "The Contribution of Parapsychology," in *Death and Eternal Life* (New York: Harper & Row, 1976), 129–46.

23. Cf. the T. H. Huxley, "Life and Letters," I, 240, cited by James in "Final Impressions of a Psychical Researcher," *MS*, 185–86: "But supposing these phenomena to be genuine—they do not interest me. If anybody would endow me with the faculty of listening to the chatter of old women and curates in the nearest provincial town, I should decline the privilege, having better things to do. And if the folk of the spiritual world do not talk more wisely and sensibly than their friends report them to do, I put them in the same category. The only good that I can see in the demonstration of the 'Truth of Spiritualism' is to furnish an additional argument against suicide. Better live a crossing-sweeper, than die and be made to talk twaddle by a 'medium' hired at a guinea a *Seance*." In fairness, such parapsychological claims as those of extrasensory perception and clairvoyance should be distinguished from "spiritualism" and "mediumship." But apart from the question of their authenticity, there still seems to be a significant qualitative difference in the lives of those who apparently possess such powers and those recognized as "mystics."

24. William James, *Talks to Teachers* (New York: Norton, 1958), 34.

25. That this is not merely an anti- or nonintellectual emotive expression on the part of James is well noted by Maria C. Madden and Edward H. Madden in their comment on this text: "It was not only the will to believe which helped him embrace the free-will view but also the removal of the belief, on good evidence, in the automaton theory. Indeed, the *will* to believe that one is free was not enough for James by any means. That option had to be made a live one for him by honestly eliminating the automaton theory, done by hard intellectual labor. His respect for scientific evidence had to be met, and it was" ("The Psychosomatic Illnesses of William James," *Thought*, Dec. 1979, p. 392).

26. Cf. also *P*, 60: "Free will pragmatically means *novelties in the world*, the right to expect that in its deepest elements as well as in its surface phenomena, the future may not identically repeat and imitate the past."

27. Three of the four experiences were similar in character, the fourth being a disturbing dream that recurred over several nights. The waking experiences are the focus of my concern, but James's conclusion regarding the dreams is well worth noting: "The distressing confusion of mind in this experience was the exact opposite of mystical illumination, and equally unmystical was the definiteness of what was perceived. But the exaltation of the sense of relation was mystical (the perplexity all revolved about the fact that the three dreams *both did and did not belong in the most intimate way together*); and the sense that *reality was being uncovered* was mystical in the

highest degree. To this day I feel that those extra dreams were dreamed in reality, but when, where, and by whom, I cannot guess" (*CER*, 511).

28. D. C. Mathur, *Naturalistic Philosophies of Experience* (St. Louis, Mo.: Warren H. Green, 1971), 62.

29. Cf. *VRE*, 157–58. Though James here attributes an experience of metaphysical terror to an anonymous Frenchman, he later admitted it was his own.

30. Cf. *TC*, II:346: "I have no mystical experience of my own, but just enough of the germ of mysticism in me to recognize the region from which their [*sic*] voice comes when I hear it." See also, *TC*, II:350: "I have no living sense of commerce with a God. . . . Although I am so devoid of *Gottesbewusstsein* in the directer and stronger sense, yet there is *something in me* which *makes response* when I hear utterances from that quarter made by others." John Smith considers this last statement "the key to the resolution of whatever paradox is involved" in James being "convinced at second-hand that only first-hand experience in religion represents the genuine article" (*VRE*, xvi).

31. Cf. *WB*, 223: "No part of the unclassified residuum has usually been treated with a more contemptuous scientific disregard than the mass of phenomena generally called *mystical*. . . . All the while, however, the phenomena are there, lying broadcast over the surface of history."

32. Cf. *VRE*, 58–59: "Such cases, taken along with others which would be too tedious for quotation, seem sufficiently to prove the existence in our mental machinery of a sense of present reality more diffused and general than that which our special senses yield."

33. James will later suggest that if the word "subliminal" is offensive "smelling too much of psychical research or other aberrations," then one might speak of the A- and the B-region of personality. The A-region is "the level of full sunlit consciousness." The larger B-region "is the abode of everything that is latent and the reservoir of everything that passes unrecorded and unobserved. It contains, for example, such things as all our momentarily inactive memories, and it harbors the springs of all our obscurely motivated passions, impulses, likes, dislikes, and prejudices. Our intuitions, hypotheses, fancies, superstitions, persuasions, convictions, and in general all our non-rational operations, come from it" (*VRE*, 381).

34. Cf. Perry, *TC*, II:273: "Again he discovered that men find within themselves unexpected resources upon which to draw in times of danger or privation. There is thus a common thread running through James' observations on religion, neurasthenia, war, earthquakes, fasting, lynching, patriotism—an interest, namely, in human behavior under high pressure, and the conclusion that exceptional circumstances generate exceptional inner power. These phenomena have a bearing on metaphysics because such exceptional power suggests the sudden removal of a barrier and the tappings of a greater reservoir of consciousness."

35. Cf. *WB*, 237: "The result is to make me feel that we all have a potentially 'subliminal' self, which may make at any time irruption into our ordinary lives. At its lowest, it is only the depository of our forgotten memories; at its highest, we do not know what it is at all."

36. Cf. Patrick Kiaran Dooley, *Pragmatism as Humanism* (Totowa, N.J.: Littlefield, Adams, 1975), 169: "Even though he felt that the existence of the self was required by man's ethical religious experiences, he maintained that the self was only *experienced* as cephalic movements of adjustment. James now proposed that this self, experienced as muscular adjustment, was only a portion of a wider self. Moreover, the

wider self was experienced in ethical and religious experiences wherein the wider self moves from the periphery (subconscious awareness) to the center (conscious awareness)."

37. From an essay on subliminal consciousness written by Frederick Myers in 1892 and published in *Proceedings of the Society for Psychical Research* 7:305. The congeniality of this text to the kind of field-self suggested in this essay is quite evident.

38. James was quite aware that in encouraging speculations such as Fechner's, one was opening a Pandora's box. Cf. *PU*, 142: "It is true that superstitions and wild growing over-beliefs of all sorts will undoubtedly begin to abound if the notion of higher consciousnesses enveloping ours, of fechnerian earth-souls and the like, grows orthodox and fashionable. . . . But ought one seriously to allow such a timid consideration as that to deter one from following the evident path of greatest religious promise? Since when, in this mixed world, was any good given us in purest outline and isolation? One of the characteristics of life is redundancy. . . . Everything is smothered in the litter that is fated to accompany it. Without *too much* you cannot have *enough* of anything."

39. Something similar is suggested by Charles Sanders Peirce:

A friend of mine, in consequence of a fever, totally lost his sense of hearing. He had been very fond of music before his calamity; and, strange to say, even afterwards would love to stand by the piano when a good performer played. So then, I said to him, after all you can hear a little. Absolutely not, he replied; but I can *feel* the music all over my body. Why, I exclaimed, how is it possible for a new sense to be developed in a few months! It is not a new sense, he answered. Now that my hearing is gone I can recognize that I always possessed this mode of consciousness, which I formerly, with other people, mistook for hearing. In the same manner, when the carnal consciousness passes away in death, we shall at once perceive that we have had all along a lively spiritual consciousness which we have been confusing with something different. (*The Collected Papers of Charles Sanders Peirce*, 8 vols., ed. Charles Hartshorne, Paul Weiss, and Arthur W. Burks [Cambridge, Mass.: Harvard University Press, 1931–35, 1958], VII, par. 577)

40. In a letter written shortly after the publication of *VRE*, James stated: "I think that the fixed point with me is the conviction that our 'rational' consciousness touches but a portion of the real universe and that our life is fed by the 'mystical' region as well" (cited in *TC*, II:346).

41. Cf. the British analytic philosopher, H. H. Price's "Survival and the Idea of 'Another World,'" in *Language, Metaphysics, and Death*, ed. John Donnelly (New York: Fordham University Press, 1978), 194: "*If* there are other worlds than this (again I emphasize the 'if'), who knows whether with some stratum of our personalities we are not living in them now, as well as in this present one which conscious sense-perception discloses?"

42. Cf. Perry, *TC*, II:676–77: "This belief was to some extent founded on normal observation, on the reports of others, and on the theory of the subliminal consciousness which he adopted from Myers. But the impression is irresistible that it was his own unusual experiences that put the seal of conviction on what would otherwise have been an alluring but open hypothesis."

43. If we read some of the more arcane Jamesian texts within such a field metaphysics, I believe we render them a bit more plausible. Try it, for example, singly and together, with two just-cited texts—"millions of years later, a similarly retrospective experience, should any come to birth . . ." and "a continuum of cosmic consciousness. . . ."

44. In a text written more than twenty years earlier, there is an anticipation of this "collectivism of personal lives," though with a more abstract and less dynamic flavor: "If idealism be true, the great question that presents itself is whether its truth involve the necessity of an infinite, unitary, and omniscient consciousness, or whether a republic of semi-detached consciousnesses will do,—consciousnesses united by a certain common fund of representations, but each possessing a private store which the others do not share" ("On Some Hegelisms," *WB,* 215).

45. Cf. also *TC,* I:526: "Nihilism denies continuity. Of the two elements of change it says one does not exist *at all* till the other has ceased *entirely.* Common sense lets one thing run into another and exist potentially or in substance where its antecedent is, allows continuity." Cf. also p. 527: "Substance metaphysically considered denotes nothing more than this: '*it is meant,*' a *plus ultra* the phenomenon. What this *plus* may be is left undecided; it may be a noumenal world, it may only be other phenomena with which the present real one is related,—it may, in a word, denote merely the *continuity* of the real world."

46. In positing a substantive sameness as characterizing the self, we must keep in mind the distinctive features of James's doctrine of personal identity described in the last chapter, in particular, the mode of "sameness" that is experientially warranted. Cf. *PP,* I:318: "The past and present selves compared are the same just so far forth as they *are* the same, and no farther."

CHAPTER 6

1. C. Stephen Evans, *Subjectivity and Religious Belief* (Washington, D.C.: University Press of America, 1982), 142. The most dramatic expression of the metaphysical and ethical implications attached to the God-question is Nietzsche's famous parable of the "Death of God." What Nietzsche so brilliantly and terrifyingly illustrates is that the loss of belief in the traditional God is not restricted in its implications to the undermining of the classical arguments for the existence of God, nor even to the denial of the existence of some transcendent Being. Rather, the "death of God" involves the dissolution of that view of reality upon which the most important and central institutions and values of Western civilization were grounded.

2. Paul Tillich, *The Dynamics of Faith* (New York: Harper Torchbooks, 1958), 45: "Whatever we say about that which concerns us ultimately, whether or not we call it God, has a symbolic meaning. It points beyond itself while participating in that to which it points. In no other way can faith express itself adequately. The language of faith is the language of symbols."

I wish to add that the symbolic character of God-language applies particularly to the use of the masculine pronouns "he" and "him." I have followed customary Western usage throughout simply because I could think of no alternative that would not be cumbersome and distracting. Needless to say, God is no more nor less "he" than "she"; nor, perhaps, than "it."

3. It is not only those working explicitly out of the pragmatic tradition who reject this simplistic dichotomy. Cf. the sociologist of religion Robert Bellah's "Religion in the University: Changing Consciousness, Changing Structures," in Claude Welch, ed., *Religion in the Undergraduate Curriculum* (Washington, D.C.: Association of American Colleges, 1972), 14:

> For the religiously orthodox religious belief systems were felt to represent "objective" reality as it really is, and thus if one of them is true the others must be false,

either absolutely or in some degree. For the secular orthodox all religion is merely "subjective," based on emotion, wish or faulty inference, and therefore false. For the third group, who take symbolism seriously, religion is seen as a system of symbols which is neither simply objective nor simply subjective but which links subject and object in a way that transfigures reality or even, in a sense, creates reality. For people with this point of view the idea of finding more than one religion valid, even in a deeply personal sense, is not only possible but normal. This means neither syncretism nor relativism, since it is possible within any social or personal context to develop criteria for the evaluation of religious phenomena and a consequent hierarchy of choices.

4. Cf. Paul Ricoeur, *Freedom and Nature*, trans. Erazím V. Kohák (Evanston, Ill.: Northwestern University Press, 1966), 476: "At this point Orphic Poetry [Goethe, Rilke, Nietzsche] leaves us unsatisfied. It conceals a great temptation, the temptation to lose ourselves as subjectivity and to sink in the great metamorphosis. . . . It is no accident that Orphism tends to a nature of worship in which the unique status of the Cogito evaporates in the cycle of the mineral and the animal."

5. Ralph Barton Perry, *The Thought and Character of William James*, 2 vols. (Boston: Little, Brown, 1935), II:358–59 (hereafter *TC*).

6. See also *P*, 40–41: "*If theological ideas prove to have value for concrete life, they will be true, for pragmatism, in the sense of being good for so much. For how much more they are true, will depend entirely on their relations to the other truths that also have to be acknowledged.*"

7. Cf. *TC*, II:273: "Again he discovered that men find within themselves unexpected resources upon which to draw in times of danger or privation. . . . These phenomena have a bearing on metaphysics because such exceptional power suggests the sudden removal of a barrier and the tappings of a greater reservoir of consciousness; and they have a bearing on ethics, since this power differs in degree rather than in kind from that moral power—that fighting and adventurous spirit, that heroic quality—which gives to life the color and radiance of value."

8. The passage elided reads, "So a 'god of battles' must be allowed for one kind of person, a god of peace and heaven and home, the god for another." I have dropped it because it distracts from the richness of James's pluralistic perspective by giving the impression that all gods must be allowed. This is in sharp opposition to his view that we must evaluate all claims, including religious ones, on the basis of their experiential fruits. I submit that whatever limited fruits belief in a "god of battles" brought forth at an earlier time, the overwhelming historical evidence points to its now being an unacceptable belief.

9. For a recognition of God's pluralistic relationship to the human community from a biblical perspective, cf. Clark M. Williamson, *Has God Rejected His People? Anti-Judaism in the Christian Church* (Nashville, Tenn.: Abingdon, 1982), 164: "If one assumes that God affects the world by offering different possibilities to different peoples in different times and places, then we may affirm that God wills diversity and pluralism." While not in conflict with a pluralism such as that suggested by Williamson the pluralism presented by James is more personalistic than cultural. It is the diversity of personal needs present even at the same time and in the same culture that James refers to several times in the *Varieties* (in addition to *VRE*, 384, just cited, see also pp. 115, 136, 127). Further, James does not restrict pluralism to that of "religious" types. In a passage left out of earlier published versions of the *Varieties*, James states: "The first thing that strikes us is that the religious man in the sense used in these lectures is only one type of man. Round about *him* are other men who say

they cannot realize this experimental commerce with the divine; and taken collectively there is no flagrant difference of worth in the two classes of persons. . . . No
one type of man whatsoever is the total fullness of truth immediately revealed. Each
of us has to borrow from the other parts of truth seen better from the other's point of
view" (*VRE,* 383).

10. This is a variation on the following: "But rationality has at least four dimensions, intellectual, aesthetical, moral, and practical; and to find a world rational to
the maximal degree *in all these respects simultaneously* is no easy matter" (*PU,* 55).

11. "The best fruits of religious experience are the best things that history has to
show" (*VRE,* 210). "Religious rapture, moral enthusiasm, ontological wonder, cosmic emotion, are all unifying states of mind, in which the sand and grit of selfhood
incline to disappear, and tenderness to rule" (*VRE,* 225). Hans Küng takes a position
similar to that of James when he points out that the existence of needs, desires, and
wishes do not prove that there is a fulfilling reality corresponding to them, but
neither does their existence exclude such a possibility: "To be more precise, could
not the *sense of dependence* and the *instinct of self-preservation* have a very *real* ground,
could not our *striving for happiness* have a very *real* goal?" Küng then cites a text from
Edward von Hartmann which denies that the psychological dimension of a belief
renders it untrue: "It is quite true that nothing exists merely because we wish it, but
it is not true that something cannot exist if we wish it. Feuerbach's whole critique of
religion and the whole proof of his atheism, however, rest on this single argument;
that is, on a logical fallacy" (Hans Küng, *Eternal Life?* trans. Edward Quinn [New
York: Doubleday, 1984], 30–31).

12. For a contrary view presented within a semi-playful context, see Stanislaw
Lem, "Non Serviam," in *The Mind's I,* ed. Douglas R. Hofstadter and Daniel C.
Dennett (New York: Basic Books, 1981), 313: "Living, we play the game of life, and
in it we are allies, everyone. Therewith, the game between us is perfectly sym-
metrical. In postulating God, we postulate a continuation of the game beyond the
world. I believe that one should be allowed to postulate this continuation of the
game, so long as it does not in any way influence the course of the game here.
Otherwise, for the sake of someone who perhaps does not exist we may well be
sacrificing that which exists here, and exists for certain."

13. For a strikingly similar image constructed by a thinker who is at the opposite
pole from James concerning the value of religion, see Friedrich Nietzsche, *The Will
to Power,* trans. Walter Kaufmann and R. J. Hallingdale, ed. Walter Kaufmann (New
York: Vintage Books, 1967), 40: "Disintegration characterizes this time, and thus
uncertainty: nothing stands firmly on its feet or on a hard faith in itself; one lives for
tomorrow as the day after tomorrow is dubious. Everything on our way is slippery
and dangerous, and the ice that still supports us has become thin: all of us feel the
warm, uncanny breath of the thawing wind; where we walk, soon no one will be
able to walk."

14. Cf. *VRE,* 367: "The genuineness of religion is thus indissolubly bound up
with the question whether the prayerful consciousness be or be not deceitful. The
conviction that something is genuinely transacted in this consciousness is the very
core of living religion."

15. John Smith claims that "the importance to James's argument of this extension
of faith to include God and the ideal order has not been sufficiently appreciated."
According to Smith, "James was calling attention to the pervasive religious belief

that the 'More,' however conceived, is never thought of as present only in the experience of the individual but is envisaged as at work in the cosmos in the form of a divine order" (*VRE*, xlvii–xlix).

16. Paul Edwards, "Atheism," in *The Encyclopedia of Philosophy*, 8 vols., ed. Paul Edwards (New York: Free Press/Macmillan, 1967), I:187.

17. Henry Samuel Levinson, *The Religious Investigations of William James* (Chapel Hill: University of North Carolina Press, 1981), 192 (hereafter *RIWJ*).

18. In a letter to James commenting on religion in *A Pluralistic Universe*, Bertrand Russell noticed "one purely temperamental difference: that the first demand you make of your God is that you should be able to love him, whereas my first demand is that I should be able to worship him" (In James, *MT*, Appendix IV, 303).

19. Cf. *PU*, 28: "The doctrine on which the absolutists lay most stress is the absolute's 'timeless' character. For pluralists, on the other hand, time remains as real as anything, and nothing in the universe is great or static or eternal enough not to have some history."

20. William James, "Reason and Faith," *Journal of Philosophy* 24 (1924):197.

21. As early as 1882, James questioned the need for an all-inclusive God. In a letter to Thomas Davidson, he wrote: "It is a curious thing this matter of God! . . . I find myself less and less able to do without him. He need not be an *all*-including 'subjective unity of the universe.' . . . All I mean is that there must be *some* subjective unity in the universe which has purposes commensurable with my own, and which is at the same time large enough to be, among all the powers that may be there, the strongest. I simply refuse to accept the notion of there being *no* purpose in the objective world. . . . In saying 'God exists' all I imply is that my purposes are cared for by a mind so powerful as on the whole to control the drift of the universe" (*TC*, I:737).

22. Cf. Marcus Peter Ford, *William James's Philosophy* (Amherst: University of Massachusetts Press, 1982), 100: "This process view of the relations between God and a given individual, or God and the World, which both James and Whitehead ascribe to, necessarily implies that God has an environment and that God is in some respects limited in power and knowledge. Both James and Whitehead accept this view of God, but for different reasons. Whitehead's understanding of God's limitations follows from metaphysical principles whereas James's understanding of God (at least as developed in *A Pluralistic Universe*) is merely an ad hoc solution to the problem of evil." I would strongly disagree with Ford on this. Granted that James does not present his case with the systematic metaphysical rigor of Whitehead, I think it is clear that even in *PU* the metaphysical pluralism advanced by James leads to a finite God. Even apart from the problem of evil, an infinite God would seem to undermine the autonomy and freedom of human activity, creativity, and novelty.

23. "Who knows whether the faithfulness of individuals here below to their own poor over-beliefs may not actually help God in turn to be more effectively fruitful to his own greater tasks" (*VRE*, 408). "I confess that I do not see why the very existence of an invisible world may not in part depend on the personal response which any one of us may make to the religious appeal" (*WB*, 55).

24. Cf. Levinson, *RIWJ*, 205: "James wanted to articulate a pantheism that admitted real *chaos* on the one hand but real *reparation* of chaos on the other."

25. Joseph Heller puts these words into the mouth of his protagonist, Yossarian, in *Catch-22* (New York: Dell, 1961), 184. Cf. Friedrich Nietzsche, *Daybreak*, trans. R.

J. Hollingdale (New York: Cambridge University Press, 1982), 52–53: "*God's honesty.*—A god who is all-knowing and all-powerful and who does not even make sure that his creatures understand his intention—could that be a god of goodness? Who allows countless doubts and dubieties to persist, for thousands of years, as though the salvation of mankind were unaffected by them, and who on the other hand holds out the prospect of frightful consequences if any mistake is made as to the nature of truth? Would he not be a cruel god if he possessed the truth and could behold mankind miserably tormenting itself over the truth?"

26. Bonnell Spencer, O. H. C., *God Who Dares to Be Man: Theology for Prayer and Suffering* (New York: Seabury Press, 1980), 4. It is significant, I believe, as David Griffith notes in his review of this work, that Spencer balks at positing a finite God. Instead he justifies God's actions on the basis of divine self-limitation and respect for the integrity of human self-determination (*Process Studies,* Fall 1983, 238). I suspect that this is an example of an unresolved conflict between an existential insight and a desire to maintain the traditional understanding of God.

27. H. D. Lewis, *The Self and Immortality* (New York: Seabury Press, 1973), 196.

28. Williamson, *Has God Rejected His People?* 150.

29. John K. Roth, *Process Studies,* Fall 1983, 236–37.

30. Cf. Lem, "Non Serviam," 316. "He who is almighty could have provided certainty. Since He did not provide it, if He exists, He must have deemed it unnecessary. Why unnecessary? One begins to suspect that maybe He is not almighty. A God not almighty would be deserving of feelings akin to pity, and indeed to love as well; but this, I think, none of our Theodicies allow." If Lem gives us a playful version of the situation, Thomas Hardy gives us a more cynical one:

> He did sometimes think that he had been ill-used by fortune. . . . But that he and his had been sarcastically and piteously handled in having such irons thrust into their souls he did not maintain long. It is usually so, except with the sternest of men. Human beings, in their generous endeavor to construct a hypothesis that shall not degrade a First Cause, have always hesitated to conceive a dominant power of lower moral quality than their own; and, even while they sit down and weep by the waters of Babylon, invent excuses for the oppression which prompts their tears. (*The Return of the Native* [New York: Harper & Row, n.d.], 455)

31. Cf. James's reply to a questionnaire concerning his views of God and religion:

> "*God*" *to me, is not the only spiritual reality to believe in. Religion means primarily a universe of spiritual relations surrounding the earthly practical ones, not merely relations of* "*value,*" *but agencies and their activities. I suppose the chief premise for my hospitality towards the religious testimony of others is my conviction that* "*normal*" *or* "*sane*" *consciousness is so small a part of actual experience. What e'er be true, it is not true exclusively, as a philistine scientific opinion assumes. The other kinds of consciousness bear witness to a much wider universe of experiences, from which our belief selects and emphasizes such parts as best satisfy our needs.* (*LWJ,* II:213)

32. Ian Barbour, *Myths, Models, and Paradigms* (New York: Harper & Row, 1976), 161.

33. Cf. Owen Barfield, *Saving the Appearances* (New York: A Harvest/HBJ Book, Harcourt Brace & World, n.d., f.p. 1956), 160. Barfield contends that history has no significance "unless, in the course of it, the relation between creature and Creator is being changed."

34. God as a presupposition for personal immortality is, of course, the view of almost all who have in any way affirmed the latter doctrine. "Almost" but not all—a

notable exception is the late nineteenth-century Hegelian philosopher, J. M. E. McTaggart; see his *Human Immortality and Pre-existence* (London: E. Arnold, 1916).

35. Cf. also *WB*, 111: "In every being that is real there is something external to, and sacred from, the grasp of every other. God's being is sacred from ours. To co-operate with his creation by the best and rightest response seems all he wants of us. In such co-operation with his purposes, not in any speculative conquest of him, not in any theoretic drinking of him up, must lie the real meaning of our destiny." Levinson expresses James's view here as follows: "When they [Theists] characterized the world as 'thou,' they pictured its deepest power as formally personal, individuated, and caring, fighting for righteousness as men understood it and recognizing each individual for the person he is. God was a 'power not ourselves' who helped people realize their best intentions because he meant to" (*RIWJ*, 41).

36. Cited by Ronald W. Clark, *Einstein: The Life and Times* (New York: World, 1971), 19.

37. For a distinguished, if unheralded, expression of a relational personalism, see the Gifford Lectures of John Macmurray, published in 2 vols., *Self as Agent* and *Persons in Relation* (London: Faber & Faber, 1957, 1961).

38. Ralph Harper, *The Existential Experience* (Baltimore, Md.: Johns Hopkins University Press, 1972), 122, 123. Harper sees the threat, if not the already realized reality, of the loss of transcendence and presence as placing the very life of the self in jeopardy. Thus he states: "Proust meant to be shocking when he said, 'We exist alone. Man is the creature that cannot emerge from himself, that knows his fellows only in himself; when he asserts the contrary he is lying' (*Remembrance of Things Past*, 2:698)." Harper maintains that "no more frightening judgment has ever been made of human existence, not even the announcement that God is dead, for it is tantamount to saying that man is dead also" (p. 82).

39. John Dewey, *Experience and Nature* (New York: Dover, 1958), 244.

40. R. H. Charles, *Eschatology* (New York: Schocken Books, 1963), 61.

41. The possibility of a continued existence apart from the body is acknowledged by Whitehead: "How far this soul finds a support for its existence beyond the body is:—another question. The everlasting nature of God, which in a sense is non-temporal and in another sense temporal, may establish with the soul a peculiarly intense relationship of mutual immanence. Thus in some important sense the existence of the soul may be freed from its complete dependence upon the bodily organization" (*Adventures of Ideas* [New York: Free Press/Macmillan, 1967], 208).

42. Luke 20:38.

CHAPTER 7

1. Joseph Butler, *The Analogy of Religion* (London: Henry G. Bohn, 1860, f.p. 1736), 328.

2. Cf. John Herman Randall, Jr., *Philosophy after Darwin*, ed. Beth J. Singer (New York: Columbia University Press, 1977), 18 (hereafter *PAD*): "Science had already destroyed the faith in personal immortality. It could of course not disprove the belief, but it could and did make it seem irrelevant to the kind of being man is." See also, Louis Dupré, *Transcendent Selfhood* (New York: Seabury Press, 1976), 80: "Indeed, even to religious believers today the thought of a future life remains far from the center of their faith, if they do not reject it outright."

3. Hans Jonas, *The Phenomenon of Life* (New York: Dell, 1966), 262 (hereafter *PL*).

4. Hans Küng, *Eternal Life?*, trans. Edward Quinn (New York: Doubleday, 1984), xiii.

5. Joseph Blenkinsopp, "Theological Synthesis and Hermeneutical Conclusions," in *Immortality and Resurrection,* ed. Pierre Benoit and Roland Murphy (Herder & Herder, 1970), 115 (hereafter *IR*).

6. Schubert M. Ogden, *The Reality of God and Other Essays* (New York: Harper & Row, 1966), 229–30.

7. William Ernest Hocking, *The Meaning of Immortality in Human Experience* (New York: Harper, 1957), xvii–xviii (hereafter *MI*).

8. Ludwig Wittgenstein, *Tractatus Logico-philosophicus,* trans. D. F. McGuinness and B. F. McGuinness (New York: Humanities Press, 1961), 151. Cf. also Wittgenstein's *The Blue and Brown Books* (New York: Harper & Row, 1965), 45: "The difficulty in philosophy is to say no more than we know." Perhaps at least one benefit and one liability would result from literal adherence to this injunction: The benefit would be that most of us, in particular philosophy professors, would be rendered almost mute; the liability might be that unless we continually strive to say *more* than we know, we will never *know* more than we now say.

9. Peirce has expressed this perhaps as succinctly as anyone: "There are three things we can never hope to attain . . . absolute certainty, absolute exactitude, absolute uncertainty" (*The Collected Papers of Charles Sanders Peirce,* 8 vols., ed. Charles Hartshorne, Paul Weiss, and Arthur W. Burks [Cambridge, Mass.: Harvard University Press, 1931–35, 1958], I, par. 141. The Kant text is found in the "Preface to the Second Edition" of the *Critique of Pure Reason,* trans. Norman Kemp Smith (London: Macmillan, 1953), 29.

10. Cf. Ian Barbour, *Myths, Models, and Paradigms* (New York: Harper & Row, 1976), 180 (hereafter *MMP*): "There is a 'holy insecurity,' as Buber calls it, in our lack of certainty about the finality of our formulations. There is a risk in acting on the basis of any interpretative framework which is not subject to conclusive proof. Faith, then, does not mean intellectual certainty or the absence of doubt, but rather a trust and commitment even when there are no guaranteed beliefs or infallible dogmas. Faith takes us beyond a detached and speculative outlook into the sphere of personal involvement."

11. Cf. Reinhold Niebuhr, *The Self and Its Dramas* (New York: Scribner, 1955), 94: "The elaboration of the meaning of the Christian revelation demanded from the very beginning that the truth about life and God apprehended in an historical revelation be brought into conformity with the truth which may be known by analyzing the structures and essences of reality on all levels."

12. Cf. Richard Neuhaus's description of Wolfhart Pannenberg's theology: "A critical faith is not a compromise with modernity. It is, rather, a more radical commitment which takes the risk of making one's faith vulnerable to refutation by further evidence" ("History as Sacred Drama," *Worldview,* April, 1979, p. 23).

The risk accompanying critical thinking is not restricted to Christians or even to "religious" believers. Cf. John Dewey, *Experience and Nature* (New York: Dover, 1958), 222: "Let us admit the case of the conservative; if we once start thinking no one can guarantee where we shall come out, except that many objects, ends and institutions are surely doomed. Every thinker puts some portion of an apparently stable world in peril and no one can wholly predict what will emerge in its place."

13. Jonathan Swift, *Gulliver's Travels,* ed. Robert A. Greenberg (New York: Norton, 1970), 177ff.

14. In Bernard Williams, *Problems of the Self* (New York: Cambridge University Press, 1976), 82ff. (hereafter *PS*).

15. Corliss Lamont, *The Illusion of Immortality,* introduction by John Dewey (New York: Frederick Ungar, 1965), 13 (hereafter, *II*).

16. The following text of Wittgenstein's is, I believe, a response to a situation similar to the one under consideration:

> There are, for instance, these entirely different ways of thinking first of all—which needn't be expressed by one person saying one thing, another person another thing.
>
> What we call believing in a Judgement Day or not believing in a Judgement Day—the expression of belief may play an absolutely minor role.
>
> If you ask me whether or not I believe in a Judgement Day, in the sense in which religious people have belief in it, I wouldn't say: "No. I don't believe there will be such a thing." It would seem to be utterly crazy to say this.
>
> And then I give an explanation: "I don't believe in . . .", but then the religious person never believes what I describe.
>
> I can't say. I can't contradict that person. (*Lectures and Conversations on Aesthetics, Psychology and Religious Belief,* ed. Cyril Barrett [Berkeley: University of California Press, n.d.], 55)

17. While not asserting that Paul Ricoeur is advancing a position identical in all respects to the one here presented, I do believe that his commentary on the following Goethe citation points in the same direction:

> If you have not understood
> The command, "Die and become!"
> You are but an obscure transient
> On a shadow of an earth.

"Highly coded language" says Ricoeur. "The incantation suggests that we dare not translate: The *no* and *yes* are bound in all things according to a dialectic law which is not at all one of arithemetical composition but one of metamorphosis and transcendence. The universe travails under the hard law of 'Die and become' " (*Freedom and Nature,* trans. Erazím V. Kohák [Evanston, Ill.: Northwestern University Press, 1966], 473).

18. Andrew Greeley, *Death and Beyond* (Chicago: Thomas More Press, 1976), 37.

19. Is this something of what Nietzsche is calling for in the following? "*The needful sacrifice.*—These serious, excellent, upright, deeply sensitive people who are still Christians from the very heart: they owe it to themselves to try for once the experiment of living for some length of time without Christianity, they owe it to their *faith* in this way for once to sojourn 'in the wilderness'—if only to win for themselves the right to a voice on the question whether Christianity is necessary" (*Daybreak,* trans. R. J. Hollingdale [New York: Cambridge University Press, 1982], 37).

20. Of course, I am employing a paradoxical mode, no novelty in questions of this sort. One might argue that in such questions as God and immortality, anything less than paradox is trivial; anything more is impossible.

21. Julius Seelye Bixler, *Immortality and the Present* (Cambridge, Mass.: Harvard University Press, 1931), 35 (hereafter *IPM*).

22. Cf. Miguel de Unamuno, *The Tragic Sense of Life,* trans. J. E. Crawford Flitch

(New York: Dover, 1954) (hereafter *TSL*). Unamuno not only refuses to accept immortality belief and tragedy as mutually exclusive but goes a long way toward making tragedy the essential character of such belief. Unamuno's style is much too florid and superheated to suit the laid-back contemporary philosopher; nevertheless, I must admit that I find myself engaged by his metaphysical wail. Indeed, without suggesting any comparison between my halting, all too tentative words and those of Unamuno, my effort might be entitled: "Unamuno without Tears." I am struggling to sing the same song, though in a much lower key and with immeasurably more prosaic music.

23. Lael Wertenbaker, *Death of a Man* (Boston: Beacon Press, 1974), 70.

24. For a strong condemnation of belief in immortality as unworthy of human beings, cf. Leslie Dewart, "The Fear of Death and Its Basis in the Nature of Consciousness," in *Philosophical Aspects of Thanatology*, 2 vols., ed. Florence M. Hetzler and Austin H. Kutscher (New York: MSS Information Corporation, 1978), I:61, 63 (hereafter *PAT*): "Thus our common thinking today begins with the premise that immortality is desirable. . . . Critical reflection should reveal not only its invalidity but also its disvalue for human development. . . . Man may well die, needlessly, from his self-imposed, mortal fear of death."

25. William Ernest Hocking and Ralph Barton Perry, both sympathetic to belief in immortality, assert that such belief does not remove the pain of death. "No doctrine of survival in any case escapes the fact of death," Hocking tells us, "nor the suffering that goes with it; these remain the data of every argument" (*MI*, 9). According to Perry, "The belief in a future life mitigates but does not destroy the menace of death, and while it provides reserves of hope it leaves abundant room for fortitude" (*The Hope of Immortality* [New York: Vanguard Press, 1945], 26; hereafter *HFI*).

26. Cf. Friedrich Nietzsche, *Ecce Homo*, trans. and ed. Walter Kaufmann (New York: Vintage Books, 1969), 261: "Ultmately, nobody can get more out of things, including books, than he already knows. For what one lacks access to from experience one will have no ear. Now let us imagine an extreme case: that a book speaks of nothing but events that lie altogether beyond the possibility of any frequent or rare experience—that it is the first language for a new series of experiences. In that case, simply nothing will be heard, but there will be the acoustic illusion that where nothing is heard, nothing is there."

27. *The Antichrist*, in *The Portable Nietzsche*, trans. and ed. Walter Kaufmann (New York: Viking Press, 1954), 618 (hereafter *PN*).

28. Cf. Walter Kaufmann, *Nietzsche*, 3rd ed. (New York: Vintage Books, 1968), 102: "To escape nihilism which seems involved both in asserting the existence of God and thus robbing *this* world of ultimate significance, and also in denying God and thus robbing *everything* of meaning and value—that is Nietzsche's greatest and most persistent problem."

29. Friedrich Nietzsche, *The Will to Power*, trans. Walter Kaufmann and R. J. Hollingdale, ed. Walter Kaufmann (New York: Vintage Books, 1967), 17 (hereafter *WP*).

30. Cf. *WP*, 3: "What I relate is the history of the next two centuries. I describe what is coming, what can no longer come differently: *the advent of nihilism.*"

31. *Thus Spoke Zarathustra*, in *PN*, 125. See also the Nietzsche note cited by George Morgan, *Nietzsche* (New York: Harper Torchbooks, 1965), 313: "We must take upon us and affirm *all* suffering that has been suffered, by men and animals, *and have a goal in which it gets reason.*"

"We justify all the dead subsequently and give their life meaning, when we form the superman out of *this* material and give the entire past a *goal*." See also texts cited by Karl Jaspers, *Nietzsche,* trans. Charles F. Wallroff and Frederick J. Schmitz (Chicago: Henry Regnery, 1965), 167: "In spite of all, he must come to us sometime, this *redeeming* man . . . who gives the earth its purpose . . . this victor over God and nothingness. . . . God has died, our desire is now that the superman live."

32. Cf. Joan Stambaugh, *Nietzsche's Thought of Eternal Return* (Baltimore, Md.: Johns Hopkins University Press, 1972), 88: "The superman is the man who is able to affirm eternal recurrence, the man who experiences eternal recurrence as his own inner being. The superman is a possibility which appears with the death of God."

33. For an insightful development of eternal return as the affirmation of the depth of the moment, see Stambaugh, *Nietzsche's Thought.*

34. I think that Bernd Magnus is right when he claims that Nietzsche does not escape a version of eternalism in his effort to overcome that kronophobia that appears to be an inescapable feature of the human condition; see Magnus, *Nietzsche's Existential Imperative* (Bloomington: Indiana University Press, 1978), 195–96.

35. Rainer Maria Rilke, himself touched by Nietzsche, wrote of his own *Duino Elegies* and *Sonnets to Orpheus:* "To presuppose the *oneness* of life and death . . . to know the *identity* of terror and bliss . . . is the essential meaning and idea of my two books" (*Briefe,* Wiesbaden, 1950, II, 382, 407; cited in Erich Heller, *The Disinherited Mind* [New York: Farrar, Straus & Cudahy, 1957], 148).

36. John J. McDermott, "The American Angle of Vision," *Cross Currents,* Winter 1965, p. 86.

37. These essays have been collected in John J. McDermott, *The Culture of Experience* (New York: New York University Press, 1976; hereafter *CE*); and *Streams of Experience* (Amherst: University of Massachusetts Press, 1986; hereafter *SE*).

38. "Time and Individuality," in *On Experience, Nature, and Freedom,* ed. Richard Bernstein (New York: Library of Liberal Arts, 1960), 225.

39. See also *SE,* 98: "Yet this was precisely what American classical philosophical tradition was proposing, namely that the very transient character of our human lives enhanced, rather than denigrated, the profound inferential character of our values, decisions, and disabilities."

40. Norman O. Brown, *Life against Death* (New York: Random House, 1959); *Love's Body* (New York: Random House, 1966); *Closing Time* (New York: Random House, 1973).

41. Unpublished note, cited by Eric Heller, "The Importance of Nietzsche," in *The Artist's Journey into the Interior* (New York: Harcourt Brace Jovanovich, 1976), 193.

42. That "all shall be well" is, of course, the essence of religious hope. The fifteenth-century mystic Julian of Norwich expresses this as a divine revelation: "At one time our Lord said: 'All things shall be well'; and at another she said: 'Thou shall see thyself that all manner thing shall be well'" (*The Revelations of Divine Love of Julian of Norwich,* trans. James Walsh, S. J. [New York: Harper, 1961], 98).

43. Rainer Maria Rilke, "The Ninth Elegy," in *Duino Elegies,* trans., with introduction and commentary, J. B. Leishman and Stephen Spender (New York: Norton, 1939), 73.

44. Charles Hartshorne, "A Philosophy of Death," in *PAT,* II:83.

45. Cf. Yeager Hudson, "Death and the Meaning of Life," in *PAT,* II:98: "A play or novel which did not end would be completely unsatisfactory." Hartshorne and

Hudson might find support for their position on esthetic grounds in the examples of "endless" soap operas. For many, however, the lack of a final ending does not seem to diminish the interest.

46. Charles Hartshorne, "The Acceptance of Death," in *PAT*, I:84–86.

47. For a diametrically opposed view, see Hocking, *MI*, 150: "The true meaning of the deed is what it means to the self which performs it; without this self the deed has no meaning at all. . . . And if this self vanishes, and all like it, meaning vanishes out of the world. No achievement can keep the person alive, but the continuance of the person is a guaranty that such values as that shall not reduce to nothing. It is the person who perpetuates the achievement, not the achievement the person."

48. A. N. Whitehead, *Process and Reality* (New York: Humanities Press, 1955), ix (hereafter *PR*).

49. A. N. Whitehead, *Science and the Modern World* (New York: Free Press/Macmillan, 1969), 192.

50. The *locus classicus* for this view of immortality is in Pericles' Funeral Oration, Thucydides 2.43–44. Andy Warhol somewhere said something to the effect that "in the future everyone will be famous for fifteen minutes." This would hardly have satisfied the Greeks and is not likely to satisfy any present or future fame seekers. The essence of belief in fame-immortality is that one will achieve or create something that will continue to endure after one's death. The radical discrepancy between the living experience and what remains is poignantly captured in the opening lines of James's "Address at the Emerson Centenary in Concord": "The pathos of death is this, that when the days of one's life are ended, those days that were so crowded with business and felt so heavy in their passing, what remains of one in memory should usually be so slight a thing. The phantom of an attitude, the echo of a certain mode of thought, a few pages of print, some invention, or some victory we gained in a brief critical hour, are all that can survive the best of us" (*MS*, 19).

51. George Santayana, *Life of Reason*, 5 vols. (New York: Scribner, 1913), III:272.

52. It must be conceded that James comes very close to agreeing with the view that survival of values or ideals is more important than survival of individuals. In *VRE*, he tells us that he did not discuss immortality because it seemed to him "a secondary point. . . . If our ideals are only cared for in 'eternity,' I do not see why we might not be willing to resign their care to other hands than ours" (*VRE*, 412). In a letter to James, Carl Stumpf, after declaring that "personal immortality stands for me in the foreground," cites the foregoing passage and comments that it "seems to me to contain a sort of inner contradiction. The realization of ideals *is* only possible on the presupposition of individual immortality." James responds: "I agree that a God *of the totality* must be an unacceptable religious object. But I do not see why there may not be superhuman consciousness of *ideals* of ours, and *that* would be *our* God. It is all very dark. I have never felt the *rational* need of immortality as you seem to feel it; but as I grow older I confess that I feel the practical need of it much more than I ever did before; and that combines with reasons, not exactly the same as your own, to give me a growing faith in its reality" (cited in Ralph Barton Perry, *The Thought and Character of William James,* 2 vols. [Boston: Little, Brown, 1935], II:343, 345). James here converges with and diverges from the views of Hartshorne and Jonas. He converges insofar as he makes survival of ideals the important matter; he diverges insofar as he does not exclude the possibility of personal survival.

53. John Hick, *Death and Eternal Life* (New York: Harper & Row, 1976), 73, 63–64

(hereafter *DEL*). See also R. H. Charles, *Eschatology* (New York: Schocken Books, 1963), 51–81.

54. Thomas Aquinas, *Summa Theologica*, I, Q. 29, Art. 3, trans. Anton Pegis (New York: Random House, 1945), I:295.

55. For an apparent counterchoice, see Mary McCarthy's novel, *Cannibals and Missionaries* (New York: Harcourt Brace Jovanovich, 1979), 293–94. A group of hijackers are in process of exchanging hostages for some great works of art. One of the hostages, sympathetically portrayed, reflects upon the "stragetic genius" of this undertaking: "If a hostage or two got killed, it had to be seen in the perspective of the greater good of the greater number. But works of art were a different type of noncombatant, not to be touched with a ten-foot pole by any government respectful of 'values.' It was in the nature of civilians to die sooner or later . . . while works of art by their nature and in principle were imperishable. In addition, they were irreplaceable, which could not be said of their owners. . . . The lesson to be derived . . . was that paintings were more sacrosanct than persons."

56. Romans 9:20–21.

57. Perhaps the most laid-back response to "the absurd" is that of Thomas Nagel in "The Absurd," in *Language, Metaphysics, and Death,* ed. John Donnelly (New York: Fordham University Press, 1978), 114: "I would argue that absurdity is one of the most human things about us. . . . It need not be a matter of agony unless we make it so. Nor need it evoke a defiant contempt of fate that allows us to feel brave or proud. Such dramatics, even if carried on in private, betray a failure to appreciate the cosmic importance of the situation. If, *sub specie aeternitatis,* there is no reason to believe that anything matters, then that does not matter either, and we can approach our absurd lives with irony instead of heroism or despair."

58. Cf. Gabriel Marcel, *The Mystery of Being,* 2 vols., trans. G. S. Fraser (Chicago: Henry Regnery, 1950–51), II:155: "What we have to find out is whether one can radically separate faith in a God conceived in His sanctity from any affirmation which bears on the destiny of the intersubjective unity which is formed by beings who love one another and who live in and by one another. What is really important, in fact, is the destiny of the living link, and not that of an entity which is isolated and closed in on itself. That is what we more or less explicitly mean when we assert our faith in personal immortality."

59. Even bracketing the question of God, the cessation of human persons must be lamented. "It is absurd for us to insist," Bixler points out, "in line with the present mood, on an educational process in which personality shall be developed and an economic order in which it can be maintained, and to profess at the same time indifference to its extinction" (*IPM*, 35). Cf. Perry, *HFI*, 11: "Whatever philosophy praises the creation of man must deplore his annihilation."

60. Cf. William Styron's novel, *Sophie's Choice* (New York: Random House, 1979), 218–19. Styron's protagonist, evidently speaking for the author, argues against George Steiner's suggestion that confronted with an evil on the magnitude of the Holocaust, "*silence* is the answer"; he adds that "Steiner has not remained silent" but has stated that "the next best is 'to try and understand.'"

61. Cf. *IPM*, 63, where Bixler cites the British idealist Bernard Bosanquet to the effect that "we shall never get a popular conception of religion that is clear and sane until this perpetual hankering after a future life as a means of recompense is laid to rest."

62. For an interpretation of resurrection that does not separate individual and community, cf. Charles, *Eschatology*, 164: "Not to a future of individual bliss, even though in the divine presence, but to a resurrection to a new life (Is. xxvi. 19) as members of the holy people and citizens of the Messianic kingdom, did the righteous aspire. The *individual* thus looked forward to his highest consummation in the life of the righteous community" (italics added). For a more recent personalist version of resurrection, cf. Rosemary Haughton, *The Passionate God* (New York: Paulist Press, 1981), 196: "Jesus talked to people about eternal life, or life in the kingdom of God, in ways which make it clear that he thought of them as being still and always 'themselves.' They would not 'merge' into the kingdom, they would 'inherit' it, live in it, have 'mansions' in it."

63. Cf. Hans Küng, *Does God Exist?* trans. Edward Quinn (New York: Doubleday, 1980), 659: "There can be a true consummation and a true happiness of mankind only when not merely the last generation, but all men, even those who suffered and bled in the past, come to share in it."

64. I am not, of course, suggesting that this *constancy* of belief in eternal life has been an *identity* of belief in all ages of the Christian community. The different modes in which this belief has been expressed through art, literature, reliquaries, altarpieces, death rites, and funerary practices is brilliantly detailed by Philippe Aries in *The Hour of Our Death*, trans. Helen Weaver (New York: Knopf, 1981).

65. Cf. James B. Pratt, *The Religious Consciousness* (New York: Macmillan, 1928), 253: "As the belief in miracles and special answers to prayer and in the interference of the supernatural within the natural has gradually disappeared, almost the only *pragmatic* value of the supernatural left to religion is the belief in a personal future life" (cited in Lamont, *II*, 6). See also Lamont, *II*, 5: "But in this fundamental identity between God and immortality priority still belongs to immortality. God would be dead if there were no immortality."

CHAPTER 8

1. John Hick, *Death and Eternal Life* (New York: Harper & Row, 1976), 24 (hereafter *DEL*).

2. H. D. Lewis, *The Self and Immortality* (New York: Seabury Press, 1973), 196 (hereafter *SI*). See also William Ernest Hocking, *The Meaning of Immortality in Human Experience* (New York: Harper, 1957), xi–xii (hereafter *MI*): "*Unless an Idea has or can have an intelligible basis in the constitution of things* it is illegitimate, whether for postulate or for faith: we must be able to say what it is we postulate or believe."

3. Cf. David L. Norton, *Personal Destinies* (Princeton, N.J.: Princeton University Press, 1976), 358: "He who affirms the worth of life does not embrace the idea of an afterlife that is the antithesis of the life he and all human beings live."

4. John Dewey, *Experience and Education* (New York: Macmillan, 1956), 51.

5. Albert Camus, *The Rebel*, trans. Anthony Bower (New York: Vintage Books, 1956), 304.

6. Christopher Mooney, "Death and Human Expectation," in *Philosophical Aspects of Thanatology*, 2 vols., ed. Florence M. Hetzler and Austin H. Kutscher (New York: MSS Information Corporation, 1978), II:151 (hereafter *PAT*).

7. For a suggestion of some convergences as well as divergences between pragmatism and the thought of Aurobindo, see Eugene Fontinell, "A Pragmatic Approach to *The Human Cycle*," in *Six Pillars,* ed. Robert A. McDermott (Chambersburg, Pa.: Wilson Books, 1974), 131–59.

8. Such a view is antithetical to any interpretation of Jesus' teaching that sees no comparison possible between present and future life. For a representative example, see Franz Mussner, "The Synoptic Account of Jesus' Teaching on the Future Life," in *Immortality and Resurrection,* ed. Pierre Benoit and Roland Murphy (Herder & Herder, 1970), 53: "It is Jesus' teaching that the coming life bears no comparison with the present life. To make Jesus a witness to a point of view that saw this life as one evolving towards the coming life, would be to misrepresent the synoptic account of his teaching."

9. Cf. Denis Goulet, "Is Economic Justice Possible?" *Cross Currents,* Spring 1981, 47: "Can any religion offer a convincing rationale why men and women should build history even as they strive to bear witness to transcendence? . . . One vital arena is how any religion values time itself: is earthly life simply a means to some paradise beyond this world, or is it rather some end having its own dignity and worth?"

10. Cf. James, *SPP,* 116: "'If we do *our* best, *and* the other powers do *their* best, the world will be perfected'—this proposition expresses no actual fact, but only the complexion of a fact thought of as eventually possible."

11. For a critique of Teilhard de Chardin on just this point, see, George Maloney, "Death and Omega: An Evolving Eschaton," in *PAT,* I:143: "Thus two great weaknesses of Teilhard's system (he never comes to serious grips with the problems) are (1) he fails to continue the evolutionary process beyond the Omega Point and (2) he does not answer how the majority of the human race, all those billions who have lived in the past, our present majority and a good deal of the future to come, how will they reach the Omega Point?"

12. Cf. Aldous Huxley, *The Doors of Perception* (New York: Harper & Row, 1963), 23–24: "That which, in the language of religion, is called 'this world' is the universe of reduced awareness, expressed, and, as it were, petrified by language. The various 'other worlds,' with which human beings erratically make contact are so many elements in the totality of the awareness belonging to Mind at Large."

13. See also *WB,* 51: "But the inner need of believing that this world of nature is a sign of something more spiritual and eternal than itself is just as strong and authoritative in those who feel it, as the inner need of uniform laws of causation ever can be in a professionally scientific head."

14. Though he would be outraged by the use James and I make of it, a somewhat similar phenomenon is suggested by Nietzsche: "We discover an activity that would have to be ascribed to a far higher and more comprehensive intellect than we know of. . . . Of the numerous influences operating at every moment, e.g., air, electricity, we sense almost nothing: there could well be forces that, although we never sense them, continually influence us" (*The Will to Power,* trans. Walter Kaufmann and R. J. Hollingdale, ed. Walter Kaufmann [New York: Vintage Books, 1967], 357).

15. There is a highly technical question attached to the notion of a plurality of worlds: namely, the possibility or conceivability of plural times, or plural spaces, or plural space-times. Speculation on this question is not confined to "tender-minded" or "romantic" thinkers. See, for example, Hocking's reference (*MI,* 210) to "Minkowski's Memoir of 1908, in which he vigorously assaulted the doctrine of monism (though chiefly for the purposes of calculation), making the radical assertion that 'from henceforth we shall speak no more of Space and Time, but of spaces and times.'"

John Hick (*DEL,* 279–95) speculates on the plurality of spaces as a prerequisite for a doctrine of bodily resurrection. The distinguished psychologist Gardner Murphy asks, "Is there a possibility that general psychology would say, 'We don't yet have a time-space reference for the study of death any more than we have a time-space reference for the study of personality?'" (*The Meaning of Death,* ed. Herman Feifel [New York: McGraw-Hill, 1965], 339).

The conceivability of plural spaces is defended by Anthony Quinton in "Spaces and Times," *Philosophy,* April 1962. And working from a radically different philosophical and cultural context, P. T. Raju states: "I think that the Upanishads are right in saying that there are different levels of space and time. There is space between one book and another; but what is the space that separates ideas of cause and effect when I think of the law of causation? What is the space that separates me and my mental images? Certainly, I am not my mental images. And what is the time that separates me as observing the first instant of a duration of five seconds and me as observing the last instant? How many problems arise here? ("Self and Body: How Known and Differentiated," *Monist* 61, no. 1 [Jan. 1978], 153–54).

16. Cf. John Shea, *What a Modern Catholic Believes about Heaven and Hell* (Chicago: Thomas More Press, 1972), 21 (hereafter *HH*): "Hope is rooted in the actuality of things. . . . If personal immortality is a true hope and not a mere wish, in some way it must be intimated in the experience of men."

17. Extrapolation is an act of imagination that should be sharply differentiated from idle fantasy. Cf. William Lynch, S. J., *Images of Hope* (New York: New American Library, 1965), 27, 209: "For one of the permanent meanings of imagination has been that it is the gift that envisions what cannot yet be seen, the gift that constantly proposes to itself that the boundaries of the possible are wider than they seem. . . . *The first task of such an imagination, if it is to be healing, is to find a way through fantasy and lies into fact and existence.*" Lynch also develops this theme, that the imagination is essentially reality-oriented, in *Christ and Apollo* (New York: Sheed & Ward, 1961).

18. Recall the previously cited statement of James: "I have no mystical experience of my own, but just enough of the germ of mysticism in me to recognize the region from which their [*sic*] voice comes when I hear it" (cited in Ralph Barton Perry, *The Thought and Character of William James,* 2 vols, [Boston: Little, Brown, 1935], II:346; hereafter *TC*).

I have made no reference to a large body of claims which are often cited as supporting immortality—those of spiritualism and other paranormal psychic experiences. The evaluation of these claims is an undertaking in itself and one that I make no pretense of doing in a footnote. Let me simply say that I share with many who have sympathetically investigated these claims the conclusion, "not proved." That is not their greatest weakness, however, for pragmatism neither asks nor expects "proof" in such instances. What it does seek are fruits in the form of the deepening, illumination, and expansion of human life. Such fruits can reasonably be said to issue from the lives of many if not all mystics but are decidedly less evident in the case of "spiritualists," particularly in their claims of communication with the dead. James, himself deeply sympathetic with and professionally supportive of such efforts, concluded, as we saw earlier, that "the spirit-hypothesis exhibits a vacancy, triviality and incoherence of mind painful to think of as the state of the departed" (*CER,* 438–39).

A figure who might be an exception here, and who commands the respect of a number of serious thinkers, is Rudolph Steiner. While I find the details of his other-world descriptions bordering on the fantastic, there is an element of insight in his writings that I think should not be dismissed. Two passages from his autobiography might be cited as most congenial to the kind of extrapolation or model herein offered: "I have tried to show in my book that nothing *unknowable* lies *behind* the sense-world, but that *within* it is the spiritual world. . . . I insisted that a person who deepens his view of the world as much as lies within the scope of his powers, will discover a universal process which encompasses the true reality of nature as well as morality" (*Rudolph Steiner, An Autobiography* [Blauvelt, N.Y.: Rudolph Steiner Publications, 1977], 215, 213). There is one other group of phenomena that I can only mention in passing—"clinical death" experiences such as those described by R. A. Moody in *Life after Life* (St. Simons Island, Ga.: Mockingbird Books, 1975). These are instances in which persons judged clinically dead, "return" to life and proceed to describe "out of body" experiences, usually as beautiful and reassuring. While these experiences might support a view of the self that avoids identifying it with the body narrowly understood, I find nothing in them that can be cited as evidence for immortality. Since the definition of "death" presupposed is suspect, there is no difficulty in accounting for these phenomena in "materialistic" terms. I share Hans Küng's conclusion concerning such cases: "What then do these experiences of dying imply for life after death? To put it briefly, nothing! . . . Experiences of this kind prove nothing about a possible life after death: it is a question here of the last five minutes *before* death and not of an eternal life *after* death" (*Eternal Life?*, trans. Edward Quinn [New York: Doubleday, 1984], 20).

19. Cf. Gottfried Leibniz, *Discourse on Metaphysics,* trans. George R. Montgomery (La Salle, Ill.: Open Court, 1947), 58: "Suppose that some individual could suddenly become King of China on condition, however, of forgetting what he had been, as though being born again, would it not amount to the same practically, or as far as the effects could be perceived, as if the individual were annihilated, and a king of China were the same instant created in his place? The individual would have no reason to desire this." A similar insight is found in Aristotle: "No one chooses to possess the whole world if he has first to become someone else . . . he wishes for this only on condition of being whatever he is" (*Nichomachean Ethics* 9.4.1166a, ed. Richard McKeon [New York: Random House, 1941], 1081).

20. Bernard Williams, *Problems of the Self* (New York: Cambridge University Press, 1976), 91 (hereafter *PS*).

21. Friedrich Nietzsche, *Thus Spoke Zarathustra,* in *The Portable Nietzsche,* trans. and ed. Walter Kaufmann (New York: Viking Press, 1968), 339–40.

22. Friedrich D. E. Schleiermacher, *On Religion,* trans. by John Oman (New York: Harper Torchbooks, 1958), 101. Cf. A. Seth Pringle-Pattison, *The Idea of Immortality* (Oxford: Clarendon Press, 1922), 136, 155–56:

> But eternity and immortality are by no means necessarily exclusive terms: on the contrary, our experience here and now may carry in it "the power of an endless life", and be in truth the only earnest or guarantee of such a life. . . . It does not follow that the attainment of religious insight in the present life involves the surrender of any hope of a personal life beyond. Why should not the apprehension of the eternal rather carry with it the gift of further life and a fuller fruition? . . . Throughout the New Testament, accordingly, even in the passages which most clearly treat "eternal life" as realized here and now, the present experience is never taken as foreclosing the possibility of a future life, but always rather as a foretaste, as an assurance, indeed, of a fuller realization hereafter.

23. Soren Kierkegaard, *Purity of Heart,* trans. Douglas V. Steere (New York: Harper Torchbooks, 1956), 35. Cf. J. Heywood Thomas, "Kierkegaard's View of

Time," in *PAT,* I:233: "The point Kierkegaard wants to make is that the eternal is the present or better that the present is the eternal."

24. George Santayana, *Soliloquies In England* (Ann Arbor: University of Michigan Press, 1967), 116.

25. See also *MI,* 71: "But if lastingness is a mark of value, is it not an absurdity of a universe in which the everlasting things are things which do not know and cannot become aware of their post of honor?" For a diametrically opposed interpretation of the endurance of inorganic entities, see Hans Jonas, *The Phenomenon of Life* (New York: Dell, 1966), 276: "If permanence were the point, life should not have started out in the first place, for in no possible form can it match the duration of inorganic bodies." Though Camus does not believe in its reality, he does recognize the efficacy of a life that endures: "It appears that great minds are sometimes less horrified by suffering than by the fact that it does not endure. In default of inexhaustible happiness, eternal suffering would at least give us a destiny" (*The Rebel,* trans. Anthony Bower [New York: Vintage Books, 1956], 261).

26. Henri Bergson, *Creative Evolution,* trans. Arthur Mitchell (New York: Modern Library, 1944), 7.

27. Stewart Sutherland, "Immortality and Resurrection," in *Language, Metaphysics, and Death,* ed. John Donnelly (New York: Fordham University Press, 1978), 206.

28. John Smith, "Dying, Death and Their Significance," in *PAT,* I:xii.

29. John Baillie, *And the Life Everlasting* (New York: Oxford University Press, 1934), 204. Cited in Louis Dupré, *Transcendent Selfhood,* (New York: Seabury Press, 1976), 81. Cf. Owen Barfield, "Matter, Imagination, and Spirit," *Journal of Religion,* Dec. 1974, 627: "I would wish to emphasize that I mean important . . . for the whole future of humanity. The issue of survival after death today has, I believe, that kind of importance as well as the personal one. But I am not very fond of the word 'survival' in this context. It has too strong a suggestion of a mere prolongation of the life we are so familiar with. I prefer 'immortality' as suggesting transition to a new and very different kind of life."

30. E. J. Fortmann, *Everlasting Life after Death* (New York: Alba House, 1976), 301 (hereafter *ELD*).

31. William Frost, "Religious Imagination," *Ecumenist,* March–April 1980, 44. Also relevant is Frost's description (p. 43) of the interpretation that the Marxist Ernst Bloch gives to "Christ's saying that he who loses his life will find it and he who seeks his life will lose it. Only those who are willing to follow the life of the soul which vibrates beyond the body and the mundane are made free for an immortality which is more than the existing form of reality. It is the trans-cosmological."

32. This, I believe, is the fundamental thrust of his *The Phenomenon of Man,* trans. Bernard Wall (New York: Harper, 1959). Teilhard also implies that human beings would not participate in a process that they knew was a dead-end one: "Man will never take a step in a direction he knows to be blocked. There lies precisely the ill that causes our disquiet" (p. 229). See also p. 231: "*Without the taste for life,* mankind would soon stop inventing and constructing for a work it knew to be doomed in advance."

33. Cf. Gabriel Marcel, *The Mystery of Being,* 2 vols., trans. G. S. Fraser (Chicago: Henry Regnery, 1950, 1951), II:157–58 (hereafter *MB*): "What we loosely call 'beyond' consists of unknown dimensions or perspectives within a universe of which

we apprehend only the one aspect which is in tune with our own organo-psychic structure."

34. F. X. Durrwell, *The Resurrection* (New York: Sheed & Ward, 1960), 126.

35. Piet Schoonenberg, "I Believe in Eternal Life," in *The Problem of Eschatology*, ed. Edward Schillebeeckx, O. P., and Boniface Willems, O. P. (New York: Paulist Press, 1969), 110.

36. Ignace Lepp, *Death and Its Mysteries*, trans. Bernard Murchland (New York: Macmillan, 1968), 188.

37. See also, Fortman, *ELD*, 135, where he describes Karl Rahner's and Ladislaus Boros's process views of purgatory. While Fortman himself is not completely antagonistic to a processive purgatory or heaven, he balks at the notion of a processive God.

38. Henri Bergson, *Two Sources of Religion and Morality*, trans. R. Ashley Audra and Cloudesley Brereton (New York: Henry Holt, 1935), 124.

39. J. P. Eckermann, *Gespraeche mit Goethe* (Stuttgart: Cotta, n.d.), cited in Rose Pfeffer, *Nietzsche, Disciple of Dionysus* (Lewisburg, Pa.: Bucknell University Press, 1972), 267.

40. See also Norton, *Personal Destinies*, 237: "Goethe said to Eckermann that he would not know what to do with an afterlife if it did not provide new tasks and new opportunities. This extrapolative propensity is supported by certain distinctive theories of immortality as exemplified in the thought of Immanuel Kant and Josiah Royce."

41. Ralph Barton Perry, *The Hope for Immortality* (New York: Vanguard Press, 1945), 8, 24.

42. It should be noted, however, that the relation between "fitness" and immortality was not a late-life afterthought for James. See *PP*, I:330: "The demand for immortality is nowadays essentially teleological. We believe ourselves immortal because we believe ourselves *fit* for immortality. A 'substance' ought surely to perish, we think, if not worthy to survive; and an insubstantial 'stream' to prolong itself provided it be worthy, if the nature of Things is organized in the rational way in which we trust it is."

43. Cf. James L. Muyskens, *The Sufficiency of Hope* (Philadelphia: Temple University Press, 1979), 72: "Unless one's sense of self and one's potential are very limited or one is uncommonly blessed with favorable conditions and knows it, death blocks one's path to genuine fulfillment. . . . At the time of one's death, self-fulfillment normally has not been attained. Much of one's potential remains untapped. If, then, death is the final curtain, it destroys the possibility of a truly meaningful life to a great many. For them, it would be reasonable to desire a life after death in the form of personal survival."

44. Cf. Marcel, *MB*, II: 153–55: "First let me quote again what one of my characters says, 'to love a being is to say, "Thou, thou shalt not die." ' . . . [This] prophetic assurance . . . might be expressed fairly enough as follows: whatever changes may intervene in what I see before me, you and I will persist as one: the event that has occurred and which belongs to the order of accident, cannot nullify the promise of eternity which is enclosed in our love, in our mutual pledge."

45. Thomas Hardy, *Tess of the D'Urbervilles* (New York: Signet, 1964), 416. Prince Andrew in Tolstoy's *War and Peace* responds differently to the separation consequent upon the death of a loved one: "All I say is that it is not argument that convinces me

of the necessity of a future life, but this: when you go hand in hand with someone and all at once that person vanishes *there, into nowhere,* and you yourself are left facing that abyss and look in. And I have looked in . . ." (trans. Aylmer Maude [New York: Simon & Schuster, 1942], 422).

46. Gabriel Marcel *Creative Fidelity,* trans. Robert Rosthal (New York: Farrar, Straus & Giroux, 1964), 152. For a fine exposition of Marcel's views on death, see Barbara E. Wall, "The Doctrine of Death in the Philosophy of Gabriel Marcel," in *PAT,* II:223–35. For a description of a "phenomenon" similar to Marcel's but interpreted radically differently, see Vivienne Thaul Wechter, "A Time to Live—A Time to Die?" in *PAT,* I:244–45: "As an addendum must be added, that though my own understanding—or wish—for death as 'the end,' has I suspect seeped through, there must be an admission of the ambivalence which is a common affliction. Though I choose to think, to intellectualize, to indeed wish for that kind of death as in the words of Epicurus 'when death is come we are not'—nevertheless I find myself relating to loved ones who have died as though they have migrated into some kind of discarnate existence, which still is in some mysterious way related to me here. And my dreams indicate that I wish to encourage this relationship."

47. See, e.g., Karl Jaspers, "On My Philosophy," trans. F. Kaufmann, in *Existentialism from Dostoevsky to Sartre,* ed. Walter Kaufmann (New York: Meridian Books, 1968), 147: "The individual cannot become human by himself. Self-being is only real in communication with another self-being. Alone, I sink into gloomy isolation—only in community with others can I be revealed in the act of mutual discovery." For an impressive and intellectually demanding exposition and evaluation of both transcendental and dialogical versions of a transactional social self, see Michael Theunissen, *The Other: Studies in the Social Ontology of Husserl, Heidegger, Sartre and Buber,* trans. Christopher Macann (Cambridge, Mass.: MIT Press, 1984).

For a subtle and unsettling suggestion of the way in which man-made mass death impacts upon the social or transactional self, cf. Edith Wyschogrod, *Spirit in Ashes: Hegel, Heidegger, and Man-Made Mass Death* (New Haven, Conn.: Yale University Press, 1985), 211: "The conception of a linguistic and corporeal transactional self holds in equipoise the individuating aspect of self, the I pole, and the objectified me. With the advent of man-made mass death this more or less harmonious unity is broken: the I pole is shattered resulting in a negative and apocalyptic subject. Each I experiences the possibility not only of its own coming to an end but also of human extinction in toto as a result of human acts."

48. Josiah Royce's ideal of the "Beloved Community," developed in *The Problem of Christianity* (1913; Chicago: University of Chicago Press, 1968) would be a rich resource for an extrapolation along the lines of the one I am suggesting. One text will indicate the direction of Royce's efforts:

> The ideal Christian community is to be the community of all mankind,—as completely united in its inner life as one conscious self could conceivably become, and as destructive of the natural hostilities and of the narrow passions which estrange individual men, as it is skillful in winning from the infinite realm of bare possibilities concrete arts of control over nature and of joy in its own riches of grace. This free and faithful community of all mankind, wherein the individuals should indeed die to their own natural life, but should also enjoy a newness of positive life,—this community never became, so far as I can learn, a conscious ideal for early Buddhism. (p. 195)

49. The metaphysical character of "struggle" is suggested by James: "The facts of struggle seem too deeply characteristic of the whole frame of things for me not to suspect that hindrance and experiment go all the way through" (*TC,* II:379).

50. Cf. Anne Carr, "The God Who Is Involved," *Theology Today,* (Oct. 1981, 314: "There is today a theological insistence, rooted in interpretations of the Bible and of contemporary experience, that the God of Christian faith, while remaining God, is intimate to the joy and the pain, the victory and the defeat, the struggle of human existence, and comes to be known precisely there." See also David Tracy, *Blessed Rage for Order* (New York: Seabury Press, 1975), 177: "Is not the God of the Jewish and Christian scriptures a God profoundly involved in humanity's struggle to the point where God not merely affects but is affected by the struggle?"

51. "For it is not against human enemies that we have to struggle, but against the Sovereignties and the Powers who originate the darkness in this world, the spiritual army of evil in the heavens" (Ephesians 6:12).

52. Cf. Hans Küng, *Does God Exist?,* trans. Edward Quinn (New York: Doubleday, 1980), 665: "*The biblical God is not a God without feeling, incapable of suffering, apathetic in regard to the vast suffering of the world and man, but a sym-pathetic com-passionate God.*" See also, Tracy, *Blessed Rage,* 177: "Is Bonhoeffer's famous cry that only a suffering God can help merely a rhetorical flourish of a troubled man? Can the God of Jesus Christ really be *simply* changeless, omnipotent, omniscient, unaffected by our anguish and our achievements?"

53. Eugene Fontinell, "John Hick's 'After-Life': A Critical Comment," *Cross Currents,* Fall 1978.

54. See Hick, "Universal Salvation," in *DEL,* 242ff.

CONCLUDING REFLECTIONS

1. For a brief description of and the relevant sources relating to "The Origins of After-Life and Immortality Beliefs," see John Hick, *Death and Eternal Life* (New York: Harper & Row, 1976), 54–77.

2. *The Epic of Gilgamesh in the Ancient Near East,* ed. James B. Prichard (Princeton, N.J.: Princeton University Press, 1958), I:64.

3. Ecclesiastes 5:17, 9:10.

4. Samuel Beckett, *Waiting for Godot* (New York: Grove Press, 1954), 57.

5. Marilyn French, *The Women's Room* (New York: Summit Books, 1977), 279.

6. Sigmund Freud, *Beyond the Pleasure Principle,* trans. and ed. James Strachey (New York: Norton, 1961), 32.

7. Cf. *VRE,* 263: "We can never hope for clean-cut scholastic results. . . . Decide that *on the whole* one type of religion is approved by its fruits, and another type condemned. 'On the whole'—I fear we shall never escape complicity with that qualification, so dear to your practical man, so repugnant to your systematizer!"

8. Jeanne Hersch, "Jasper's Conception of Tradition," in *The Philosophy of Karl Jaspers,* ed. Paul A. Schilpp (New York: Tudor, 1957), 603–4. Of course, Hersch is not suggesting—nor am I—that it is either possible or desirable to return to an earlier mode of religion, whatever the richness of life that ensued from it.

9. Cf. Gabriel Marcel, *The Mystery of Being,* 2 vols., trans. G. S. Fraser (Chicago: Henry Regnery, 1950, 1951), II:146: "There is no doubt but that the appalling error

of which a certain sort of spiritualism is guilty, lies in denying to death this gravity, this at all events *apparent* final value, which gives to human life a quality of tragedy without which it is nothing more than a puppet-show. There is a mistake which balances this one; it is even more serious and much weighter with consequences; it is that which lies in a dogmatic affirmation of the final character of death."

10. Cf. Norman Malcolm, *Ludwig Wittgenstein: A Memoir* (London: Oxford University Press, 1958), 71: "Wittgenstein once suggested that a way in which the notion of immortality can acquire meaning is through one's feeling that one has duties from which one cannot be released, even by death."

11. See James's letter to Perry in Ralph Barton Perry, *The Thought and Character of William James,* 2 vols. (Boston: Little, Brown, 1935), II:475: "Certainly a doctrine that encouraged immortality would draw belief more than one that didn't, if it were *exactly as satisfactory* in residual respects. Of course it couldn't prevail against knock-knock-down evidence to the contrary; but where there is no such evidence, it will incline belief."

12. Ecclesiastes 9:3. Cf. Max Horkheimer, *Die Sehnsucht nach dem ganz Anderen,* an interview with commentary by H. Gumnior (Hamburg, 1970), 61–62; cited in H. Küng, *Does God Exist?,* trans. Edward Quinn (New York: Doubleday, 1980), 491: "Theology . . . is the hope that this injustice which characterizes the world is not permanent, that injustice will not be the last word . . . that the murderer will not triumph over his innocent victim."

13. For a similar version of this argument, see James L. Muyskens, *The Sufficiency of Hope* (Philadelphia: Temple University Press, 1979), 74–75.

14. Cf. *The Brothers Karamazov* by Dostoevsky and *The Plague* by Camus for an example of two persons perceiving with great insight, intensity, and sensitivity the irreducible absurdity of the sufferings of innocent children but responding with different modes of hope.

15. Cf. A. N. Whitehead, *Adventures of Ideas* (New York: Free Press/Macmillan, 1967), 286: "Decay, Transition, Loss, Displacement belong to the essence of the Creative Advance."

16. Glenn Cunningham, the great miler, through persistent effort, overcame severe leg burns suffered as a youth.

17. Cf. the reflections of Hans Jonas, who, though unable to accept personal immortality, nevertheless desired that the victims of Auschwitz achieve some mode of immortality through being a spur to an effort that will transform human life. The refusal to forget them serves as the way in which they are incorporated in the living process.

18. Some years ago, I concluded an essay on "Faith and Metaphysics" with the following:

> The Christian of today, unlike his believing forerunners, will no longer expect or seek superficial aid or comfort from the Other, not even the certain assurance of His existence. It might be suggested that a distinct advantage of such an approach would be the avoidance of the characteristically Christian mode of self-deception, i.e., the affirmation of the noblest values as a blind for a spiritual egotism, for a selfish individual obsession with personal immortality which the contemporary world has quite properly designated as unworthy of man. This last will jar Christians, but if we were to put it simply we might ask which is the more noble, a man who loves his fellowman in order to avoid hell-fire or one who loves him because he is his fellow-man. This is by no means a radically new insight, for it is already

contained in the story of the saint who encountered an angel walking down the road with a torch in one hand and a pail of water in the other. When asked what they were for he replied, "The torch is to burn down the castles of heaven and the water to put out the flames of hell and then we shall see who really loves God." (*Cross Currents,* Winter 1966, 39–40)

19. Something along these lines seems to be suggested in the letter Peirce wrote to James's son on James's death: "I think we have a *full logical right* to entertain high *hopes* of a future life, a life of work, long or perhaps endless. But it is clear to me that it has not been intended (so to speak) that we should *count upon* it too implicitly" (cited in Thomas Knight, *Charles Sanders Peirce* [New York: Washington Square Press, 1965], 23).

20. The priority of life over meaning is expressed in the following exchange in Dostoevsky's *Brothers Karamazov:*

"I understand too well, Ivan. One longs to love with one's inside, with one's stomach. You said that so well and I am awfully glad that you have such a longing for life," cried Alyosha. "I think everyone should love life above everything in the world."

"Love life more than the meaning of it?"

"Certainly, love it regardless of logic as you say, it must be regardless of logic, and it's only then one will understand the meaning of it. I have thought so a long time. Half your work is done, Ivan, you love life, now you've only to try to do the second half and you are saved."

"You are trying to save me, but perhaps I am not lost! And what does your second half mean?"

"Why, one has to raise up your dead, who perhaps have not died after all." (trans. Constance Garnett [New York: Modern Library, n.d.], 239)

It is this passage that Camus probably had in mind when he remarked: "One must love life before loving its meaning, says Dostoevsky. . . . Yes and when the love of life disappears, no meaning can console us" (*Notebooks* 1949, cited in Germaine Brée, *Camus* [New Brunswick, N.J.: Rutgers University Press, 1959], 57).

21. No one has expressed this charge more passionately and vividly than Nietzsche. See *The Birth of Tragedy,* trans. Walter Kaufmann, (New York: Vintage Books, 1967), 23: "Christianity was from the beginning, essentially and fundamentally, life's nausea and disgust with life, merely concealed behind, masked by, and dressed up as, faith in 'another' or 'better' life."

22. For a similar call from one located at the other pole of the dialogue, see Michael Harrington, *The Politics at God's Funeral* (New York: Holt, Rinehart & Winston, 1983), 197, 202: "Can Western-Society create transcendental common values in its everyday experience? Values which are not based upon—yet not counterposed to—the supernatural? . . . My answer is clear by now: there is no way back—or forward—to a religious integration of society on the model of Judeo-Christianity in any of its manifestations. But there is a need for the transcendental. That is why the conflict between religious and atheistic humanism must now be ended."

Index

Absolute, the, 91, 107, 143, 150, 207, 262 n.15; and evil, 216; James's critique of, 144–48
Action, in Barbour, 259 n.32
Activity: and action, 97; character of, in fields, 42
Amphitryon 38, 173–74
Aquinas,St.Thomas,190,252 n.21,277n.54
Arendt, Hannah, 183
Aries, Philippe, 278 n.64
Aristotle, 3, 281 n.19
Associationism, 86, 90–91
Atomistic individualism, xiii, 11, 17, 27, 46, 157
Aurobindo, Sri, 203
Ayer, A. J., 35, 242 n.23

"Bad faith," 48, 167, 175, 216. *See also* Self-deception
Baillie, John, 209, 282 n.29
Barbour, Ian, 20, 155, 236 nn.13–14, 238 n.31, 259 n.32, 270 n.32, 272 n.10
Barfield, Owen, 270 n.33, 282 n.29
Beckett, Samuel, 222, 285 n.4
Belief, 166, 172, 177, 223, 238 n.26, 263 n.25; and arguments, 232; in fame-immortality, 276 n.50; in God, xi, 101, 134–35, 137–38, 141, 152, 156, 174, 179–80, 190, 197, 200, 226, 231, 257 n.58; in higher presences, 148; in human annihilation, 173; and immortality, 286 n.11; of James, 113; and needs, 270 n.31; in other worlds, 206;

psychological dimension of, 268 n.11; religious, 114, 178, 266 n.3, 268 n.15; and resurrection, 195–97; in the resurrection, 167; and risk, 232; and self-deception, 223–24; in superhuman life, 206; Wittgenstein on, 273 n.16
Belief in personal immortality, xi–xiv, 8, 202, 204, 205, 210, 232; Bixler on, 194; and Christianity, 196–98; and compensation, 228–29; and consolation, 224, 229; and its counterbelief, 189–90; and death, 174, 274 nn.24, 25; as demeaning, 229–30; Dewey on, 172, 182; Dostoevsky on, 22; as energizing or deenergizing, 171–72, 231; as expression of expectancy, 130; fading of, 222; and field-self, 132; fruitfulness of, 182, 225–26; and God, 101, 132, 133, 156, 158, 159; and a growing world, 99; hope or hindrance, 199; and illusion, 173; and James's critique of the Absolute, 144; and justice, 227; in Marcel, 277 n.58; McDermott on, 179–80, 184; and meaning, 230; and metaphysical dualism, 168; and model of the self, 45; and a moral universe, 226–27; and "new life," 200; Nietzsche's critique of, 177–79; and personal identity, 81; and pragmatic evaluation, 15, 19, 232; as "reasonable," 169–70; and science, 271 n.2; Smith on, 209; and tragedy, 173–75, 274 n.22; and Western religion, 194; and wider consciousness, 115